THE POLITICAL ECONOMY
OF UNEMPLOYMENT

THE POLITICAL ECONOMY
OF UNEMPLOYMENT

*Active Labor Market Policy
in West Germany and the United States*

THOMAS JANOSKI

UNIVERSITY OF CALIFORNIA PRESS
BERKELEY   LOS ANGELES   OXFORD

University of California Press
Berkeley and Los Angeles, California

University of California Press, Ltd.
Oxford, England

© 1990 by
The Regents of the University of California

Library of Congress Cataloging-in-Publication Data

Janoski, Thomas.
   The Political economy of unemployment : active labor
market policy in West Germany and the United States /
Thomas Janoski.
     p.   cm.
   ISBN 0-520-06885-8 (alk. paper)
   1. Manpower policy—United States. 2. Manpower
policy—Germany (West)   I. Title.
HD5724.J36 1990
331.12'042'0943—dc20   89-49053
                                    CIP

Printed in the United States of America

1 2 3 4 5 6 7 8 9

The paper used in this publication meets the minimum re-
quirements of American National Standard for Information
Sciences—Permanence of Paper for Printed Library Materials,
ANSI Z39.48-1984 ∞

To Linda Klink and Andrew

Contents

List of Tables

List of Figures

Acknowledgments

During the several years of this research, I received stimulation and support from faculty and friends at the University of California at Berkeley as well as researchers and government officials in West Germany and the United States. My greatest intellectual debt is owed to Harold Wilensky who provided the impetus for me to do comparative research. Working with him on his Welfare State and Equality Project at Berkeley gave me innumerable insights into the methods and substance of comparative political economy. As a teacher and supervisor of my dissertation, and as a rigorous and critical reader of successive drafts of this book, he imposed the high scholarly standards evident in his own work. This book could not have been completed without his help.

I also thank Reinhard Bendix who provided the theoretical stimulus for much of my citizenship rights approach to social policy. Neil Smelser offered comparative and theoretical advice on several chapters, and Michael Wiseman guided me in the time-series analysis. Gerald Feldman gave critical commentary on the sections dealing with the Weimar Republic. In addition, I thank George Strauss, Glenn Carroll, Gary Gereffi, Edward Tiryakian, and Joel Smith.

Troy Duster, David Matza, and Janice Tanigawa (at the Institute for the Study of Social Change) provided essential social and intellectual resources throughout my research. I also thank Russell Ellis for his timely and optimistic early-morning advice.

I offer special thanks to a group of colleagues that provided critical readings of each chapter: Robert Yamashita, Basil Browne, Steven Gold, Betty Lou Bradshaw, and Davida Weinberg. Often these chapters were rough drafts, and although I was horrified when they said that my 160 tables would make a good appendix, I eventually cut them. Their help was invaluable in conceptualizing and completing the book.

Nan Sand of the Institute of Industrial Relations at the University of California at Berkeley actively assisted me in locating materials; she and Marjorie Morrissette gave me unfailing encouragement. Joan Lewis provided administrative help, and her brave outlook in the face of death was an inspiration to me.

In West Germany, my greatest debt goes to Dr. Günther Schmid at the Wissenschaftszentrum in West Berlin. Upon presenting myself at his doorstep with little more than a calling card, he arranged my access to materials and information throughout West Germany. Werner Sengenberger at the Institut für Wissenschaftlicheforschung in Munich afforded me the use of his office for two weeks and provided critical introductions at federal offices, and Jürgen Kühl of the Bundesanstalt für Arbeit helped me navigate the Federal Institute of Labor. Professor Evelies Mayer at the University of Darmstadt and Bernard Casey at the Wissenschaftszentrum also provided help.

In the United States, Robert Lipman of U.S. Employment Service, Joseph Krauth of the Employment and Training Administration Budget Office, Mary Bugg of U.S. Employment Service, and Richard Ruzzio of the Department of Labor supplied leads and statistical data. Professor Malcolm Cohen at the University of Michigan gave me his data on job placement in the United States. Appreciation also goes to Christine Heuberger who helped me with German translations and field work. At Duke University, I would like to thank Martha Dimes Toher for editorial assistance and Anita Hume, Elizabeth Wing, and Judith Dillon for technical support.

I am grateful for financial support provided by the National Science Foundation (Grant SOC 77-13265, directed by Harold L. Wilensky), the Ford Foundation, the Institute of International Studies, the Institute of Industrial Relations, the National Institute of Mental Health, the University of California Regents, the Graduate Division at the University of California at Berkeley, the Social Science Research Bureau at Michigan State University, and the Swedish Bicentennial Fund.

And finally, I thank Linda Klink for her overt and subliminal pressure to finish this project despite countless broken deadlines.

Abbreviations

GERMAN AND INTERNATIONAL ABBREVIATIONS

ABM   Work creation measures

AFG   Work Promotion Law of 1969

A für A   The Bundestag Committee on Labor (Ausschuß für Arbeit)

ALMP   Active labor market policy

AMAG   Labor Market Adjustment Law, proposed in 1966

BAA   Federal Institute for Labor, formed in 1969

BAVAV   Federal Institute of Unemployment Insurance and Labor Placement, formed in 1952 and became the BAA in 1969

BBiG   Federal Vocational Education Act of 1969

BDA   Federation of German Employers Associations

BDI   Federation of German Industry

BIBB   Federal Institute for Vocational Education, started in 1970

BR   Bundesrat, the legislature composed of state representatives

BRD   Federal Republic of Germany

BT   Bundestag, the legislature composed of federal representatives

CDU   Christian Democratic Union (political party)

CGB	Christian Trade Union Federation
CSU	Christian Social Union (political party)
DDR	East German Republic
DAG	Federation of German White Collar Employee Unions
DBB	Federation of German Professional Civil Servants
DGB	German Federation of Trade Unions (ADGB in Weimar)
DIHT	Association of German Chambers of Industry and Commerce
DP	A liberal party of the early 1950s that merged with the FDP
Dr.	Druchsache, or volume number for Bundestag reports
DZ	*Die Zeit*, weekly German newspaper
EEC	European Economic Community
FDP	Free Democratic Party (political party)
FRG	Federal Republic of Germany (see also BRD)
HHSG	Budgetary Structure Law passed in 1975
IG Metall	Metal Workers Union, including auto, steel, and others
ILO	International Labor Organization
JUSO	Young Socialist Organization of the SPD
OECD	Organization for Economic Cooperation and Development
OPEC	Organization of Petroleum Exporting Countries
ÖTV	The Public Employees and Service Workers Union
STW	Short-time work
SPD	Social Democratic Party of Germany
SZ	*Süddeutsch Zeitung*, major newspaper of Munich, West Germany
USPD	Communist party during the Weimar Republic
WTB	The DGB's Keynesian spending plan during the Weimar Republic

U.S. ABBREVIATIONS

AFL-CIO	American Federation of Labor and Congress of Industrial Organizations
AVA	American Vocational Association
ARA	Area Redevelopment Act of 1961
APW	Accelerated Public Works Program of 1962
CCC	Civilian Conservation Corps
CEP	Concentrated Employment Program
CETA	Comprehensive Employment and Training Act, passed in 1973
CETA I	Initial CETA job-training programs
CETA IIBC	Later CETA job-training programs
CETA IID	Job creation programs aimed at structural unemployment
CETA III	Various national programs for Native Americans, migrants, and others
CETA VI	Job creation programs aimed at cyclical unemployment
CORE	Congress on Racial Equality
CQ	Congressional Quarterly
DOL	Department of Labor
ECRP	Economic Report of the President
EDA	Economic Development Administration for Appalachian Redevelopment
ETA	Employment and Training Administration in the Department of Labor
ETRP	Employment and Training Report of the President, previously named the Manpower Report of the President
GAO	Government Accounting Office
HIRE	Help through Industrial Retraining and Employment
ICESA	Interstate Conference of Employment Security Agencies
JTPA	Job Training and Partnership Act

M1 and M2   Narrow and wide definitions of the money supply

MDTA   Manpower Development and Training Act of 1962

NAB   National Association of Businessmen

NAM   National Association of Manufacturers

NJTC   New Jobs Tax Credit Program

NYC   Neighborhood Youth Corps

PATCO   Professional Air Traffic Controllers

OEO   Office of Economic Opportunity

OJT   On-the-Job Training

OMAT   Office of Manpower, Automation, and Training

OSHA   Occupational Safety and Health Administration

PEP   Public Employment Program

PIC   Private Industry Councils

PSC   Public Service Careers

PSIP   Private Sector Initiative Program

PWA   Public Works Administration during the New Deal

Rep.   Representative in U.S. House of Representatives (or West German Bundestag)

STIP   Skill Training Improvement Program, started in 1977

SYEP   Summer Youth Employment Program

TJTC   Targeted Jobs Tax Credit

UAW   United Automobile Workers

USES   United States Employment Service

VA   Veterans Administration

WIN   Work Incentive Program

WPA   Works Progress Administration during the New Deal

YACC   Young Adult Conservation Corps

YEDPA   Youth Employment and Demonstration Project Act of 1977

YETP   Youth Employment and Training Program

YCCIP   Youth Community Conservation Improvement Projects

YIEPP   Youth Incentive Entitlement Project Program

Preface

This book describes and explains the formation of active labor market policy in Germany and the United States. It sets programs of education, job training, job creation, and job placement in a historical context and covers developments since World War I in detail with some attention to earlier centuries. The analysis does not aim to show the deleterious effects of unemployment. It assumes these effects, which are substantiated in an ever growing sociological literature on the unemployed worker's downward slide in morale, income, and conviviality.[1] Instead, my purpose is to uncover the causal forces that brought governments to intervene into employment problems in the labor market.

I first became interested in this topic while working as a compliance surveyor for the Veterans Administration. Day after day I would go into vocational schools, universities, and apprenticeship establishments that varied considerably in their quality: from a diving school on the Pacific Ocean that placed all its graduates in high-paying but dangerous jobs to a business school apparently run by gangsters with an "honest ignorance" of what learning entailed. I also saw how schools could avoid the Veterans Administration's 50 percent rule on the job placement of graduates; for example, a music school graduated two of five hundred students and then placed a single student on a one-night stand sing-

1. For recent surveys of the literature on social psychological effects of unemployment, see Jahoda (1982), Hayes and Nutman (1981), and Fryer and Payne (1986).

ing engagement, hence, meeting the 50 percent rule. My interest in this topic was redoubled during the oil crisis when my hometown of Detroit experienced massive layoffs and long-term unemployment.

In my explanation of government intervention in labor markets, I have attempted to fuse historical and quantitative materials—to show that quantitative models of "work" and "socialization" fit well with documentary evidence of the passage of legislation concerning active labor market policy. In this way, I have provided context for and put meaning into quantitative models. This kind of analysis integrates two research traditions in political economy from within sociology and history. Such scholars as Richard Titmuss (1963), Harold L. Wilensky and Charles Lebeaux (1965), T. H. Marshall (1964), Asa Briggs (1961), Gunnar Myrdal (1960), Gaston Rimlinger (1971), and, more recently, Margaret Weir, Shela Orloff, and Theda Skocpol (1988) provide a rich structural and historical account of the development of welfare states, but they generally avoid quantitative analysis.

Alexander Hicks (1984), Peter Flora (1983, 1986), Douglas Hibbs (1977), Hibbs et al. (1982), Nathaniel Beck (1982), and other political economy analysts provide a rigorous statistical time-series analysis of a number of welfare state variables, but their work seems devoid of the rich contextual analyses of the previous studies. Comparative data on welfare states with single country time-series analyses are somewhat infrequent because the analyst must concentrate much effort on the incredibly difficult task of collecting comparative data. Nonetheless, I have tried to integrate the strong points of these somewhat disparate styles of research in a "synthetic" rather than simply "combined" fashion (Ragin 1987, pp. 69–71).

I have also attempted to fuse the theoretical explanations of the welfare state put forth by T. H. Marshall and Reinhard Bendix in their citizenship rights theory, Theda Skocpol and Ann Shola Orloff in their state centric theory, and Walter Korpi and Michael Shalev in their power resources theory. With the example of Harold Wilensky in mind, I have integrated these theories by looking at a range of variables and causes from labor market pressures to forms of neocorporatist policy making (Wilensky 1975, 1976, 1981). The result is not eclecticism but a comprehensive theory that focuses on four causal forces: social demands, state formation, citizenship rights ideology, and external events. A consequence of this approach is that some causal forces work in one country but not the other. This may distress some, but I simply do not believe that the comparative analysis of welfare states is ready for monocausal theories.

A major purpose of this book is to understand how social and political structures and ideologies shape labor market policies. By placing American institutions next to those of a similar country with strong active labor market policy one can learn which policies and programs might be transferred to the United States. It may seem that since Ronald Reagan took office, active government intervention into the American economy became a thing of the past. (Some believe that has been the case in Europe, but, as I show, that belief is misguided.) Indeed, with the drastic reduction of job creation programs in 1983, active labor market policy at the federal level in the United States has given way to small state programs restricted to job training. However, this has not been without a price. As Jesse Jackson was fond of saying in the 1988 primaries, we have opted for "welfare and jailcare." The current problems of drug dealing in the streets in poor neighborhoods point out the lack of job programs for disadvantaged teenagers often facing 50 percent unemployment rates. The active labor market policy programs of the 1960s and 1970s could have employed many of these now criminalized teenagers. As the problem of unemployment among youth has become more urgent, the U.S. government has chosen largely to either ignore it or moralize about it. The federal government has also chosen to deemphasize wider investments in the bottom half of America's human resources. I will directly address these and related issues within the comparative context of restoring U.S. competitiveness.

In the book I first pursue the pre-World War II roots of active labor market policy. Chapter 1 introduces the problem of labor market policies and my theoretical framework. Chapters 2 and 3 examine the beginnings of the employment service, the bases for job-training policy in the Berufschule and the high school, and the early Weimar and New Deal job creation policies.

In the next three chapters, I examine the implementation and effectiveness of post-World War II active labor market programs.

Chapter 4 analyzes the employment service and its job placement efficiency. Chapter 5 compares the education systems of both countries and then focuses on the job-training programs of the United States and West Germany. Chapter 6 examines job creation policies, which are politically vulnerable and expensive in both countries.

The last three chapters deal with the causes of legislation and expenditures on active labor market policy. Chapter 7 on West Germany and Chapter 8 on the United States follow laws regarding active labor market policy through the corridors of power; in each chapter, I ground interest groups in their social bases and then explain the enactment of major post–World War II laws. In Chapter 9, I present a systematic analysis of expenditures in active labor market policy from 1950 to 1984. The West German work model—centering on left party power, unemployment rates, and the manufacturing sector—is contrasted with the American socialization model of demographic and service sector change. These two models, cast in the framework of social demand and state formation, are put into an overall path model. Finally, in an effort to contribute to continuing debates about both social justice and international competitiveness, I conclude with policy recommendations to address unemployment and other labor market problems.

Chapter One

Introduction

High unemployment means low industrial productivity and an inefficient use of industrial and social capital. Unemployment multiplies inefficiency by degrading workers' skills and destroying motivation. In an era of increasing international competition that demands both high productivity and impeccable quality, advanced industrial nations cannot waste human resources. Nor can they forego flexibility in the work force by overlooking transitional measures to help vulnerable workers move from older industries using obsolete skills to newer industries requiring advanced skills. Nations competing in export markets cannot trade off equity and efficiency or legitimation and accumulation in a zero sum game. Survival in the global marketplace requires that equity and efficiency reinforce each other to produce positive sum results. When applied correctly, active labor market policy (ALMP) allows flexibility in labor markets for firms needing highly skilled workers and equity for workers left unemployed or stuck in declining industries.[1]

But the reactions of advanced industrial nations to efficiency and equity may differ considerably—from passively giving com-

1. I use the broadest measure of productivity (gross output per worker per year in the manufacturing sector) to justify the productivity statements in this paragraph. This measure includes the unemployed from the manufacturing sector, while other measures based on hours worked would exclude the unemployed. Although one could envision a society with mass unemployment and highly efficient industries, such a country would certainly be wasting its human resources. For more details on productivity measurement see Kendrick 1977; Denison 1967, 1979; and Dertouzos et al. 1989.

pensation payments to the unemployed, to indirectly stimulating the economy through macroeconomic policies, or to directly attacking unemployment through government intervention into labor markets. Although most governments do all three with varied emphases, some governments choose active labor market policy to supplement passive compensation programs and uncertain macroeconomic policies by placing the unemployed in jobs, retraining laid-off or vulnerable workers for new jobs, and creating jobs for those who need them. ALMP cannot substitute for sensible fiscal and monetary policies, eliminate the need for unemployment insurance, or overcome stagnant growth, but it can be a valuable tool in enhancing the long-run productivity of the labor force and reducing unemployment. But even with ALMP alone, the range of commitment to ALMP differs greatly between nations (see Table 1). In 1980 and 1985, Sweden spent 2.2 percent and 3.3 percent of GNP, respectively, on ALMP; the United States consistently spent less than 0.5 percent, despite having twice the unemployment rate.

Divergent commitments to ALMP have a dramatic impact on individual workers. In a country with strong ALMP—Sweden or West Germany—a worker threatened with unemployment can obtain critical help from the state. When the possibility of layoff emerges, the firm must notify the worker, the union or works council, and the employment service well in advance of the "possible" layoff. The union, firm, and employment service avoid layoffs by subsidizing work or training within the firm through short-time work or other measures. If the firm cannot avoid the cutback, the employment service provides job counseling and planning well before the layoff. While the worker receives full pay for the one to six months before the layoff, a well-staffed employment service does everything in its power to place the worker in a new job. During a recession and even during industry-specific slumps, the employment service authorizes public works projects. If these job efforts fail, the worker may enter one of many labor market training schools and receive a subsistence allowance high enough to live on. At last resort, the worker receives unemployment insurance, while looking for a job at an employment service that lists most job vacancies. This active approach leads to the constant upgrading of skills that keep

TABLE 1 *Government Expenditures on Active Labor Market Policy over GNP[a] (in percentages)*

Country	1960	1965	1970	1975	1980	1984	1987
Sweden	0.63	0.76	1.13	1.40	2.17	3.30	1.86
Ireland	—	—	—	0.17	—	—	1.45
Denmark	—	—	0.20	1.51	—	—	1.14
Belgium	—	—	0.70	—	—	—	1.10
Netherlands	—	—	0.22	0.42	—	—	1.08
W. Germany	0.19	0.15	0.31	0.58	0.61	0.62	0.99
U.K.	—	—	0.43	0.72	—	—	0.89
Finland	—	1.36	0.56	0.71	1.18	—	0.76
France	—	—	0.17	0.28	—	—	0.74
N.Z.	—	—	—	—	—	—	0.65
Canada	—	—	0.44	0.51	0.58	0.66	0.57
Italy	—	—	—	—	—	—	0.46
Norway	—	—	0.90	0.63	0.63	—	0.41
Austria	—	—	0.05	0.15	—	—	0.41
Australia	—	—	0.30	0.34	—	—	0.32
U.S.	0.03	0.10	0.18	0.28	0.30	0.16	0.24
Switzerland	—	—	—	—	—	—	0.17
Japan	—	—	0.43	0.72	—	—	0.17

Sources: For the United States and West Germany, see appendix; Sweden, from Johannessen and Schmid (1980) and Johannesson (1989); Austria calculated from Soldwedel (1984, p. 93); Ireland calculated from Dineen (1984, p. 269); Belgium from OECD (1974, p. 53); Finland calculated from Finland (1966–82); Canada calculated from Berg andSmucker (1989); all 1987 figures are from the OECD (1988, p. 86); remaining countries and years from OECD (1978 and 1982).
[a]Countries are ranked according to 1987 expenditures over GNP.

people involved in work and amenable to the technological changes that lead to higher productivity.

In the United States, a worker is often told of a layoff with little or no warning. If protected by union seniority rules, the worker may take a job from a fellow worker with less seniority. Without a union, the "fire-at-will" doctrine simply allows the employer to discharge workers.[2] If the employment service handles his or her

2. The erosion of the "fire-at-will" doctrine—workers winning discharge cases in court—has a short history and uncertain future because employers have become more cautious about promising job tenure (see Holloway and Leach 1985).

type of work, the discharged worker visits an understaffed employment office for unemployment insurance and placement services. The employment service places workers in only a small percentage of jobs open in the economy (5.7 percent in 1982); and most workers will also have to visit private employment offices, temporary work registries, union hiring halls, or individual employers, as well as read the want ads and consult with friends and relatives.[3] In short, the layoff may be sudden and swift, but state support for job search, retraining, and job creation may be slow, uncoordinated, and hard to get. The passive approach creates immediate productivity losses and allows for the deterioration of workers' skills that leads to long-term productivity losses. This approach also causes workers to be defensive about technological change because it may lead to layoffs.

Sweden and West Germany do everything in their power to help every citizen find work, but the United States does little. In 1980, this difference in help was reflected in ALMP expenditures as a percentage of GNP: Sweden spent more than seven times the money as a percentage of GNP than did the United States. Unlike pensions and similar entitlements, which require automatic expenditures, ALMP as a discretionary policy does not demand a uniform response. Western countries can vary in their use of ALMP as a weapon against unemployment. Given this discretion, why are American expenditures so low?

In pursuing the answer to this question, I chose to compare the weak ALMP of the United States with the strong ALMP of West Germany. West Germany provides realistic policy alternatives and matches the United States on many important political dimensions, despite some obvious differences in culture and history. Although Sweden funds the most effective ALMP anywhere, it has done so because its Social Democratic Party, dominant in a highly centralized and neocorporatist system, helps produce peak bargains between capital and labor on economic and social policies. The United States, of course, is highly unlikely to develop a dominant left party, utilize a neocorporatist bargaining framework, or organize 90 percent of the labor force into a few, powerful, trade union federations. However, both the

3. The 5.7 percent figure is computed from data discussed in Chapter 4.

United States and West Germany have opposing political parties that have alternated in power during the last thirty years, the burden of high defense expenditures, and a federal system of government where the states have wide powers to enact and implement social policy.[4] The political structure of the United States and West Germany demands that ALMP operate under tough conditions. At the same time, the two countries differ greatly on ALMP commitment. For instance, West Germany passed more effective ALMP legislation in the 1960s and spent twice as much money on ALMP as a percentage of GNP in 1980 than did the United States.

Contrasting national commitments to full employment in West Germany and the United States reveal three major differences in ALMP. First, the West German employment service controls all organized job placement, bans most private agencies, and operates as an umbrella organization for nearly all ALMP programs. But the U.S. employment service has a marginal role in other ALMP programs and also struggles against private employment offices and even competes with public agencies—college placement offices and civil service information centers. Second, West German job training produces highly skilled, manual workers or raises the skill levels of lower-skilled workers through job training with paid leaves of absence. U.S. job-training programs target low-skilled jobs and provide little advanced-skill training. They tend toward socialization training—how to behave during job interviews, how to use an alarm clock, and how to "get your mind right" for a job. Third, West German job creation often focuses on industries afflicted with high unemployment; for instance, the government subsidizes the construction industry to provide jobs during the winter when most firms shut down and sets up short-time work programs so that firms can avoid lay-offs during a temporary downturn in the economy. The United States ignores specific-industry subsidies, does not stabilize jobs,

4. On defense expenditures as a percentage of GNP in 1974, the United States ranked first among OECD countries, while West Germany ranked fourth (Harold Wilensky Welfare State and Equality Data Set and Wilensky 1975, pp. 76–77). On federalism, Katzenstein states that "only the United States has a federal system that accords to the individual states the prominence granted to the eleven states in the Federal Republic" (1987, pp. 15–17).

and tends to put laid-off workers on extended unemployment compensation.

Through my analysis of these policies, the U.S. approach to productivity and equity in the increasingly competitive world economy is shown wanting. The United States has ignored the bottom half of the labor force for far too long and must provide these workers with the tools and flexibility to handle the nation's needs for the twenty-first century. The threat, of course, is to be buried economically by the East Asians (especially Japan) and Western Europeans (because of European integration coming in 1992). The United States excels at higher education and basic research and development, but it is abominable at vocational or below college education. Over the course of the last century, American neglect of the noncollege worker has given a competitive edge to engineer-controlled mass production which primarily relies on unskilled workers. But Dertouzos and coauthors state that mass production is an "outdated strategy" (1989, p. 46). This system produced a mass of goods at a low price in the shortest possible amount of time, with little attention to either workers or the quality of their efforts. As many third world countries have caught up with the United States in basic education and economic development, they are taking over these largely semi- and unskilled industries. The United States must compete in terms of higher skill or suffer a major decline in per capita income. Many European countries like West Germany have produced noncollege workers who are highly skilled in multiple areas to depths unknown in the United States. This gives them a competitive advantage in worker-controlled and flexible production, and consequently they tend to make small numbers of highly complex machines in response to ever-increasing market changes. Moreover, they have developed job placement and job-retraining programs to move workers from declining industries to growing firms needing new skills.

Of course, the United States may look to Japan for management techniques, from quality control circles to just-in-time inventory, but the likelihood of transferring labor market norms and values from such a different, homogeneous population to a multicultural society is highly unlikely. Although the United

States and other countries will adopt some Japanese techniques, the model for American revival is much more likely to come from across the Atlantic than the Pacific (Becker 1989; Peters 1989). The basis for this renewal will involve the educational, re-training, job placement, and job creation institutions discussed in the following pages. Other parts of the new American model will be connected to flexibility and teamwork within the firm. This book provides the basis for understanding one side of the renewal equation—flexibility in labor markets through training, placement, and avoiding unemployment. I uncover the political and social forces that led to American problems with education and job placement and show how and why we stand where we do today. In the next section, I discuss both the data that forms a basis for each chapter and the theoretical framework for this study.

DEFINITIONS, DATA, AND METHODS

ALMP is a relatively new term, rarely compiled by governmental authorities or international agencies. It can often slip through definitional boundaries because almost any policy that affects the labor market could be considered a labor market policy. I restrict ALMP to state intervention into labor markets with the purpose of reducing unemployment for persons who are ready to work. ALMP is job placement (matching people to jobs), job training (teaching new skills to people to eliminate shortages of skills or production bottlenecks), and job creation (direct government ef-forts to create jobs). ALMP excludes several policies commonly viewed as affecting unemployment. Subsidies for relocating firms, which lead into regional redevelopment and industrial policies, may simply subsidize businesses and not decrease unemploy-ment. Methods to reduce the labor supply—lowering the retire-ment age, raising the age of compulsory schooling, curtailing immigrants, or increasing military recruitment—are indirect in-terventions. Affirmative action policies redistribute rather than increase work. Reductions in business regulation aim to increase economic growth, but their effects on the labor market are often unpredictable. Trade restrictions, even if they work, may create jobs in the short run but disastrous backlashes in the long run. Finally, I exclude training of veterans and vocational rehabilitation benefits in the United States because they were not mainly intended to reduce unemployment and they have different political roots than ALMP. These and other policies are too indirectly related to the major task of ALMP—direct intervention in labor markets to reduce unemployment.

ALMP data was easier to collect in West Germany because it has a more unified conception of ALMP than the United States. I collected West German ALMP data from *Bundesanstalt für Arbeit* records that provided expenditure figures with comparable categories for more than thirty years. There was only one exception; from 1965 to 1968 I used Ministry of Labor sources (see Appendix).[5] American expenditures came from the U.S. *Budget of the U.S. Government* and *Employment and Training Report of the President.* But even the President's Report unaccountably aggregated expenditures and submerged program categories. Therefore, disaggregated figures from the U.S. budget and an internal Department of Labor memoranda were crucial (see Appendix).

In most of the text, I refer to the levels of expenditures divided by GNP and, in a few instances, correlations between variables. In the penultimate chapter, I use time-series analysis corrected for autocorrelation and narrow the definition of ALMP to make it strictly comparable in the two countries (see Chapter 9 for more details on time-series methods). This results in excluding programs unique in the two countries: youth stay-in-school programs in the United States, and speech training for guest-

5. These two time series are unique because other analyses have not divided expenditures into job placement, job training, and job creation over the entire post–World War II period. Günther Wittich collected West German ALMP data from 1950 to 1961 in his 1966 dissertation. Günther Schmid presents Bundesanstalt expenditure data from 1968 to 1978 (1980, p. 250). A consistent opponent of ALMP, Rüdiger Soltwedel, lists data from 1972 to 1980. Gert Bruche and Bernd Reissert (1985) examine expenditures and revenues from 1973 to 1983. I know of only one previous effort to collect U.S. ALMP data. Peter Gottschalk (1983) looked at U.S. data from 1964 to 1983. His data neither include job placement nor divide job training from job creation measures.

workers, foreign visitor training, construction industry support, and short-time work in West Germany.[6]

This book uses two methodologies in order to provide a "synthetic research strategy" (Ragin 1987, p. 69). First, a comparative/historical approach follows Mill's indirect method of difference to set up a research design of most similar cases (Smelser 1976; Mill 1936). This analysis detects structural constants that explain policy differences. Thus, much of the historical analysis especially points to: (a) the effects of past events that happened once but have a continuing effect, for instance, the linkage of labor organizing to the movement for the political franchise; and (b) the effects of social or governmental structure that also do not change year by year but are constantly present during subsequent years (for instance, the different consequences of proportional and winner-take-all election procedures). Second, I use time-series analysis in later chapters to show the incremental effects of yearly changes in political and economic variables on the labor market's expenditures. In the following analysis, these two kinds of causes are often combined, but social demands tend to fall into the incremental category and state formation into the structural constant category.

THE CAUSES OF SOCIAL POLICY

In providing explanations for different periods with diverse evidence, I use a Weberian theory of class and status group power with the independent influence of state structures and citizenship ideologies. Thus, three factors—social demands, state formation, and external effects—along with the subordinated influence of the ideology of citizenship rights under parties and coalitions explain the development of social policy. First, socially rooted demands emanating from class and status group struggles are often used to explain policy, especially concerning the labor unions' push to be recognized and to extend the welfare state. Second, the formation of the state, which consists of administrative, judi-

6. Whenever I speak of total expenditures, I will be referring to the narrow definition that excludes the above mentioned policies (see Appendix). I will specifically refer to these unique job creation expenditures when they are discussed in Chapter 6.

cial, educational, military, and representative institutions, also explains major comparative differences between nations.[7] Because ALMP is a discretionary policy, rather than an automatic policy responding to demographic pressures, state structure is especially important. Third, external events in terms of international wars and economic crises may have different effects on nations if their experiences with these matters significantly differ. Finally, I add the ideological influence of citizenship rights as a subordinated factor between social demands and state formation because it tends to straddle interest groups (social demands) and parties (state formation); as such, it represents the influence of ideas. My causal model for the first historical period can be seen in Figures 1 and 2 for each country (Skocpol and Orloff 1986, pp. 241–43; Korpi 1989; Quadagno 1987; Sewell 1985; Burstein 1981, p. 311). Subsequent historical periods follow the same model.

These processes set the stage for social policy during the Weimar Republic and the New Deal. In this formative period, social policy was parceled out to particular bureaucracies allied with interest groups brandishing their own specific ideologies. In Germany, social demands from unions coupled with a strong state tradition led to a powerful Ministry of Labor administering social policy for both labor and employers in a comprehensive welfare state. In the United States, third-party bureaucrats administered a fragmented and narrow welfare state by relying on social workers, but employers and unions were left to their own devices. As a result Germany held a "work orientation" toward social policy that emphasized strong social demands over state formation; and in the United States, a "socialization orientation" revealed muted social demands and the negative influence of state formation. After World War II, each country's social demands and state structures passed largely intact from Weimar and the New Deal to provide the structural constants for the more recent developments in ALMP. In this section, I delineate the social demands of developing class and status groups that led to ALMP. In the next sections, I deal with state formation and external events.

---

7. State formation refers to differential state structures in a comparative context and to the relatively autonomous interests of state bureaucrats. I discuss this in more detail at the end of Chapter 1.

1. The Formation of Labor Market Policies in Germany Before World War II

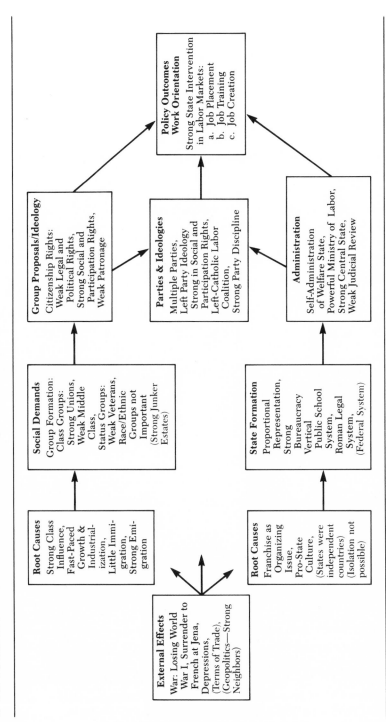

Note: Factors are listed in order of importance, and items in parentheses are less important causes for ALMP not mentioned in the text.

2. The Formation of Labor Market Policies in the United States Before World War II

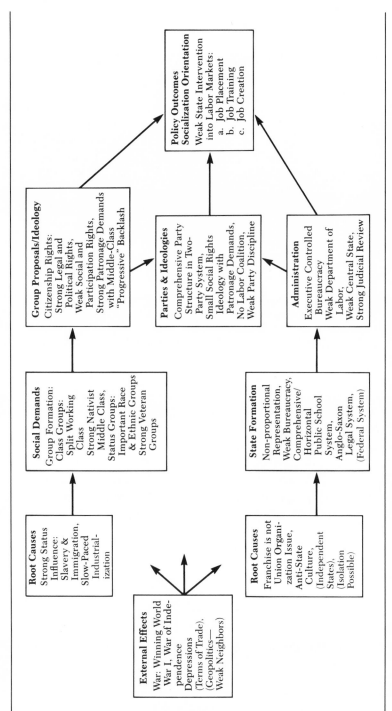

Note: Factors are listed in order of importance, and items in parentheses are less important causes for ALMP not mentioned in the text.

Social Demands

Social demands come from class and status group processes, although states can occasionally bestow rights.[8] In Imperial and Weimar Germany, the "worker question" dominated social policy discussion. Critically observing the harsh living and working conditions of propertyless workers in Saxony and Berlin, Karl Marx and other scholars directed attention to the growing importance of workers.[9] Although different social groups approached the worker question from many perspectives, they all focused on the industrial working class. When liberal and leftist intellectuals raised the worker question, they referred to the working conditions, poverty, and the political potential of German nationals who had lived on the land only a few decades ago but were thrust penniless into factories, mines, and mills. When union leaders raised the worker question, they demanded decent wages, better working conditions, and greater political power. Conservative moralists, concerned about the breakup of community bonds, even condemned industrialization. The middle classes and artisans defended their position in society, as did the employers. Although each group had a different perspective, the worker question guided their responses toward social policy.

Late and rapid industrialization led to strong trade unions that avoided major craft/industrial conflict. Industrial growth also emphasized manufacturing, whose factories were easier for unions to organize. Immigration did not cause a status split in the labor force between nativist and immigrant unions, and the anti-Socialist law delayed but unified union organizing. The sudden and monolithic rise of capitalism, accentuated by a relatively homogeneous labor force and the repression of union organizing efforts, led to industrial unionism with its broader goals and values

8. One should be careful on this point. All too often social scientists leap too quickly to this conclusion. As I argue later concerning Bismarck's pensions and as Aldon Morris (1984, pp. 31, 281–82) argues concerning the civil rights movement, the easy assumption of unilateral state action (benevolent or manipulative) without extensive social demands is usually off the mark.

9. The propertyless worker was most evident in the Berlin and Saxony areas because former peasants from semifeudal estates could only sell their labor while workers or their families from Baden-Württemberg and Bavaria also worked farms.

encompassing craft unionism (Ritter and Tenfelde 1975). After
the antisocialist law was repealed, union membership grew by a
factor of eleven in two decades, from less than one million in
1901 to nine million by 1920 (Bry 1960, p. 32).

Although Germany had ethnic tensions, immigrating masses
did not threaten to overwhelm German society as they did in
America. The Polish immigration across the Elbe into secondary
labor markets worried Max Weber, but the number of Poles were
few in comparison to the myriad of immigrants entering the
United States at the turn of the century.[10] The Jewish question
caused ethnic tensions but few labor market problems because
Jews were established in jobs, sometimes well educated, and often totally acculturated to German customs and language. Thus,
neither Poles nor Jews were a factor in the formation of German
institutions of social policy.

Aristocratic elites and parts of the middle class in Germany resisted working-class franchise and favored class closure, which
helped the unions and the Social Democratic Party to convert the
franchise into a "worker issue" and mold the isolated industrial
workers into a working-class subculture. The emigration of ambitious Germans reduced the impact of social mobility within Germany, while aristocrats on large feudal estates in East Germany
controlled peasants in farming. Where German farmers were independent, like most farmers in the United States, or industrial
workers kept their ties to the land, as in Baden-Württemberg,
the unions had a hard time recruiting workers. But independent
farmers were few in Prussia and other states. When landless and
unskilled peasants fled the estates for Berlin and other cities,
they quickly assimilated into unions and left parties. Thus, desperate immigrants and upwardly mobile workers in craft unions
did not divide the German labor movement.

Although the Imperial government kept a watchful eye on the
worker question and attempted to forestall workers' protest with
social rights programs, World War I demolished aristocratic
power, temporarily weakened capital, and gave control of the

10. Polish workers in the Ruhr area were allowed to declare their citizenship
in 1922 under the Treaty of Versailles, but this was more involved with reestablishing the Polish state than German citizenship (Murphy 1983, p. 170).

state to the democratic left and its unions.[11] The Social Democrats pressed for participation rights in codetermination and self-administration, and the worker question blossomed into many new social policies and bureaucracies: labor courts, workers' councils, and employment services. The state, which had feared the worker question, welcomed workers' representatives on labor courts and pension boards. Although Weimar politics were chaotic, the worker question and worker participation dominated social policy. By 1927, the worker question had produced a neocorporatist welfare bureaucracy, a strong Ministry of Labor with a wide range of policies, and a "work ideology" of participation and solidarity.

In the United States, the dominant social problem at the turn of the century was the "immigrant question," soon to be followed by the "race question." Leaders saw the immigrating stranger's lack of socialization as the cause of most social problems. Control and socialization of immigrants was the solution, and training workers became secondary. A substantial minority of urban immigrants did not need to learn skills; they had brought considerable skills with them. The vast majority of immigrants also did not really need skill training because they were destined for menial jobs. However, this mass of immigrants needed to learn the customs, language, and government of the new country. Philanthropic organizations, churches, and local governments attempted to solve the socialization problems by providing settlement houses and other missionary organizations to help the culturally bewildered immigrants.

Weak unions developed in the United States because of immigration, high wages, and longer and slower paced industrialization. Skilled workers, who only understood the new immigrants enough to know that they were willing to work for less and occasionally break strikes, backed away from immigrants and built nativist unions.[12] These skilled craft unions developed gradually, dominated, and then competed with industrial unions composed

11. See Maier (1975, pp. 61–62) and Feldman (1970) on the Stinnes-Liegen Agreement where labor and capital worked out many issues of social policy.

12. Unions often have difficulties in understanding immigrants because their troubles extend beyond the workplace to housing, discrimination, and other issues (Sabel 1982, p. 133).

of more recent and unskilled immigrants. As a result, craft unions followed economistic goals under the leadership of AFL President Samuel Gompers, but industrial unions awaited the New Deal to organize the CIO. When trade unions gained strength within their industries after World War II, many constructed a welfare state of their own based on private sector pensions and health benefits. After visibility peaked from 1890 to 1919, the worker question was dispersed into a privileged and segmented welfare state (Jacoby 1989; Brody 1983; Davis 1980; Lipset 1977).

Citizenship Rights and Social Demands

Rights of citizenship provide a useful tool for assessing class or status group struggles in social policy because they can easily incorporate conflicts within both class and status groups (race, ethnicity, and gender). Building on Marshall and Bendix, I expand citizenship rights to include participation rights: workers' rights to democratic participation in firms, labor markets, and capital markets. Established groups and emerging social movements battle over these and other citizenship rights (Marshall 1964; Bendix 1964).

Following lines of development in Bendix, I derive participation rights. Bendix defines legal rights as political existence or being, political rights as political action or doing, and social rights as economic existence or being (that is, programs that ensure the ability to compete economically). Being means that one has rights, while doing means that one has the meta-right to create rights.[13] Bendix implies a cross-classification of social institutions (public and private) and social action (being and doing), without presenting the last cell of Figure 3 (1964, pp. 78–79). Participation rights form the last cell representing private or economic action.

The four rights are shown in Table 2. Legal rights for individuals include the freedoms of speech, property, religion, and association. The individual rights to association bring organizational

13. This classification comes from the legal distinction between "status" and "capacity" in Graveson (1953).

3. Citizenship Rights as a Dichotomy of Action and Institution

	Social Institution	
	Public Arena (Political)	Private Arena (Economic)
Passive Being or having rights	(1) Legal Rights	(2) Social Rights
Active doing or creating rights	(3) Political Rights	(4) Participation Rights

Social Action

TABLE 2   An Expanded Citizenship Rights Model of Social Policy

Legal Rights: Having Rights	Political Rights: Creating Rights	Social Rights: Having Rights	Participation Rights: Creating Rights

A. *Personal Rights*
1. Liberty of person
2. Freedom of speech
3. Freedom of religion
4. Property rights
5. Contracting rights
6. Association rights
7. Rights to equal treatment
	A. *Personal Rights*
	1. Enfranchisement for:
	  a. Nonpropertied (class)
	  b. Women and gender groups
	  c. Ethnic groups
	  d. Racial groups
	  e. Age categories
	  f. Immigrants/foreigners
	2. Rights to hold office
	3. Secret ballot
	4. Rights to join a party
		A. *Enabling or Preventive Rights* (health and family care)
		1. Health care services
		2. Family allowances
		3. Personal and family counseling
		4. Physical rehabilitation
			A. *Labor Market Intervention Rights* (distribution of work)
			1. Job creation programs
			2. Job placement services

B. *Organizational Rights* (firm, union, bureaucracy, and association rights) 1. Employee organizing 2. Business incorporation 3. Federation rights 4. Political party organization	B. *Organizational Rights* (party, interest group, and social movement rights) 1. Political lobbying 2. Political fund raising 3. Legislative and administrative consultation 4. Political bargaining 5. Social movement and protest rights	B. *Opportunity Rights* 1. Preprimary education 2. Primary and secondary education 3. Higher education 4. Vocational education 5. Educational assistance for special groups	B. *Firm/Bureaucracy Participation Rights* (control or participation by workers and/or clients) 1. Job security and redundancy 2. Codetermination and workers councils 3. Client participation in agencies 4. Affirmative action and comparable worth 5. Collective bargaining 6. Wage and income policy
C. *Legal Enforcement and Access* 1. Access to courts (legal aid) 2. Expansion of the courts 3. Law enforcement	C. *Legal Enforcement* 1. Election monitoring 2. Fund-raising controls 3. Lobbying controls	C. *Distributive Rights* (transfer payments) 1. Old-age pensions 2. Public assistance 3. Unemployment compensation 4. Work injury insurance 5. War injury pensions	C. *Capital Intervention and Participation Rights* (democratic control over decisions) 1. Wage earner and union funds 2. Capital escape laws 3. Regional investment policy 4. Antitrust and merger laws

legal rights into existence. Political rights involve the procedures for creating new laws, including voting, running for office, and casting secret ballots. For private organizations, political rights are the powers of political action such as fundraising, nominating candidates, lobbying, and even protesting. Social rights are public interventions into the private sphere to support citizens' claims to economic existence. They alter the distribution of resources through transfer payments and services and provide basic survival minimums for individuals, including public assistance, compensation payments, family allowances, health care, and educational benefits. Just as political rights are the legal power of doing, participation rights are the private power of doing. They represent the private or economic creation of action and refer to rights to a job and involvement in economic decision making by controlling markets, firms, and capital. Thus, the essence of public (political) democracy resides in legal and political rights, while the heart of private (largely economic) democracy exists in social and participation rights.

Participation rights constitute the extension of Bendix's and Marshall's theory of citizenship rights. Viewed substantively, participation rights focus on three parts of the economy. Labor market intervention rights concern job creation and placement programs to provide for full employment and rational use of human resources. Firm participation rights provide worker and public participation in the control of firms or bureaucracies (i.e., workers' councils and codetermination laws). Capital participation rights involve workers' and public participation in decisions about investment in firms and capital flows within and outside the country (i.e., wage earners' funds in Sweden). These rights may be either indirectly advanced by government efforts to promote citizen interests or directly exerted by workers participating in decisions in firms and public bureaucracies. ALMP largely involves the labor market intervention rights exerted by the government.[14]

14. Midway between intervention rights and direct participation rights would be representation of labor and management on self-administered organizations, much like the West German state welfare boards where labor, employer, and government representatives guide policy.

U.S. and German citizenship rights demonstrate two distinct sequences of enactments with entirely different ideologies of social policy. In the United States, Marshall's progression is more or less followed: legal, political, social, and minor participation rights. However, rights overlap considerably in their time frames. For instance, political and legal rights often emerge concurrently, and social rights develop with the assistance of legal rights (i.e., legal aid and NAACP lawsuits during the War on Poverty). Reverses are short-lived, and many citizenship rights remain despite political tides. In Imperial Germany, more social rights were passed than in most other Western democracies, but political rights were restricted (Flora and Alber 1981, pp. 68–71). Weimar Germany developed participation rights to a much larger extent than Anglo-Saxon countries, but political and legal rights in Germany were tragically destroyed during the Nazi regime. Clearly, the United States and Germany followed different patterns of citizenship rights development.[15]

The progress of citizenship rights depends on battles by interest groups over social policy and particular patterns of state formation. The emerging interest groups—powered by class, race, religion, or gender claims and concerns—push for expanding citizenship rights against groups already in the power structure (Turner 1986, p. 92). Interest groups representing these emerging citizens may be empowered or reduced by economic, demographic, ideological, or international developments. As a result,

---

15. Citizenship rights theory has been criticized for its evolutionary theory of rights (Rimlinger 1971, p. 339; Mishra 1981, pp. 31–32; Dahrendorf 1974; Giddens 1982, p. 172). Marshall's original article on citizenship rights did not mention reverses or skipping stages in citizenship rights because few major regressions had occurred in three hundred years of English social history. Nevertheless, Marshall recognized that citizenship rights can regress because they depend in large part upon the fluctuating political and economic powers of interest groups. He discusses how civil rights may be more important than political rights in controlling authoritarian governments (1981, pp. 141, 156); how command economies develop social rights but repress political and civil rights (p. 138); and how social movements may make a "direct break-through" with political rights, rather than pursuing legal rights (p. 150). Similarly, Bendix's version of citizenship rights claims that countries establish their own sequence of enactments in transforming citizenship rights over time (1964, p. 76). Turner states that criticisms of evolutionary theory are a "plausible" deduction in Marshall's original essay; however, Marshall did not use an "evolutionary perspective" (1986, p. 46).

citizenship rights can easily regress when interest group power is weak. Trade unions in both countries have historically embodied many of these rights. But because of different divisions of class and status groups, citizenship ideologies in these two countries are vastly different.[16]

Ideology of Citizenship

In Germany, a coherent ideology of workers' social policy developed with an intellectual base in "participation rights." Fritz Napthali (1928) provided the structure and goals of self-administration, and Eduard Heinemann (1929) proposed the social theory of capitalism. Napthali saw self-administration pervading all social policy and thought that the 1927 employment service law would lead to an overall change in the welfare state, with all government functions being democratically administered in bi- or tripartite councils. Unions developed special schools, libraries, and cultural institutions to spread this ideology in the worker subculture, which was particularly strong compared to other countries (Schneider 1975b; Lidtke 1985). After World War II, the ideology of work and participation rights continued to dominate social policy. Self-administration in the welfare state and codetermination in production spread in the West German economy. The West German welfare and labor market programs tend toward including the working class as a whole, and its programs were less punitive toward the poor than those in the United States (Liebfried 1978, p. 74).

Well-known West German academic works on social policy and social welfare emphasized the ideology of work. For instance, in *Social Policy: A Problem Oriented Introduction* (1980), Backer et al. use the following "threat" areas to organize the book: income, employment, training, health, and age. In *The Compendium of Social Policy* (1979), Anton Burghardt addresses four major sections: interventionistic social policy, wage policy, the labor market, and social insurance. In *Practice and Problems of Social*

16. Conflict enters into citizenship rights theory at two entirely different levels. First, newly emerging and established interest groups battle over extending "personhood" to new citizens and advancing citizenship rights. Second, inherent theoretical conflicts can occur between rights.

Policy (1970), Ludwig Preller puts employment policy first on the agenda of social policy. American social policy rarely places employment, wages, or the labor market at the center of its analyses of social policy; it often prefers to examine poverty, deviance, discrimination, delinquency, and health problems.

In the United States a socialization ideology developed for social welfare.[17] The native working class did not develop an extensive subculture because it was busy pursuing social mobility to occupations above those of immigrants and blacks. Instead, ethnic and racial groups established their own cultural and self-help organizations. Even the blue-collar communities that formed around factories were often based on ethnic origins rather than class (Kornblum 1978). Ethnic groups frequently exerted their influence on social policy through urban political machines that had little influence in Washington, and ethnic and racial subcultures supplanted a working-class subculture (Wilson 1980; Katznelson and Weir 1985).

After World War II, the ideology of work and welfare continued in a socialization vein. Race replaced ethnicity as the dominant defining force in social policy, and the code word for social problems and unemployment became "poverty." Although poverty is amenable to many techniques and definitions, it is particularly susceptible to the social rights approach. The poor could not be expected to exercise participation rights, so services and transfer payments were provided. Nixon began dismantling the one attempt at participation rights, the Community Action Program, when its programs were less than four years old. During the 1970s, emphasis on job creation appeared a step away from this social rights approach to poverty, but job creation lasted only about eight years before it was eliminated. A theoretical justification for labor-controlled social policy withered in obscurity. Instead, under the banners of opportunity and individualism, the ideologies of "interventionist and self-help" social work and "economistic and job control" unionism developed together (Perlman 1928). In the end, the United States has avoided participa-

17. I use "socialization" in the typical sociological way to refer to the inculcation of norms, values, and training to immigrants. This should not be confused with Esping-Andersen's use of the term in socialist discourse, which refers to the socialization of the means of production (1985, pp. 191, 201).

tion rights and even lagged behind in social rights (Wilson 1987, pp. 3–18; Donovan 1980; Lander 1971).

STATE FORMATION

In my explanation of ALMP, state formation refers to the administrative structures of welfare bureaucracies, the form of political parties, the type of judicial system, and the power of various segments of the bureaucracy.

Self-Administration or Professional Control of the Welfare State?

In Germany, the unions and employer associations administered social policy in a neocorporatist structure of social welfare emphasizing participation rights. Pensions for manual and white-collar workers, industrial injury benefits, health insurance, and other social programs were all managed by bipartite labor-management boards.[18] Self-administration had emerged with the *Knappschaftskassen*—mutual aid funds formed by miners and encouraged by Frederick the Great. Prussian legislation in 1854 and 1865 formalized and extended these funds to other industrial sectors.[19] Workers and employers had an equal say in electing the fund executives; together they controlled fifty-three funds (Tenfelde 1977, pp. 90–98).

To forestall workers' protest and political power, Bismarck sought a pension and health system run by executive bureaucracies but funded by employers and unions. Ignoring employer and union traditions, Bismarck introduced an accident liability law in 1871 that replaced self-administration with state management. The law passed in 1871, but employers and workers regarded it as unfair. When the Reichstag rejected a similar accident bill in 1881 and another in 1882, Bismarck finally abandoned the idea of total state administration. Self-administration won and was for-

18. Handwerk, skilled artisans often owning their own shops and businesses, and the free professions were not covered by such policies before World War II.

19. The Prussian Industrial Code of 1845 provided for self-administered pension funds for craftsmen, and legislation followed in other German states after 1850.

mally introduced in the German welfare state with the third accident law and initial health insurance bill in 1883.[20] Courts of
Arbitration for liability were also established with tripartite control over health insurance in 1911. Thus, union and employer's
preferences for self-administration triumphed over Bismarck's opposition (Tennstedt 1977; Hentschel 1983; Huber 1981).[21] Over
time, the unions directed their members from company-based
insurance funds to local sickness funds and other contributory insurance funds. Union representatives replaced the employers or
foremen as directors of the funds. Soon the institutions became
known as the "third pillar" of the German labor movement. As
Heidenheimer comments,

by 1912 many of the 3,000 full-time sickness fund positions were held
by trade unionists, who provided for the labor "subculture" resources of
expertise that paralleled those of the "regular" German *Beamtentum*.
The German unions chose the option of infiltrating and winning control
of the soon dominant insurance administration. (1981, pp. 8–9)

The social funds were administered in executive and general
meetings with members elected by employers and workers in
proportion to their payments: one-third employers and two-thirds
labor (Dawson 1912, p. 72; Syrup 1939).

German social work played little or no role in formulating labor
market policies because it diverged into separate religious paths.
The Protestant movement, allied with the state as early as 1873,
maintained its highly religious deacon's training into the 1920s.
Workers naturally distrusted it.[22] The Catholic movement developed in opposition to the state due to Bismarck's *Kulturkampf*.

20. The Imperial Insurance Office still maintained small amounts of regulation. For more details, see Dawson (1912), Huber (1981, 4:1191–204, 6:1057–
1101), Kaim-Caudle (1973, p. 134), Katzenstein (1987, pp. 170–75).

21. The Socialist Law, passed in 1879, made direct Social Democratic influence minimal, but pressure by both workers and employers was necessary for
the law's passage.

22. The founder of German social work, Johann Wichern, built the Protestant "Rough House" in 1833 for orphans and wayward boys, and in 1845 he
began social training for deacons. He founded the "Inner Mission" as a general
social work organization that still exists today. Wichern and the movement were
tied to the state evangelical church, and Wichern himself became a permanent
adviser on prison affairs in the Prussian Ministry of Interior until 1873 (Friedlander and Myers 1940; Landwehr and Baron 1983).

Instead of supporting public social work institutions, the Catholics developed their own trade unions, political parties, and social work institutions.[23] Although professional social work schools developed for Catholics in 1899 and some Protestants in 1905, neither thrived. An interventionist social movement could not separate itself from religion, infiltrate the universities, or avoid being partially coopted by the state (Friedlander and Myers 1940, p. 3).

After World War II, the new government reestablished self-administration of labor and management over the welfare state as social work hit a "null point" (Pfaffenberger 1981, p. 63). Ideas about social work oscillated between the social help system of Weimar and the reform ideas of the Anglo-Saxon victors, but West Germany eventually returned to the Weimar model. In the 1960s and 1970s, social work tried new training and examination reforms, but it remained divided into social pedagogics and social work and dominated by religious associations (Pankoke 1981; Flamm 1974; Katzenstein 1987, pp. 74–75).[24] Nevertheless, social work became popular as the percentage of social workers in the labor force increased steadily: 0.29 percent in 1950, 0.37 percent in 1961, 0.59 percent in 1970, and 1.17 percent in 1982 (Karr and Leupoldt 1976; BRD Minicensus 1982). But diverse educational backgrounds and weak occupational controls over the profession—unusual in a society that closely regulates most occupations—continued to plague the profession.

23. Catholic concern for workers started in 1864 with Archbishop Keheler of Mainz writing on "the Worker Question and Christianity." After World War II, Catholic workers became part of the left wing of the Christian Democratic Party.

24. New social work regulations in the 1960s included the following: welfare guardians (nurses and welfare workers) from the welfare schools were replaced by social workers taught in the College for Social Work (Fachhochschule); schooling was extended from two to three years; the preparatory practicum—a low-level apprenticeship as an aide—and the narrow training of child, health, and occupational care were dropped in favor of a general academic curriculum; and a professional colloquium was required before the state certificate was granted. In the 1970s, four changes were proposed: more professional training in the graduate schools of social work (advanced Fachhochschule); centralized training and funding in the•larger schools; more flexible academic work with both research and training; and combining social work and social pedagogics—teaching in hospitals, boys' homes, and day care centers—in the same schools. Still, the profession was disorganized under social pedagogics and social work.

A noted scholar of social work laments that social work education "is more heterogeneous than most occupations, i.e., more diverse and fragmented. The system of education is above all not a single system, but one of systemlessness. To those who endure it, it appears as chaos, and for those who must work with it, a labyrinth in which one can hardly find one's way" (Pfaffenberger 1981, p. 61).

The glue that holds the West German welfare system together is self-administration by the unions and employers, not the social work profession. Protestant workers embraced the Social Democratic Party and rejected social work; Catholic workers favored their own union route to social policy. The unions took over what appear to Americans to be social work tasks in the social security system. For example, union social offices provided practical advice to workers on pensions, health insurance, accident insurance, and other benefits. Rudolph Wissell, before becoming Minister of Labor during Weimar, was one of many local union advisers who provided social services to workers. Self-administration, with its long history, pervaded the structure of *Sozialpolitik* (Friedlander and Myers 1940; Sagarra 1977, p. 218; Buck 1983; BMA 1972; Katzenstein 1987, pp. 58–76).

In the United States, social welfare was fragmented with a social rights emphasis. Labor had a weak voice in the administration and formulation of social welfare. Veterans' pensions supplied benefits for native workers in the late 1800s and under an independent agency in 1930, and the Social Security system provided old age pensions beginning in 1935. Gaps in the welfare state gave private pension plans a substantial foothold. National health insurance in the United States has yet to develop, despite efforts in the 1950s and 1960s. Social welfare administration was divided between the state—local and federal governments—and the private sector—firms, churches, and philanthropic organizations. Even the New Deal could only establish a marginal federal welfare system (Wilensky and Lebeaux 1965; Fink 1942). During the 1980s this fragmentation of welfare further increased through underfunding and the privatization of some public programs.

Social work in the United States has played a strong role in the welfare state because it broke its religious ties, avoided the domination of business, which promised a ready source of philanthropic income, and established an independent identity. The social workers developed a professional ethic of their own rather than relying on religious views or the efficiency ethic of business (Wilensky and Lebeaux 1965, p. 162). Social workers found ready employment in the county, city, church, and philanthropic organizations, and they saw the integration of immigrants and poor blacks as their primary task. Social work eventually dominated service provision in welfare bureaucracies, and social workers even held the top leadership positions in the Works Progress Administration and Department of Labor during the New Deal.

After World War II, the social work profession gained in status, income, and prestige. Many efforts were made to secure professional status in licensing for family, psychiatric, drug, genetic, and other types of counseling. The U.S. system of public welfare, comprising numerous single constituency agencies, made referrals to and from social workers a necessity. Schools of social work developed advanced degree programs, offering both the master's degree and the doctorate as well as administrative programs; this system promoted the principle that only social workers were capable of managing social workers. Eventually social workers became the mainstay of the massive welfare state bureaucracies in authority and expertise if not in numbers. Although their reforming zeal eroded as some social workers became more professionalized and espoused therapeutic and referral methods, the 1960s saw a resurgence of community, but not labor, organizing. The right-wing federal adminstrations of the 1980s brought no small erosion of social worker leadership, but for the most part social work remained in control of welfare institutions (Brilliant 1986, pp. 326–27). Thus, U.S. social work has been professionalized with a consistently ordered system of education, firmly ensconced in the social policy bureaucracy, and dominated by the socialization world view based on social rights programs.

In none of this discussion of unions and social work, however, do I imply that unions or social workers dominate government activities because in both countries it is lawyers who clearly have the largest occupational base in state formation. Nevertheless, the major differences between these two countries can be seen in the differential access and power of unions and social workers in the government.

Political Structure and Political Parties

Although federalism supplies a basis for comparison, the political assumptions and structures in these two nations are different. In Germany, the state was born at the surrender to the French at Jena and even further back in the Swedish invasions and the forging of the Prussian nation from land with few geographical demarcations (Droz 1983). In contrast, the United States was founded on a distrust of government intrusion into private life. As a consequence, German citizens' prostate bias allows the belief that the state could accomplish many tasks, while U.S. citizens' antistate bias follows revolution against a world power and centers on self-reliance. The American view carried over into social welfare by seeing inequality as an individual problem and the state's role as limited.

The political structure of each state led to entirely different consequences for party formation. The German parliamentary structure, a precondition for a labor party because it allowed proportional representation, enabled new parties to start with a small percentage of the vote. The system also led to party discipline and encouraged an issue rather than personality or opportunistic approach toward politics. Even though being forced underground by Bismarck, the Social Democrats gained strength in the early 1900s and took power in 1918. The absence of a labor party in the United States can be partly blamed on nonproportional elections. New American parties were very difficult to sustain because losers lose everything, rather than being represented on the basis of the proportion of votes they received. In the long run, third parties were either prophetic, and their issues were absorbed by the major parties; or they were symbolic, and their issues were ignored, forgotten, or suppressed. The two major parties became consensus organizations subject to fluctuating interest groups and social movements, rather than developing specific ideologies and party discipline (Lowi 1984; Lipset 1977, pp. 58–64; Brody 1983).

A major factor in the Social Democratic Party's drive was its ability to combine the demand for working-class franchise with union organizing. This gave the Social Democratic Party society-wide legitimacy as a mass party (often despite their rhetoric) rather than a restricted workers' movement. But American democracy was well established before industrialization. The unions and radical parties could not make the franchise a working-class issue and thus lost a major strategic advantage.

The possibilities for coalitions were propitious for the labor party in Germany. The Social Democrats found allies in the Center Party and the Christian Trade Unions. This coalition can be seen in the compatibility of the two ministers of labor who symbolized the "practical Weimar coalition" of SPD leaders and Center Party radicals who worked together to produce advances in social policy and participation rights. Minister Heinrich Brauns (1920 to 1928) was a Catholic prelate with close ties to the Christian Trade Unions, a Center Party politician, and a leader of the reformist Popular Society for a Catholic Germany. Brauns helped engineer both labor exchange laws and the labor court law as leader of the left coalition within the Center Party that frequently sided with the unions and the SPD.[25] Rudolph Wissell (minister from 1928 to 1930) was a union bureaucrat and SPD politician who presided over the Ministry of Labor during its 1928–30 crisis. Under these two men with strong union ties, the Ministry of Labor during Weimar controlled a large range of worker-oriented social policies.

While the paternalistic social welfare position of the Catholic Church was compatible with moderate left politics in Germany, protestant moralism dominated Catholic paternalism in U.S. social policy, probably due to the low status of the Catholic immigrants, who spent much of their money supporting churches and schools rather than influencing national politics. The indigenous, regionally based Catholics in Bavaria and Baden-Württemberg clearly had the time and resources to enter the political arena. Although U.S. Catholics had a small role in the union organizing drives of the 1930s, Catholics as a group have not publicly criticized the economy until recently, and they are still far from having a progressive social policy agenda (Lipset 1977; Davis 1980; Brody 1983; Wilensky 1981).

In the United States, instead of working-class coalitions, the nativist middle class became the major reform element with the

25. The Center Party used Brauns as liberal cover for Catholic workers, while the party as a whole drifted to the right.

Progressive Movement. Left parties had a very difficult time, and
the Populist Movement suffered the fate of many third parties—
issue absorption by the two-party system. The Republican party
did not develop a labor wing, and the Democratic party wavered
between the liberalism of the North and the conservatism of the
South. The result was ambiguous ideology susceptible to attack
from the right.

Judicial Review and the Structure of Legal Systems

Judicial review is the least visible part of state formation because
it operates sporadically; nevertheless, American judicial review
prevented extensive government intervention into the economy,
while German judicial review did not. American judicial review
prevented labor placement monopoly, eventually voided the National Industrial Recovery Act, and, from 1870 to 1937 limited
the power of the states and the federal government to regulate
private economic activities (Melone and Mace 1988, p. 12). Germany had weak norms of judicial review that did not prevent
government intervention partly because Germany had a Roman
law system and partly because the Weimar constitution was
forged under defeat (Kommers 1976, p. 35). The power of judicial
review, attained by the Weimar courts on April 19, 1929, only
applied to future cases and was usually restricted to intergovernmental conflicts. The constitution, hardly societal bedrock, contained ambitious goals that were difficult to enforce (e.g., full
employment as a right), allowed easy preemption by legislation,
and provided many supreme courts that confused issues of ultimate authority (Blair 1981; Lenior 1940). Thus, a Roman legal
system with weak judicial review allowed government intervention in the economy, while an Anglo-Saxon legal system did not.

The Bureaucracy: Civil Service, the Cabinet, and Labor

The natural history of the bureaucracy and the franchise have
critical consequences for social policy. Where the bureaucracy
precedes the franchise, a powerful organizational precedent is set
for a strong ministry of labor and self-administration. Where the
franchise precedes the bureaucracy, government jobs become

subject to patronage, and in the long run labor has a much weaker position in the government. The formation of self-administration in Germany was aided by the early formation of an elite bureaucracy under aristocratic rule. However, this elite bureaucracy was penetrated by trade union and employer representatives in the institution of self-administration, partly because the franchise was an organizing issue. In contrast, the American franchise was granted well before any definitive federal (and even local) bureaucracy was put into place. As a result, patronage was so widespread in American bureaucracies that the Progressive Movement lashed back against corruption with a vigorous reform agenda. Not only did the Progressives promote social work and the high school to socialize the immigrants, but they also demanded a civil service with merit employment. The civil service guarded against corruption but latently prevented labor-management participation (Skocpol and Orloff 1986, pp. 241–43; Schefter 1977, pp. 423–29).

Furthermore, the Ministry of Labor was powerful in Weimar Germany (Barclay 1974, p. 248).[26] From 1918 to 1933, it administered a wide array of policies: social insurance, public assistance, veterans' benefits, public housing, health insurance, labor and child welfare law, unemployment compensation, job creation policies, and some job training programs. This range of policies completely outstripped the U.S. Department of Labor and the labor ministries of most other countries. But in addition to a large range of duties, the ministry had power—final say over arbitration in industrial strikes.[27]

After World War II, the West German government reestablished a powerful Ministry of Labor that assumed many of the same duties as it had during Weimar, plus new duties including vocational rehabilitation, family allowances, regulating guestworkers, payments to war victims, and the "equalization of burdens."

26. The importance of ministries of labor applies only to contentious governments. Sweden spends about 5 percent of central governmental expenditures on the Ministry of Labor, but Prime Minister Palme has stated that all Swedish ministries are ministries of labor (Meidner 1984; Swedish Government 1976).

27. The longest serving minister, Heinrich Brauns, commented that the ministry "has now practically obtained the significance of an interior ministry," which was the most powerful ministry under the Kaiser (Barclay 1974, p. 248).

From 1960 to 1982, the ministry consumed an average of 20 per-cent of federal expenditures—rivaling the Ministry of Defense as the most heavily funded ministry. Its budget was huge. In com-parison, the U.S. Department of Labor always received less than 6 percent of total federal government expenditures, and its allot-ment was only 2 percent even at the peak of the War on Poverty (U.S. *Budget of the U.S. Government* 1950–84; BRD *Bunde-shaushaltsplan* 1952–82).[28]

In the United States, the Department of Labor has always been weak. Although Congress established the Bureau of Labor in 1884 and the president combined the Department of Com-merce and Labor in 1903, a cabinet-level Department of Labor was not established until 1913. Its mission was not entirely clear, in that it brought together the Bureau of Naturalization, the Chil-dren's Bureau, the Division of Conciliation, and later the Em-ployment Service, but it focused mainly on immigrants and labor conflict (Robertson 1981, p. 80).

Rather than expanding from 1913 to 1946, the Department of Labor suffered one setback after another. It lost duties to inde-pendent agencies: railroad industrial relations to the National Railway Labor Board (1934), union organizing to the National La-bor Relations Board (1935), coal mining problems to the National Bituminous Coal Administration (1935), and industrial disputes to the Federal Mediation and Conciliation Service (1935). It lost other duties to other departments: immigration to Department of Justice (1940), the Children's Bureau to the Federal Security Agen-cy (1946), and job creation programs to the Public Works Admin-istration, the Works Progress Administration, and other agencies (1933–36). Even the employment service was lost for a time to the Federal Security Agency, and pensions and work rehabilita-tion for veterans were permanently given to the Veterans Admin-

28. Even though control of the Ministry of Labor alternates between Social Democratic and Christian-Democratic representatives, union interests are strongly represented. The ministers of labor were: (a) from the Christian Dem-ocratic Party: Anton Storch, 1949–57; Theodore Blank, 1957–65; Hans Katzer, 1965–69; and Norbert Blüm, 1982–present; and (b) from the Social Democratic Party: Walter Arendt, 1972–76; Herbert Ehrenberg, 1976–April 1982; Heinz Westphal, April 1982–October 1982 (Schindler 1983, pp. 337–38). The conser-vative parties have never held the ministry.

istration in 1930 (Grossman 1969; Lombardi 1942). Theodore Lowi comments on the attrition of the Department's duties:

On the eve of the Roosevelt revolution, labor was a microscopic cabinet department whose only significant governing activity was the Immigration and Naturalization Service. During the 1930s, government expanded its relation to the laboring man in many ways, but little of this involved the laboring man's department. On the contrary, the department declined relative to virtually every other sector of public activity. (1979, pp. 81–82)

In the 1950s and early 1960s, the Department of Labor remained marginal, with minuscule expenditures of 0.5 percent to 0.6 percent of the total federal budget. Most social policy was handled by the Department of Health, Education and Welfare, which had taken over in 1953 from the Federal Security Agency, and administered social security, public assistance, child welfare, education, vocational rehabilitation, and public health. And special constituency programs for social policy existed for Native Americans in the Department of the Interior, railroad pensions in the Railroad Retirement Board, and returning soldiers in the Veterans Administration. None of these other agencies invited labor-management participation, though some granted the states wide latitude with funds.

The Department of Labor was bypassed when federal social policy expanded in the mid-1960s, grew slightly in the 1970s, but dropped again in the 1980s. The Office of Economic Opportunity (OEO) received the funds for most 1960s social programs and implemented them through the community action agencies. Although OEO contracted out some programs to the Department of Labor, the agency's budget only rose to about 2 percent of total federal expenditures. In the 1970s, the Labor Department's authority and budgetary expenditures suddenly increased when it received the job creation and job-training programs housed in OEO. The Labor Department also gained expenditures for job creation and safety programs—the Occupational Safety and Health Administration and the Mine Safety and Health Administration. With new programs, the Department of Labor share of the federal budget rose to 5 percent, still less than one-quarter of the German labor ministry. However, the Department of

Labor's expanding authority proved short-lived because job creation programs were dissolved and safety programs were severely curtailed in the 1980s. In sum, the Department of Labor has been marginal.

THE IMPACT OF EXTERNAL EVENTS

Finally, social policy can be influenced by external events such as war and international economic crises. In this section I focus on war and postpone discussion of the oil crisis until later chapters. Losing World War I discredited German capitalists and aristocrats, blunted the influence of veteran and military interests, and temporarily propelled the SPD into power. As a result, the Weimar governments passed many participation rights and universalistic labor market programs. After returning victorious from World War I, U.S. veterans pressed for and eventually obtained the Veterans Administration welfare system—mainly for native workers—while diluting demands for universalistic welfare and labor market programs.[29] Thus, losing World War I strengthened universalistic welfare policies in Germany, and winning the war weakened overall support for the welfare state in the United States.

Since the Second World War, these same differences produced a unified welfare state in West Germany, but they intensified the segmented and uneven welfare state in the United States. Unknown in West Germany, veterans' benefits in the United States provide the most privileged and generously funded of the state welfare programs. Overlapping with active labor market policies, veterans' educational benefits constitute a special labor market policy that establishes a legal claim to subsidized job training and affirmative action programs in government labor markets. In most cases, veterans have thirty-six months of tuition and subsistence allowances to attend the educational institution of their choice, and they have special affirmative action programs entitling them to five to ten preference points on one-hundred-point civil service exams. These preference points often allow veterans to score

29. Even before that, Northern Civil War veterans had gained pension benefits that effectively excluded southern veterans and the massive wave of immigrants that came around the turn of the century (Sanders 1980).

beyond the maximum test result and eliminate nonveteran competition. Veterans also have reemployment rights to their old jobs, while a special veterans' counselor at the employment service provides job placement information. Finally, indigent veterans without service-connected disabilities can avoid the stigma of public assistance and receive "veterans' pensions" and free medical care at Veterans Administration hospitals. The political consequence of war is that American veterans as a status group siphon off political support for universalistic social policies, while West German veterans support the welfare state. Thus, where wars either are fought on home soil or are lost, veterans' groups have fewer claims to privilege because all social groups were subjected to death and the hazards of war (Dryzek and Goodin 1985, p. 10).[30]

In sum, in Germany class groups motivate social demands, and state structures are favorable to social policy; but in the United States status groups crosscut social demands, and state structures are negative toward the welfare state. Germany represents a class-divided society that has found solutions to its major social policy problems through strong labor unions, a powerful Ministry of Labor, and extensive participation rights. The United States represents a more status-based social order where the welfare state is segmented into separate components with competing constituencies—the white working class, blacks, ethnic immigrants, and veterans. A causal model of these factors can be seen in Figures 1 and 2 where two causes are at work. First, concerning social demands, class closure with emigration versus class openness with immigration is the dominant factor. Differences concerning social demands in these two countries boil down to class-versus-status group issues. The presence of a frontier and the lack of a feudal past are epiphenomenal. What separates the United States from the Anglo-Saxon countries is a double dose of status conflict: massive central and eastern European immigration, and the past importation of slaves. But second, social demands are not enough. Particular processes of state formation cause unusual

30. Titmuss (1963) and others emphasize the positive solidarity of sharing burdens, but they fail to note the negative solidarity of groups who pursue their own agenda.

constraints on social policy formation. Self-administration, the structure and ideology of parties, the structure of school systems (see next chapter), judicial systems, and the overall strength of bureaucracies all influence the formation of social policy. And third, external events can produce major differences in social policy, especially with veterans returning from wars.

Consequently, this study of active labor market policy extends our knowledge of social policy in three ways: First, ALMP is discretionary rather than automatic. This study examines what happens when politicians have real policy choices, whereas most studies of social policy address pensions or other more automatic entitlement programs. Second, ALMP involves a unified theoretical approach extending citizenship rights. By embedding citizenship theory in a broader theory of social demands, state formation, and external events, this study advances understanding of social policy within a comprehensive framework of social policy. Third, this book combines both qualitative and quantitative evidence in a synthetic approach to support its case. I apply this theoretical framework of diverse methods to the following analysis, beginning with the roots of labor market policy.

Chapter Two

The Roots of ALMP:
Job Placement
and Job Training

Why did Weimar Germany develop a strong employment service, while the United States developed a weak one? Why did Germany develop a job-training policy based on high skill training in a continuation school system, while the United States developed the high school that provided little or no specific skill training for manual workers? My discussion focuses on the issues raised by these two questions.

GERMAN JOB PLACEMENT BEFORE 1945

In the 1920s Germany developed a strong employment service with independence as a public law corporation, monopoly over organized placement, tripartite (i.e., labor, management, and government) self-administration, and a centralized structure at the national level. The contrast with the weak U.S. Employment Service (USES) could not be greater. A left-Catholic coalition deftly negotiated the federal system of jealous states to produce a powerful employment service embodying traditions of self-administration.

Early Developments in Germany

In medieval Germany, workers found jobs through parental ascription in paternalistic guilds that controlled placement, training, and production. Labor exchanges were not necessary.[1] The growth of cities brought a demand for labor exchanges as early as 1421 in Nuremberg, and private employment agencies began to expand in the 1800s. By the 1840s, complaints about private agencies led to public employment offices in Dresden and Leipzig (Weigert 1934, p. 33).

Business cycles with alternating labor shortages and unemployment inspired different kinds of labor exchange. Private employment agencies provided jobs for servants, retail sales workers, farm laborers, sailors, and actors. Police control and state licensure soon followed because of private agency abuses—for example, the sale of nonexistent jobs for fees. Moral institutions— religious societies, communes, and relief stations—included labor exchange services with their help for the poor. Skilled laborers established artisan exchanges, and the nascent industrial unions started labor exchanges. Employer labor exchanges developed in large cities for metal, pottery, textile, and building trade workers, but they sought nonunion workers. Joint labor exchanges emerged out of the few firms and unions that would work together (Weigert 1934; Bogart 1908, pp. 367–72).[2]

These organizations constituted a quiltwork of agencies that operated with different and often contradictory purposes: private agencies pursuing profit were subject to many abuses; religious and relief agencies, with police assistance, sought the moral control of the unemployed poor, beggars, and deviants; skilled craft agencies tried to control competition and protect their jobs; industrial unions aimed to build membership and oppose management control; employers' agencies looked for workers untainted by unions and socialism; and the few joint employer-worker organizations, started by liberal employers and moderate unions, tried to avoid the excesses of the other agencies. The demand for

1. During the plague, the English state tried to regulate labor mobility but not through public labor exchanges. Prussia tried to hold the rural population on the land with government edicts similar to the Statute of Artificiers enacted by Edward III in England. However, both failed (Garraty 1978, pp. 21, 37).

2. In 1895, Prussia had 5,216 private agencies, but only 230 union agencies. In the 1890s, Germany as a whole had 1,707 relief stations—the equivalent of the English work houses—734 guild exchanges, and 46 joint offices. Employer offices and union exchanges were few (Weigert 1934; Bogart 1908).

free public employment services grew against this background of competing and overlapping labor exchanges.

Public agencies emerged under municipal control in Esslingen as early as 1884, and a social congress in Frankfurt endorsed public municipal employment exchanges. But the most significant public agencies began in Munich and Berlin. Munich developed a public employment exchange in 1895 as a cooperative venture of the municipality; three employer representatives, three employee representatives, and the chairman of the Munich Trade Council held considerable administrative control. This free agency, financed by the city, absorbed other employment offices. It served as a model for many city exchanges—Württemberg, Stuttgart, Frankfurt, Nuremberg, Straussburg, and Mannheim.

The Berlin office was semipublic because the city provided a small annual subsidy, but voluntary associations of employers and employees also covered the costs of labor exchange where contributions and user fees were paid by workers. Düsseldorf and Cologne had intermediate forms between the Munich and Berlin labor exchanges, with decentralized policy direction (like Berlin) but municipal administration and funding (like Munich). Each model used some form of self-administration (Beveridge 1908, p. 7; Weigert 1934, pp. 33–35).

However, a national labor exchange did not emerge until the early twentieth century. Bismarck ignored proposals for a national employment exchange and opposed unemployment compensation because it could not be actuarially predicted (Henderson 1975; Kitchen 1978). Germany, a federal system aggregating states that were protective of their independence, also faced regional barriers to a centralized labor exchange system. Nevertheless, the Association of German Employment Offices recommended an imperial labor exchange (Bogart 1908, p. 75), and the unions, though initially skeptical, increasingly supported the idea. In 1894, the Prussian government created employment offices with worker-employer supervision in cities of more than one hundred thousand people (lowered to twenty thousand in 1902), but this was still not a national system (Weigert 1934, p. 34).

In 1914, the government established the Federal Office for Placement to coordinate the employment offices throughout the country. Despite the booming war economy, unemployment still increased. The "truce of the fortress" assigned political parties and unions to help relieve unemployment and promote labor exchanges.[3] A Central Information Office was established, and on June 14, 1916, a Reichsrat order gave the states the power to establish jointly supervised public offices in communities with more than ten thousand people. Thus, a national exchange haltingly emerged.

Weimar and the 1922 Labor Exchange Law

Immediately after World War I, the German nation writhed in defeat and chaos. The interim SPD government instituted demobilization regulations with "forced hiring" and "prohibited firing" decrees to restore production and employment. Labor placement changed hands from the local districts to the Commission on Demobilization. After five million job seekers swamped the public and private registries in 1919, the Labor Ministry submitted the first draft of an unemployment law and a year later organized the temporary Federal Placement Office (Fischer 1981, pp. 95–101; Huber 1981, 6:1099–101).[4]

The Labor Law Committee of the Reichstag reworked the Labor Ministry draft for a national labor exchange that included tripartite self-administration by labor, management, and government; decentralization with few federal controls; public monopoly over labor placement abolishing private labor exchanges within two years;[5] and control over vocational counseling, apprenticeships, and labor market research. The draft also contained two requirements: employers must hire new workers through the employment service, and workers must use the service to find jobs and apply for unemployment benefits.

3. The SPD and its socialist unions had to change the most in order to participate in the truce's reformist course. The SPD/USPD schism soon followed in 1917 with the USPD moving toward communism and the SPD toward reform (Feldman 1966, pp. 118–19, 274; Schorske 1955, pp. 293–302; Breitman 1981, pp. 13–14).

4. Responsibility for labor placement was transferred on May 1, 1919, to the Ministry of Labor, but the federal placement office was organized later, in January 1920.

5. Professional exchanges would be allowed for ten years, but they would not receive compensation, as did the other exchanges.

The powerful employment service sketched by the draft encountered opposition. The trade union federations—the blue-collar DGB and the white-collar Afa Bund—saw the utilization requirement as necessary to administer unemployment insurance and end individualizing job searches. Employer associations and conservative unions rejected the utilization requirement because of its cost. Furthermore, the DGB rejected job referrals to striking plants, while the employers wanted referrals to continue. The unions and employers also wanted joint control (without government participation) based on the precedent of the pension and health funds, but the local governments wanted control because they provided public assistance—a payment closely linked to unemployment compensation. Finally, three groups opposed placement monopoly: Christian Trade Unions wanted a white-collar registry, Handwerk Chambers wanted artisan placement of apprentices, and the Catholic Church wanted control over the poor. Given the draft's far-reaching proposals, strong opposition was not surprising.

In 1922, the Wirth government revised the bill. Bowing to community wishes, legislators accepted moderate self-management by unions, employers, and the communities. To reduce the impact on labor registry owners, they accepted an incomplete public labor exchange monopoly—old exchanges could continue under extensive regulation, but new exchanges were prohibited.[6] Reacting to the employers, the government dropped the utilization requirement but kept a mild reporting requirement for unemployment relief. Ignoring Handwerk, the government made the labor registry responsible for counseling and apprentice referral. With these concessions, the innovative draft became law on July 22, 1922 (Stürmer 1967; Preller 1949; Huber 1981, vol. 6).

The Reichanstalt, the new labor placement office, with twenty-two state and numerous local offices, also gained responsibility for job creation, company shutdowns, and handicapped quotas. The central Reichanstalt had extremely loose controls allowing local offices to cooperate with municipal welfare agencies. Furthermore, the law gave local "associations of unemployed workers"

---

6. The 1922 law allowed existing private nonprofit exchanges, but new exchanges were prohibited; and all nonprofit exchanges were required to operate under Reichanstalt regulations (Weigert 1934, pp. 35, 129–32, 163).

the right to protest district decisions and policies. Although the Reichanstalt was begun with weak federal controls during a period of runaway inflation, war debts, and serious social dislocations, it did a reasonable job in labor placement.

Nevertheless, serious problems arose with decentralization: coordination was lacking between levels, tripartite self-administration was awkward at the local level, and the areas of coverage for labor exchanges were often too small. Moreover, unemployment insurance covered only a fraction of the needy, and the "associations of unemployed workers" caused considerable disruption in some urban offices. White-collar workers, who had lost most of their savings in the postwar hyperinflation, faced increasing unemployment due to office rationalization. A January 17, 1926, law included more white-collar employees under unemployment compensation, but then the seasonal workers became an issue. Social Democratic politicians and DGB leaders soon realized that unemployed workers without benefits of any kind outnumbered those sheltered by the state. Unemployment compensation and the labor exchange would have to change (Preller 1949; Faust 1984).[7]

The Pillar of Participation Rights

In 1925, the government drafted a new law centralizing the labor exchange and reintroducing short-time work—subsidizing jobs in threatened industries by paying full-time wages for part-time work. The employers disliked the high contribution requirements, and the communities opposed centralization. The DGB, the Center Party, and the German National Party wanted a national employment service with a central labor-management board over both unemployment insurance and labor placement. It would be

7. Labor exchange and unemployment insurance became politically intertwined. From 1920 to 1927, the legislature tried in vain to deal with occupational coverage, financial responsibility, and payment distribution of unemployment insurance. Federal decrees—October 15, 1923, October 30, 1923, and February 16, 1924—were needed as the legislature failed to reach a decision. The unions dropped their demands for general unemployment relief and finally accepted the insurance principal without a means test. Employers remained ambivalent about unemployment insurance because they wanted to keep the means test, but they did not want to expand general relief. One basic problem was that unemployment payments at the time were not adjusted to wage levels, so that some low-wage workers received unemployment payments higher than their previous wages (Preller 1949, pp. 276–82, 365).

similar to the bipartite administration in the pension and health funds. However, the white-collar employee federation wanted the health funds to dispense unemployment insurance.

The depression of 1926 increased demands for a centralized employment service because the local offices had trouble handling work creation, labor placement, and unemployment relief. Although Bavaria had many strong labor exchanges, the Prussian exchanges, especially in the eastern areas, were inefficient and poorly organized. The depression had severely tested all of them. On March 11, 1926, Labor Minister Heinrich Brauns sent "strengthening professionals" to rationalize, relieve, and support the local exchanges. The "strengthening professionals" produced an exaggerated report on local failures, charging the labor exchanges with demarcation disputes, uncoordinated placement, conflicts with firms, and ambitious financial schemes; some communities complained of grandiose labor market plans. These professionals demanded the end of local control over labor exchanges.

The report circulated during negotiations on the labor exchange and insurance law in the Reichstag and renewed pressure for change. Support for separating labor exchanges from the communities came from the DGB in particular, the employer associations who had abhorred the left's seizure of power in some urban registries, the Christian and Hirsch-Dunker unions, the Labor Ministry, and even the white-collar employee federation. In fact, a centralized employment service seemed to generate little Reichstag opposition.

Consequently, in February 1927, the Reichstag Labor Committee requested that the government set up guidelines for converting the decentralized Reichanstalt into a new and centralized organization. The federal guidelines supported an executive bureaucracy with federal, state, and local self-administration. Following the clever strategy of the DGB, Center Party Rep. Thomas Esser introduced the bill with the federal recommendations as a private proposal. As neither a SPD opposition bill nor a Center Party–Bourgeois coalition-government bill, a private bill in the Reichstag would bypass the community interests opposed to centralization in the Reichsrat.

However, opposition was still sharp from the communities who claimed that a centralized Reichanstalt would meddle in local affairs creating unwanted reform and that welfare and unemployment would remain closely linked to the communities despite the new law. To soften the opposition, the Labor Ministry set up three community meetings. In Munich, on April 22, 1927, counterproposals, although they did not contest centralization, demanded community presence in local self-administration and a separate public law corporation, rather than an executive bureaucracy. At the May 23–25 meeting in Hamburg, the community welfare delegates emphasized their social approach to unemployment rather than the "lopsided" economic approach of the federal government. From June 2 to June 4 in Dresden, the National Labor Registry Conference not only emphasized the social aspects of unemployment but also endorsed the federal reorganization. Although federal centralization was somewhat limited by local self-administration over budget determinations and independence for the employment service as a public law corporation, community bitterness was muted through the clever maneuvers of the DGB and the Labor Ministry. The law was passed by a large Reichstag majority on July 16, 1927; only the Nazi, Communist, and German National Party representatives voted against it. Social Democratic theoretician Fritz Napthali referred to the new employment service as the pillar of economic democracy in Weimar social policy (Napthali 1928, p. 151; Preller 1949, pp. 366–75; Huber 1981, 6:1099–101).

The 1927 law placed the administration of the Reichanstalt in the hands of labor, business, and government, rather than local communities and the "associations of unemployed workers." The new Reichanstalt became a public law corporation (like the U.S. Federal Reserve Board); contributions from employers and employees, not general revenues, supplied its income. Labor exchange was in a national system under thirteen districts, while profit labor exchanges were to be abolished by July 1, 1931 (Weigert 1934, pp. 38, 60–63, 131).[8] Its passage demonstrates trade unions' social demands exerted through the SPD–Center Party

8. Private labor exchanges for theatrical employees were allowed to continue (less than 110). At the end of 1930, there were 1,473 private commercial agencies that handled artistic professions, domestic servants, agricultural workers, and restaurant workers, down from 17,730 in 1929. Over time, nonprofit agencies declined, and only a few profit exchanges remained.

coalition, plus an ability to control the political power of state structures and bureaucracies.

After Democracy, 1930 to 1933

The governments of the 1930s weakened and then disabled the employment service. The Brüning government decree of March 21, 1932, took budgetary power away from the local offices, disabled self-administration, centralized administration, and made the Reichanstalt president the dominant decision maker (Weigert 1934, pp. 151–61). Battles over funding of unemployment compensation and the Nazi rise to power caused the Reichanstalt to further decline as an effective institution (Zöllner 1982, pp. 49–51; Eyck 1967).[9] The Nazis started extreme controls: labor books to trace worker movements, purges of Jewish and politically undesirable employees, and forced labor in concentration camps. At first the Nazis used the Reichanstalt for creating job programs, but they soon gravitated toward their own United Labor Front.

JOB PLACEMENT IN THE UNITED STATES
BEFORE 1945

The United States developed an ineffective employment service on the fringes of the labor market. The employment service lacked centralization, autonomy, placement monopoly, and labor-management cooperation; it was a weak organization in a weak cabinet department.

9. As unemployment increased during the depression, the Reichanstalt became known as the "stamping place" (*Stempelstellen*) because it validated unemployment compensation forms. The Reichanstalt revenues could not even handle the unemployment claims of the previous year. Obviously, these legislators had envisioned unrestrained economic growth (Weisbrod 1981). Repeated battles over raising rates of contribution and cutting levels of benefit were fought after 1927. The following changes were made in benefit levels and contribution rates of employers and workers: contributions were raised to 3 percent and benefits were cut in 1929; contributions were raised to 3.5 percent, 4.5 percent, and then to 6.5 percent along with two benefit cuts in 1930; benefits were drastically cut in 1931; and benefit levels were reduced, the duration of benefits was cut, and crisis relief was repealed in 1932. Rosenhaft (1981, pp. 220–24) claims that the new law did not eliminate the massive antagonisms between workers, bureaucrats, and police in the Berlin Reichanstalt offices.

Early Developments with Private and State Agencies

In early American settlement, severe labor shortages forced employers to recruit workers from Europe and Africa. Recruiters solicited workers in English towns for servant ships, agents sold indentured servant contracts to ship captains and kidnappers, and slave ships supplied blacks for the southern auction blocks. Formal employment agencies emerged indigenously around 1820 with the Employers and Servants Protestant Agency for domestic servants and the wagons that patrolled rural areas seeking young farm girls for the mills. By 1846 in New York, Thomas Spink began to specialize in agencies for female domestics and manual workers, and in 1863 the American Immigrant Company recruited its own immigrants (Martinez 1976).

By the 1890s, the United States developed a number of private employment organizations. General employment agencies placed middle-class workers in white-collar jobs (teachers, nurses, actors, barbers, engineers, and bookkeepers) and working-class workers in unskilled jobs (manual laborers, cooks, maids, waiter/ waitresses, and servants).[10] Ethnic agencies recruited new immigrants at home and abroad, and racial agencies specialized in blacks from cities and rural areas in the South. Moral institutions such as churches, the YMCA, the YWCA, and charity organizations conducted labor exchanges without fees.[11] Skilled unions often operated labor exchanges, and some chambers of commerce sponsored employer agencies (Martinez 1976, pp. 32–33, 137; Wilensky and Lebeaux 1965, pp. 51–55).

These private agencies were more fragmented and less combative than those in Germany. The employer-union competition over labor exchanges was limited, and employee-employer cooperation was rare. Abuses by private agencies soon emerged; these included misrepresenting the existence and pay level of jobs (especially in isolated and distant areas); fee splitting between

10. General employment agencies were numerous in large cities and some states by the end of the 1890s: Boston had 119 agencies, Chicago 110, California 69, Colorado 21, and St. Louis 12. In a detailed 1908 study of Chicago, Abbott found 33 female agencies, 56 manual agencies, and 21 mixed agencies (1908, p. 293).

11. Moral institutions were fewer than other private agencies: Boston had fourteen and New York four (Bogart 1908, pp. 347–49).

employers and agents, with workers being fired after paying placement fees; raiding other employers for workers; discriminating on the basis of race, sex, religion, and national origin; and urban slavery, sometimes connected to prostitution (Martinez 1976, pp. 43–56; Dembo 1983, pp. 72–73; Davis 1920; Ringenbach 1973). By 1890, the people demanded public labor exchanges.

Such exchanges started at the state level. In 1890, upon returning from the Paris International Exposition, W. T. Lewis, the Ohio commissioner for labor, helped draft a labor exchange bill based on the French system of intelligence offices.[12] Having passed the Ohio state legislature, the "Ohio Idea" provided the nation's first public employment exchange (Guzda 1983). Twenty other states soon instituted employment offices, but they and the independent city placement offices were usually starved for funds. Private employment offices also skimmed off the better job applicants, leaving public offices with people more difficult to place.

By 1924, twenty-four states had tried direct regulation of private exchanges to make job placement more rational and efficient, but they were frustrated by the state and federal supreme courts. In the 1904 case of *Ex Parte Dicky*, the California Supreme Court decided that although the state could regulate dangerous and unhealthy occupations, private employment agencies were innocent and beneficial. In the 1916 case of *Brazee vs. Michigan* the Michigan Supreme Court ruled that regulation was legal, but it left the extent of the regulation murky. In the decisive *Adams vs. Tanner* case (1916), the U.S. Supreme Court ruled by a five-to-four margin that regulation was permissible but the abolition of a lawful enterprise was unconstitutional under the Fourteenth Amendment. Justice Louis Brandeis concluded in the dissenting opinion that eliminating private employment agencies was necessary to establish a useful employment service (Martinez 1976, pp. 57–80). If these state laws had been upheld, legislation would have flowed from Congress to control private employment agencies. But judi-

12. The "Bourses du Travail" in 1914 existed in 144 French cities. A city would generally give a small amount of money to a local alliance of unions to pay for a building. The unions would then conduct a labor exchange for the city as a whole. From 1887 to 1888, Bourses were founded in Paris, Marseille, and Niems (Shorter and Tilly 1974, pp. 166–67).

cial restraint of government intervention into the economy was not unusual for Anglo-Saxon countries. Democracies with Anglo-Saxon law—the United States, Canada, New Zealand, and Australia—prohibited placement monopoly, while countries with Roman law—West Germany, Netherlands, Austria, and Sweden—permitted it.

At the same time, Terrence Powderly, head of the Immigration Service, founded the Division of Information to help immigrants relocate to the interior of the country rather than "bunching" around cities. By mid-1917, the Division of Information had ninety-three offices that concentrated on a "beneficial distribution of aliens" to farm areas, but it encountered resistance from farmers who opposed dumping immigrants into their communities. The division soon disappeared (*Adams v. Tanner* 1916, p. 607). Throughout this period the Department of Labor spent 80 percent of its budget on immigration problems and largely ignored demands for labor exchange and unemployment relief.

The job placement issue repeatedly emerged in American policy debates prior to World War I. In 1914, the American Association for Labor Legislation demanded a national system of labor exchanges in its "Practical Program for the Prevention of Unemployment," and one year later the American Association of Public Employment Offices repeated the demand. Also in 1914, the House Committee on Labor reported Victor Murdock's plan for national labor exchanges; but Congress saw job placement as a temporary immigration or depression problem. Senator John Nolan proposed and President Woodrow Wilson supported a national exchange system in 1916, but war hysteria drowned out congressional interest (Robertson 1981, pp. 105–7).

The Development of the U.S. Employment Service

In January 1918, by executive order Woodrow Wilson created the U.S. Employment Service (USES) out of the old Division of Information. Employment offices were established in forty states, but the 1917–18 strike wave—the highest in U.S. history—threatened its future. Many employers thought USES would spread a pro-union credo, some employers found the new organization ineffective, and even labor voiced some dissatisfaction. In an effort to forestall complaints, USES established state advisory boards composed of workers, management, and the state director. The boards gave advice on personnel and policy, but the secretary of labor retained control. After the advisory boards expanded to 1,386 local offices, labor and management viewed the employment service in a more positive light. But support was still weak. Indeed, unions were fighting for their lives, while employers were trying to crush the strike movement (Lescohier 1919, p. 193).

After World War I, Senator William Kenyon (R-Iowa) and Rep. John Nolan (R-Calif.) introduced legislation for employment offices. Thomas Blanton (D-Tex.) led the fight against it, with arguments for cutting the budget after an expensive war. Interest group opposition came from private employment agencies, detective agencies, and big antiunion employers. The AFL, at the high point of its voluntaristic stage, gave little support. President Wilson's Industrial Conference (1919–20) and Secretary of Commerce Herbert Hoover's Unemployment Conference (1921) made favorable recommendations. Although hearings were held, the bill was not put to a vote.

During the Hoover administration USES further deteriorated: it had been cut to a skeleton system; it published unemployment figures that predicted "prosperity just around the corner" when the depression was deepening, and its director was implicated for illegal patronage.[13] USES was in trouble (Guzda 1983, pp. 14–17; Robertson 1981, pp. 130–31). Senator Robert Wagner (D-N.Y.) reopened the labor exchange issue in 1928 and reintroduced the Wagner-Peyser Bill for labor exchanges in 1930; however, Secretary of Labor Doak disliked the bill and submitted his own proposal to revamp the existing system. Although Doak's bill was defeated in the House, he persuaded President Hoover to pocket veto the Wagner-Peyser bill after it had passed both the House and the Senate.

When Roosevelt became president, he appointed Francis Perkins as secretary of labor, and she quickly fired the head of USES. Roosevelt, however, needed immediate recruitment capabilities for the Civilian Conservation Corps. Rejecting the military and ignoring USES, he had Secretary Perkins set up the National Re-employment Agency to fill the void until a compre-

---

13. John Alpine, the USES director, was accused of creating seven phony mail room jobs at six times their regular salary.

hensive solution to job placement could be achieved (Robertson 1981, p. 108).

In 1932, the Wagner-Peyser bill was reintroduced into the legislature with opposition from conservative Republicans and Southern Democrats. Senator Hiram Bingham (R-Conn.) and Representative George Graham (R-Pa.) led the Republican opposition against Wagner-Peyser in 1931. The AFL and Chamber of Commerce supported the plan, as did the "social welfare intellectuals"—institutional economists (Donald Lescohier, William Leiserson, and John B. Andrews), social researchers (Mary Van Kleeck and Mary La Dame), and social workers (Paul Kellogg and Samuel Joseph). Overall, the urban reform group of social welfare intellectuals was the dominant force behind the Wagner-Peyser Act.

The AFL's approach to labor exchanges passed three contradictory stages: before 1917, the AFL opposed a national employment office system; from 1917 to 1932, the AFL was lukewarm with its "voluntaristic anti-policy stand"; and only after November 1932 did the AFL back the Wagner-Peyser Act. Even worse, the AFL did little to get the law passed and remained poorly informed on its provisions. While the AFL was maintaining a low profile on the act, veterans, a crosscutting status group, successfully pressured Congress to create the Veterans Administration and give veterans special considerations in the Wagner-Peyser Act (Robertson 1981, pp. 130–47).[14]

Business was split between large and small employers. The National Association of Manufacturers (NAM) opposed the bill because of its reliance on "federal coercion of the states"—a weak objection—but their opposition was mainly attributed to hostility toward labor. The Chamber of Commerce supported the bill. The National Civic Federation may well have been in accord with such a bill, but little evidence points to their interest.

The Wagner-Peyser Act, becoming law on June 6, 1933, set up a voluntary confederation of state offices with loose federal controls, rather than a comprehensive and centralized employment service. Furthermore, USES did not spread to most states

14. The Veterans Administration was formally established in 1930—two years into the depression. This formalized the veterans' constituency, which had been strong since the Civil War, under a separate government agency. Reagan has elevated veterans' interests to the cabinet.

until 1938 (Robertson 1981, p. 108). Although the Democratic party was near the peak of its power, it could only produce a weak employment service act due to the constraints of state structures: hostile courts and social demands unable to control state interests.

GERMAN EDUCATION AND JOB TRAINING
BEFORE 1945

The German "work orientation" produced a school system for the workers and taught specific skills in apprenticeship programs, as opposed to the U.S. system of homogeneous and social skill training.

By the sixteenth and seventeenth centuries, mercantilist governments moved to eliminate guild power in Germany, and by 1850, factory workers, who were growing four times faster than guild artisans, dominated the labor market (Stearns 1967, pp. 142–46; Kieser 1989, pp. 555–56). In the twentieth century, German artisans continued to train workers in their *Handwerk* organizations—the traditional craft trades—but their political power was weak. Indeed, the socialist unions tried to unionize workers in Handwerk, organize the state-run workshops, and take apprenticeship control away from the artisan masters (Domurad 1981, p. 178). However, the state and private firms, rather than the unions, took control of apprenticeship training.

While the German state demanded economic growth, employers needed more highly skilled workers, and they eventually converted religious Sunday schools into the occupational *Berufschule* (continuation school). The Sunday schools, first set up in Württemberg in 1559, were intended for persons who had completed their elementary education. By 1846, Württemberg had over seventy Sunday trade schools. As the primary school became almost universal in Germany in the 1850s, the Sunday trade schools shifted to weekdays (Ringer 1979, p. 33). By the 1870s, the Sunday schools had been renamed the Berufschule, and a general curriculum was added. Attendance became compulsory in Saxony in 1873, in Württemberg in 1895, and soon thereafter in most other German states. The German system used apprentice training in the firm and the Berufschule for general education, with the trade being the major pedagogical example. The Berufschule became the dominant school for German workers.

The early Berufschule used Herbartian principles designed to cover a broad range of topics with extensive memorization, but Georg Kerschensteiner, the pioneering director of education in Munich, opposed these methods.[15] From 1900 to 1914, Kerschensteiner reorganized the Munich Berufschule according to new principles. First, his Berufschule explained life through the trade and practical work. The curriculum consisted of the practice, theory, and history of the trade; the trade itself became the major pedagogical example. Second, because learning the trade was somewhat egotistical, it needed to be supplemented by altruism developed through team work projects, moral/religious education, empathy for others by understanding one's own trade history, and education for world citizenship; that is, the student learned the purpose and function of the state, commercial law, union rights, and aid to underdeveloped countries.[16] Third, the Berufschule would be a regularly scheduled day school accompanied by an apprenticeship, not a residual night school for overworked apprentices (Toews 1955, pp. 100–110, 162–66; Simons 1967, pp. 16–21, 54).

Although other continuation schools had been started in Baden by Friedrich Rucklin and in Leipzig by Oskar Pache, Kerschensteiner's model became dominant. After 1907, the Berufschule was made compulsory in Munich (Simons 1967, p. 74). Most German states followed Kerschensteiner's Munich plan, and the Berufschule became the most prevalent form of education for the masses.[17] From 1900 to 1930, the United States, United King-

15. Herbart (1776–1841) despised practical training and emphasized a moral education with a wide curriculum. Thus, history focused on desirable individuals in order to teach moral traits. Both Kerschensteiner and Herbart pursued moral education; however, Kerschensteiner's quote of Goethe makes his practical emphasis clear: "to know and to practice one thing well has a greater educative value than to have a smattering of a hundred" (Simons 1967, p. 70).

16. Kerschensteiner saw his concept of "education for citizenship" being distorted into German nationalism by focusing on slavish obedience. Others saw his concept naturally amenable to this (Roman 1930, p. 286).

17. The Reich made the Berufschule compulsory in 1911, and the Weimar Republic tried to make it compulsory in 1920 (Article 145 of the New Constitution) and in 1925. However, each attempt failed (Toews 1955, p. 110; Roman 1930, p. 225).

dom, and other countries sent delegations to Munich to study Kerschensteiner's continuation schools.

The apprenticeship system existed in three areas: Handwerk with apprentices working in small craft firms being tested (circa 1920) by the Handwerk Chambers; small- to medium-sized firms where training was moderate; and large firms with apprentices attending the modern and well-equipped *Lehrwerkstatt*—a private industry school located in the workplace and noted for excellent instruction. Developing from the Prussian railway schools (1879), the Lehrwerkstatt quickly spread to large private industries. But in each case, employers firmly controlled all in-the-firm training (Behr 1982, 1985; Tollkühn 1926).

The state, especially Bavaria and Prussia, and industry were the prime movers behind the Berufschule. Prussia gave Kerschensteiner a prestigious award before his appointment as director of Munich schools and then tried to hire him after 1906 (Toews 1955, p. 116). Apparently the industrialists and craft workers were the first groups to push the Berufschule, but the state soon took over in the interests of economic growth. Because Catholics and Protestants were split over segregated religious schools, they had little effect on vocational education (Roman 1930, p. 211).

Labor was divided. The Berufschule offered the unions skill as a protection against the assault of mass production. However, the firm controlled the apprenticeship, and the state controlled the school. The *Gymnasium* and other forms of higher education were out of reach for workers, and the Berufschule tended to reinforce this separation. But labor simply waited too long. By 1919, when the tenth union conference demanded a comprehensive vocational education training law, the state and industry had already set up the dominant system (Schöfer 1981, p. 185).

The SPD wanted democratization of the universities and development of their own *Arbeitschulen*—worker schools. During the Weimar Republic, the SPD also proposed the *Einheitschule* (unity school) as a comprehensive school with differentiated instruction centering around core courses. However, these and other comprehensive schools failed during Weimar and the reform-minded 1960s. Either employer and middle-class opposition was too strong, or SPD advocacy was too weak (Heidenheimer 1983; Hearndon 1974, pp. 47–49).

In sum, with export-oriented industrialization and its demand for skilled workers, the state took over classroom education and employers controlled the apprenticeship. The employers clearly favored the Berufschule, but the unions acted too late. The middle and upper classes supported the *Realschule* and *Gymnasium* but curtailed their expansion to maintain their elite status. The Berufschule instructors, coopted into the privileged civil service, made little effort to expand their internal bureaucratic empire. In the end, the social demands of employers backed by the state won out over the SPD and labor's late cry for more integrated education.

AMERICAN EDUCATION AND JOB TRAINING
BEFORE 1945

The United States rejected the skill-producing continuation school in favor of the comprehensive school. In the high school, most students learned the same general subjects rather than a specific trade. Thus, specific job training was unavailable either in the schools or through the employment service. First, I focus on the comprehensive school, which dominated education through its socialization orientation; then I consider three minor exceptions to the rule.

Although most American colonies adopted a traditional apprenticeship system, craft organization declined until a stable niche for apprenticeship was negotiated in the twentieth century. Continuous labor shortages in the new nation undermined apprenticeship controls because runaway apprentices easily obtained skilled work. Later, immigration continually increased the supply of cheap labor. By the 1850s, the merchant capitalist system effectively destroyed many trades upon which apprenticeship systems were based, and industrialization destroyed many more; thus, many workers were driven from craft to factory work (Rayback 1966, pp. 18–75). Gordon, Edwards, and Reich conclude that by mid-century "the system of independent craft production was in total disarray and retreat" (1982, p. 64). However, industrialization also created new crafts and skilled labor. After 1900, a labor-management accommodation was made that left the mass industries to the corporations, and the crafts that were difficult to mechanize, such as construction, to the craft unions (Benenson 1982; Gordon, Reich, and Edwards 1982, p. 159).

Consequently, the main educational system for American manual workers developed out of the high school, not crafts or apprenticeships. In the 1890s, the high school was still a minor segment of the educational system, oriented more toward the university than the general public. By the end of the century, however, the high school changed drastically. In 1892, the Committee of Ten on Secondary Education emphasized that the high school should prepare students for life, that is, educate terminal high school students rather than breed potential college students. In 1906, the Massachusetts Commission on Industrial and Technical Education found that twenty-five thousand of the state's children aged fourteen to fifteen worked inefficiently at industrial jobs with no hope of advancement because of low skills. These recommendations and findings started the movement toward the comprehensive school.

The critical moment for comprehensivism came with the 1913 Cooley Bill, an Illinois proposal for a dual system of separate comprehensive and continuation schools. Among the bill's opponents was John Dewey, who claimed that business favored children dropping out of school and irresponsibly charged public schools with Bolshevism. Dewey called for an "alliance between educators and settlement house workers" to fight the continuation school concept that was "calculated to promote the interests of the employing class." Dewey, educators, and social workers in a "social welfare–intellectual" alliance clearly promoted comprehensivism (Wirth 1971, pp. 208–10; Wrigley 1982, pp. 60–90; Hogan 1985, pp. 167–81; Dewey 1914, p. 11). By 1918, Clarence Kingsley and the National Education Association Committee on Reorganizing Secondary Education came out in favor of the high school, and it spread throughout the country (Kantor 1988, pp. 98–106).

Employers were divided on the school issue. The National Association of Manufacturers favored the continuation school system over the high school. Their 1905 report depicted the continuation school as absolutely necessary in the race for international commercial supremacy, while full-time vocational schools were ruled out as too expensive. The continuation schools were cheap, bypassed labor's meddling, and gave control to business through apprenticeship. However, the National Civic Federation—a progressive alliance dominated by major business interests and reformers—supported comprehensive schools in 1916. The NCF expected the high school to educate and socialize immigrants, in-crease labor-management cooperation (with or without unions), and train good citizens (not anarchists or socialists) (Weinstein 1968, pp. 128–34; Wirth 1971, pp. 23–42).

The AFL was slow to reach an opinion on training. Some craft leaders wanted apprenticeship to continue without change; Gom-pers felt that because technology demanded new skills, union schools might be the answer. But a 1908 AFL convention's reso-lution rejected trade or continuation schools in favor of the com-prehensive school. At the convention, one AFL leader voiced a widely held opinion about the two groups advocating secondary education proposals:

One of the groups is largely composed of the non-union employers of the country who advance industrial education as a special privilege un-der conditions that educate the student or apprentice to non-union sym-pathies and prepare him as a skilled worker for scab labor. . . . The other group is composed of great educators, enlightened representatives of organized labor and persons engaged in genuine social service, who advocate industrial education as a common right to be open to all chil-dren on equal terms to be provided by general taxation and kept under the control of the whole people. (quoted in Wirth 1971, p. 54)

A 1910 AFL report mentioned labor's social mobility aspirations: the high schools would make it possible for the offspring of labor to enter management. But many other union leaders had an apprentice mentality, favoring narrow craft education. While the AFL vacillated, the movement for comprehensive schools gained momentum, and eventually the federation jumped on the band wagon. By 1913, the AFL vigorously opposed the Cooley bill for dual school systems (Wirth 1971, pp. 24–29, 38, 53–57). High school enrollments subsequently increased, almost doubling each decade.[18]

Germany had set the international example for continuation schools, and pragmatic Americans could have been easily per-

---

18. In 1890, 6.7 percent of fourteen- to seventeen-year-olds were in high school; in 1900, 10.2 percent; in 1910, 15.4 percent; in 1920, 32.3 percent. The causes for this include the increase in per capita income, the increase in white-collar jobs, and the imposition of child labor laws (Church and Sedlak 1976, p. 289).

suaded to such a system of vocational education. However, a continuation school did not appear in the United States for three reasons. First, the predominantly Protestant middle class who dominated the reform movement wanted to socialize the unruly Catholic immigrants and provide social mobility for their offspring. Socially conscious elites, some politicians, scholars, and industrialists were also concerned with social order and industrial discipline. Given the ineffective melting pot of ethnic groups in America, these leaders sought socialization in the comprehensive high school. By putting everyone in the same school social classes mingled; and by differentiating courses good students progressed, and poor students survived. Activities, clubs, sports, and student government would further increase social mingling, and teaching English and civics to immigrants would speed their assimilation.

Second, the status gap between the high school teacher and college teacher had increased, so that high school teachers no longer joined professors at conferences. High school teachers saw the comprehensive high school as a way to promote their interests by expanding the scope and institutional prestige of the high school (Church and Sedlak 1976, pp. 308–9; Spring 1972). German secondary school teachers, as members of the privileged civil service, had no such incentive because their power rested on scarcity, not possibilities for expansion. And third, the indecisive AFL and most workers were converted to the comprehensive school by arguments of social mobility for their offspring (Hofstadter 1955). Separate vocational schools would have violated American notions of equal opportunity.[19]

Thus, the differentiation of academic courses satisfied the middle classes, while the combination of practical vocational education along with the possibility of academic education—even if that only occurred when lower-class students rubbed shoulders with middle-class students—persuaded or at least split the working classes. David Snedden, a major proponent of industrial education, recognized privately that the comprehensive school was a

19. These achievement arguments were held by skilled nativist workers, rather than the unskilled immigrant workers who were "would-be-craftsmen," not latent second generation bureaucrats, managers, or professionals (Sabel 1982).

poor way to offer vocational education: "real vocational training required specialized schools" and comprehensive schools can "give only an imitation of vocational education" (Spring 1972, p. 109). But no one could deny that the high school was an effective way to socialize immigrants.[20]

There were three exceptions to the dominant socialization emphasis of the comprehensive school: vocationalism in the high school, apprenticeship, and black education. First, the 1917 Smith-Hughes Act added vocational courses to the high school by paying for vocational teachers and materials. Its passage is attributed to progressive reformers, the democratic public in search of meaningful education, and the middle-class interest group now called the American Vocational Association (AVA). But vocational education in the high school was ineffective because it provided no clear certification (the high school diploma was general), no demonstrable skill, few systematic connections to the world of work, and outmoded training in declining fields like agriculture and home economics.[21]

Second, craft unions carved a niche outside the high school for apprenticeship training by informal agreements and then government-sanctioned programs. In 1911, Wisconsin enacted apprenticeship controls through an industrial commission that required classroom instruction of at least five hours a week. After obtaining national immigration controls in the 1920s, employer, labor, and educational officials began a concerted effort to regulate apprenticeships nationally. The Federal Committee on Apprenticeship was appointed in 1934 to recommend policy on apprenticeship, and in 1937 the National Apprenticeship Law, the Fitzgerald Act, was passed to regulate and standardize apprenticeship training. The Bureau of Apprenticeship and Training in the Department of Labor promoted and publicized apprenticeships but did not control them. However, apprenticeship programs constituted only a small part of the U.S. labor force, and

20. The comprehensive school was left untouched by the New Deal although enrollments continued to rise—47 percent in 1930, 80 percent in 1940.

21. There were other training programs. The Morrill Act (1862) established land grant colleges. The Hatch Act (1887) and the Smith-Lever Act (1914) established agricultural experiment stations and educational outreach (Kirkland 1951, p. 470; Cremin 1961, p. 105).

their importance primarily followed their dominance in construction (U.S. DOL 1979).

The third deviation from the accent on socialization was black vocational education. From 1870 to 1915, the "Negro Industrial Training Movement" promoted agricultural and mechanical education, but in reality the movement intended to produce black teachers who would transmit the Puritan work ethic to southern blacks. The industrial normal schools were built under the banner of vocationalism, but the first industrial training certificate at Hampton was not awarded until 1895 (Anderson 1982, p. 186). From 1890 to 1920, the Morrill Act established some black high schools and new land grant colleges to produce first-class workers, shopfloor supervisors, and craft teachers. The schools were patterned after industrial normal schools offering trade certificates in carpentry, brick laying, and tailoring. However, the vocational courses were sparsely attended because discrimination dampened enthusiasm for the trades.

In the 1920s, massive black migrations to the North caused major curriculum changes and segregation in high schools.[22] Lieberson (1980) shows that the propensity of northern blacks for education before this time was similar to that of whites. But high school enrollments in northern cities expanded at tremendous rates for both blacks and whites: 210 percent from 1910 to 1920, 150 percent from 1920 to 1930, and 170 percent from 1930 to 1940. By 1920, whites began to guide the northern ghetto toward segregation. The curriculum for blacks changed in most high schools from academic courses to manual training. Even vocational electives such as bookkeeping and stenography were dropped, and in some schools the home economics courses were changed to laundry work. While the schools shifted to vocational education for blacks, the skilled unions closed off apprenticeships—a problem still addressed with difficulty (Katzman 1973, pp. 124–25). In turn, black interest in education began to decline (Kusmer 1976, pp. 184–98). Catholic immigrants also flooded the

22. From 1910 to 1920, Detroit's black population increased by 611 percent, Cleveland's by 308 percent, and Chicago's by 148 percent (Kusmer 1976, p. 157). From 1910 to 1930, Chicago's black population increased by 430 percent (Anderson 1982, p. 199).

United States at this time, but what discrimination they faced in schools was partially tempered by private parochial schools.

From 1930 to 1950, the black vocational guidance movement arose. Counselors discovered that an "alarming" number of black high school seniors planned to go to college and that black college students intended to do graduate work or professional studies. Counselors felt this trend would lead to undue stratification among blacks and disappointment in the labor market. What blacks needed was "the help of men trained in the technique of vocational adjustment, to help them find their way in the vocational world" (Anderson 1982, p. 202). The movement tended to blame the schools and neglect the labor market. Although Roosevelt promoted the guidance movement, black educators shifted focus to new occupations.

Black education has gone in circles: no education, no jobs; without jobs, education is not worth providing. The state's role was to acquiesce to and at times promote a dual racial education system, to ignore black educators' hopes for a well-developed system of black mechanical trade schools, and to convert black land grant colleges into institutes of manual labor.[23] Paradoxically, blacks received a racial socialization education under the banner of vocational education, while whites received a general socialization education in the comprehensive school.

Although the comprehensive school overwhelmed other forms of secondary and vocational education, its victory has not been met with accolades. Vocational training in high schools has produced "few positive results," and vocational graduates have "no significant occupational advantages" (Kett 1982; Semple 1986; Reubens 1974; Berg 1970). Misused vocational training in black and women's programs has tainted its reputation, and the additional Smith-Hughes expenditures themselves did little to increase vocational courses. Thus, in most states vocational education was underfunded, while the bulk of state educational revenues went to colleges and the comprehensive high school.

Three negative results emerged from the comprehensive school victory. First, the U.S. manual work force has low skill

23. Samuel Cornish started the black push for mechanical trade schools in 1829 (see Anderson 1982, pp. 181, 195).

levels, despite the years spent in high school. Vocational education was downgraded in the eyes of both whites—"it's mostly for low status whites and negroes"—and blacks—"it's mostly heavy toil and disappointment."[24] White flight to higher education for social mobility resulted.

Second, social discrimination formalized and recreated secondary labor markets. The education system and labor market, especially for blacks, produced the structurally unemployed work force that subsequent ALMP sought to serve (Anderson 1982, p. 195). Third, the homogeneous skill structure had a supply side effect. Although the high school produced literate workers with possibilities for social mobility into white-collar jobs, it failed to produce workers with manual skills. The homogeneous manual work force graduating from the high school gave the United States a competitive advantage in mass production for domestic markets but a disadvantage in batch production of capital goods for export markets where greater manual skills were needed. Thus, job training in the United States from 1920 to 1950 was limited to basic skills—reading, writing, and arithmetic—and above all socialization skills, including deference to management authority, punctuality, and American customs. Skill training for the bulk of the labor force was done on the job or not at all.[25]

Thus, the high school emerged from the interests of educators and social welfare intellectuals close to the state; meanwhile employers were divided, and labor—crosscut by race, ethnic, and other status divisions—was too late in pushing the issue.

24. Anderson says this was more powerful than the Washington-DuBois debates in molding black attitudes toward vocational education.

25. Arguing in the opposite direction, Grubb and Lazerson (1982, pp. 130–31) claim that vocational courses in the high school have worked well because office jobs and clerical work have been served by the provision of literacy and typing, economic returns to schooling became substantial, and political movements concentrated on access to schools, rather than calling for their abolition. However, from 1920 to 1960, most vocational funds went into agriculture and home economics, which had little to do with office jobs. Whatever economic returns to schooling that occurred during this period were the result of general education, not specific vocational training. Political emphasis on access to higher education points to vocational education being ignored rather than succeeding. And finally, they ignore the role of vocational education in retarding the progress of blacks and women during this period.

Chapter Three

The Roots of ALMP:
Job Creation
and Systematic Comparison

Job creation was the last labor market policy to be widely implemented in both countries. But why did Germany invest early in job creation, while the United States, even under the most dire economic circumstances, avoided and then tentatively embraced job creation? After dealing with this question, I systematically compare the roots of ALMP in this formative period of institution building.

GERMAN JOB CREATION BEFORE 1945

In the early 1920s, Germany was ahead of the United States and other countries in instituting a wide range of national job creation policies—for instance, "productive unemployment relief" and "short-time work" programs. In 1926 and later, German job creation policies were permanently housed in the employment service. But only the Nazis could deliver massive funding for policies that created jobs. In both countries, democratic governments had great difficulties implementing major job creation programs.

Work creation began during World War I when small public works projects were started in armament industries (Barclay 1974, p. 68). After the war, the demobilization decrees imposed extreme controls on hiring and firing, but they were lifted by 1920. Article 163 of the Weimar Constitution, adopted July 31,

1919, declared work an individual right and obligation and required the state to provide relief. During the next five years, the state tried to live up to this promise through five types of job creation programs: productive unemployment relief, the *Deutsche Werk*, short-time work, compulsory work, and national work creation programs (Moses 1982, p. 298; ILO 1931).

First, productive unemployment relief, instituted by decree in 1920 and then legislated in the 1922 labor exchange law, replaced unemployment compensation with grants and loans for relief workshops and public works. The grants went to local governments, public utilities, and private organizations for transportation, construction, and agricultural work. The government strongly defended this policy: it provided valuable work that would not otherwise be done, invested where few banks or firms would invest during risky periods, discouraged workers from quitting private jobs for new jobs with excessive wage rates, and covered less than 10 percent of the unemployed.[1]

Second, the Deutsche Werk provided union-sponsored, joint stock companies owned by the public. To avoid massive layoffs and to satisfy Allies' demands, the individual states and industrial unions converted old armament factories into collective concerns producing civilian goods. In June 1920, thirty thousand employees started work in Deutsche Werk; but it was forced out of business in 1926 by the Allies' insistence on destroying "war" machines, private industry's "capital strike," and a lack of customers (Barclay 1974, pp. 232–36).

Third, the short-time work program paid support to bring workers' incomes up to full pay, while the work week was shortened to produce more jobs. This innovative program had a checkered career. Short-time work was first limited to six weeks,

1. Many changes were made in productive work relief measures. The October 15, 1923, order reduced the rate of pay; the April 30, 1925, order defined state job creation as relief, making it ineligible for works councils and other welfare state protections. On July 16, 1927, the Employment Exchange Act again emphasized "productive unemployment relief" with public utility and noncompetition with the private sector. Loans and subsidies could not exceed 50 percent of the project, and all government payments could not exceed 80 percent of total costs. All these job creation programs were small, and enrollments decreased from 11.6 percent (51,919 persons) of the unemployed on relief in 1925 to 3.6 percent (45,457 persons) in 1929 (ILO 1931, pp. 129–32).

discontinued in April 1924, and then revived in March 1926 without time limitations (Preller 1949, pp. 366–70).

Fourth, compulsory work was introduced in 1923 to make young relief recipients earn their keep, much in the manner of contemporary "workfare" programs in the United States. Some communities combined it with youth training courses at occupational and adult schools. Unions and the SPD opposed the programs, while the Nazis, National Clerks Association, and the Young German Order supported it. But it remained marginal throughout Weimar (Preller 1949, p. 368).[2]

Finally, the government instituted national work creation programs during the 1926 depression. Countercyclical expenditures of 200 million RM, covered by a mortgage guaranteed loan, were to stimulate the economy. The program, too small to have a major effect, hardly made a dent from June 1926 to January 1927, although some blamed its failures on infighting between the states and federal government. This was the last democratic effort at job creation.

The three emergency governments from 1930 to 1933 also failed to reduce unemployment through job creation programs. The Brüning government (March 1930 to May 1932) ignored job creation until the end of its term, when it was too late. Brüning banned overtime, increased public schooling, and proposed public works programs in railway and road building.[3] However, these policies, where initiated, were counteracted by the Russian trade deals, reparation negotiations, reductions in social security payments, and general attempts to limit expenditures (Schneider 1986, p. 181; Schneider 1975a, pp. 167–92). Brüning's right hand negated his left (Wolffsohn 1981, pp. 220–21).

The Papen government (May 1932 to December 1932) initially focused its job creation effort on tax credits. Papen negotiated a narrow course between labor, industry, and agriculture, but he

2. The Nazi regime reintroduced compulsory work with forced work for war prisoners in armament factories and for Jews and others in some death camps.
3. The "Additional Works Program," drawn up by the Brüning cabinet in mid-1930, proposed 272 million RM for railways, 200 million RM for postal services, and 100 million RM for building houses. Little is known about how much of this was spent. The second plan, prepared in 1932, included employment vouchers and bonuses for employers; it was to spend 750 million RM, but less than half was actually used (ILO 1935, p. 14).

tended to discuss, not implement, tax relief and indirect incentives for job creation. As leader of the third emergency government (December 1932 to January 1933), Schleicher appointed a commissioner for work creation and solicited liberal employers, labor, and the Nazis. Schleicher's "supplementary employment premiums" failed, and his late 1932 public work creation measures lost the support of industry and banking because they feared a centrally planned economy. Schleicher's work creation policies thus "fell between all stools" (Wolffsohn 1981, p. 237; Abraham 1981, p. 173; Schneider 1975a, pp. 192–202).[4]

Enacted funds and money spent during these three administrations always fell far short of proposed expenditures because of delays in legislative voting and tardiness in implementation (ILO 1935, p. 17). Job creation took a back seat because these three governments all bowed to fiscal restraints demanded by industry and at times agriculture.

But Germany had strong advocates for public works policies. In the early 1930s, Wladimir Woytinsky, Fritz Tarnow, and Fritz Baade formulated the WTB Plan to inflate the currency and increase consumer demand through government spending on public works and relief. The DGB finally endorsed this plan in 1932, but SPD President Otto Wells opposed it because he believed the SPD's first obligation was to the employed. Wells thought that because so many unemployed were supporting the communists, the communists should take care of the unemployed (Garraty 1978, p. 194). Furthermore, Rudolf Hilferding—the Social Democratic finance minister and author of *Finanzkapital*—strongly opposed the WTB plan and deficit spending because "capitalism does not work that way" (Barclay 1974, p. 326). Brüning even commented in his memoirs that "with this socialist [Hilferding] I have found more understanding for the principles of the capitalist banking system than with all the leaders of the greatest banks" (Gates 1974, p. 212). Although trade union leaders had overcome skilled workers' lack of interest in the unemployed, the SPD had bought the neoclassical deflation argument

4. The Gerecke plan under Schleicher's government provided for 500 million RM in loans for work encouragement for municipalities, public corporations, and others. Of the 535 million RM appropriated, only 230 million were spent (ILO 1935, p. 14).

and became "the staunchest defender of the status quo" (Pollard 1974, p. 246; Schneider 1975a, pp. 45–165; Woytinsky 1961).

When Hitler came to power in 1933, he found many job creation measures planned at the national and local levels. Having no real job creation policies of his own, he activated the Social Democratic programs and other proposals (Stachura 1986, p. 22). The Reinhardt National Socialist Program increased direct job creation expenditures to 1,071 million RM—more than five times the Brüning promises, four times the Papen proposals, and twice the Gerecke plan. The Reinhardt Program was soon supplemented by an unemployment reduction program (500 million RM) and a road-building project (1,400 to 2,000 million RM). Altogether the Nazi government spent 4.6 percent of GNP in 1934 on job creation programs, while prior governments proposed about 1.5 percent of GNP and spent less than half that.[5] The Nazis emphasized infrastructural improvements, subsidies for business investment (which did not stem the decrease in private investment) and house repair, tax repeals on new vehicles, and a major boost in government employment. Labor was controlled by reducing work hours, shrinking wage rates, withdrawing youths from the labor market, encouraging women through marriage loans to have children and leave the labor force, and forcing Jews and others out of jobs (Guillebaude 1971, pp. 45–46; Maier 1987, pp. 96–104; Schneider 1975a, pp. 202–13; Bry 1960, pp. 233–65). These expenditures and social controls were massive.

There is "no doubt about the temporary success of these measures" (Neumann 1966, p. 293). In 1932 Germany had six million unemployed; in 1936 Germany had a labor shortage. Programs creating civilian jobs reduced unemployment by 63 percent from January to November 1933 but slowed to a 16 percent reduction in the next twelve months. After the draft began in March 1935, unemployment resumed its rapid decline. Job creation programs clearly reduced unemployment in the first two years of the Nazi regime, but after 1934 the effects of the war economy and forced labor overcame the effects of job creation programs. Although it is difficult to measure the specific effects of the job creation pro-

5. Nazi figures always need to be approached with suspicion; however, I have not found substantial disagreement on these figures, and Neumann also seems generally to accept the success of the early Nazi job creation efforts.

grams, the civilian expenditures alone greatly boosted the economy (Neumann 1966). This "positive aspect" of the Nazis led to the political legitimacy that supported later atrocities (Maier 1987, pp. 96–104; Allen 1966, p. 272).[6]

Although the left began job creation programs in the early 1920s, they could not implement them in sufficient quantity during the worldwide depression. The DGB and Social Democratic Party established a wide range of work creation policies in the early 1920s, and these moderate successes were important because opposition from the middle class, hardest hit by inflation, was strong. During democratic Weimar, the unions had considerable control over implementing policies because they were administered through the employment service. In the late 1920s and early 1930s, however, the DGB gingerly formulated the WTB plan, but the SPD chose not to back it. Even Social Democratic politicians followed budget-balancing advice, and in effect, abandoned the unemployed. From 1930 to 1933, nondemocratic governments retrenched social policy and flirted with job creation policies. The Nazis opened the floodgates of job creation programs to vastly reduce unemployment, but by 1936 they relied more on repression and the war economy.

JOB CREATION IN THE UNITED STATES BEFORE 1945

American job creation programs, when they finally came in the 1930s, were highly funded in comparison to many countries, but they were much smaller than German and Swedish programs.

---

6. The effect of Hitler's programs has produced intense debate (Stachura 1986, p. 22; Maier 1987, pp. 96–104). Some claim that unemployment was reduced only through military expansion. Others claim that the early programs were legitimate job creation efforts that other governments could have followed. I believe that the evidence supports the success of civilian job creation in the first two years of the Nazi regime. These programs had only a small military component, and they reduced unemployment by 43 percent in 1933–34 and 21 percent in 1934–35 (calculations here are from the *European Historical Statistics;* calculations in text are based on different dates in Stachura). It appears plausible that Hitler perceived a weakness in the effects of civilian job creation policies in the 1934–35 statistics and sought to increase employment through war related measures. With the draft, unemployment was reduced by 26 percent in 1935–36 and 43 percent in 1936–37. Unemployment was reduced by 53 percent in 1937–38 and 72 percent in 1938–39. Note that the American PWA was also involved in military production before 1936, e.g., building battleships.

Job creation programs were initially self-financed, capital intensive projects that later competed with labor-intensive "put 'em to work" programs. But the employment service and the Department of Labor were continually bypassed for these job creation projects, leaving an institutional void after World War II.

Although early American governments had a positive attitude toward creating public work, such programs were strenuously resisted after the Civil War (Schlesinger 1986). In the depression of 1873, when unemployment reached three million, demonstrations in New York demanded public works programs. But the city ignored job creation and persuaded the Relief and Aid Society to open its coffers to the unemployed (Rayback 1966, p. 130). Despite further depressions and the American Association for Labor Legislation's call for systematic public works programs, the federal government did not make real proposals on public works until the 1928 depression (Robertson 1981, p. 100; Sautter 1986).[7]

By 1930–31, most large cities had instituted crude job programs, which burdened their budgets. When the public increased pressure on President Herbert Hoover for national action, the National Unemployment League proposed spending $3 billion on public works. Hoover rejected this plan but appointed the Woods Committee to come up with a better proposal; it recommended a $0.8 billion spending program, which Hoover also rejected. In 1930, federal expenditures for public works, set in a ten-year plan, amounted to only $0.2 billion, while the states and cities at the time were spending $2.9 billion. Hoover vetoed another congressional bill for $2.3 billion in public works. Finally, in 1932, Hoover reluctantly signed the Emergency Relief and Construction Act that authorized him to use the Reconstruction Finance Corporation to loan $0.3 billion to states and cities for creating jobs. This program for small loans mainly took effect after Hoover left office (Kesselman 1978, p. 157).[8]

In 1933, Roosevelt, who had stressed Hoover's failure to balance the budget, looked like an opponent of job creation pro-

7. The association voiced its job creation programs along with the employment service proposals in the 1914 "Practical Program for the Prevention of Unemployment." See Feder (1936) for other plans at the state level.

8. Unemployment was about 24 percent in 1932, and private construction dropped from $8.7 billion in 1929 to $1.4 billion in 1932.

grams. Many of Roosevelt's aides described him as "frankly leery" of job creation because during the campaign he had repeatedly backed away from their plan for a $5 billion work creation program (Kesselman 1978, pp. 159, 166). Doubting that enough useful projects existed for real jobs, Roosevelt had long argued against the multiplier effects of job programs.

But his attitude toward job creation changed when Senator Hugo Black proposed a bill to create jobs by reducing the work week to thirty hours in jobs connected to interstate commerce. After the Senate passed Black's bill, Roosevelt intervened with the National Industrial Recovery Act. Although Roosevelt told Black that his Thirty Hour Bill would be included in a larger employment package, Roosevelt objected to the bill because it was inflexible toward seasonal work, restricted production when it should be expanded, and constrained rather than courted industry. In the end, the work hour reduction plan was dropped.

Nevertheless, Black's bill also pressured Roosevelt to implement the Civilian Conservation Corps (CCC), a program for single men, eighteen to twenty-five years old, from needy families. The CCC paid them up to $30 each month, with an additional monthly $25 family allowance. Then in 1933, despite previous reservations, Roosevelt accepted his cabinet's recommendations and created the Public Works Administration (PWA). Loans and grants were used by federal, state, and local bodies for construction to stimulate heavy industry. PWA Director Harold Ickes concentrated on projects of permanent value, which often delayed expenditures because of extensive planning. The Federal Emergency Relief Administration in 1933 provided grants for more direct unemployment relief and work programs, and its administrator, Harry Hopkins, pushed hard for work-oriented relief in light construction and programs based on financial need. The slow progress of the PWA and fears of rising unemployment led to the Civil Works Administration, a pump-priming measure combining recovery and relief. Hopkins also headed the Civil Works Administration, and it temporarily became the nation's largest job creation program.

In summer 1933, big business leaders, such as Dupont and Sloan, formed the American Liberty League to defeat Roosevelt, unions, and social welfare causes. In February 1934, Roosevelt issued an executive order that supported majority rule in the National Labor Board and appeared to clear the path for labor's participation in collective bargaining. As business support dwindled, Roosevelt and the Democrats looked to the unions and unorganized labor. Labor helped Roosevelt win an overwhelming victory in 1934 and establish a mandate for solving mass unemployment (Berkowitz and McQuaid 1980, p. 90; Fine 1963, p. 219).

But the mandate was not necessarily for creating jobs. Roosevelt had to conceal the "major" job creation effort of the New Deal—the Works Progress Administration (WPA)—in the flexible but vague Emergency Relief Appropriation Act. This act authorized Roosevelt to dispense $4 billion of work relief money in as yet unplanned programs. All public works programs were to be self-liquidating—that is, they were designed to pay their own way. The bill easily passed the House but was caught with amendments in the Senate. Informed testimony was sparse: Ickes had no idea who would administer it, Hopkins said he had just seen the bill, and Admiral Christian J. Peoples—the official Roosevelt spokesman—was so uninformed that he thought the bill would fund federal gas stations. After Roosevelt gave verbal promises about flexibility and wages, the emergency act passed in April; Roosevelt immediately established the Rural Electrification Administration and the National Youth Administration.[9] In May, Roosevelt set up the WPA by federal order to handle coordination and investigation. Thus, Roosevelt used the entire force of his electoral mandate to slip the major work creation program of the New Deal past legislators representing both conservatives and employers who abhorred the state's interference with the capitalist system.

Roosevelt appointed Harry Hopkins as WPA administrator to promote massive work creation programs. This began the conflict between Harry Ickes—permanent projects of value—and Harry Hopkins—"put 'em to work" no matter what the project. As with the PWA, the WPA officially was supposed to create capital-intensive projects that were self-liquidating, that is, generate revenues like electric bills in rural electrification or rent in public

9. The National Youth Administration provided jobs for youth, especially for college students, because they were barred from other New Deal programs.

housing. But self-liquidation contradicted Hopkins's position of creating as many jobs as possible:

Never forget that the objective of this whole program . . . is . . . taking 3.5 million people off relief and putting them to work and the secondary object is to put them to work on the best possible projects we can; but don't ever forget that first objective. (Jerrett and Barocci 1979, p. 7)

Hopkins soon expanded the WPA into the largest New Deal work creation program. Although no formal difference between the PWA and the WPA existed and yearly expenditures varied, the WPA spent about three times more than the PWA on job creation from 1934 to 1943 (Kesselman 1978, p. 158).[10]

However, the WPA had diverse goals: reduce unemployment, stimulate the economy, and relieve national disasters. In budgetary fights over the WPA, Roosevelt usually discovered what Congress would accept and then let WPA battle it out with the conservative treasury and budget office. The WPA budget—the largest of all programs—was much smaller than the president's advisers wanted, perhaps because Roosevelt's support was lukewarm. Nevertheless, Roosevelt obtained "light public work creation" with few political costs by gradually twisting self-liquidating and capital-intensive work measures into totally subsidized and labor-intensive programs.

Congress, nevertheless, retained many controls over the WPA. Because transition to the private sector remained a goal, the WPA workers had to leave the WPA if private jobs at wages greater than WPA wages were available. With the media and conservatives playing up "careers on WPA," Congress enacted legislation to rotate WPA workers with eighteen months' tenure off the WPA for at least thirty days, whether or not jobs existed (Briscoe 1972); this measure also met considerable criticism. For example, the mayor of Detroit protested that "it's pretty hard to rotate your appetite" (Jerrett and Barocci 1979, p. 8). Congress continually cut the WPA budget and interfered with its administration by writing exceptions and qualifications into law. Finally, the WPA was neither permanent, nor were its duties transferred to another agency. Secretary of Labor Perkins was somewhat up-

10. During this period the WPA spent $13.4 billion and the PWA $4.5.

set that the job creation programs were not housed in the Department of Labor, but given that she was in "everything a states righter" and her moderate opposition to centralized job creation programs, her interest in absorbing the WPA was ambivalent (Berkowitz and McQuaid 1980, p. 99).

Although never formally evaluated, the WPA received considerable attention. The National Appraisal Commission and the National Resource Planning Board claimed that the WPA created dead-end jobs, mixed relief payments with work, and provided work of dubious utility—for instance, leaf raking and make-work. It was indeed true that Hopkins emphasized the quantity rather than the quality of jobs. WPA projects were labor-intensive; nearly 90 percent of costs and 1.4 billion dollars went into wages each year for two million families. Although WPA programs did not end the depression, they put vast numbers of needy people to work and completed useful dams, buildings, and less capital-intensive projects. But opinions on the WPA were divided. In a 1939 public opinion poll appraising programs of the New Deal, people listed the WPA as both the best and the worst program. Evaluations of the WPA depended on one's economic position: that is, if you were in dire need of work, you thought the WPA was a lifesaver; but if you were employed in the private sector and supplied the revenues for job creation programs, you thought the WPA was a disaster (Jerrett and Barocci 1979, p. 10).

In sum, effective job creation programs finally reached the unemployed masses through the WPA, whereas the early New Deal programs created jobs for only a small fraction of the unemployed. But even after Roosevelt had won a large electoral mandate, he still had to camouflage his major job creation bill as "fiscally responsible" public works in order to spend unprecedented sums of money on unemployed workers (MacMahon et al. 1941, pp. 121–65, 276–78; Sipe 1981, p. 23). Thus, state structures with conservative interests in the legislature constituted a difficult hurdle that could be only sporadically overcome, despite the social demands inherent in a large Democratic victory.

COMPARING THE ROOTS OF U.S. AND GERMAN ALMP

The historical development of ALMP shows strong divergences between these two countries. Secondary schools could hardly be more different than the Berufschule and the high school. Furthermore, in 1930, the Reichsanstalt spent $12.79 per worker, while the U.S. Employment Service spent only 49 cents (Deutsche Reich 1932; U.S. Government 1932).

The employment service, as the central organization of labor market policy, developed in different directions on all major dimensions—labor market power, participation in administration, employment service autonomy, and organizational centralization. From 1910 to 1930 most nations moved to regulate or abolish private labor exchanges. Germany's employment service monopolized power in the labor market. But why did the German courts allow labor placement monopoly while the U.S. courts rejected it? In part, Germany had a Roman law system with weak political norms of judicial review and a constitution to match these norms (Kommers 1976, p. 35; Blair 1981; Lenoir 1940).

Judicial review in the United States was active, severely restricting intervention in the labor market during this period of institution building. After twenty-four states failed to control directly or ban altogether private employment agencies, Senator Robert Wagner (D-N.Y.), defensive on placement monopoly, denied that his 1932 bill had anything to do with private employment agencies. Social welfare intellectuals, reversing Gresham's Law, thought that the "good" public agencies would drive the "bad" private agencies out of circulation. For instance, La Dame predicted the public agencies' "complete absorption" of the private agencies, and Senator Douglas spoke of "co-optation" (Robertson 1981, pp. 140–41). Despite their confidence, private employment agencies thrived, especially in white-collar labor markets. Moreover, the National Employment Association successfully lobbied to keep the employment service limited to blue-collar, black, poor, and disadvantaged workers. As a result, a monopoly on labor placement was absent in the United States.

Strong self-administration gives both labor and employers a stake in directing a labor exchange, rather than leaving them to complain about or ignore the employment service. The 1922 German employment service law gave labor, management, and the local communities control over local administration. The 1927 Reichanstalt law restricted local community participation and spread tripartite participation to federal and state levels.

Throughout the history of job placement, the Social Democratic Party and the DGB pushed for self-administration, while employers eventually sided with the unions.[11]

In contrast, the United States had weak self-administration, although tripartite administration of the employment service was not always ignored. Tripartite councils existed during World War I, but Secretary of Labor Wilson deleted them from the 1919 Nolan Bill because councils would risk a "feeling of discontent and disloyalty" within USES (Robertson 1981, p. 155). Ohio Director of Placement Croxton, future Secretary of Labor Perkins, and Secretary of Labor Doak discounted these councils as unnecessary.[12] The Wagner-Peyser Act established weak federal and state advisory councils composed of employer, employee, and public representatives. However, the federal councils met too infrequently to give expert advice or to "allow members to become fully cognizant of the problems confronting USES" (Robertson 1981, p. 121). Perkins and others in the Department of Labor left the councils to languish in obscurity, while they pushed the introduction of the civil service into USES.[13] Ironically, the federal government sued the states on the civil service issue but ignored the advisory councils, despite their statutory basis in the Wagner-Peyser Act. Thus, American labor's participation was excluded in two ways: the advisory councils were ignored, and jobs that might have gone to many labor bureaucrats went instead to middle-class civil servants. Instead of being impartial and respected, USES became dominated by bureaucratic self-interest

11. Rosenhaft (1981, pp. 220–24) implies that the neocorporatist elements of the 1927 law may have derived from a desire to suppress the association of unemployed workers and place administrative control into the hands of employers, unions, and the government. Because employers were upset with the radical takeover of many labor exchanges and the DGB unions were similarly threatened by the presence of a strong USPD (communist) influence among the unemployed, the implication is plausible. However, her evidence is only for Berlin.

12. No one advocated the use of councils more than John Commons. He believed that industrial society needed to create consensus among organized labor and capital, and further to control bureaucracy. But despite Commons's views, the "Commons Group" let merit selection prevail over the councils (Robertson 1981, pp. 151–55; Shalev 1985; Commons 1928).

13. The introduction of the civil service was a governmentwide movement at the time, not isolated to USES.

and a defensive posture toward labor and management (Robertson 1981, pp. 150–55).

Autonomy allows an employment service to do its job without interference. The 1922 German Reichanstalt was too decentralized for national independence, but the 1927 Reichanstalt became an independent public law corporation. Community representatives rather than labor and capital pushed for an independent Reichanstalt. In contrast, USES lacked autonomy. The early proposals of social welfare intellectuals had suggested autonomy: John Commons saw the employment service as a fourth branch of government; Commons's student, policy activist William Leiserson, proposed a "Federal Labor Reserve Board"; and economist Donald Lescohier, another student of Commons, suggested a "Central Employment Council" with limited connections to interest groups (Robertson 1981, pp. 158–60).[14] Over time, as support for autonomy weakened, the AFL wanted USES moved under the Department of Labor; eventually it became a third-tier organization within that bureaucracy.

Why was USES made a dependent agency when the Federal Reserve Board, National Labor Relations Board, Federal Trade Commission, and Securities and Exchange Commission were independent? First, these agencies were small, centralized bodies with professional constituencies, whereas an autonomous employment service would view the entire labor force as its constituency and require thousands of local offices. A large autonomous agency would be politically powerful and set a new precedent. Second, no independent agency had the power to dispense mass transfer payments then or now, so an autonomous agency dispensing unemployment checks was difficult to imagine.[15] And third, employers disapproved of an independent employment service because an effective labor exchange would reduce their power in the labor market. Thus, the public employment service was passed around

14. The power attributed to labor board "advice" is sometimes baffling. Lescohier (1919, p. 224) proselytized the employment service with councils having "real, rather than nominal participation in the management of the Service." However, he then described real participation as "power to suggest changes," "should be consulted," "should cooperate," and "power to make recommendations."

15. The departments that issue transfer payments for social security and veterans are under the direct control of the president.

six times to other departments and directly supervised by the individual states.

The 1927 German law established an effective and flexible centralized system. Local offices could create and dissolve subsidiary offices—branch, control, and auxiliary offices—to meet fluctuating problems (Weigert 1934, p. 41). Organizational flexibility allowed the national system to work from a centralized base; the SPD and DGB pushed hard for this centralization, while the communities and states opposed it. But USES is necessarily decentralized; the individual states control their own employment services. The Wagner-Peyser Act established a weak federal advisory role with enforcement power to withdraw federal funds—a drastic all-or-nothing-at-all step. As a result of weak federal controls, interstate clearance and coordination were ineffective. For example, when in 1942 the South Carolina employment service made referrals to another state—a legitimate interstate clearance action—the governor of South Carolina threatened employment service employees with arrest, stopped interstate referrals, and forced the resignation of the state employment service director. The states' rights politicians and the Interstate Conference of Employment Security Agencies strongly supported state control of the employment service because they claimed the states know better their specific problems, offer more creative solutions, and work more efficiently. But many experts claim that state offices simply duplicated services and produced stagnant bureaucracies that differed just enough to make interstate clearance difficult. The Interstate Conference, an interest group representing states and their employment bureaucracies, even opposed raising state workers' salaries for doing the same work as more highly paid federal workers during World War II; it was also accused of lobbying against appropriation bills for the employment service in 1947 (Butler 1951, pp. 52–53, 72, 332).

In the second major area of ALMP, job training, the German work orientation produced vocational training with specific skills. The Berufschule and apprenticeship training targeted skills and work experience at the same time. The government's formalization of apprenticeship made the "job" the central focus of at least 50 percent of secondary education. In the United States, the socialization orientation sought to avoid specific training and provide a common experience for native and immigrant students. Comprehensive education put some immigrants into channels of upward mobility, but it left most manual workers undifferentiated upon the labor market. Thus, the comprehensive high school avoided specialization as much as possible and graduated students with a generic diploma. Black education was sold as specialized vocational education, but it segregated blacks in the secondary labor markets and led to the degradation of vocational education.

Job creation policy constitutes the third area of ALMP. Germany accepted policies for job creation as a continuing need, developed many preventive and protective policies, and housed them in a permanent organization. Germany also developed short-time work programs, but the United States did not. In the United States, work creation programs were absent in the 1920s and less creative than German programs when they eventually appeared in the 1930s. They were housed in temporary agencies that disappeared after World War II, leaving USES and the Department of Labor without job creation precedents.[16]

A comparison of "Nazi versus New Deal" job creation programs shows some similarities in content but strong differences in funding. From 1933 to 1939, the German national debt increased by a factor of 3.3, while the U.S. debt increased by 1.8. According to Garraty, the Germans' heavy deficit financing was one reason for their greater success in reducing unemployment (1973, p. 944).[17] In job creation expenditures over GNP, the Nazi government in 1934 spent 4.6 percent of GNP while prior governments spent less than 1.5 percent. Job creation expenditures in the United States hovered below 2.8 percent before the WPA, rose to 4.5 percent in 1935, but then declined to 1.5 percent of GNP in 1937. The New Deal and Nazi Germany unleashed a flood of funds, but the American funds came more sporadically and may have simply replaced local efforts. Yet points of similarity remain, and even Hitler claimed that American efforts against unemployment followed his example.

16. Some weaknesses of U.S. job creation policies may be due to the low unemployment rate in the United States in the 1920s, while Germany had much earlier encounters with high unemployment in 1924 and 1926.

17. Between 1933 and 1939, the German national debt increased from 12.9 billion RM to 42.7; while the U.S. debt increased from $22.5 billion to $40.4.

However, the comparison of job creation programs under Weimar and the New Deal suggests the limitations of democratic regimes in vigorously creating jobs. Weimar failed to implement extensive job creation schemes, whereas only the Nazis were able to unleash the flow of funds. Roosevelt needed a landslide victory to enable him to sneak the WPA past Congress; even then his programs were often curtailed.

In sum, during this formative period, the strong social demands of both German unions and the state structures of bureaucratic self-administration and a strong Ministry of Labor led to extensive job placement and early job creation policies. The bureaucracy and state interests were otherwise overcome by social demands. However, these demands failed in the face of the worldwide depression. U.S. social demands from labor were splintered by status divisions, and the Progressive movement had much more influence on the outcomes of labor market policy before Roosevelt. After Roosevelt died, structural constraints had already been initiated, despite short-lived job creation programs that were temporarily allowed by an overwhelming electoral mandate during the depression. The weak state structures of the Department of Labor did little to promote either job placement or job creation policies. However, job training seemed to elude unions' social demands in both countries; German employers had strong influence, and the state appeared more autonomous, especially in the United States.

Given these roots of ALMP, one can better understand the strengths and weaknesses of ALMP programs after World War II.

Chapter Four

Job Placement
and the Employment Service

In 1974 during the oil crisis, a West German worker walking into the public employment service had a 25 percent chance of getting a job, while an American worker had only a 10 percent chance—an immense difference when it was difficult to place workers. The West German employment service is more effective in both its vacancy penetration rate—a measure that shows how far the employment service goes in obtaining listings of vacancies throughout the economy—and its external placement rate—the percentage of persons placed by the employment service out of all job vacancies, regardless of the listing.[1] That the West German employment service is more than twice as effective in job placement than its U.S. counterpart has important consequences for labor market programs and national competitiveness.

One major factor contributing to this difference in effectiveness over three decades is size and funding. For every one thousand unemployed workers in West Germany there were forty-two job placement personnel to help them at the employment service, while there were only four persons to help the unemployed at U.S. offices. Of course, West German funding has been as high as ten times greater than U.S. expenditures. A second reason for

1. The internal placement rate—persons placed as a percentage of job vacancies listed at the employment service—only measures internal efficiency. I do not use it because it is the same whether the employment service places one of two or five hundred thousand of one million workers.

these differences is the organizational strength of the employment service through its stability, flexibility, autonomy, and labor market clout.[2]

WEST GERMAN JOB PLACEMENT

AND EMPLOYMENT SERVICE

The West German Bundesanstalt für Arbeit,

1952 to 1968

The Federal Institute of Labor Placement and Unemployment Compensation, or Bundesanstalt, followed the organizational patterns of Weimar.[3] As a public law corporation, it had primary duties to place persons in jobs, counsel people on these vocational choices, and administer unemployment compensation programs. Although some smaller programs were set up for job training and job creation, the dominant duties simply reflected the organization's name: labor placement and unemployment insurance (Green 1966, p. 20). Three aspects of organizational structure gave it unusual strength and coherence: monopoly power in the labor market over job placement, autonomy in operation with a centralized structure, and a tripartite form of self-administration.

The Bundesanstalt had a clear monopoly over placement in the labor market. Following the example of the Weimar Reichanstalt, monopoly over placement was reintroduced, and private employment agencies were disallowed. Workers did not go to private agencies, university placement offices, or any other kinds of intermediaries; rather, they went to the employment service or simply relied on informal means of job information.

Although the Bundesanstalt was an independent, public law corporation that generated most of its own funding, financial problems could limit autonomy. Unemployment compensation funds were to come entirely from employers and workers; however, during the crisis of the early 1950s, general tax revenues were needed

2. The figures in the two introductory paragraphs come from the following years: size—1980, effectiveness—1975, and funding—1953.

3. The initial Bundesanstalt was established in 1952 by the Law on Labor Placement and Unemployment Compensation, whose amendments in 1957, 1961, and 1968 did little to change its original structure.

to support relief and job creation programs. Since then, Bundesanstalt budgets have always had two income sources: unemployment insurance funds from workers and employers, and additional funds from the federal government. Although the Bundesanstalt avoided deficits in the early 1950s, unemployment contribution rates were continuously cut, and deficits appeared in recessions (1957, 1967–68) and even in good times (1962–63). Deficit spending and federal funding limit Bundesanstalt autonomy. Autonomy decreases when legions of unemployed workers begin demanding payments instead of making contributions, and the federal government, backed by its bailouts, plays a stronger role in policy decisions. Autonomy increases when Bundesanstalt coffers overflow from the contributions of a fully employed work force.

The 1952 employment service law allowed more federal government supervision than specified in the 1927 law. The budget for the labor exchange was contingent on federal government approval, and the federal audit office controlled managerial appointments. A "hearing law" technically allowed employer and union objections to federal intervention, but it saw little use (Höckerts 1980, p. 158). The Ministry of Labor reviewed and sometimes denied regulations that were not within the law and constitution.

In sum, Bundesanstalt autonomy was limited by financial controls by the Bundestag and the federal audit office, regulatory control by the Ministry of Labor, and federal government appointment of Bundesanstalt leaders. Although the employment service never enjoyed complete autonomy from the Federal government, its freedom was immense compared to a bureaucracy under direct executive control or under dual state/federal management as in the United States.

The Bundesanstalt's governing structure consisted of tripartite self-administration in two councils and an appointed president. The most important organ, the Administrative Council, had thirty-nine members, with thirteen representatives each from unions, employers, and government. The federal council developed general policy on employment, formulated the budget, and represented the Bundesanstalt in Labor Committee meetings in the Bundestag. The council chair was elected annually; representatives of employers and labor alternate years. Similar councils also existed at regional and community levels. The Executive Board,

with nine members from labor, employers, and government, issued internal directives and made administrative rulings. Although it represented the Bundesanstalt on legal matters and
presented the budget to the Bundestag, it did little lobbying.
Day-to-day management was delegated to the president.

Individual state governments, with little control over the employment services, were represented on the national administrative council, as only one part of the government's delegation.
States were represented on the administrative councils at regional and local levels, although the central office directly supervised these subdivisions.[4] The president clearly ran the
Bundesanstalt with constraints set by the administrative council
and the federal government. Thus, the power of West German
states over the placement service was severely curtailed, compared to the state/federal power struggle in the United States.

When the postwar economic crises had subsided, job placement and unemployment insurance activities became routine at
the local level. Central headquarters initially controlled 12 state
offices and 209 local offices, which were reduced in 1966 to 9 regional offices and 146 local offices.[5] These regional and state offices controlled and financed small job creation programs,
approved job-training programs, adjusted central Bundesanstalt
regulations to local conditions, and monitored local office finances. The federal Bundesanstalt evaluated service performance
(Krautkramer 1978, p. 25). Local offices had four departments:
placement, vocational counseling, unemployment insurance, and
administration. The director of the local office delegated opera-
tional tasks and paved the way for programs by speaking to employers, unions, and the public. A group head performed internal
supervisory duties, and department heads arranged job creation
and sometimes job-training measures. In the placement depart-

4. The states are not represented on the executive council.
5. A change and efficiency drive consolidated the Rheinland-Pflaz and Saar-
land offices into one office, and the Bremen and Hamburg offices into the
Holstein-Schleswig and Niedersachsen regional offices. Bavaria received two offices for the north and south. But specialized centers later added employees: a
placement office for professionals in Frankfurt; recruiting stations in Turkey, Italy, and other countries; administrative training centers in Lauf and Münster-
Mecklenbeck; and a welfare center in Nuremberg (Bruche and Kroker 1982,
p. 34).

ment, agents spent half their day obtaining vacancies from employers and the other half placing persons in jobs. This basic structure changed little over the years.

The Bundesanstalt was a large organization. Beginning as the third largest civilian agency in the West German federal government—after the post office and the state railways—the Bundesanstalt had a staff of 36,123 in 1952. The employment service clearly needed a large staff to handle job applicants during the mass unemployment of the 1950s, but as unemployment receded in 1960, Bundesanstalt employees were reduced to about 30,000. A 1961 rationalization drive cut back over 10,000 white-collar employees, but employment stayed at earlier levels because of new duties. Although the size of the employment service varied with the business cycle, it remained large.

The Bundesanstalt was clearly an effective actor in the labor market. The vacancy penetration rate, ranging from 37 percent to 49 percent in the 1960s, shows that the Bundesanstalt reached a major portion of the labor market. The U.S. rate was only 18 percent. The external placement rate—the percentage of placements made by the employment service out of all vacancies—was 25 percent in the 1950s, rising to about 28 percent in the 1967–68 recession. The West German external placement rate was not only high by international standards but also more than double the U.S. rate of 10 percent (Kühl et al. 1980, p. 52).

The AFG Recreates the Bundesanstalt, 1969 to 1974

The Bundesanstalt was changing before and after the new law. In April 1967, the Bundesanstalt president Anton Sabel, nearing the end of his career, appointed Dieter Mertens to head the new Institute for Labor Market and Occupational Research. In May, a prominent Christian-Democratic politician, Dr. Josef Stingl, became the new Bundesanstalt president. Stingl, a wily politician and genuine supporter of ALMP, held the post for sixteen years, shaping and protecting the organization.[6] In 1969, the Labor Promotion Act (AFG) increased ALMP funding and programs and

---

6. Stingl was sometimes referred to as *Baroccolandfürsten*, that is, the king of a baroque principality—the employment service.

soon authorized a new central office building surrounded by decorative glass towers with flowing water—nicknamed the *Wasserkopf* or fountainhead.[7]

The Bundesanstalt weathered a number of threats during this period. First, monopolistic powers were somewhat threatened by thousands of recruiting agencies that had sprung up to place guestworkers. The Bundesanstalt was to decide their fate, but it lacked the staff to review all the new agencies. Delays led to mild protests about Bundesanstalt's monopoly powers in the early 1970s; but eventually the private agencies diminished, and questions about monopoly powers died down. Second, national self-administration appeared unaffected by the AFG. At the local level, however, self-administrative councils gained more control over job creation measures as they became more important after 1975. Third, autonomy was threatened by increased federal government revenues in the Bundesanstalt budget. With deficits and federal subsidies from 1970 to 1972 and 1974, the federal government assumed greater leverage over the Bundesanstalt. The oil crisis increased unemployment and forced the Bundesanstalt to emphasize unemployment benefits over ALMP. Nevertheless, the Bundesanstalt retained most of its autonomy because employers and unions lobbied hard for ALMP.

After the passage of the AFG, the Bundesanstalt experienced both federal centralization and local decentralization. The Bundesanstalt national and state offices assumed more control over job placement by emphasizing interstate labor referral. Job placement at the local level changed little; the director continued wide-ranging contact with employers, while agents made more specific contacts to place individuals. The federal Bundesanstalt also centralized its power over local and state budgets and appointments of lower-level presidents. Regional offices continued to make most decisions on job creation including recruitment, approval, and funding. But the local offices took over school approvals from the state offices. The approval process was tedious because thousands of job-training organizations existed in each region, and the Bundesanstalt only approved programs on a case-

7. The "Bundesanstalt" was also renamed from the *Bundesanstalt für Arbeitsvermittlung und Arbeitslosenversicherung* (1952–69) to the *Bundesanstalt für Arbeit* (1969–present).

by-case basis after application. Although the local offices did not receive additional staff, they assumed more control of school approvals (Krautkramer 1978, pp. 123–29).

The Bundesanstalt grew under the AFG. Division I—covering labor market policy, vocational placement, counseling, and the medical service—split, leaving six divisions in 1970; the Research Institute was fully staffed for the first time. The 1967–68 recession stimulated an increase of Bundesanstalt employees to about 32,000 employees, and the reorganization and the AFG brought the Bundesanstalt to 37,465 employees in 1971.[8] Bundesanstalt's steady growth contrasted with the stagnation and organizational confusion at the U.S. Employment Service.[9]

Efficiency declined as the Bundesanstalt started to concentrate more on disadvantaged workers and as citizens began to feel the oil shock. The external penetration rate, which had stayed around 25 percent from 1969 to 1972, dropped to 23.2 percent in 1974. Placements over seven days in absolute numbers were fewer each year than in the early 1960s and continued to drop. Registered vacancies decreased from 46.2 percent in 1969 to 36.1 percent in 1974. Although these penetration rates are still much higher than those of the United States, specific programs were implemented to improve work registration and occupational measures from 1969 and 1974.

Interstate placement, as a national or regional task that covered large labor markets, was handled by the Central Office for Placement in Frankfurt.[10] It provided interstate and general placement for foreign, hotel, and restaurant workers, but unlike USES, it also placed managerial and media personnel. These specialized offices, most of which were founded in 1954, have not

8. The increase seems top heavy because few employees were added to the local offices where the new duties were implemented. The number of regional and branch offices remained the same (9 and 146), while the special suboffices increased from 501 to 571 (BAA *Geschaftsbericht* 1984, p. 15).

9. The 1973 Employment and Training Act in the United Kingdom created a new organization, while the 1969 AFG adapted an old organization. Although some countries separated compensation from job placement, the AFG clearly kept them together.

10. A small, common market placement agency—*Systeme europeen de diffusion des offres et demandes d'emploi enregistre en compensation internationale*—also made international placements (Bruche and Kroker 1982).

been as successful as the employment service in general. Their placement success was 20 percent for most specialized workers, and only 4 percent for higher-, 7 percent for middle-, and 11 percent for lower-management employees (Bruche and Kroker 1982, p. 43). Despite these figures, it is significant that the employment service also covers this broad range of higher-level occupations where network contacts are important.

The West German Bundesanstalt in Crisis, 1975 to the Present

The oil crises of 1974 and 1979 presented the Bundesanstalt with an entirely new and overwhelming set of problems. Josef Stingl provided strong leadership for the Bundesanstalt until his retirement in 1984, when Heinrich Franke was appointed in his place.[11] Because the oil crisis brought higher unemployment, ALMP was increased in 1974, but as deficits mounted in 1975, the federal government restricted ALMP. Under Bundesanstalt protest, the government continued to cut ALMP budgets, to emphasize unemployment insurance, and to concentrate the little remaining money on job creation measures.

The monopoly over job placement remained intact. In 1983, the Free Democratic Party (FDP), a constant opponent of ALMP during the crisis, asked for private employment agencies. They reasoned that private agencies would provide better service because the employers would pay the fees.[12] But the FDP plan failed to gain political support because of strong public sentiment that the government should look after the structure of employment, which private agencies would not do. Furthermore, no one was compelled to use the Bundesanstalt because individuals could always conduct their own job searches.

Although monopoly powers in the labor market remained strong, the recessions and Bundesanstalt deficits severely cur-

---

11. While Stingl provided strong leadership during a period of low unemployment and high ALMP growth, Franke began office with high unemployment and restricted ALMP programs. His decision—the *Franke Erlaß*—to deny unemployment compensation to workers indirectly affected by the 1984 "short-work time" strike also made for a rocky start.

12. This FDP plan was tied to private universities, which were actually created.

tailed organizational autonomy. The Budgetary Structure Law of 1975 started the attack on the federal deficit by reducing federal government subsidies to the Bundesanstalt. The government also enacted eligibility restrictions and changed training rights to discretionary privileges. In 1976, job-training expenditures were reduced by 10.2 percent and unemployment policies by 9.9 percent, while other areas of social policy actually increased; children's benefits increased by 0.9 percent and invalid health benefits by 12.8 percent (BMA 1984, p. 101). Clearly ALMP bore the brunt of the budgetary cuts. Budgetary laws, introducing a new way to amend labor market policy, were also passed in 1983 and 1984 (Krautkramer 1978, pp. 120–21; Gagel 1984, pp. 22–28).

But the budgetary laws did not eliminate Bundesanstalt deficits, which rose to almost 9 million DM in 1975 and 2 million DM in 1976. Although the labor market budget momentarily hit the black with a 0.3 million DM surplus in 1977, higher unemployment caused the deficits to rise over 2 million DM in 1979 and 8 million DM the next year. The Labor Market Promotion and Consolidation Law cut the deficits in 1983, but at that point ALMP could no longer be considered countercyclical.

The Bundesanstalt's first obligation was to pay unemployment compensation; and second, it could use the remaining revenue for ALMP. However, during the recession, unemployment compensation consumed much more of the budget. Despite the Bundesanstalt's vigorous protests, the remaining funds were subject to federal control through the Ministry of Labor. Little flexibility existed in shifting funds because excess money accumulated in the unemployment compensation fund had to be carried over into the same category next year. The Bundesanstalt also wanted to expand ALMP, but the finance minister would not subsidize it. Thus, the federal government gained control over the Bundesanstalt and reduced ALMP in the later 1970s (Kühl 1984).

Trends toward decentralization continued, aided in 1975 by a "commissioned course system" that allowed the local labor office to target special groups. Instead of approving each course and paying each student. the local office budgeted a course, found a carrier, and then paid a fixed sum to the school, regardless of the number of people enrolled. The commissioned course system allowed faster start-up, reduced risks to schools, and permitted the local Bundesanstalt offices to be more active. However, only 15 percent of all courses were commissioned this way (Krautkramer 1978, p. 127). During the same period, private firms could for the first time offer the schooling side of job-training courses if they agreed to take outside students. But as of 1977, only 5 percent of all trainees participated in firm courses.

After 1975, with job creation becoming the Bundesanstalt's most important ALMP task, local labor offices were given the power to allocate job creation measures up to 500,000 DM. Because most job creation programs tended to be small—a few people at the police department, the public assistance office, or the hospitals—these additional duties greatly expanded the power of the local office. However, despite the placement director's increased discretion with funds, the local offices had not nurtured the entrepreneurial abilities that the job creation measures and commissioned courses demanded.[13] Furthermore, placement programs were reoriented toward hard-to-place and less motivated workers. Finally, because the local offices were still understaffed, the local offices tried to learn new duties with overloaded work schedules and strained personnel. In late 1981, the job placement staff was further taxed because the Bundesanstalt transferred many employees from placing people in jobs to processing unemployment claims (Bruche and Kroker 1982, p. 40).

Although the regional employment offices still allocated funds to the local offices and interpreted regulations for local conditions, regional duties were clearly decreasing. Some local-level employees even questioned the continued existence of the regional Bundesanstalt offices arguing that the state offices not only lacked sufficient duties but also failed to perform their current duties (Krautkramer 1978, pp. 23–24). For example, the local offices had to implement the November 1976 special placement program on the basis of newspaper clippings, while state offices took more than three months to interpret the new regulations.

13. The Swedish Labor Market Board (AMS) has pushed decision making to the lower levels, and as a result it has started to develop an entrepreneurial mentality among its placement officers. For instance, in June 1989, job placement counselors at a local Stockholm office set up temporary shop in their local subway, where they connected a bank of computers listing jobs and directly connected telephone lines to four employers looking for employees.

In summary, increasing federal control over the Bundesanstalt forced it to centralize budget decisions. But at the same time, discretionary power flowed from the state offices to the local offices.[14] The central office lost autonomy, but local offices gained power.

The administrative council watched the federal government press the Bundesanstalt executive into a budgetary straitjacket but allowed local councils to maintain some power. For instance, the law was amended in the late 1960s so that general job creation policies could not be implemented by local communities where unemployment was below a minimum level. The administrative council of the Bundesanstalt ignored these decisions and let the local offices operate on their own. Consequently, local governments remained sponsors despite low unemployment and the law's intent. In the opposite direction, a local administrative council in another city blocked the implementation of public job creation programs for over a year by delaying it in a subcommission. Thus, self-administration retained some power despite strong federal influence (Reissert 1984, p. 217; Maier 1982).

The Bundesanstalt remained structurally stable, and the size of the organization grew during the crisis. At the central office, staff positions were shuffled in 1975 into a new central division that handled planning, information services, coordination, and the Bureau of Self-Administration. Another bureau was also added to the research division.[15] From 1975 to 1981 the total number of permanent Bundesanstalt employees increased by 16.9 percent because of increased unemployment compensation rather than ALMP. In 1984, the local offices had 93 percent of all employees, the states 5 percent, and the national offices 2 percent.[16]

But effectiveness declined because of the oil shock and lower employer confidence, which may have been due to targeting disadvantaged workers. The vacancy penetration rate, after a high of

14. Unemployment initiatives and the city's job creation measures constituted further decentralization, but the Bundesanstalt did not implement these programs.

15. Regional and local offices remained constant at 9 and 146 during the period while the number of branch and temporary offices decreased from 570 in 1966 to 501 in 1979 (Green 1966; BAA *Geschaftsbericht* 1984; Krautkramer 1978, p. 21).

16. The figures are central—812, state—2,481, and local—44,149; these were obtained from the Bundesanstalt budget committee by Jürgen Kühl.

40.2 percent in 1975, declined to an eighteen-year low of 30.6 percent in 1979. The number of jobs registered at the Bundesanstalt dropped from a high of 3.2 million in 1968 to 1.9 million in 1979, while total vacancies remained constant. The external placement rate fell to nearly 20 percent and reached 19.4 percent in 1979. In 1976, new placement incentives targeted persons over forty-five years old and the long-term unemployed with mobility allowances, grants for removal expenses, and resettlement aids (Kühl et al. 1980). However, the programs were too small to affect placement rates greatly.

As yet, the Bundesanstalt has not developed a computer system for nationwide job placement. An experimental program in three labor offices exists for a decentralized placement system that covers daily commuting distances. However, interstate placements are still handled by referring "slow to place vacancies" to the central Bundesanstalt office where microfiches are made for local labor offices. On the whole, computerization has a great potential for increasing the efficiency of the employment service (Bruche and Kroker 1982, pp. 35–37).[17]

JOB PLACEMENT AND EMPLOYMENT SERVICE IN THE UNITED STATES
The U.S. Employment Service from 1947 to 1960

The federal government made many attempts to jolt USES into improving its job placement rates and overall effectiveness. In the late 1940s, the Department of Labor issued a "Six Point Program" mandating the employment service to improve job placement services.[18] In the late 1950s, two task forces reviewed the public image and management of USES and proposed that it im-

17. Although routine job vacancies were not computerized, some computerization exists for professional and special programs. Complete computerization has been achieved in Sweden where employers are mandated by law to report vacancies.

18. The Six Point Program called for placement for all employers and workers; employment counseling; a local veterans' employment representative; management services to employers; labor market information on occupational trends; and employment development with state and local organizations. It emphasized management needs, information gathering, and community services.

prove placement and counseling, target the unemployed, conduct more manpower research, and start community economic development programs. However, these reforms largely failed.[19]

The public employment service simply lacked the organizational strength that makes the West German Bundesanstalt so effective, and it faced a growing number of competitors—private employment agencies, union hiring halls, civil service departments, and college placement services. The government made little effort to regulate this burgeoning market of employment agencies, except for limited self-policing by the National Employment Association and licensing by the states. The USES had neither monopoly powers nor a strong position in the labor market.

The public employment service developed without a clear and effective management structure. In 1945, Executive Order 9617 dissolved the War Labor Board and transferred USES from the Federal Security Agency to the Department of Labor. In 1948, an appropriations bill moved USES back, but finally in 1949 it was permanently placed in the Department of Labor (Adams 1969, pp. 32–33). The local and state offices were returned to state control, where they stayed even when the federal employment service was transferred to the Office of Defense Mobilization during the Korean War. The state offices were autonomous, varying in their cabinet status from independent departments in right-to-work states to subsections of the labor department in other states. USES clearly lacked management authority over state and local offices (Butler 1951; Klatzky 1970).

After World War II, USES experienced two difficulties in funding its programs. Requirements for federal matching funds were dropped for USES because federal administrators feared that many states would not cooperate. And further, funds were diverted from the Unemployment Insurance Trust Fund, even though these earmarked funds were not supposed to go into general accounts. Al-

19. The response was mixed. USES tried harder to sell itself to employers through more professional placement (109 offices), extensive testing, and increased staff training at all levels. A few states tried special programs for older workers, minority groups (eight states), handicapped workers, and veterans. Thirty-nine states surveyed employer needs for skilled workers and started local industrial development projects (Adams 1969; Haber and Kruger 1964, pp. 33–34).

though diversions of earmarked funds violated the trust fund principle, such diversions were frequently made in the United States but rarely seen in West Germany.[20] Both difficulties made USES funding subject to severe financial constraints.

Self-administration has not had success in the United States. The secretary of labor appointed federal advisory councils from the ranks of employers, labor, and the public; they were intended to provide advice on old and new policies, insure impartiality, and protect against political influence (Adams 1969, p. 24). If the state deemed it necessary, similar councils could be established at the state and local levels. However, the advisory councils were preoccupied with unemployment insurance.

From 1946 to 1949, the Truman administration cut USES budgets. One thousand jobs were lost at USES headquarters in fiscal 1947, and most labor market research was transferred to the states. Total employment service employees in the 1950s settled to about 45,000, which if staffed at German levels, would have been 105,000 employees. In two major recessions during the 1950s, expenditures increasingly focused on unemployment insurance, while job placement was ignored. The number of workers at the employment service working on job placement hovered around 17,000, with unemployment insurance workers making up the rest. Clearly USES ranked low on the list of America's largest bureaucracies.

The public employment service listed only a small percentage of available vacancies; therefore, its vacancy penetration rate was extremely low. Criticism of ineffective job placement activities arose. In early 1949, Robert Goodwin, director of the Bureau of Employment Security, compared the employment service's marginal penetration rates to Canada's higher rates achieved under similar conditions in the labor market. But criticism stalled for ten years until Secretary of Labor Mitchell in 1958 chided USES for not keeping pace with the changing labor force. He asked whether a public service restricted to such a small number of working Americans could be justified, but nevertheless Congress provided a $2 million funding increase (M. Johnson 1973, p. 15).

20. Although trust fund diversions in West Germany are rare, pension money was sent to the Bundesanstalt in the late 1970s (Lampert 1983).

USES reacted with skill surveys, batteries of new aptitude tests, workshops on employer relations, a book called *Twelve Steps to Placement Operations*, and a revision of the *Dictionary of Occupational Titles*.

These minor activities did little to change organizational goals, weaknesses in the labor market, and a decentralized and dualistic organizational structure. The minority counselor—"a miracle worker without a wand"—was especially ineffective because an employer-oriented placement service could easily overlook qualified black workers (Preston 1984, p. 28). Although the secretary of labor sought to serve the whole labor force, USES primarily assisted the white lower-middle and working classes. As Adams laments, "With no nationally established and accepted goals for the placement process, there . . . was confusion in the states over which groups of persons and employers should receive the most attention and which part of the employment security program should have priority" (1969, p. 53). During the 1950s, USES was mired in "eleven years of stalemate, if not progressive decline" (M. Johnson 1973, p. 16).

The Employment Service during the War on Poverty,
1960 to 1971

In 1961, President John Kennedy directed the secretary of labor to expand counseling and placement in depressed areas with high unemployment (U.S. President 1964). These programs targeted the young, old, and technologically dislocated (Adams 1969, p. 55). Kennedy expanded USES funding and pressed for "community manpower centers" that would consolidate human resources activities, increase counseling, promote communities' economic growth, and assist in educational curriculum planning. Although private employment agencies and some employment service officials resisted these proposals, Congress enacted funds to improve USES.

During the social policy explosion of the 1960s, USES encountered stiff competition not only from rival organizations in the labor market but also from new agencies that sought to supplant what many liberals saw as a racist or ineffective bureaucracy. Competition from other labor market agencies became stronger as college placement offices, professional associations, federal civil service information centers, and private agencies grew. But the employment service played a minor role in the War on Poverty. It was loudly criticized on the one hand by civil rights activists and liberals, who felt that USES was incompetent to handle the disadvantaged, and on the other by states rights and private employment agency representatives, who feared the alteration of the racial order and bureaucratic centralization. Only the AFL-CIO demanded a centralized public employment service in a federal system (Beimiller 1966).

In 1965, Secretary of Labor Willard Wirtz appointed a task force that recommended Comprehensive Manpower Service Centers. These centers would develop occupations, provide special counseling, enter into community economic planning, and exceed the current "casual one-shot" placement psychology. The centers would also separate job placement and unemployment insurance and expand interarea placement, especially with multimarket recruitment centers for professional and skilled workers. All these changes required intensified research in counseling, employers, and labor markets. A labor market information officer would disseminate research to employers, unions, and the public. These centers would serve all workers by reaching out to disadvantaged groups and cooperating with private employment agencies. At the same time the National Commission on Technology, Automation and Economic Progress called for similar changes (Adams 1969, pp. 146–72).[21]

But two bills with many of the recommendations failed. The states and conservatives ignored or resisted attempts to change USES. In October 1968, Wirtz reorganized Department of Labor regional offices so that apprenticeship, training, and employment security would be under a regional manpower administrator. However, state employment service directors caused President Lyndon Johnson to countermand Wirtz. Secretary of Labor George Shultz was successful with a much less ambitious program in 1969 because he used USES personnel in the key supervisory positions (Hallman 1977, p. 62). The employment system was highly resistant to change.

21. The task force also recommended an emergency planning unit and a new advisory and review committee for USES (Adams 1969, pp. 146–72).

In 1960, the Unemployment Trust Funds were removed from federal budget negotiations over general revenues and strictly earmarked for employment security. The result from 1961 to 1967 was a funding splurge that demonstrated the positive effect of employment service autonomy. However, under the pressure of the Vietnam War the trust funds were put back into the federal budget in 1968 (Beideman 1976, pp. 3–82).

During the 1960s, the organization of ALMP faced massive confusion and continuous reorganization. First, four agencies competed for the new duties contained in the 1962 Manpower Development and Training Act (MDTA). Although only USES had a nationwide network of local offices, it was a third-tier organization in the Department of Labor that faced possible reorganization, and the ICESA—an interest group for state-dominated employment service offices—opposed many duties for the organization. The AFL-CIO supported on-the-job training (OJT) under the Bureau of Apprenticeship Training. The new secretary of labor had just created the Office of Manpower, Automation and Training, which was eager to implement MDTA, but it had no field or constituency support. And even the Department of Health, Education and Welfare had an interest. MDTA duties were finally divided between four organizations: USES referred trainees to programs; the Manpower, Automation and Training Office set up experimental demonstration projects and developed fourteen city offices; the Bureau of Apprenticeship Training supervised apprenticeship and OJT programs; and the U.S. Office of Education, along with the latter two agencies, handled school approvals. This division of duties was filled with conflict.

Second, the Department of Labor added further bureaucratic confusion by frequently reorganizing its offices for employment security. It created the Office of Manpower Policy, Evaluation, and Research in 1966; the Bureau of Work Training Programs in 1968; and the U.S. Training and Employment Service and the Unemployment Insurance Service in 1970 (U.S. Government Manuals 1960–70).

Third, the Economic Opportunity Act bypassed the employment service, and in 1967 the Concentrated Employment Program directly competed with the public employment service. It created its own manpower delivery system with Employability

Development Teams to place disadvantaged workers. The Office of Economic Opportunity contracted community action agencies to centralize outreach, counseling, prevocational training, and job placement. Half its staff, drawn from disadvantaged areas, often represented the self-determination of blacks or other minority groups. Besides the employment service the community action agencies subcontracted services from local community agencies, such as the Opportunities Industrial Centers, Urban League, and skills centers.

In 1969, the Concentrated Employment Program was reorganized giving USES control over subcontracting for Employability Development Teams. This intensified the conflict between USES and community action personnel—that is, between white professionalism and black advocacy—that escalated from strained cooperation to outright hostility. The tension resulted in disruptions to program services and criticisms that the employment service could not help the poor and disadvantaged (M. Johnson 1973, p. 155). Community action agencies and minority representatives even opposed turning job creation programs over to the states because the programs might fall into the insensitive hands of USES (Mirengoff and Rindler 1978, p. 91). Shirley Chisholm (D-N.Y.) received a standing ovation at Senate hearings when she attacked the employment service:

The whole reason manpower programs came into existence in the first place is that the state employment services were not doing their jobs. It seems ludicrous to me to reward them for their failure just because it fits someone's philosophical scheme of decentralization. (Davidson 1972, p. 26)

As a result, USES yielded to the community action agencies, then to the local governments, and finally to the community-based organizations.

The advisory councils mandated by the Wagner-Peyser Act continued to concentrate on unemployment insurance, but the MDTA brought new manpower advisory committees at the national, state, and local levels. The federal advisory committee, with Department of Labor agenda and staff, commented on policy and appointed subcommittees to study specific problems. State advisory committees had vaguely defined duties and did little, while the local advisory committees obtained some employer commitments for job placement. On the whole, these councils were powerless and rarely worked together. A USES directive illustrates the agency's adversarial attitude toward the committees: "It should be clearly understood by all members that the committee may act only as an advisory body. . . . It does not have the authority to require or to veto the establishment of training programs" (quoted in Mangum 1968, p. 70). As a result, the committees had little effect.

From 1960 to 1963, personnel in USES increased dramatically from 19,318 to 26,197, mainly from the autonomous control of funds and new duties from MDTA. Increases were less impressive during the War on Poverty with employees growing by only about 4,000 workers from 1963 to 1969. As placement activities were coopted by other organizations, the employment service stagnated.

Although complete data on the penetration and placement rates during this period are not available, Sheppard and Belitsky (1966) report a vacancy penetration rate of about 16 percent in 1960—low compared to continental placements in the 25 percent range. Competition from other job placement agencies in the later 1960s most probably led to low penetration and placement rates.

The U.S. Employment Service during the Crisis, 1971 to 1984

Having suffered during the 1960s, USES entered the 1970s determined to change. Computerization of job openings and free access to job listings were designed to facilitate increased placements, which in turn would increase organizational power. President Richard Nixon's Executive Order 11598 of 1971 required all federal contractors and first-tier subcontractors to list their job openings under $18,000 a year with USES. The order became law in 1972 under the Vietnam-Era Veterans' Readjustment Assistance Act (Baum and Ullman 1976, pp. 1–6). Furthermore, job creation programs under the Public Employment Program had to list with USES forty-eight hours before informing other agencies (Roomkin 1974, p. 64; Hallman 1977, pp. 76–79). Although public job creation hiring was complicated by the civil service and public unions and shared with many other community organizations, USES had gained ground in job placement. When the Economic Opportunity Act manpower programs were reassigned to the Department of Labor, the employment service had even higher hopes of expansion.

By 1973, the public employment service had two direct competitors for labor market programs: prime sponsors and community-based organizations. Under the Comprehensive Employment and Training Act (CETA), federal and most state "single-issue programs" were decategorized and placed under local prime sponsors' control. Prime sponsors—cities, counties, consortia of cities and/or counties, and less frequently states—were to develop a comprehensive approach to manpower policy. Most prime sponsors were attached to the executive's office, with a new human resources department or an expanded personnel department. Although personnel departments easily reoriented their recruiting efforts toward job creation programs, job training had to be subcontracted to the skills centers, the public schools, and community agencies (Snedecker and Snedecker 1978, p. 187). Thus, as Mirengoff and Rindler point out, "a new administrative layer emerged between program operators and regional offices" of the Department of Labor (1978, pp. 100–16).

Prime sponsors faced formidable obstacles. They had to create and train a new staff, control and monitor subcontractors, balance local political interests, and adjust to a major source of uncertainty—the federal government. Difficulties from Washington included: funding fluctuations and delays, federal audits, constantly changing regulations especially for veteran's preference and equal employment opportunity, and even doubts about the future of CETA (Mirengoff et al. 1982, p. 26). Prime sponsors subcontracted with public agencies including USES and a variety of schools, but they increasingly ignored the skills centers, which declined by 35 percent (Snedecker and Snedecker 1978, pp. 161–65; Mirengoff and Rindler 1978, p. 109).

Community-based organizations were increasingly funded from 1974 to 1975: the Urban League increased by 60 percent; Service, Employment and Redevelopment by 24 percent; and the Opportunities Industrial Centers by 29 percent. Community-based skills centers remained at prior funding levels if run by the Urban League or the Opportunities Industrial Centers. As prime sponsors took over outreach, placement, and employability programs community action agencies lost these duties. Sometimes community action staffs were simply transferred to prime sponsor payrolls. Thus, national community-based organizations assumed a larger role, while community action agencies disappeared (Snedecker and Snedecker 1978, pp. 166–71).

But CETA—the most important labor market legislation of the 1970s—did not make USES its automatic delivery mechanism for trainees and public service workers, as had been the case under MDTA. Prime sponsors could subcontract placement services to agencies of their own choosing, and many, especially in large cities, ignored the employment service. The cities that did contract with USES reduced their service requests by 62 percent, as compared to precontract levels. Prime sponsors avoided the employment service, perhaps because of its inflexible and insensitive reputation but also because prime sponsors wanted power over as many CETA functions as possible (Mirengoff and Rindler 1978, pp. 87–89; Davidson 1972, pp. 25–30). With little effect the Department of Labor pushed coordination with USES in field memos that emphasized efficiency.

The 1976 CETA amendments increased the USES role in expanding job creation programs because the employment service could easily access the pool of public assistance and unemployment insurance claimants. The law pressured prime sponsors to enter into agreements with the employment service. As an incentive, prime sponsors were exempted from liability for illegal payments if the public employment service handled the placement. In one study of twenty-eight prime sponsors, twenty-four such agreements were signed (Mirengoff et al. 1980, pp. 68–72).

The size of USES rose in 1977–78, and "employment service–prime sponsor" relations improved; but when CETA was accused of abuses, the 1978 CETA Reauthorization Act strengthened auditing controls and removed the incentive to use the employment service. As a result, prime sponsors took over job placement and established their own internal monitoring units. They also began to abandon CETA because of new auditing penalties and pressures to hire the disadvantaged. The community-based organizations that took over CETA responsibilities had less political clout, which left CETA politically vulnerable (Nathan 1983, p. 49; Mirengoff et al. 1982, pp. 41, 61–64).

As in the 1960s, the Department of Labor and especially its Employment and Training Administration went through confusing reorganizations creating the following new offices: in 1972 the Office of National Projects Administration and the Office of Public Service Employment; in 1973 the Office of National Projects and the Office of Employment Development Programs; in 1974 the Office of Manpower Development Programs; in 1975 the Office of Policy, Evaluation and Research; and in 1976 the Office of Comprehensive Employment Development Programs. The Reagan administration brought more reorganizations: the Office of Employment Security, Office of Trade Adjustment Assistance, Office of Job Training Programs, Office of Strategic Planning and Policy Development, Office of Financial Control and Management Systems, Office of Program and Fiscal Integrity, and Office of Regional Management (U.S. Government Manuals 1970–86). Until 1980, presidents simply reshuffled new offices in the same deck of programs. The Reagan reorganizations were a little different because they added bureaus of budgetary management and eliminated job creation offices.

Self-administration made some initial strides in the community action agencies with maximum feasible participation but declined thereafter. Nixon removed the community action agencies and much of the War on Poverty. Congress responded by reformulating the community action concept into decentralized and local human resource planning with ALMP delegated to prime sponsors. CETA established State Manpower Services Councils— composed of local prime sponsors, USES, educational agencies, business, labor, and client groups—to systematically monitor prime sponsors; however, the councils had little authority (Mirengoff and Rindler 1978, pp. 93–94). The 1978 CETA Reauthorization Act attempted to make the councils more effective by broadening the membership and requiring that prime sponsors formally justify when rejecting council recommendations. The reauthorization also created Private Industry Councils—composed of business, labor, community-based organizations, and schools— and Youth Councils. But instead of giving power to existing councils, Congress and the Department of Labor simply created more powerless councils, causing further fragmentation and duplication of effort (Mirengoff et al. 1982, p. 49).

Although USES gained some employees with job creation programs, the employment service as a whole declined to low levels. After reaching a post–World War II peak in 1971 with 31,000 employees, it became only one competitor among many in the CETA era. Because USES lost many contracts to place CETA enrollees, employment was cut; for instance, New York City lost 150 USES workers. By 1976, total personnel dropped to 27,500 (Snedecker and Snedecker 1978, pp. 151–58). After Reagan eliminated 3,000 employees in 1980 and 5,000 more in 1982, USES job placement totals hit bottom with 23,000, a figure not seen since 1962.[22]

Placement effectiveness also reached new lows from 1971 to 1982. One study showed that of all persons looking for work, 27.6 percent used USES but only 5.6 percent found a job there. The employment service's share of vacancies was equivalent to private employment agencies, while informal channels of finding work—personal contacts, relatives, and direct application—continued to dominate (CAMIL 1975, pp. 1–60). Another study showed that 31.3 percent of white youths and 41.8 percent of black youths used the public employment service, but only 3.2 percent and 4.8 percent of each group obtained jobs there (Holzer 1987a). Although 20.1 percent of employers in 1982 used USES, only 2.6 percent of most recently hired employees were actually hired through the agency (Holzer 1987b).

The vacancy penetration rates that I calculated from systematic data showed that the access of USES to the stock of job openings declined from a high of 18.4 percent in 1975 to a low of 12.6 percent in 1982. The external placement rate also declined from 10.2 percent in 1975 to 5.7 percent in 1982. This drastic drop is partly due to the recession; however, the absolute number of USES placements showed a steady decline as the labor force grew with women and baby-boom workers. Thus, USES has withered away in size and effectiveness while actual job openings have grown. Because of this decisive erosion, the Government Accounting Office even recommended that job seekers use private employment agencies (GAO 1986).

22. Employees in unemployment insurance, however, did not suffer such a fate, due to the high unemployment. Their figures reached a new high in 1983 at 56,000.

4. Expenditures for Job Placement, Job Training, and Job Creation as a Percentage of GNP in the United States and West Germany

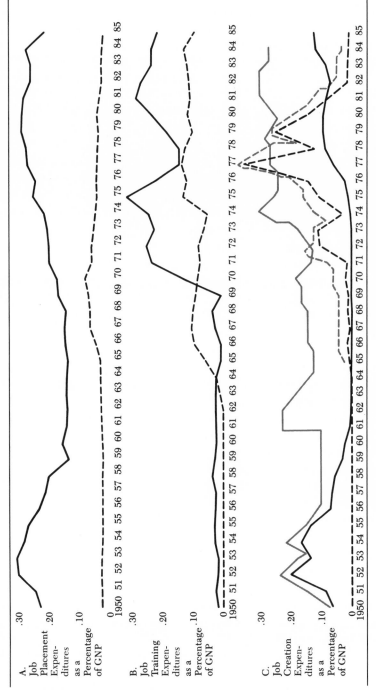

A.
Job
Placement
Expen-
ditures
as a
Percentage
of GNP

.30

.20

.10

0
1950 51 52 53 54 55 56 57 58 59 60 61 62 63 64 65 66 67 68 69 70 71 72 73 74 75 76 77 78 79 80 81 82 83 84 85

B.
Job
Training
Expen-
ditures
as a
Percentage
of GNP

.30

.20

.10

0
1950 51 52 53 54 55 56 57 58 59 60 61 62 63 64 65 66 67 68 69 70 71 72 73 74 75 76 77 78 79 80 81 82 83 84 85

C.
Job
Creation
Expen-
ditures
as a
Percentage
of GNP

.30

.20

.10

0
1950 51 52 53 54 55 56 57 58 59 60 61 62 63 64 65 66 67 68 69 70 71 72 73 74 75 76 77 78 79 80 81 82 83 84 85

Note: ━━━━ = ALMP/GNP in the United States, ━━━ = ALMP/GNP in the Federal Republic of Germany,
━ ━ ━ = U.S. ALMP plus youth programs that start in 1965, ━━━ = West German ALMP plus job maintenance programs.

COMPARING THE U.S. AND GERMAN
EMPLOYMENT SERVICES

Of all ALMP programs, job placement and the employment service show the greatest contrast between these two countries. Job placement policy in West Germany has been handled by a single bureaucracy (renamed once), with autonomy as a public law corporation. Although the Bundesanstalt has less autonomy when unemployment and deficits are high, it remains largely independent. Despite fluctuating size and centralization, the Bundesanstalt remains a stable, growing organization. Labor-management-government cooperation through real policy-making decisions on self-administrative boards has consistently contributed to effective policy implementation. The results have been vacancy penetration rates and external placement rates at least twice as large as those in the United States. West German job placement expenditures were ten times U.S. expenditures in the 1950s, four times in the 1960s, three times in the early 1970s, and seven times in the 1980s (see Figure 4–A and Table 3, column 1). Thus, West Germany has developed strong and stable labor market institutions.

In the United States, job placement has been handled by an ever-changing mélange of public and private organizations. USES—the primary job placement agency—has a confused mandate with its line of managerial authority passing through both the state and federal governments. The Department of Labor has constantly reorganized its ALMP activities, and the public employment service was largely supplanted by other agencies and organizations. A parade of short-lived implementing organizations—including community action agencies, community-based organizations, prime sponsors, private industry councils—has contributed to organizational confusion in the labor market. Not only job placement expenditures as a percentage of GNP but also the absolute number of employees have declined in size since 1973. And despite the proliferation of advisory councils, the United States has ignored real labor-management participation in job placement. As a mere shadow of the Bundesanstalt, USES remains a singularly intractable and declining organization (Preston 1984, pp. 24, 45–48).

TABLE 3 *Comparison of West German and U.S. Expenditures as a Percentage of GNP: Job Placement, Job Training, Job Creation, and Total ALMP Over GNP*

Year	Job Placement		Job Training		Job Creation		Total ALMP	
	WG	US	WG	US	WG	US	WG	US
1950	0.228	0.025	0.015	0	0.060	0	0.303	0.025
1951	0.243	0.025	0.023	0	0.085	0	0.350	0.025
1952	0.299	0.028	0.016	0	0.197	0	0.511	0.028
1953	0.306	0.028	0.015	0	0.131	0	0.452	0.028
1954	0.281	0.024	0.025	0	0.165	0	0.471	0.024
1955	0.269	0.022	0.027	0	0.134	0	0.430	0.022
1956	0.231	0.025	0.025	0	0.073	0	0.329	0.025
1957	0.211	0.025	0.022	0	0.067	0	0.300	0.021
1958	0.199	0.025	0.033	0	0.060	0	0.292	0.025
1959	0.136	0.023	0.026	0	0.032	0	0.194	0.023
1960	0.156	0.026	0.020	0	0.024	0	0.190	0.026
1961	0.144	0.027	0.023	0	0.007	0	0.174	0.027
1962	0.140	0.030	0.024	0	0.003	0	0.167	0.030
1963	0.141	0.031	0.024	0.010	0.003	0	0.168	0.041
1964	0.139	0.032	0.024	0.024	0.003	0.000	0.166	0.058
1965	0.137	0.033	0.009	0.055	0.002	0.008	0.148	0.097
1966	0.145	0.046	0.009	0.092	0.001	0.015	0.156	0.153
1967	0.147	0.067	0.026	0.101	0.000	0.007	0.173	0.175
1968	0.142	0.066	0.037	0.098	0.000	0.008	0.180	0.172
1969	0.169	0.071	0.006	0.088	0.003	0.011	0.234	0.171
1970	0.175	0.081	0.129	0.082	0.002	0.021	0.307	0.185
1971	0.198	0.060	0.232	0.072	0.003	0.017	0.432	0.149
1972	0.198	0.061	0.249	0.078	0.003	0.104	0.449	0.243
1973	0.206	0.054	0.223	0.061	0.003	0.111	0.463	0.226
1974	0.215	0.048	0.242	0.051	0.005	0.032	0.462	0.131
1975	0.250	0.042	0.312	0.128	0.015	0.109	0.577	0.279
1976	0.243	0.045	0.220	0.118	0.024	0.145	0.487	0.308
1977	0.270	0.044	0.141	0.133	0.061	0.355	0.472	0.531

TABLE 3   (continued)

Year	Job Placement		Job Training		Job Creation		Total ALMP	
	WG	US	WG	US	WG	US	WG	US
1978	0.273	0.041	0.142	0.122	0.088	0.121	0.503	0.284
1979	0.289	0.038	0.181	0.098	0.095	0.249	0.565	0.385
1980	0.288	0.043	0.232	0.115	0.093	0.144	0.613	0.302
1981	0.282	0.037	0.283	0.105	0.084	0.076	0.649	0.218
1982	0.259	0.028	0.266	0.110	0.070	0.014	0.594	0.153
1983	0.257	0.029	0.235	0.117	0.084	0.014	0.577	0.160
1984	0.272	0.027	0.236	0.125	0.116	0.012	0.549	0.166
1985	0.214	0.022	0.212	0.092	0.123	0.010	0.549	0.124

Chapter Five

Education and
Job Training

West German job-training programs focus on highly skilled jobs, while U.S. job-training programs concentrate on socialization programs—remedial education and job orientation skills for disadvantaged workers—in unskilled jobs. Furthermore, West German job-training expenditures have been much higher than U.S. appropriations through much of the post–World War II period. But one must understand the structure of the education systems in these two countries because general education and ALMP job training critically interact. ALMP job training builds on general education with initial schooling—a base that is systematically different in these two countries. Consequently, I first present the general education system of each country and then focus on ALMP job-training programs and their evaluation.

WEST GERMAN JOB TRAINING

After World War II, the "Dual System" of the Berufschule and firm apprenticeship training was reestablished, along with the academic *Gymnasium* and the technical *Realschule*. The states regulated the Berufschule, and the Conference of State Education Ministers coordinated national policy. Although the Weimar constitution had not enforced compulsory attendance for the Berufschule, every state in the Bonn Republic soon passed and enforced laws on vocational education attendance (Münch 1984, p. 54; Führ 1983).[1]

In their recovery from the tremendous physical and social damage of the war, the West Germans stressed the need for practical apprenticeship programs to boost economic production. In-firm training workshops had dropped from 5,000 in 1944 to 1,034 in 1952. The government made the apprenticeship system work and increased workshops to 1,658 by 1958. Apprentice training and the Berufschule became the most prevalent form of education in the 1950s, encompassing 69 percent of all secondary school students (Münch 1984, p. 49). By 1960, the basic system of education in apprenticeship programs had solidified.

After trade unionists and educators criticized the apprenticeship system for blocking opportunity for working-class students, the government created the *Berufsaufbauschule* in 1962 and the *Fachoberschule* in 1969. Although these schools provided new paths to higher technical education for working-class students, they stayed within the bounds of its vertical system. One must understand this basic system to grasp the nature of West German job-training programs.

Although the eleven states are responsible for education and produce, to some extent, eleven different systems, the various systems in the 1960s can be generalized into one system as outlined in Figure 5. The West German vertical school system separates students at a fairly early age, while the horizontal system in the United States keeps students together until the age of seventeen.[2]

1. The 1949 Basic Law gave responsibility for education to the states. After a brief American attempt to impose comprehensive schools, the Germans reinstated their school system in the 1955 Düsseldorf Agreement (Münch 1984, pp. 39–60; Hearndon 1974; Max Planck Institute 1984, p. 107; Führ 1983). However, the Chambers of Industry and Commerce (1947–49), the Office for Vocational Training of the Association of Industry and Commerce (1949–52), and the Office of In-Firm Vocational Training (1952–69) regulated apprentice training in the firm. In the late 1940s, the unions demanded more comprehensive regulation of vocational training but with little success. West Berlin enacted a law to regulate apprenticeship (1951), and the federal government passed the "Law to Regulate the Craft Trades" for in-plant training (1953).

2. The horizontal American school system is also called a comprehensive school system. The West German vertical system can be called a "continuation" school system, but that label applies more to the Berufschule than to other schools.

5. The West German School System

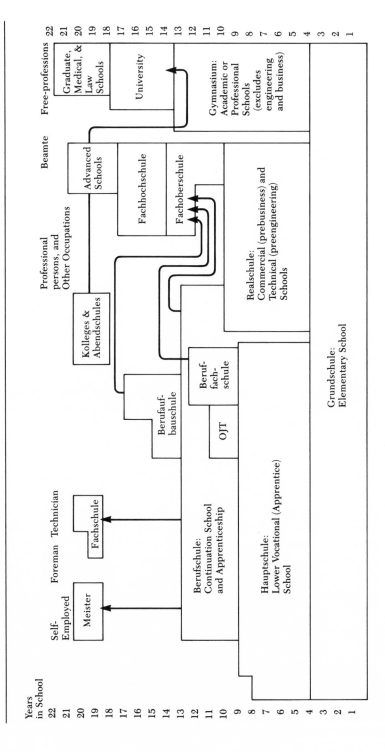

The basic school system consists of the *Grundschule*, an elementary school that everyone attends, and three secondary school tracks. In the vocational track, the *Hauptschule* teaches basic educational subjects, similar to the junior high school in the United States, except that all its students intend to enter apprenticeship programs. The *Berufschule* is a part-time school for students who graduate from the Hauptschule and obtain an apprenticeship in industry or commerce; however, those who do not obtain an apprenticeship must still attend the Berufschule. The Berufschule provides technical training in a particular apprenticeship, along with general political, religious, and citizenship instruction. The *Berufsfachschule* gives basic training for vocational programs lasting a variable number of years equivalent to apprenticeship training and the Berufschule. The apprenticeship is completed by an examination after about three years (Hamilton 1985).

In the second track, the *Realschule* provides technical and commercial training with more rigor than the Hauptschule. It could be viewed as a specialized junior and senior high school leading to work or advanced study in engineering, business, or other vocational subjects. The third track involves the *Gymnasium*—the rigorous academic secondary school—that teaches basic, classical, and advanced subjects and provides the only entrée to the university. From an American perspective it combines the junior high school, high school, and the first two years of college. Transitions from the Realschule and Berufschule to the Gymnasium are difficult because their curricula are vastly different.

The complex postsecondary school system is divided into vocational and academic tracks. The vocational track has two parts. The *Berufsaufbauschule* offers technical training to graduate apprentices and a transition to higher technical training in the *Fachoberschule* for one year before entering the *Fachhochschule* for four years. The *Fachschule* provides either six-month to two-year full-time courses or two- to four-year part-time courses for middle-level technical occupations. The Fachschule requires two to three years of experience beyond the apprenticeship and in some cases beyond Realschule education. Thus, the Berufsaufbauschule provides a transition to higher technical training, and the Fachschule supplies advanced technical training.

Higher education is divided into professional and academic schools. The *Fachoberschule* is an intermediate school leading to the Fachhochschule, where the equivalent of a college degree in engineering or other technical and business occupations can be obtained. Students may directly enter the Fachoberschule from the Realschule, complete two years of training, and then enter the Fachhochschule. Students with apprenticeship training complete the Realschule, the Berufsfachschule, or the Berufsaufbauschule; spend only one year in the Fachoberschule; and then attend the Fachhochschule. The *Fachhochschule* is the professional school for engineering, commerce, social work, social pedagogics, fine arts, and other vocational courses. The *Universität* begins after the Gymnasium. The four-year university degree is equivalent to the master's degree in the United States; a bachelor's degree does not exist. Consequently, the gap between college and apprenticeship graduates in West Germany is much greater than the gap between B.A.s and high school graduates in the United States. The *Abendrealschulen* and *Abendgymnasium* are evening schools with part-time courses for Realschule or Gymnasium diplomas; *Kolleges* are full-time schools leading to a Gymnasium diploma. These secondary paths are time-consuming but allow a trickle of working-class students into higher education.

This educational structure has prevailed despite some structural and enrollment changes. From 1970 to 1974, enrollments at the university almost doubled, and the Gymnasium and Realschule continued their moderate growth.[3] Vocational enrollments (the Berufschule and Berufsfachschule) declined to postwar low points; nevertheless, the vocational track has remained the largest. From 1974 to 1984, the school system stabilized. The decline of the Berufschule was slightly reversed with enrollment levels at 38 percent, and the growth of the Gymnasium and Realschule slowed down.[4]

3. West German educational reforms have not been particularly successful. The lack of educational opportunity in the country led to a movement for the *Gesamtschule*, a comprehensive secondary school much like the high school. However, after peaking from 1969 to 1974, it failed to dent the dominant system (Heidenheimer 1983). Furthermore, the transitional schools did not work well: the Berufsaufbauschule—providing entrance into the Fachoberschule—declined from its peak enrollments in 1968; and "the second path" of adult education—providing a Realschule or Gymnasium diploma—remained minuscule.

4. The slowing of university enrollments was not due to lack of demand. Overcrowding caused the government to ration positions through the "numerus clausus."

But the apprenticeship system has come under attack. Educators and the government were increasingly dismayed at the shortage of teachers, the declining quality of instruction, inadequate facilities, and the paucity of apprenticeship slots offered by industry. Training programs were also thought overspecialized; for example, electricians had over seventeen separate apprenticeships. *Handwerk* training slots far outweighed the actual number of jobs available, and industrial apprenticeships fell well short of available industrial jobs. Firms were unable to provide sufficient training slots, while the government was unable or unwilling to provide its share of positions. Some employers even ignored training schedules, prevented apprentices from attending the Berufschule, assigned too much irrelevant or menial work, physically abused apprentices, and imposed overly strict hair and dress codes.

These problems were addressed by the 1969 Vocational Education Act and the 1976 Training Place Promotion Act. The 1969 act provided the first comprehensive regulation of apprenticeship training in firms, while the individual state laws regulated school instruction (Münch 1984, p. 67).[5] The legislation attempted to improve the competence and suitability of trainers, the adequacy of the training facilities, and firm compliance with training ordinances. These regulations applied only to firm regulation, not to the schools or financial allowances.[6] The 1976 law proposed special taxes for employers who did not provide a minimum number of new apprentice slots, and the administration of apprenticeship by the Ministry of Education rather than the Ministries of Labor and Economics. The combined effects of regulation reduced the number of official trades to avoid narrow specialization, offered a school-based *Berufgrundschuljahr* in place of the first year of apprenticeship, increased federal spending for training facilities for small firms by over one billion DM, and started experimental programs (Jochimsen 1978, p. 206). Although the act was declared unconstitutional in December 1980, an almost identical act without the punitive employer tax passed in December 1981.

5. The federal Vocational Education Law is a labor and commercial law rather than an education law.
6. This law also established in 1970 the Federal Institute for Basic Vocational Education Research (BIBB 1983, p. 1).

Despite these innovations, the viability of apprenticeship has been questioned because of fast-paced economic change. The major problem of any vocational education system is to predict accurately the occupational structure and provide up-to-date courses. The weakness of apprenticeship is that journeymen workers must already exist in industry for the system to work among a large number of apprentices. Vocational schools, it is claimed, can adapt more easily to totally new industries (Reubens 1973, p. 14; OECD 1979, p. 9).[7] However, vocational teachers are often recruited from practitioners receiving high wages because of their scarcity. As a result, vocational schools may be even slower in providing competent training than apprenticeships in the field. Furthermore, vocational schools always have problems obtaining up-to-date equipment, to which apprenticeship programs in high-growth firms have easy access.

The jury is still out on the apprenticeship-vocational school controversy, but clearly apprenticeship programs contribute to the success of West German job training and highly skilled production success. The majority of workers needing job training already have a strong skill base (the neophyte worker that emerges from the U.S. high school is rarely seen in West Germany) upon which to pursue ALMP job-training programs.

WEST GERMAN ALMP JOB TRAINING
Modest West German Job Training, 1950 to 1969

Job training during the 1950s was small because the labor market was highly competitive and workers could not afford time for training when material needs were pressing. Consequently, training in the 1950s focused primarily on retraining the disabled or workers whose prior jobs were destroyed by the war. Bundesanstalt expenditures ranged from 0.023 percent in 1951 to 0.027 percent in 1955 of GNP, well below the surge of training expenditures in the late 1960s.

During the economic miracle in the early 1960s, the West German approach to job training changed. Industrial expansion demanded labor, while the Berlin Wall (and later détente) made

7. OECD has questioned the modern relevance of apprenticeship and cites figures showing that it is declining (OECD 1979, p. 9).

labor scarce by discouraging escapes from behind the Iron Curtain. In response to labor shortages, employers and eventually the federal government pursued a two-fold strategy that lasted until 1974: recruit foreign workers for menial work and the less skilled jobs vacated by German workers and put German workers into training slots for jobs difficult to fill or requiring higher levels of skill. With job-training expenditures nearly doubling compared to the 1950s, this strategy upgraded the skills of the native work force, provided social mobility to the working class, and supplied wide consensus for ALMP.[8]

The 1967–68 recession trebled the unemployment rate and triggered demands for changes in job training.[9] Although the recession was temporary and mild—indeed, it had lower rates of unemployment than the American boom of the late 1960s—the recession had a decided social impact. In 1967, the Bundesanstalt increased existing job-training programs, and by 1968 job-training expenditures were three times the 1965 level. But these increases provided advanced training programs for master craft, industry foremen, and new businessmen, and initiated financial support for individuals and institutions (Dückert 1982, p. 105). The Bundesanstalt pushed advanced training for persons recently unemployed by the recession, but it ignored retraining for the hard-core unemployed—Ruhr miners and steel workers—until well into 1968. The increased training was more a response to employers' needs for highly skilled workers and the unions' demands for social mobility. Moreover, job training was available only at the discretion of the Bundesanstalt, not considered an individual right, and the Bundesanstalt could neither finance the total demand for training nor claim the legal basis for doing so.

The Dominance of Job Training in Labor Market Policy, 1969 to 1974

The 1966–67 recession led to the Labor Promotion Law (AFG) that answered the labor market problems of the early 1970s with

8. These early figures include some vocational rehabilitation and labor placement, as well as job-training expenditures; however, the additional figures are so small that the error is not great.

9. Unemployment then settled down to 1.5 percent in 1969 and 0.7 percent in 1970.

an emphasis on job training. The discretionary power of the bureaucracy over job training allowed the worker rights to job training, whether the worker was unemployed or not. Job-training
programs were redefined into four categories: initial job training
for those unable to obtain education; retraining for workers
whose jobs had been made obsolete by technology or economic
adjustments; advanced training for the social mobility of workers
and the technical needs of employers; and OJT training for more
narrow jobs in specific firms.

The balance of programs initially favored retraining but soon
gave way to advanced training. Job-retraining programs increased
the most at first, especially for workers in Rhineland-Pflaz, Saar-
land, the border areas on the DDR, and the economically depressed steel and mining industries in the Ruhr. Initial job
training, which had been provided in fairly large amounts, was
continued and increased but not as much as the other programs.
The emphasis on retraining programs, however, soon shifted toward advanced training, which, in 1969, was almost equal to retraining, but in 1970 and 1977 it doubled and trebled job
retraining.[10] There were two major reasons for the change: the
unemployment rate drastically dropped, reducing demands for
retraining, and employer needs for skilled workers increased requests for advanced training.[11]

Support payments for workers in job-training programs greatly
increased in the 1970s, but other programs were smaller. Support
subsidies amounted to a reasonable percentage of prior wages
and accounted for about half of all job-training expenditures in
1973.[12] Bundesanstalt financing of training institutions for groups
of smaller firms and OJT for disadvantaged workers were much
more modest. Although the Bundesanstalt does not list OJT expenditures, OJT enrollments frequently exceeded their limit of 7
percent of all trainees. As in the United States, OJT was cheap
because it relied on private sector funding (BAA Förderung 1973,

10. From 1969 to 1970 advanced training more than doubled, and by 1977 it
was five times the 1969 rate. Retraining was less than half advanced training in
1977.

11. Unemployment dropped from 2.1 percent in 1967 and 1.9 percent in
1968 to below 1.2 percent from 1969 to 1973 (BMA 1983, p. 65).

12. Support payments have gone from 80 percent of wages in the late 1960s
to 68 percent in 1980.

pp. 18–24); nevertheless, it was restricted in favor of apprentice-ship in West Germany.

All told, the increases in ALMP job training expenditures were dramatic. If we compare the three years prior to the AFG with the three years after the AFG for five job-training categories (eliminating 1969 as a transitional year), the increase in job-training programs was an explosive 900 percent. The implementation of these programs was mainly handled by employers (47 percent), along with vocational associations (11 percent), academies and scientific societies (8 percent), schools (7 percent), and Handwerk Chambers (5 percent) (BIBB 1983, p. 10).

Problems with job training concerned targeting the areas of need and regulating the quality of vocational education. However, little evaluation research was done on Bundesanstalt job training because advanced job training seemed to be fulfilling its function. OJT was so small that it attracted little attention, despite the program's modest goals.

Bäthge and coauthors (1976) did the principal evaluation research on job retraining with comparable control groups. They found that more than half the retraining graduates were placed in their new specialized areas. But some firms, not trusting the trainees' newly acquired skills, placed many trainees in their old skill areas (1976, pp. 5–6). Bäthge also indicated that placement efforts for job retraining were not sufficiently individualized. However, wages for all retrained workers exceeded those of the control groups, which points to success despite placement in un-related occupations. Bäthge criticized some aspects of training quality: vocational goals were often overlooked; courses were often reduced to the lowest common denominator; theory and practice were insufficiently integrated; and even motivated trainees found retraining a cold and somewhat alienating experience. Re-trainees had more prior training experience than nontrainees, tended to come from families of skilled workers, were half as likely to accept unfavorable jobs, and were twice as optimistic about the future as nontrainees.[13] According to Bäthge's view, re-training reached a motivated and skilled group of needy work-ers who had a family background of skilled work, but retraining

13. Nontrainees had little confidence in retraining and job placement programs.

was less effective in reaching disadvantaged and unemployed workers (Bäthge 1976, pp. 295–97).

Thus, job training was effective and highly funded from 1969 to 1974. The financial stability of the Bundesanstalt job-training programs seemed assured for many years, but this mild euphoria was punctured by the oil crisis.

The Crisis and Attack on Job-Training Policies, 1974 to 1984

The oil crisis hit hard because West Germany was critically dependent on Middle East oil. Unemployment reached 2.6 percent in 1974, 4.6 percent in 1975, and an unprecedented postdepression rate of 7.5 percent by 1982. These increases—initiated by the oil crisis and then sustained by technological and industrial change—made the low rates of 0.7 percent in the 1960s and early 1970s appear utopian.

The initial and optimistic response of the government to the oil shock was to increase ALMP job training and to restrict labor supply—send guestworkers home. Proponents of this approach anticipated a short recession, not long-term stagnation. When unemployment caused large Bundesanstalt deficits, the government's strategy changed toward cutting expenditures wherever possible. The new strategy balanced the Bundesanstalt budget, emphasized job creation, and drastically cut job-training funds and support payments. The strategy made its debut in the 1975 Budgetary Structure Law, which led to an absolute decrease in training expenditures for 1976 and 1977, with the largest cutbacks coming in training support. By 1977, job-training expenditures represented only 39 percent of their 1975 figure.

The effects on enrollments proved drastic and unbalanced. The number of persons entering training dropped from 270,853 in 1975 to 135,926 in 1977—a 50 percent decline. By 1980, total training enrollments were still below the 1975 level. Retraining gradually surpassed its 1975 enrollment figures by 1980, while advanced training did not. OJT programs were spared, although they were never very large (BAA Förderung 1979, p. 14).

By 1978, the first oil shock had subsided, and the government showed that more training was needed: 55.5 percent of the unemployed were unskilled, while employers could not fill many skilled positions (BT SB. 8/2624, p. 17). In 1979, the Fifth Change in the AFG tried to increase job training, improve vocational training for problem groups, and abolish abuses by training carriers. Job training increased from 1979 to 1980: 29 percent for advanced training, 42 percent for retraining, and 27 percent for training support payments.

But when the second oil shock arrived, the Labor Market Consolidation Law, reacting to new economic tremors, cut job-training expenditures in January 1982. For most people, support payments were now regarded as loans, which reduced the incentive to train, and employers' demands controlled the worker's choice of training fields. The 1983 and 1984 Budgetary Accompanying Laws reinforced the cuts (Gagel 1984, pp. 22–28).

The shrinkage of job-training programs most affected women and youth. Job training was restricted to unemployed persons who had contributed to the unemployment compensation fund for the required time periods. This change effectively excluded many women who had recently entered the labor market and young persons who had just come of age (Weitzel 1983). The number of job trainees under the age of twenty declined precipitously: 2,270 in 1975, 98 in 1976, 443 in 1977, and 711 in 1978. Trainees from twenty to twenty-five years also declined from 44,582 in 1975 to 16,091 in 1976, but older age groups were not affected (BAA Förderung 1981, p. 47).

Job-training targets shifted markedly toward the unemployed. In 1973, only 5.8 percent of new trainees were unemployed before starting their courses, but the percentage of previously unemployed trainees rose dramatically to 31.1 percent in 1975, 39.1 percent in 1977, 43.7 percent in 1980, and 64.3 percent in 1983. This is a tremendous increase; however, the rule may have been more vigorously applied to women in 1978 because 60.9 percent of women had been unemployed before training, while only 36 percent of the men were previously unemployed (BAA Förderung 1981, p. 12; Sauter 1984, p. 174).

Evaluation research indicated that the job-training programs worked rather well.[14] Bundesanstalt studies from 1974 to 1979

14. However, the validity of much of this research is debatable. Data were taken from Bundesanstalt records, and control groups were used; however, the comparability of control groups is in question. Other studies done by Infratest and the census office were not much of an improvement. Hofbauer states that comparable control groups have yet to be constructed (1984a, 1984b).

showed that 92.8 percent of trainees were employed after training and that 87.9 percent of the trainees who were previously
unemployed also found work. The weakest program was retraining, where 89 percent of all trainees were employed, much
higher than U.S. placement rates for job training. The 11 percent
of trainees that were unemployed after retraining mainly came
from the youngest (under twenty) and oldest (sixty to sixty-five)
groups. Advanced training also had problems within these age
groups, but had only half as many unemployed workers. The very
small OJT programs had the best record, placing 98.8 percent of
all trainees and 97.9 percent of those previously unemployed
(Hofbauer 1984a, pp. 515–29, 1984b).[15] Although job training suffered many cutbacks and ceased to be viewed as the answer to
crisis levels of unemployment, it was still a success that benefited
many workers and society as a whole.

U.S. JOB TRAINING

After World War II, the dominant American secondary school,
the high school, changed little. Although some federal funds
were disbursed for shop, typing, business, and home economics
classes, the vocational content of the high school remained
minimal.[16] Periodic changes occurred in curriculum toward science in the late 1950s, toward relevance in the 1960s, and back to
basics in the 1980s, but curriculum changes neither affected the
structure of secondary education nor introduced rigorous vocational programs.

Because the U.S. high school provided only shallow vocational
education and students cannot claim certification in specific vocational areas upon graduation, vocational training actually begins
after high school. Consequently, the United States has developed
a wide range of postsecondary job-training programs. Figure 6
shows how American students funnel into postsecondary training
options after high school. The postsecondary schools fall into
six broad areas of education: private vocational, apprenticeship,

15. Earnings increases are not a major goal of Bundesanstalt ALMP programs because earnings are a collective bargaining issue.
16. Exceptions to this statement are big city high schools with specialized
curricula: Cass Technical High School in Detroit, Brooklyn High School of Science, the New York High School of the Performing Arts, and Aviation High
School in New York.

6. The U.S. School System

Years in School

Graduate and Professional Schools

University and College Bachelor's Degree

Community College Associate Degree

Vocational Ed. in Community Colleges

Private Vocational Schools

VA

Military

Apprentice

OJT

ALMP

Skills Center

Adult Schools

High School

Junior High School

Elementary School

military, public vocational, university, and ALMP training (discussed in detail in the next section).

Despite claims of fragmentation, corruption, and antiunionism by educators and union leaders, privately financed vocational education has grown since the late 1800s. Private proprietary schools vary tremendously in quality from frauds with poor prospects of placing graduates to exemplary schools with effective placement records; many have thrived on indirect federal funding (Wilms 1981, pp. 30–31).[17] In the 1950s, the GI Bill gave private vocational schools a major boost when public vocational education was small. Since the late 1960s, Basic Educational Opportunity Grants along with veterans' benefits often provided substantial funding for many private schools despite efforts to avoid dependence.

Apprenticeship training was formalized in the 1937 National Apprenticeship Act that specified procedures for labor and management to voluntarily work together under state auspices. After World War II, three environments for apprenticeship training evolved: thirty states ratified the federal law with formal programs; twenty states ignored the law, but the Bureau of Apprenticeship Training certified programs upon request; and employers can establish informal programs without registering them (Christian 1964, pp. 624–30). By budgeting the funds in collective bargaining agreements, labor unions and management primarily finance apprenticeship programs. The government funds additional classwork at community colleges through either the Vocational Education Act or sometimes through the Department of Labor's Apprenticeship Outreach Program, which promotes minority entry into the skilled trades (Riche 1964, p. 146). However, both unions and employers restrict apprenticeships: "Apprenticeships will continue to play a minor role in skill acquisition because of restricted entry. . . . The limits to apprenticeship stem both from employers' reluctance to plan and from labor's interest in controlling the supply of craftsmen" (Wilms 1981, p. 40). These structural limitations do not exist in West

17. This leads Wilms to comment that "despite a century or more of ostracism by public educators, proprietary schools have not only survived but flourished" (1981, p. 31). Wilms's comment on "flourishing" should be taken institutionally (schools are growing), rather than educationally (quality is high).

Germany, where apprentices as a percentage of the civilian labor force overwhelm U.S. figures by factors of seventeen in 1955 to twelve in 1974 (OECD 1979; Glover 1974, pp. 64–70).[18]

With over half a million men and women, the military is probably the largest single training institution in the United States, spending almost seven billion dollars each year (Wilms 1981, p. 38). Specialized skill training, accounting for about 50 percent of military training, is carried out through many advanced individual training centers and service schools. About 85 percent of the military occupations are estimated to have direct civilian counterparts. Based on these figures, I estimate that the armed forces devote about 42.5 percent of all training to specialized skill training that has direct civilian applications (Wilms 1981; Mangum and Ball 1987, p. 428).

The Department of Education finances vocational education by distributing federal funds to the states. Large numbers of children were enrolled in federally financed high school vocational courses (half of all high school students in 1977) in such subjects as typing, home economics, mechanics, shop, and agriculture.[19] The Vocational Education Act of 1963 increased the financing and flexibility of high school programs, targeted 10 percent of its moneys for "research starved vocational education," and initiated area vocational schools and work study programs (Barlow 1971, pp. 18–24). The act also created a major vocational presence in the public community colleges, adding associate degrees and certificate programs in courses ranging from nursing to automobile repair (Wilms 1981, pp. 20–21). Amendments in 1968 and the Vocational Education Act in 1976 increased planning, and other changes have raised the pay for teachers and promoted new courses.

Universities and colleges are entirely oriented toward the primary sectors of labor markets in skilled white-collar, professional, and some skilled blue-collar work. The states supply most of the financing, with the federal government subsidizing large research

18. Because of informal apprenticeship, U.S. statistics are understated, but West German figures are comparatively understated because of their older work force.

19. These vocational high school statistics include college prep students who take typing courses and thus inflate vocational education figures.

programs and indirectly funding many programs through veterans' benefits and Basic Educational Opportunity Grants. Enrollments in the university and academic tracks of community college programs have increased greatly since the 1960s. As a result the United States has one of the world's highest percentages of working-class students in higher education—five times the West German rate in 1960 and twice that in 1970 (Robertson 1981, p. 199).[20]

Finally, the Department of Labor financed the heart of ALMP Job Training, which will be detailed in the following section.

U.S. ALMP JOB TRAINING

U.S. Veteran Job Training and the Lack of ALMP, 1950 to 1962

ALMP job-training programs, the sixth broad area of education, were virtually nonexistent in the 1950s (see Figure 7). Most persons eighteen years old and younger graduated or left high school for the labor market. Only a few went on to college, apprenticeship, the military, or private vocational schools. After the "GI Bill of Rights" passed in 1944 to provide educational benefits, the backlog of World War II veterans, educated in high schools before the war, drove postsecondary enrollments to new heights.[21] But veterans' programs were not formulated to prevent unemployment because they were seen as "war readjustment" for the nation and "equity" for the soldiers who had suffered grave hardships. Thus, veterans' benefits were not ALMP and constituted a separate labor market policy.

Furthermore, no job-training program in this period bore a positive relationship to unemployment. Although expenditures for both vocational rehabilitation and veterans' educational benefits steadily declined from a high of 0.99 percent of GNP in 1950 to a low of 0.04 percent of GNP in 1962, neither program

---

20. The data for this comparison are from Harold Wilensky's set.

21. The government subsidized the operations of private and public educational establishments but did little to police them. The GI Bill led to abuses similar to job creation or public assistance programs, but the public accepted them.

7. U.S. Job-Training Programs within Active Labor Market Policy

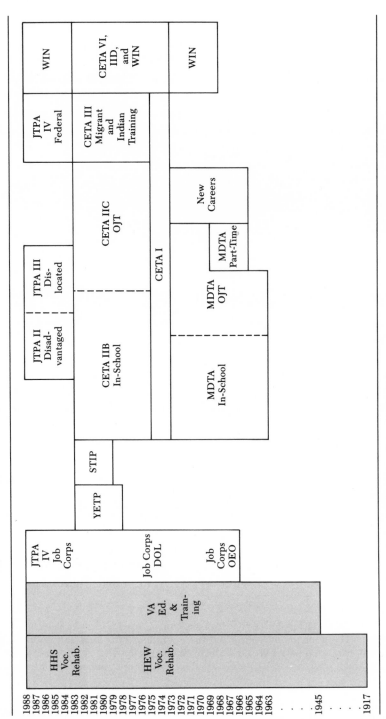

Note: Screened areas represent programs related to Active Labor Market Policy.

increased with unemployment rates. The only other programs close to ALMP were the small vocational rehabilitation programs that were run by the states and partially funded by the federal government. But vocational rehabilitation grew very slowly, while veterans' educational benefits operated procyclically—that is, they increased when unemployment went down. The government was not fighting unemployment with either policy.

The Birth of ALMP Job Training, 1962 to 1972

The economy boomed in the mid-1960s, but the memory of the high unemployment during the two recessions of the 1950s lingered.[22] ALMP job-training programs began with the Manpower Development and Training Act of 1962 (MDTA); this legislation passed with Congress assuming that automation was not only destroying old jobs but also creating new and highly skilled employment.[23] MDTA had two roles: to train displaced blue-collar workers and the hard-core unemployed for those new jobs, and to provide testing, counseling, job placement, and living allowances equal to average unemployment compensation payments in each state. MDTA job training consisted of both in-school and on-the-job (OJT) training.

In-school vocational training under MDTA started slowly. Three types of training processes gradually evolved: single-occupation classes, skills centers including multioccupational centers, and individual referrals to community colleges and vocational schools. In 1963–64, groups of trainees were sent to existing vocational schools for single occupational classes. Using existing vocational education courses and schools was cheap; however, adult and sometimes disadvantaged students required special attention not offered in vocational schools. Many vocational

22. While unemployment climbed to 5.5 percent in 1954, 6.8 percent in 1958, and 6.7 percent in 1961, it dropped to low points of 3.8 percent and 3.5 percent in 1966 and 1969. Real gross national product grew 20.5 percent from 1952 to 1961 and 28.4 percent from 1962 to 1971.

23. The Area Redevelopment Act passed before MDTA, but it had little job training.

schools also offered a poor choice of courses and left MDTA resources underutilized.[24]

Skills centers and multioccupational centers established a new subsystem especially geared to the disadvantaged and dropouts from the traditional education system. The skills centers offered adult and/or disadvantaged trainees a flexible approach: entry at any time of the year, a mix of training in core clusters of occupational courses, self-paced instruction at one's best level of learning, training to variable depths, and exit throughout the school year if the trainee found work. Establishing the skills centers was expensive due to staff, facilities, and equipment, but the centers filled a gap in the educational system. By 1973, seventy established skills centers served 17 percent of all MDTA instructional enrollments.

The centers had specific requirements: It was necessary to serve an area with at least 160 trainees, operate during prime hours, and employ an independent administration. A varied curriculum was essential, but automotive mechanics, autobody repair, welding, machine operation, office occupations, food service, and health occupations were required. Finally, the skills centers offered requisite services, such as remedial education; job assistance involving prevocational orientation, employment counseling, placement, and follow up; and personal aid ranging from housing assistance to child care. Thus, the skills centers provided both a varied curriculum and a full complement of support programs. The multioccupational centers offered fewer courses and services than the skills centers, but they accounted for 23 percent of enrollments in MDTA institutional training in 1971 (Robertson 1981, p. 200; Mangum and Walsh 1973, pp. 54–61).

Where the small number of trainees did not justify a whole course and individual needs were too specialized for the skills centers, the MDTA provided individual referral and contracting. MDTA institutional training sponsored trainees at other schools without special services or counseling. On the whole, individually referred students were less disadvantaged than others and

24. By 1971, single occupational classes made up 51 percent of total MDTA institutional enrollees (Mangum and Walsh 1973, p. 78).

amounted to only 9 percent of all institutional enrollees in 1971 (Mangum and Walsh 1973).

Under OJT, the second form of MDTA training, the federal government provided $25.00 a week for twenty-six weeks or a $650.00 payment to employers to cover training costs (but not wages) of trainees, who then learned by watching and working. Although MDTA attempted "coupled programs" similar to apprenticeship training, the OJT program consisted of work experience with little formal training. Consequently, American OJT clearly lacked a formal approach like the Berufschule with exit examinations. The government relied on the Bureau of Apprenticeship and Training in the Department of Labor to place persons in OJT positions, but such placements were slow in coming. As a result, contracts were negotiated with national trade associations and communities to increase the number of trainees, especially the disadvantaged. Although OJT provided greater certainty of placement for trainees at only 25 percent of the cost of institutional training, the OJT program was difficult to expand because of its dependence on employers.

The Economic Opportunity Act of 1964 created the next group of job-training programs under the Office for Economic Opportunity (OEO) rather than the Department of Labor. The Job Corps was designed to provide job training and increase the mental concentration of disadvantaged trainees by isolating them from their environment in a residential program. Training included counseling, basic education, skill training (electronics assembly, drafting, automotive repair, etc.), and job placement. The Job Corps had a high dropout rate due to homesickness, which challenged its underlying premise of isolation. The Nixon administration closed fifty of eighty-two conservation centers and seven of seventeen women's centers, replacing them with twenty-five new urban centers. Nixon also cut the budget from $280 million to $180 million in his first year of office, but the program has continued (Goldberg 1975a, pp. 397–98; Perry 1975b, p. 14; Levitan 1976, p. 10).

The Economic Opportunity Act also started New Careers to break professional and other highly skilled occupations into jobs for which disadvantaged workers could be trained. A small number of students trained for two or more years as health techni-

cians, assistants in law, social work, and teaching, vocational
rehabilitation specialists, police community service aides, or
mental health workers (Matlack 1975a, p. 216; Cohen 1976).

Finally, under the 1967 amendments to the Social Security
Act, the Work Incentive Program aimed at putting welfare recipients, particularly welfare mothers, to work. The program was
voluntary until the 1971 Talmadge amendments required welfare
recipients with employment potential to participate. This became
the largest ALMP job-training program; it mixed job training,
support services—remedial and vocational education, job placement, and follow-up services—and public assistance (Amons
1975, pp. 360–61).

MDTA had much higher expenditures and enrollments than
the other job-training programs. Except for one year, MDTA in-
school training consistently enrolled more students than the OJT
programs. The Department of Labor tried to increase OJT slots,
but it was difficult to obtain positions from private industry and
hard to motivate the Bureau of Apprenticeship Training to market
OJT. Thus, four times as much money was spent on in-school
training as on OJT training. The Job Corps' small enrollments
peaked in 1967 and, with the cutbacks during the Nixon administration, settled at roughly one-eighth of the MDTA programs.
Job Corps' funding per capita, however, was higher than other
programs because of its expensive room and board costs. The
Work Incentive Program had the highest enrollments and expenditures, but it included questionable prevocational counseling
and holding tank expenditures.

The evaluations of job-training programs showed moderate success, despite some initial criticism. Although the studies may be
disputed for methodological reasons, many used control groups,
and the comparative results usually demonstrated positive earnings and employment effects for trainees. Perry (1975c) summa-
rized studies of MDTA. Benefits have exceeded costs in MDTA
programs by ratios of 1.3 or 3.5 to 1, depending upon the study.
OJT is far more cost effective with ratios often exceeding 3 to 1,
while institutional training has ratios of below 2 to 1 (pp. 151–58).
Earnings increased for males by $1,447 per year in institutional
training and $1,743 per year in OJT, and for females $1,182 per
year in institutional training and $1,426 per year in OJT. Rates of

increase for blacks were comparable though wages start and end at lower levels (p. 162). Perry finds that wage rates increased by 30 cents to 50 cents per hour in the 1960s but showed a "marked drop" to 16 cents in 1972 (pp. 168–69). Finally, trainees were increasingly employed in more stable jobs; in fact, the yearly earnings' gains reported were due to employment increases of 55 percent (more hours per week), employment stability increases of 25 percent (fewer layoffs), and wage increases of only 20 percent (p. 176). MDTA has had only a marginal impact on overall unemployment rates and a negligible impact on shortages of skilled workers; however, it has clearly increased earnings and employment for disadvantaged and unemployed workers (p. 162). Many other studies report similar earning results (see Borus 1980 for a summary).

With a more disadvantaged population, the Job Corps increased annual earnings by only $187.20 to $259.60. Increases in wage rates ranged from 10 to 30 cents an hour, but Job Corps graduates were employed 10 to 17 percent more than before training. These early 1966–67 studies were only marginally favorable to the Job Corps, and their methods were highly suspect (Goldberg 1975a, pp. 410–14). But public opinion about Job Corps was poor because it cost $4,987 per trainee as opposed to about half that amount in MDTA training (Borus 1980, p. 34).

The New Careers program, the only high skill program among the four job-training programs, had moderate placement rates but high wage increases, ranging from $2.00 to $3.00 per hour. Its problem was that trainees were often placed in less than the promised, paraprofessional jobs (Matlack 1975). Increases in wages for work incentive graduates ranged from 15 cents to 50 cents, and placement rates were high at 76 percent, including program dropouts, and 66 percent to 72 percent excluding dropouts (Amons 1975, p. 372).

With the exception of New Careers, a program that carefully screened its trainees for highly skilled paraprofessional training, job-training programs were at low-skill levels. U.S. job-training programs often followed traditional "socialization training," providing extensive moral and social messages, while imparting few occupationally related skills; however, additional factors contributed to the tilt toward low-skill and socialization training: unions in construction, printing, and sewing opposed skill training in their occupations; most training was limited in duration (twenty-nine weeks in MDTA and Job Corps programs); skills centers lacked current occupational equipment and teachers; and OJT often degenerated into work experience with little formal training. Former cultural traditions of socialization training that began in the high school, structural factors of short-term policy measures, and weak labor market institutions played into the low-skill levels of American job training. Thus, the U.S. made a diverse and moderately successful effort to promote job training in the 1960s, but the training was generally at a low level of skill and took place in increasingly segregated school settings.

The Retrenchment of U.S. Job Training, 1974 to 1981

During the 1970s, few major programs or institutions of any permanence were started, although some demonstration projects were effected for a short time. Congress consolidated training programs in the 1973 Comprehensive Employment and Training Act (CETA) so that most job training fell into four categories: CETA IIBC institutional job training, CETA IIBC on-the-job training, the Job Corps, and the Work Incentive Program (see Figure 7).

CETA IIBC institutional training continued MDTA training in predominantly low-skilled jobs: clerical work, health care, automotive repair, welding, machine operation, building service, and food service. Although some higher-skilled job-training programs—computer operation, office machine repair, and licensed practical nursing—were added, CETA restricted course length to thirty-six weeks with an average of twenty-six weeks (Levitan and Mangum 1981, pp. 17–22). CETA IIBC training occurred with individual referrals to varied institutional settings (in decreasing order of usage): public postsecondary schools such as community colleges, skills centers, community-based programs (especially Opportunities Industrial Centers), and private vocational schools.

CETA IIBC on-the-job training enrollments continued to lag behind institutional training. The success of programs depended on national marketing efforts by the U.S. Employment Service, community-based organizations (especially the Urban League), and the National Alliance of Business (Levitan and Mangum 1981, p. 24). But such efforts were small. The Job Corps, after being retrenched during the Nixon administration, continued on a stable level with the same curriculum (Levitan and Johnston 1975). The Work Incentive Program operated under the Talmadge amendments, requiring public assistance recipients to register for work and added "intensive employment services" (ETRP 1980, pp. 50–51).

Enrollments in CETA IIBC in-school training programs followed the MDTA experience, with first-time enrollments stabilizing around 150,000 each year. CETA OJT enrollments showed a decline to about one-third or one-fourth of previous levels because of the recession. Expenditures increased significantly for both programs. Job Corps training stayed remarkably stable, with expenditures and enrollments increasing only in 1979–80. Work incentive enrollments continued their increase, but again the actual number of work incentive enrollees in training, as opposed to those waiting for a program, was questionable. On the whole, job-training expenditures and enrollments increased moderately when job creation programs exploded.

The evaluation of job-training programs showed that they increased earnings and employment. The vast majority of studies in the 1970s and early 1980s showed annual earnings increases among CETA IIBC institutional trainees of $300 to $500 (Barocci 1980, p. 126; Borus 1980, p. 32). Like the MDTA gains, the CETA gains came from decreased unemployment and greater hours worked, rather than wage rate increases. In later studies, Barnow finds highly positive ($200 to $1,000) increases in earnings in six cases, mixed results in two cases, and negative results in three cases (1987, p. 101). CETA training returned $1.14 in benefits for every dollar invested and placed 44 percent of its graduates in jobs (Taggart 1981a, p. 111). Thus, CETA IIBC institutional training worked well, given its limited objectives.

Other programs were also beneficial. Five of six CETA IIBC on-the-job training studies showed earnings increases one year after training, which were double the institutional increases for white males and black females and six times the figure for black males. OJT programs produced $2.18 per dollar invested— almost double the institutional figure (Taggart 1981a, p. 111). In ten of eleven OJT studies, yearly earnings increased by as much as $500 to over $1,000, but six of the classroom studies showed $500 to $1,000 increases (Barnow 1987, pp. 161–75). Clearly, OJT training seems to have worked well. Although Job Corps evaluation studies were mixed, black males, the largest group in Job Corps training, had major increases in earnings. Furthermore, evaluation research with a longer range and wider scope showed that the Job Corps provided a net gain to society of $2,271 per trainee through less crime, less welfare, and more tax revenue (Long, Mallar, and Thornton 1981).

All the job-training programs benefited most of their trainees, and the MDTA and CETA IIBC in-school programs had the largest impact in terms of earnings and enrollments. OJT was more efficient, but it reached a smaller number of people, while the Job Corps achieved its goals with a very disadvantaged target group. The Work Incentive Program affected the most people; but many programs are not ALMP, and its overall effectiveness remains an open question. Like the 1960s programs, the CETA era produced moderately effective job-training programs.

Cutback and Privatization in U.S. Job Training, 1982 to 1985

CETA was replaced by the Job Training and Partnership Act (JTPA) in October 1982. While CETA III (migrant and native American), CETA IVB (Job Corps), and the Work Incentive Program were continued, CETA IIBC training programs, which had replaced the MDTA training programs, were merged into JTPA II for disadvantaged workers and JTPA III for dislocated workers.

Under JTPA, the states took over job training from local community organizations. Instead of balanced self-administration, more than half the average private industry council was represented by business, and the remaining members were divided between government, unions, and other community groups (Levitan and Gallo 1988, p. 39). The Department of Labor gave the private industrial councils planning grants so they could deal with local governments in establishing programs. At the local level, the business community and the local government negotiated agreements to train workers. JTPA restricts administrative costs and "socialization" support services to 30 percent of funds, a small amount compared to CETA; this "no-frills" program is oriented toward needs of employers.

JTPA programs have generally been evaluated as successful. In the JTPA's first year, training programs targeted fewer high school dropouts than CETA (21 percent compared to 38 percent of total enrollments) and initially placed only 37 percent of trainees (Bailey 1988, pp. 305–11). In 1985, the disadvantaged JTPA program had low targeting of high school dropouts (27 percent) and low wages (little over the minimum wage), but the overall JTPA placement rate rose to 62 percent. The dislocated worker program during the same year had even lower targeting on high school dropouts (19 percent), but its placement rates were over 68 percent. However, after completing the program wages actually declined from pre-enrollment rates in seventeen of twenty-nine states, and overall wages were only 70 percent of the 1981 real CETA average wage. Under federal direction, the Job Corps targeted heavily on high school dropouts (79 percent) and had the highest placement rate (74 percent) for program completers. Enrollments in the disadvantaged program were the largest (752,900) with the dislocated worker program (95,600) and the Job Corps (hovering around 100,000) falling well below that number. JTPA had only a microscopic effect on unemployment because states did not even take full advantage of the small amounts of funds available to them (Levitan and Gallo 1988, pp. 98–153; NCMP 1987, pp. 98–115, 175–224).

On the whole, the JTPA is designed to look good to both business and the public. With private industry councils that give participation rights to employers, the program appears to take an easier route toward evaluation success with more effectively screened (creamed) enrollees and relaxed reporting requirements. JTPA does, however, use performance criteria to let individual programs know what kinds of placement and wage rates are expected. Relying on business rather than community groups or labor, the JTPA program was established on a permanent basis, unlike CETA, and surprisingly enough its evaluation performance is not that different from CETA results (Levitan and Gallo 1988; Guttman 1983, pp. 3–7). But we must recognize that CETA lived through two oil shocks, while JTPA operated in a moderate economic recovery.

COMPARING U.S. AND WEST GERMAN JOB TRAINING

Both countries established job-training programs after World War II, but each followed a different course. West Germany built upon the extensive skill training present in their apprenticeship system with retraining and even advanced training. Because the United States had no such base of vocational skills to build on, American job training often began with remedial, low-skilled, and socialization programs for trainees lacking previous experience in vocational education (the U.S. high school tends to discourage vocational pursuits). Thus, the growth of job training in West Germany has been based on a high initial level of skill and in the United States on a low level of vocational knowledge.

The growth of ALMP job-training programs has consequently differed; some superficial similarities are due to the business cycle. West German ALMP job-training programs, operating since 1950, have built on their use of labor, management, and government self-administration. Training has been widely available under one program for a diversity of citizens including veterans and persons on public relief. Allocation of training expenditures emphasized initial training in the 1950s, advanced training in the later 1960s, and a rough balance of advanced and retraining after the oil crisis. Retraining in an apprenticeship is long and technical; it lasts two to four years, not three to six months. On the whole, West Germany has spent much more money on job training than the United States (see Figure 4–B, and Table 3, column 2).

American job training, begun ten years after that in West Germany, was based upon executive bureaucracies usually without labor or community participation rights. U.S. job-training programs *and* service providers came and went with regularity, even to the point of introducing demonstration projects intended to quickly disappear. Even these institutions are financed by many sources: unions and management, the Departments of Labor, Education, and Defense, the Veterans Administration, and state and local governments. The institution building of much of the 1960s simply vanished, except for the skills centers, which could be viewed as a segregated and stigmatized reenactment of the industrial normal school. The balance of advanced training and retraining is not meaningful in the United States because higher skilled programs, like New Careers, have been severely limited in practice and duration. Finally, expenditures have not risen above 0.014 percent of GNP, while West German expenditures have often been twice as high.

Although evaluation research is a somewhat murky area where social scientists continually disagree and often invalidate previous findings, both countries show positive results.[25] West German job-training programs have been evaluated successes, with workers finding highly paid jobs after training. However, West German programs could use additional counseling because they are administered in a cold bureaucratic style; and although workers find jobs, they do not always get jobs in the fields of their training. American job-training programs, despite media and political critiques, have been more moderate successes with increased earnings and placement rates at half the West German level. This success is remarkable, given the programs' extensive organizational confusion and focus on disadvantaged workers left untrained by the high school.

25. Differences in evaluation research between these two countries results in an uneven comparison, and this secondary analysis of evaluation studies cannot possibly resolve the internal problems of each country, much less the problems of comparison between countries. Many problems exist with experimental controls, and some think only mass experiments are the answer (see Director 1979, Burtless and Orr 1986, Fraker and Maynard 1987, Barnow 1987, and Björklund 1988). Others criticize the use of earnings gains (Bishop 1989), which make little sense in West Germany because wages are much more centrally bargained. In the end, however, placement rates are the most reliable means of comparison in this study.

Chapter Six

Job Creation Programs

Job creation policies demonstrate the least contrast between West Germany and the United States. Of course, there are plenty of differences in actual policies, but the results are similar. In each country, the state's creation of economic activity is problematic because of two kinds of substitution effects. With job substitution, state-created jobs simply replace or compete with private sector jobs; there is no net increase in employment. In cases of fiscal substitution, local governments shift part of their wage budget to the federal government, transforming a locally financed job into a nationally financed job. Job substitution threatens the capitalist system, causing private employers to complain bitterly, while fiscal substitution is more of an intergovernmental shell game. In either case, job creation, prone to heavy political fallout, is difficult to sustain on a large scale. In the end, the most efficient and cautious programs, as in West Germany, prove most defensible. Inefficient and confused programs, as those in the United States, prove uncontrollable in the short run and vulnerable in the long run.

JOB CREATION IN WEST GERMANY

German job creation programs peaked in the early 1950s, developed a specific focus toward the structurally unemployed during the labor shortages of the 1960s, and peaked again during the oil crisis. West German job creation programs addressed a wider range of instruments than American programs, but American job creation expenditures were higher than West German expenditures in the late 1970s.

West German Job Creation Programs, 1950 to 1959

The government took a two-pronged approach toward its extensive job creation policies in the 1950s: a capital accumulation program to boost private industry, and an ALMP job creation program to directly employ workers.[1] The Act of Pressing Social Needs imposed a tax on certain property and mortgage gains resulting from the currency devaluation in 1949. The Immediate Aid Agency administered these funds and set aside 150 million DM for loans to promote job creation, with a stipulation that the jobs last eight years (later reduced to five years). A total of 111 million DM was distributed from 1949 to 1952, but the program ended in 1956.[2] In the 1950 Employment Creation Act, the government tried to reduce unemployment and stimulate the economy by spending; 3,400 million DM were provided in the form of low-interest loans aimed at construction, railroads, export financing, and small business. A "key-point" program focused on financially weak states and regions. Although most of the program was directly related to business promotion, the key-point program provided 300 million DM for 70,000 permanent jobs in private industry and labor-intensive public works.

The second approach directly implemented ALMP. The Emergency Program of 1951 reactivated the "productive unemployment assistance" concept of the 1920s. This plan anticipated passage of a labor exchange bill and diverted unemployment insurance and relief funds to emergency public works programs. Thus, financing fell into two categories: basic support consisting of grants financed from unspent unemployment insurance and relief payments, and intensified support providing long-term, low-interest loans for large projects of considerable public interest. The Labor Exchange Law of 1952 reestablished the employment

1. The capital accumulation policy was backed by the relatively new ideology of the "social market economy" and ORDO-Liberalism, which Ludwig Erdhard (1963) advocated in politics and Eugen Eucken (1951) promoted in economics. It matched well with the nation's distaste for Nazi intervention and acceptance of allied free market economics.

2. Because the program was not administered by the Bundesanstalt, expenditure figures are not available (Wittich 1966, p. 127).

service, and the Bundesanstalt took over job creation by administering the Emergency Program. In addition, the Bundesanstalt started their own "productive unemployment assistance," sheltered workshops, and short-time work programs.[3]

Total job creation reached its highest point in 1952, two years after unemployment peaked and economic growth began. Pure job creation expenditures ranged from 0.06 percent to 0.17 percent of GNP from 1950 to 1954—the highest figures in the post–World War II period. Enrollments in the early 1950s were even more impressive, employing more workers than at any other time.[4] Nonetheless, the Employment Creation Act of 1950 was criticized for its indirect relation to job creation, slow implementation in the face of peaking unemployment, and small size. Labor also criticized the Emergency Program of 1951; it was too small, ineffectively implemented, and a little too late.

Notwithstanding criticism, these programs were large and effective compared to American efforts. From 1950 to 1956, the Employment Creation Act and the Emergency Program created 70,000 and 50,000 permanent jobs out of the total 820,000 jobs attributed to all economic measures (Wittich 1966, pp. 127–51). Both laws, along with capital accumulation measures, helped reduce the unemployment rate. Job creation expenditures averaged about 0.12 percent of GNP from 1950 to 1956—much larger than expenditures during the oil shock. In summary, the well-funded 1950s job creation programs were important for their sheltered workshops for disabled workers and short-time work payments.

New Job Creation Programs during Full Employment, 1959 to 1969

The labor shortage stemming from the economic miracle reduced unemployment to less than 1 percent from 1961 to 1966 (BMA 1983, p. 65). Meanwhile export-led growth continued with manufacturing income as a percentage of GDP rising from 52.4 percent in 1959 to 54.6 percent in 1967 at a time when the manufacturing

3. Short-time work provided wage subsidy payments to employers. For example, a firm could put twenty workers on half-time work, rather than dismiss ten workers. The government then pays the firm money so that they can pay the twenty part-time workers close to their full-time wages. The purpose of the program was to keep people on the payroll rather than lay them off.

4. This comparison excludes job maintenance programs.

sector was shrinking in other countries (Dückert 1982, pp. 93–101). Labor shortages rendered large job creation efforts superfluous, as the government recruited foreign workers and some women into the labor force. Meanwhile, productive unemployment assistance and other job creation measures faded away.

At this time, the government encountered three specific areas with severe labor market problems: the construction industry, West Berlin and the border areas of East Germany, and the Ruhr coal and steel industries. First, the construction industry faced continuous work stoppages because of poor weather, and even worse, it led most economic downturns. Consequently, skilled construction workers often left construction jobs for semiskilled factory work that promised continuous employment, improved safety, and assured holidays and vacations. Wages were lower in the semiskilled work, but continuous employment made up for the discrepancy. The high unemployment rates in the early 1950s had concealed the problems of construction workers, but by the late 1950s construction unemployment rates stood out at 50 percent.[5]

Second, West Berlin and the areas bordering East Germany were often neglected by investors who saw border areas as politically unstable and risky investments. Restricted access and limited markets—Iron Curtain towns are not on trade routes—contributed to an unprofitable reputation. And third, unemployment in the Ruhr coal and steel industries remained a problem despite the 1959 European Economic Community Treaty that established the European Coal and Steel Community and provided for job-training allowances, mobility allowances, severance pay regulations, and wage supplements.

The government attacked construction unemployment with job maintenance programs. In 1959, the second amendment of the Labor Placement Law—the law over the "Promotion of Year Round Employment in the Construction Industry"—created bad weather

5. Wages are not particularly high in construction work because construction unions are not privileged craft unions. The construction industry's union negotiates industrywide wage contracts at the regional level. Thus, wages are subject to neither site wage bargaining nor site strikes. Wage rates in construction are roughly equivalent to wages in other industrial sectors at similar skill levels (Marsden 1980, p. 79).

payments for work during inclement weather and short-time work payments to prevent layoffs by subsidizing full-time wages for employees working less than forty hours a week. Funds for these two programs rose to 0.013 percent of GNP for the construction program and 0.0037 percent for short-time work payments (Kühl et al. 1980, p. 68). Pure job creation focused on devising new jobs, while job maintenance programs attempted to preserve jobs already in existence. In the 1950s, pure job creation constituted almost all such expenditures (94 percent in 1954); but by 1960, pure job creation was small (3 percent in 1962 and 5 percent in 1975), and job maintenance programs dominated.

West Germany's job maintenance programs had mixed success. The construction programs were highly effective in reducing male unemployment rates for construction workers from 57 percent in 1957 to 26 percent in 1966. Although the programs did not eliminate construction unemployment, they significantly stabilized that industry. And many construction and short-time work programs were allocated to West Berlin and the border areas (Dückert 1982, p. 102).

But the Ruhr coal and steel areas went untouched by job creation measures in the 1960s because of less demand for mining and steel employment. Construction was growing and needed more workers, but heavy industry was declining and had an excess of workers. The government wanted to get coal and steel workers into other jobs. Consequently, heavy industry workers were laid off, retrained by the Bundesanstalt, and placed in new jobs rather than being subsidized in old jobs. For example, a rationalization act provided indemnities of 2,000 to 5,000 DM to workers and required mining companies to draw up social plans for plant closures. A 1971 directive from the Economics Ministry enlarged allowances for workers over fifty years old (paid for by the European Common Market), and many of these workers entered job-retraining programs. Thus, the policy toward the coal and steel industries supported retraining and relocation, not job creation.

The Bundesanstalt focused on structural unemployment because cyclical job creation policies were unnecessary during most of the 1960s, but cyclical unemployment emerged when job creation measures failed to react to the 1967–68 recession. The Bundesanstalt job creation programs had a static emphasis on chronic, structural unemployment and could not automatically adjust to cyclical demands. The AFG was passed to correct these problems.[6]

West German Job Creation Built Anew, 1969 to 1975

To replace the old programs of the 1950s, the Labor Promotion Act (AFG) of 1969 introduced two new work creation programs: integrative allowances and general work creation measures. The AFG had a profound effect on job creation policies because it targeted the disabled and hard-to-employ workers with special job creation policies and also tried to stimulate overall demand through countercyclical job creation policies.

The integration allowance supplied wage subsidies for hard-to-place workers: the long-term unemployed, disabled workers, older workers with few prospects, and young persons without skills.[7] The government provided employers with a wage subsidy of up to 80 percent during the initial period of employment, which could last from two months to two years (the average duration was nine months). The amount of subsidies doubled from 1973 to 1979 in real DMs, and participants increased by a factor of ten from 1973 to 1977.[8] Although integration allowance subsidies were expensive and briefly discontinued in 1979, they constituted a major job creation program.

General Work Creation Measures were intended to create temporary work for all unemployed workers. If employers, government agencies, and nonprofit agencies provided new or additional jobs, the government agreed to subsidize up to 80 percent of the costs. Subsidies ranged from 60 percent to 120 percent of wage costs, which sometimes amounted to 90 percent of the total project costs (Reyher, Koller, and Spitznagel 1979, p. 100).[9]

6. Formal evaluations were not done on these programs during this period. Major research programs began in 1968 (Schwanse 1982; Derlien 1990).

7. These specially targeted groups did not include foreign workers, nor did they specifically mention female workers.

8. Participants increased from 7,000 persons in 1973 to 103,000 persons in 1977.

9. Additional laws followed in the footsteps of special targeting and countercyclical measures. The Bundestag passed "A Special Structural Program" of 900 million DM in early 1974 for regions with serious unemployment problems and

When the unemployment rate rose from 0.7 percent to 4.8 percent during the first oil crisis, job creation efforts automatically increased, unlike the reaction to the 1966–67 recession. The Bundesanstalt's three basic programs of job creation—general job creation, construction industry job maintenance, and short-time work support payments—doubled from 1969 to 1975 as a percentage of GNP. But the three programs developed unevenly. Aid to the construction industry actually decreased from 1969 to 1975 by 29 percent. The major increases came in short-time work and general job creation, which rose by factors of twenty-four and five, respectively, in the same period. Participation in pure job creation programs expanded from 1,500 persons in 1972 to 16,000 persons in 1975, and short-time work participants increased from 44,000 persons in 1973 to 773,000 persons in 1975. The automatic operation of countercyclical provisions created by the AFG caused this growth.

Job creation programs were successful. General job creation measures produced about two additional jobs for every job funded. When we consider substitution effects (persons in the program who were previously employed), the increase was still about one additional job for every funded job. Although short-time work was primarily a job maintenance program, it also contributed to positive employment gains and a sizable but smaller decrease in unemployment. However, the short-time work programs and construction aid programs were expensive, while general work creation programs were small and consequently inexpensive. When the first oil shock hit, the countercyclical funding of job creation measures quickly expanded beyond budgetary limits, and general tax revenues were required in addition to employer and worker contributions (Kühl et al. 1980, p. 30).

West German Job Creation Under Stress, 1976 to 1984

West Germany expected a quick recovery from the oil crisis and the resumption of their full employment economy. The 4.7 per-

---

another special program for 950 million DM for employment support. In late 1974, a 600 million DM program provided wage subsidies and mobility allowances and extended short-time work from one to two years. All these special programs supplied additional funding rather than programmatic change.

cent unemployment rate of 1975 was supposed to go away after a
year. However, as unemployment rates hovered around 4 percent
from 1976 to 1980 and then rose above 5 percent in 1981 and 7
percent in 1982, the country began to face mass unemployment.
Der Spiegel (1982) referred to these figures as "horror rates"
(BMA 1983, p. 37).

As the manufacturing sector began to decline, firms laid off
younger employees and were much more conservative about hiring new workers; thus, teenagers and foreign workers bore the
brunt of unemployment (Streek 1982; Windolf 1981). Actions of
firms and conditions in the labor market resulted in increased
labor market segmentation. More senior, native workers kept their
jobs, but younger and less skilled workers faced disappearing industrial apprenticeships and unemployment. By 1974, foreign
worker restrictions had made guestworkers drop from 4.1 million
in 1975 to 3.9 million in 1977. But by 1982, family reunifications
and the coming of age of children caused the number of foreign
workers to rise to 4.7 million. And, of course, a foreign (especially Turkish) youth was doubly disadvantaged.

Job creation programs were the chosen means of labor market
policy in a recession, but they were financially strained after their
full use in 1975 and smaller than one might expect. As unemployment reduced ALMP contributions in 1974, three federal programs raised revenues in Bundesanstalt coffers by 2.4 billion DM.
In early 1976, a specific job creation program provided 200 million DM for underqualified young persons and disabled workers.
In April 1977, a larger job creation program provided 270 million
DM for social service jobs, especially for women looking for part-
time work, but it also increased the penalties for refusing work.[10]
In early 1978, 100 million DM were provided for disabled workers' job creation and job training. But these ALMP expenditures
were much less than the March 1977 investment program of 16
billion DM and another large capital investment program initiated in September 1977. Despite job creation being the favored
policy tool, pure job creation expenditures were much smaller
than job maintenance and job training programs throughout the

10. Women's participation in the labor force continued its slow growth, from
30.9 percent in 1975 to 33.9 percent in 1983.

period (Reyher and Spitznagel 1979; Reyher, Koller, and Spitznagel 1979).

In July 1979, the Fifth Change of the AFG introduced two new job creation programs. First, the Special Employment Program of Job Creation Measures, similar to the general measures, increased job creation wage subsidies to 100 percent, raised the maximum subsidy period from one to two years (with the possibility of three years in North Rhine–Westfalia), and directed job creation toward social service and infrastructure jobs in public and nonprofit agencies. The program was considered successful, although it drained participants from the general job creation measures. Second, the Grants for Research and Development Program provided wage subsidies of 40 percent for the creation of new and the maintenance of old white-collar research and development jobs in small- and medium-sized firms. Schmid states that the effective program was an ideal "integrated supply-and-demand" instrument (1981, p. 14).

These positive changes in 1979, conceived during a mild economic upturn, gave way to more restrictive changes within several years. In 1981, the Labor Market Consolidation Act, followed by numerous budgetary laws, led to extensive cuts in program and budget. Consequently, job creation measures as a whole in the 1980s just barely surpassed their 1975 peak.

The balance of pure job creation and job maintenance policies inched toward pure job creation in the 1980s. Though construction job maintenance stayed constant, short-time work was cut back to below one-fifth of its 1975 level. The only programs that grew were the pure job creation programs, which in 1980 represented over six times the 1975 level. Enrollments in pure job creation measures rose from 16,000 in 1975 to 51,192 in 1979, but short-time work dropped from its 1975 peak of 773,000 to 550,000 in 1982. The emphasis in job creation programs shifted from construction and office work to public service jobs.

Two totally new programs, started in the 1980s, were not reflected in expenditure figures. Unemployment Initiatives allowed groups of unemployed workers to form an association, propose a job creation project, and then receive the money to put themselves to work. For instance, the Unemployment Center in Hannover was formed to provide self-help and special services for the unemployed including its own newspaper (*The Ear*) and a cafe staffed by unemployed workers (Blanke, Heinelt, and Macke 1984). Churches, unions, parties, and even some firms sponsored many of these initiatives (Grottian and Paasch 1984, p. 333; Kommunalverband Ruhrgebiet 1983).[11] And the Second Work Program combined Bundesanstalt unemployment pay and assistance with matching funds from cities—Munich, Bremen, and Hamburg—for local job creation programs. This decentralized revival of the "productive unemployment assistance" program of the 1920s and early 1950s offered workers who stayed in the municipal program for two to three years a chance to reestablish their eligibility for unemployment compensation.

Despite the new programs and job creation's preference as a policy tool, low funding was the major problem for job creation programs. With the cuts in job training, job creation could have been increased much more. In fact, however, pure job creation remained a small program, compared to the older aid programs for the construction industry. In enrollments, construction programs were three times the size of pure job creation in 1980, and short-time work was twenty-two times larger than pure job creation.

During this period program evaluators criticized job creation for job and fiscal substitution.[12] Some critics claimed that new jobs competed with private jobs, without increasing employment. For instance, general work creation measures to clean up parks and plant trees, it was argued, competed with garden shops that could have been called in to do this work. However, this criticism is considered weak, and on the whole the degree of competition was low.[13] Other critics argued that cities and nonprofit agencies simply transferred their fiscal burdens to the federal government. For example, Duisburg laid off surveyors only to hire new surveyors with federal subsidies, thus reducing the city's wage bill. Charges

11. The "unemployment initiative" groups attempted to come together to form a more unified pressure group, but due to their diversity this proved impossible.

12. Policy makers debated whether unemployment was a regional or general problem. From 1974 to 1979, policy makers emphasized regional policy, but by 1980 unemployment became so high that job creation programs were opened up nationwide.

13. This information comes from Jürgen Kühl at the Bundesanstalt.

of fiscal substitution were also made against employers in short-time work programs.

However, one major factor worked against widespread fiscal substitution. The ÖTV—the service workers union and second largest union in the German Federation of Trade Unions (DGB)—vigorously opposed such abuses, and the cities needed union consent to implement ALMP programs because the ÖTV and other unions were represented on the administrative boards of the Bundesanstalt at local, regional, and national levels. The ÖTV rejected abusive programs, and private employers on the boards had little incentive to act differently. The Bundesanstalt closely watched programs on this issue and did not allow extensive abuses in job creation programs. As a result, fewer criticisms were hurled at job creation programs than at unemployment compensation and its work refusal penalties.

The promise of countercyclical job creation programs, set forth in the 1969 AFG and the 1967 Stabilization and Growth Act, was clearly broken after 1976. In the face of rising unemployment, Bundesanstalt expenditures and enrollments for total and pure job creation programs failed to rise above the cuts in job training. These shortfalls in providing for the unemployed invited comparisons with the 1920s and 1930s, and advocates of ALMP claimed that "Bonn is not Weimar" (Klönne 1984, p. 210). However, West German expenditures continued into the 1980s at a moderately high level, unlike American job creation expenditures.

A Final Note on German Job Creation

In an area closely connected to job creation policies, required reporting by workers' councils and firms helped prepare for ALMP and job creation policies in particular, and these notification and consultation procedures were widened throughout the post–World War II period. The 1952 Works Constitution Act required that works' councils, composed of workers and management, participate in decisions about layoffs in the iron, steel, and coal industries. Although the employers still had the upper hand, firms were pressured to balance employer and employee interests (Sengenberger 1982; Gennard 1979). The Protection Against Dismissal Act of 1969 required employers to inform the works' council in detail and in advance about collective dismissals. The firm and the works' council would work together to avoid or reduce the hardship of dismissals through a "social plan" (or face compulsory arbitration).[14] The 1969 AFG also requires that an employer send notification of mass dismissals, along with the works' council opinions, to the local employment office thirty days before the dismissals are scheduled.[15] Besides extending works' councils to a larger range of firms, the 1972 Amended Works Constitution Act required that employers speedily notify and inform the works' council about mergers, work force reductions, product changes, and new technology.[16] And the 1978 Amended Protection Against Dismissal Law extended some coverage on individual and collective dismissals.

Notification and consultation give the Bundesanstalt time to design and implement job creation and maintenance programs. The absence of notification makes program implementation slow, and in the case of job maintenance, even impossible. West Germany has such notification laws, but the United States does not (Tarullo 1989).

14. The Protection Against Dismissal Act also only allowed firms to dismiss workers for justifiable reasons (i.e., urgent firm operating requirements or worker misconduct). Workers could sue for twelve to sixteen months of pay (but not reinstatement) in the social courts where the employer bore the burden of proof. Of the 10 percent of all dismissals that went to court, 60 percent led to the payment of compensation to employees, although maximum payments were rare.

15. Under the AFG, the notice applied to firms in three categories: dismissal of five to twenty-four workers in a firm with twenty to sixty workers; dismissal of twenty-five or more workers or 10 percent of the work force in firms with sixty-one to five hundred workers; and dismissal of more than thirty workers in firms with over five hundred workers. The local employment office had two enforcement weapons: delaying the firm's dismissals for an additional thirty days, and requiring the firm to pay the costs of retraining, counseling, and job creation (Sengenberger 1982; Gennard 1979).

16. During the early 1970s, firms and unions negotiated industrywide rationalization agreements, including economic decline contracts that continued some housing benefits and pensions payments, and extended dismissal protection to a younger group of workers (i.e., as low as forty years of age). But a loophole existed in the job security system. Redundancy accompanied by severance pay was not legally considered a "dismissal"; it was a "quit" because the worker voluntarily accepted unemployment along with severance pay. Consequently, these workers were not protected by job security agreements and laws, and they had to suffer four-week unemployment compensation penalties.

JOB CREATION IN THE UNITED STATES

The job creation policies of the New Deal left neither institutions nor programs operating after World War II. U.S. job creation policies seem to have really existed only in the 1960s and 1970s (see Figure 8 for a summary of programs). The only policy even remotely resembling job creation in the 1950s was Truman's Defense Manpower Policy Number 4 of 1952, which shifted defense procurements to areas of current or prospective unemployment (Jerrett and Barocci 1979, p. 15). Consequently, job creation began in the 1960s.

Job Creation during the War on Poverty, 1962 to 1970

In the 1960s, ALMP job creation started somewhat weakly with a number of regional programs in Appalachia. The 1961 Area Redevelopment Act created the Area Redevelopment Administration under the Department of Commerce and provided funds for creating jobs in depressed areas. The 1962 Accelerated Public Works Program added more funds, and the 1965 Public Works and Economic Development Act consolidated these programs and established the Economic Development Administration. These programs were intended to create jobs for the unemployed through public and civilian construction; however, only 22 percent of the jobs were filled by the unemployed and disadvantaged workers, and 48 percent were filled by skilled and 30 percent by moderately well-off workers (Jerrett and Barocci 1979, p. 30). A large portion of the budget (17 percent) went for business loans, only half the industrial parks built under the act were ever used, and many private firms were reluctant to move into isolated areas with disadvantaged populations. Only a small part of these policies can actually be considered ALMP because their funds went for purposes other than putting the unemployed to work.

In 1964, the War on Poverty soon established job creation programs with four major public programs. First, the Neighborhood Youth Corps provided work for teenagers in order to help disadvantaged students stay in school. Goldberg (1975b, p. 423) outlines the four main goals of the program: to increase employment among disadvantaged teenagers; to provide training, work experience, and incentives to stay in high school; to reduce teenage crime and delinquency; and to redistribute income in the direction of

8. U. S. Job Creation Programs within Active Labor Market Policy

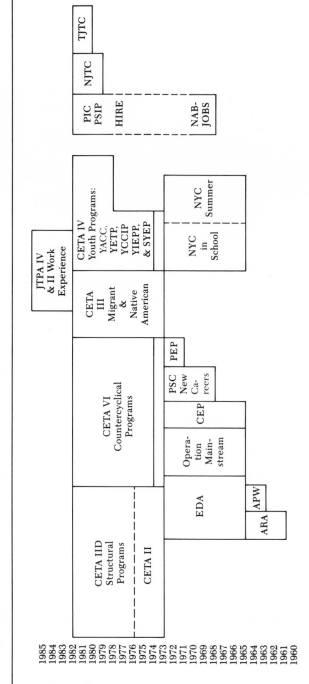

Note: JTPA did not enact job creation programs per se, but work experience programs under Titles II and IV (disadvantaged workers and migrant/Native American workers) can be interpreted as job creation programs. Nonetheless, these programs are small.

the poor. The Youth Corps consisted of an in-school program providing part-time jobs for students (i.e., preventing dropouts) and an out-of-school program consisting of work experience (i.e., improving self-discipline and work attitudes);[17] in addition, another program provided large numbers of teenagers with summer jobs (i.e., improving self-discipline and increasing the chances students would return to school in the fall). Although the Youth Corps provided a job, Goldberg said that it functioned "as a combination income maintenance and maturation device to help youths stay out of trouble until they are old enough to get a sustaining job or enroll in a training program" (1975b, p. 449). Indeed, 56.7 percent to 89 percent of trainees were under nineteen years old, in the ninth to eleventh grades of high school (Goldberg 1975b, p. 424).

Second, Operation Mainstream provided jobs for workers over fifty-five years old, especially in rural areas with high unemployment. The work consisted of public and nonprofit jobs for poorly educated farm workers and the older rural poor in services, community improvement, beautification, and in 1969 housing rehabilitation. The program also provided enrollees with counseling and basic education. Although few of its workers intended to enter the open labor market, it created jobs for older adults who needed them. Enrollments in Operation Mainstream tripled from 1967 to 1972; however, the program was less than 4 percent of the size of the Neighborhood Youth Corps Summer Program.

Third, Public Service Careers grew out of the New Careers program in 1970. It attempted to provide employment and employment upgrading in federal, state, local governments, and nonprofit agencies receiving federal funds. Enrollments and expenditures in this program were small.

And fourth, the National Association of Businessmen JOBS Program tried to place disadvantaged workers into meaningful jobs in the private sector using a "hire-now-train-later" approach. The program consisted of private jobs for disadvantaged workers, private training programs with services (supportive and prevocational), and federal subsidies for employers to cover the additional

---

17. When the program was later reoriented to skill training, it became less of a job creation measure.

costs of hiring and job training. The overall aim was the long-term integration of disadvantaged workers into the company. The Department of Labor and National Association of Businessmen jointly administered the program. After two years of sporadic operation, the program began to fade in 1970, leaving a small Jobs for Veterans and Disadvantaged Workers Program.

Evaluation research on these four job creation programs has been spotty, but the programs showed positive benefits. In the Neighborhood Youth Corps, white males gained about $600 and women slightly less in yearly earnings after termination, but black gains were as high as $1,245 for men and $1,031 for women (Borus 1980, pp. 32–34; Goldberg 1975b, p. 450). Operation Mainstream did reasonably well in providing employment to poor people over fifty-five, but because it was more of a transfer payment and mental health program, positive results disappeared when enrollees left the program (Matlack 1975b, pp. 469–73). Public Service Careers has had only one evaluation of interest. An RMC Corporation study shows outstanding benefits: full-time workers earned about $3,000 above prior annual earnings, 68 percent of enrollees received a pay raise—upgraded enrollees averaged a 9.6 percent raise—25 percent won promotions, 50 to 59 percent of enrollees obtained permanent positions, and 93 percent of enrollees had at least temporary jobs (Matlack 1975a, pp. 211–12). However, Public Service Careers was the only high-skill program, and it probably skimmed higher ability workers. The National Association of Businessmen JOBS program had little evaluation research because the reporting requirements were relaxed to encourage firm participation, but a 1971 Government Accounting Office study found that it creamed extensively, which probably accounts for most of its gains in yearly earnings after completion—$108 for white males to $1,640 for white females, with blacks squarely in between (Perry 1975a, p. 192).

On the whole, job creation programs had done well, but they were small—one-fifth of job-training expenditures—and were incidental to the War on Poverty.

The U.S. Job Creation Boom During the Crisis, 1971 to 1982

In 1971, the Congress passed the Emergency Employment Act, and the Department of Labor established the first extensive job creation program since World War II. CETA Titles II and VI soon followed in 1973, and job creation policies were off and running. During this period there are six major programs to consider.

First, the Public Employment Program provided either transitional public service employment when for three months or more the national unemployment rate exceeded an average of 4.5 percent or public service jobs and special emergency assistance when city and county unemployment rates topped 6 percent. It targeted unemployed veterans, persons over forty-five years old, migratory workers, immigrants, displaced workers, and disadvantaged workers. Pay was limited to $12,000 a year, and no more than one-third of the jobs could be in professional positions (teachers excluded). Although program services were heavily restricted, the Public Employment Program was the first extensive job creation program after World War II, and it paved the way for greater job creation programs under CETA (Sparrough 1975, pp. 252–57).

Second, the structural unemployment program (CETA IID) funded prime sponsors to hire the unemployed in public service jobs in areas with unemployment of 6.5 percent or higher for three consecutive months. The program expanded quickly because national unemployment exceeded 7 percent in 1975, and most areas met the basic criterion. Prime sponsors included the states (29 percent), cities (19 percent), counties (19 percent), and consortia (33 percent). Each participant was supposed to use the CETA job as a stepping stone to unsubsidized employment. Vietnam veterans, former manpower trainees, and the long-term unemployed were given preference. Hiring for public service employment required that sponsors not lay off other persons in order to fill the CETA IID jobs—no fiscal substitution effects— and that applicants be unemployed thirty days prior to being hired. However, persons who had lost their jobs through legitimate cutbacks could be reemployed. CETA IID participants were only 36 percent black, and 74 percent had a high school education or more—evidence of creaming highly skilled workers and avoiding the disadvantaged (Mirengoff and Rindler 1978, pp. 27–39, 160–75, 215).

The structural program was revised and amended in 1978 to address its avoidance of the disadvantaged, its perceived substitution of CETA jobs for regular jobs, and its lack of job training. Public service jobs soon became more heavily oriented toward the poor, long-term unemployed, and welfare recipients. Maximum wages on CETA jobs were lowered from $7,800 to $7,200 despite rising inflation, and the length of CETA jobs was limited to eighteen months. But many jobs were discontinued because the post-1978 trainees lacked skills for professional, technical, administrative, and law enforcement jobs. Other jobs were restructured to meet the lower level of skill among new trainees (e.g., laborer aides and custodial trainees). By 1980, participants were predominantly disadvantaged; however, the new rules made sponsors less interested in job creation, and positions fell drastically (Mirengoff et al. 1982, pp. 13, 40, 194–200).

Enrollments in the structural program started high, dipped from 1976 to 1977, and peaked again in 1979. Expenditures were also high, with peaks in 1977 and 1979, but the structural programs' expenditures over GNP on average were only half the size of the countercyclical expenditures.

Third, the countercyclical program (CETA VI) began one year after the structural program. It aimed at unemployment caused by the oil crisis and boosted the whole economy rather than targeting the hard-to-employ. As the recession grew, Title VI soon soared above other programs. In 1976, Congress passed the Emergency Jobs Program Extension Act, which authorized a further expansion of Title VI from 300,000 to 600,000 jobs (Mirengoff et al. 1980, pp. 20–21).

The countercyclical program authorized prime sponsors to provide public service jobs for all unemployed workers according to unemployment rates: 25 percent of funds went to moderate, 50 percent to high, and 25 percent to severe unemployment areas. It also gave priority to veterans, disadvantaged workers, and workers no longer eligible for unemployment compensation. Requirements for placing trainees in unsubsidized employment were relaxed through waivers (Mirengoff and Rindler 1978, pp. 30, 160–61). After the 1978 Reauthorization Act redirected CETA to the poor and disadvantaged, the countercyclical and structural programs hardly differed. The 1978 amendments also tightened countercyclical program eligibility requirements from two- to four-week unemployment to ten- to twelve-week unemployment in depressed areas and reduced wages including TitleVI's special supplemental program for higher wage jobs (Mirengoff et al. 1980, pp. 20–21, 32, 204).

Enrollments in the countercyclical program became the largest in CETA, except for the transitory summer programs, and peaked in 1978 with 457,900 persons. Expenditures reached 0.28 percent of GNP in 1977 and 0.14 percent of GNP in 1979; CETA was thus the most heavily funded ALMP program since World War II, almost on a par with veterans' educational benefits.

Fourth, Youth Employment Programs continued the tradition established in the Neighborhood Youth Corps. The Summer Youth Employment Program had the highest enrollment of any single program (averaging about 800,000), but its expenditures were much lower than other CETA job creation programs because enrollees were only employed for the summer. The Youth Community Conservation and Improvement Projects began in 1977 and provided work in construction, weatherization, beautification, and other projects for out-of-school and disadvantaged teenagers. Enrollments amounted to only 28,700 in 1978 and 38,500 in 1979, and expenditures totaled about $100 million each year. The Youth Incentive Entitlement Pilot Project, also begun in 1977, guaranteed disadvantaged teenagers a twenty-hour-a-week job during the school year, and a forty-hour full-time job during the summer if they attended high school or took the General Education Development test. About 30,000 jobs were provided in 1977–78, but the project was discontinued in August 1980. Expenditures amounted to $223 million for the whole three-and-a-half-year period. In 1977, the Young Adult Conservation Corps began, like the Civilian Conservation Corps, to employ out-of-school and unemployed teenagers (actually aged sixteen to twenty-three) in wildlife, recreational, and cleanup projects. As of September 1978 27,000 youths were enrolled, and expenditures averaged about $200 million (U.S. ETRP 1978, p. 80; 1979, p. 41; 1980, pp. 35–36; 1981, p. 37).

Fifth, Community Service Jobs for Elderly Americans followed in the footsteps of Operation Mainstream in providing jobs for elderly workers, often in rural America. As a result, it had little hope of high placement rates and earnings increases.

And sixth, job creation programs included government subsidy programs for workers in the private sector. In the Help through Industrial Retraining and Employment (HIRE) program, employers gave the unemployed jobs and training, and the federal government reimbursed the employers for their training costs. HIRE-1 pledged 100,000 jobs and spent 30 million dollars in 1978. HIRE-2 received 90 million dollars (U.S. ETRP 1979, pp. 46–47, 1980, p. 43). The New Jobs Tax Credit Program (NJTC), enacted in 1977, provided a tax credit of 50 percent of the first $6,000 in wages paid to each additional fifty workers hired in excess of 102 percent of the previous year's employment level. The general tax credit program did not specifically target the disadvantaged, but an additional subsidy was available for workers earning lower wages (Haveman 1979, p. 5). The Targeted Jobs Tax Credit (TJTC) program was similar to the previous program, except that workers had to be veterans or disadvantaged workers; the subsidy fell from 50 percent to 25 percent in the second year, and the 102 percent employment threshold was lifted.

Job creation programs are more difficult to evaluate than job-training programs. While job-training evaluators do not appear concerned with substitution effects, job creation evaluators frame substitution effects as paramount. Ironically, an employee with newly acquired skills can be substituted just as easily for an employee already at work. Furthermore, "success" in job creation can mean four different things: net increase of jobs (created jobs minus substitution effects), effectiveness in reaching the disadvantaged, job placement success after public service employment, and earnings gains after program completion.

First, given that some intended or unintended fiscal substitution effects occur, the evaluation question concerns the actual net increase in jobs.[18] Early estimates of substitution effects ranged from 46 percent to 54 percent (Fechter 1975, p. 17; Snedecker and Snedecker 1978, p. 236). After the 1978 Reauthorization Act shifted CETA from highly skilled workers to disadvantaged workers, prime sponsors could no longer substitute federal for local funding to pay their existing work force. Prime sponsors had to find new jobs for unskilled workers, and, as a result, fiscal substitution rates dropped to 22 to 35 percent (Briggs 1982, p. 260). Cook et al. (1985, p. 59) even show job displacement rates de-

---

18. I am ignoring job substitution effects because studies have not estimated the effects of public job creation programs replacing private jobs or pulling people out of nonemployment into job creation programs.

clining to 18 percent and 11 percent in 1977 and 1980, based on the Brookings-Princeton Field Study (Nathan et al. 1981). As public service continued to restrict themselves to unemployed and disadvantaged entrants, substitution rates declined even further. If we conservatively assume that substitution effects ranged from 25 percent to 50 percent, public service employment programs, both structural and countercyclical, led to a reduction in the 1979 unemployment rate of about 0.4 percent to 0.6 percent. Had these programs not existed, the unemployment rate would have been higher, at 7.4 percent to 7.2 percent instead of 6.8 percent.[19] And studies of the tax credit programs show an increase of 400,000 new jobs (+/−180,000) in one year despite the slow diffusion of information to employers during the life of the NJTC program (Rehn 1982, pp. 71–72).[20] Thus, these job creation programs were large enough to have a positive impact on the overall unemployment rate.

From 1975 to 1977 only about half the structural and countercyclical enrollees were from targeted groups (Mirengoff and Rindler 1978, p. 204).[21] After the 1978 CETA Reauthorization Act retargeted the hard-core unemployed, Title IID and VI disadvantaged enrollees rose from 73 percent of CETA totals in 1978 to 86 percent and 95 percent in the next two years (Mirengoff et al. 1982, pp. 194–200; U.S. ETRP 1980, p. 270). Achieving this second goal was a considerable feat, especially when one considers that about 15 percent of the enrollees in 1979 to 1980 were veterans who needed little proof of being disadvantaged.

Transition to jobs after public service employment was a third major CETA goal. Requirements for job placement rates after

19. If I used Cook et al. (1985) fiscal substitution effect assumptions—substitution rates of 11 to 18 percent rather than 25 to 50 percent—the unemployment rate would be 8 percent rather than 6.8 percent. Although the Cook et al. study was certainly well done, I have not used their rates because their figures are the lowest reported.

20. The tax credit programs are difficult to evaluate because reporting requirements were weak, employers' decision making was ambiguous, and calculations could not be made on employer tax reductions, worker tax revenue increases, and reduced unemployment benefits. Thus, this result should be considered tentative (Rehn 1982, pp. 71–72; Haveman 1979, p. 6; U.S. ETRP 1980, p. 62).

21. The actual figures from 1975 to 1977 are: IID: 48 percent, 47 percent, 48 percent; and VI: 44 percent, 44 percent, and 66 percent.

public service employment were initially stiff in 1975, but they were quickly watered down. Consequently, job placement rates were extremely low, ranging from 18 percent to 24 percent in Title IID and 20 percent to 34 percent in Title VI for 1975 and 1977. The 1978 CETA Reauthorization Act strongly reemphasized job placement after public service employment, and most job placement rates rose above 30 percent. When inter-Title CETA transfers are excluded and thus not treated as failures, job placement rates often exceeded 40 percent for the structural and 30 percent for the countercyclical programs. These rates later increased to 50 percent and even 80 percent (Mirengoff et al. 1982, p. 303). Placement rates of 40 percent and above indicate a major achievement, given the redirection of CETA's job creation toward the disadvantaged population during a recession. Placement rates for job creation, however, are still lower than job-training rates, mainly because CETA IIBC job-training placement rates included OJT programs, which had a 63 percent job placement figure. Given high unemployment rates and a focus on the disadvantaged, placement rates for job creation programs show moderate success.

Fourth, gains in earnings after job creation are a stringent evaluative criterion. The Westat studies of fiscal 1976 showed wage gains for public service employment enrollees from $200 to $1,000 per year more than comparison groups. Later studies showed similar results, with one study showing CETA gains over control groups of in excess of $1,600. Eight studies of eleven reviewed by Barnow (1987, pp. 161–183) showed positive results for men, and ten of eleven showed positive results for women. Only the Dickinson, Johnson, and West study showed strong negative results for men, but it included enrollees who participated for less than eight days in CETA public service employment, and the pre-enrollment earnings of this study's control group differed significantly from those of the CETA group (1984, pp. 70–72; see Bishop 1989 for a general critique). Geraci looked at post-CETA earnings from 1977 to 1979 and found strong and positive wage increases for women, but "no clear pattern for men" (Barnow 1987, p. 175). Thus, in a period of rising unemployment, CETA job creation programs in comparison with control groups clearly increased female earnings in subsequent jobs but only moderately increased male earnings.

Given these results, U.S. job creation programs were successful, especially when measured against the costs of unemployment compensation and public assistance.

COMPARING U.S. AND WEST GERMAN
JOB CREATION POLICIES

Job creation in West Germany has been in effect continuously from 1950 to the present with extensive firm and union participation. Employer input in the administration of the Bundesanstalt promotes job creation because employers are more knowledgeable about job creation programs; their participation allows managers to alter the designs of job creation programs for more favorable implementation, especially short-time work programs. Union participation helps keep job creation programs honest because they monitor fiscal substitution effects and misuses of funds. By combining job creation and job maintenance program expenditures, West German funding, except for 1977, was consistently greater than the U.S. job creation policies including youth stay-in-school programs (see Figure 4–C, and Table 3, column 3). However, excluding short-time work in West Germany and youth stay-in-school programs in the United States, pure job creation expenditures were higher in America than in West Germany from 1965 to 1980. The period of U.S. leadership in job creation expenditures derives from both West Germany's low unemployment in the early 1970s and its reluctance to expand the public sector during that decade. Despite their relatively small size, however, West German job creation programs have successfully initiated 1.5 net additional jobs for every job created, and short-time work programs have created 0.25 new jobs for each job maintained.[22]

U.S. job creation did not exist until 1963 when Democratic administrations began small categorical programs for the disadvantaged and other workers. But substantial job creation programs

22. Unlike job placement and training evaluation research, job creation results do not allow a real comparison. West German results are sparse and difficult to compare to U.S. results, especially because estimates of substitution effects are not available. I can only conclude that the job creation policies had positive effects in both countries.

arrived in the 1970s, when job creation expenditures hit their highest levels, peaking in 1977. Reagan than dismantled job creation in the 1980s. Public service employment has successfully reduced unemployment rates by about 0.5 percent, targeting the disadvantaged for 50 percent of enrollments, placing 30 percent to 40 percent of its enrollees in subsequent jobs, and increasing annual earnings by $200 to $600. Despite the clamor about substitution effects, U.S. job creation has been a moderate success, outspending West Germany on pure job creation measures from 1965 to 1980.

U.S. job creation suffered from instabilities of uncertain funding and continual administrative changes. The 1978 CETA Reauthorization Act squeezed overloaded sponsors by tightening monitoring and increasing punishment for mismanagement, while simultaneously reducing the usefulness of public service employment to prime sponsors with caps on time, wages, and skills (Briggs 1982, p. 263). Ironically, U.S. job creation was the most politically vulnerable when it operated with higher economic efficiency and targeted the most needy workers (Nathan 1983, p. 49).

COMPARISONS OF WEST GERMAN AND U.S. ALMP

West Germany clearly spent more money on all ALMP policies (see Figure 9 and Table 3, column 4) and enrolled more persons per capita. Each aspect of ALMP, however, tells a different story. The dominant theme in job placement was the clear stability of West German labor market institutions and the bureaucratic confusion of U.S. programs. The West German employment service was the dock upon which many ALMP programs were secured, while U.S. institutions provided uncertain mooring and allowed programs to be buffeted by political currents. West German rates of job placement and penetration into the labor market were two to three times the U.S. rates. As further testimony to this comparison, Bundesanstalt publishes detailed monthly expenditures, while the United States issued an assortment of incomplete annual figures, indicating that the government itself was not always sure where the money was going. Few American policy analysts really understand the American ad hoc approach to institution building that weaves a maze of programs and organizations with

9. Total Active Labor Market Policy Expenditures as a Percentage of GNP in the United States and West Germany, 1950 to 1985

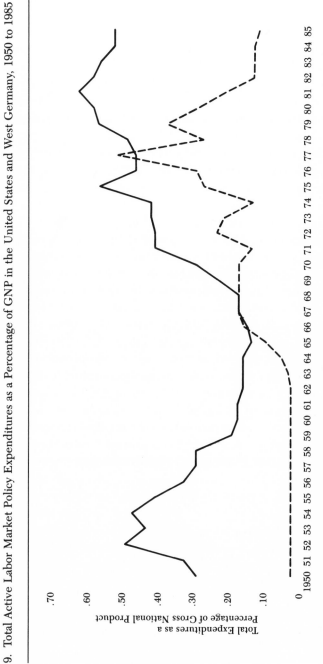

Note: ------ = Total ALMP/GNP in the United States, ——— = Total ALMP/GNP in the Federal Republic of Germany.

little concern about how they fit together. Strong West German labor market institutions predisposed legislators toward ALMP because these programs were efficient and effective.

Participation in policy making by labor and management brought greater expenditures and emphasis on high skill in West German job-training programs. Although job training was effective in both countries, placement rates in real jobs in West Germany were often more than double U.S. placement rates. Despite symbolic but powerless advisory councils, the United States either ignored labor and management in the school programs or granted control to management in the 1980s Private Industry Councils. Although job training suffered from fragmentation and lack of planning, the federal government was reluctant to endorse any meaningful system of self-administration.

However, both countries proceeded gingerly with job creation. During the oil crisis, the West Germans timidly funded pure job creation measures and boldly paid short-time work payments to hundreds of thousands of workers. The universalistic principle— the more people directly affected by the policy or problem, the more popular policy action will be—supported short-time work but mitigated against pure job creation policies because they apply to such a small fraction of the labor force. However, even short-time work was soon reined in. U.S. job creation programs peaked in the late 1970s, only to be demolished in the 1980s. Both the West German and U.S. cases suggest the limits of job creation programs in a capitalist political economy. Thus, West Germany used caution in funding its job creation programs, while the U.S. overextended and then destroyed CETA. Nonetheless, job creation effectively fought unemployment in each country.

Chapter Seven

The Passage
of ALMP Legislation
in West Germany

When the SPD entered the Grand Coalition in 1966 and the U.S. Democratic party came to power in 1960, far-reaching ALMP laws were passed in both countries. However, social demands represented by left party power alone do not explain the large differences between West German and American ALMP. To account for these differences I rely on three basic explanations. First, left party power with its particular ideologies can make a large difference in the quality and quantity of ALMP. Where participation rights are on the left's agenda, ALMP is strong; where social and legal rights dominate left party platforms, ALMP is weak. Second, a state formation process leading to fragmented legislative procedures subject to vetoes at multiple points, restricts ALMP, while more streamlined legislative procedures produce more ALMP. Status groups (e.g., veterans' associations) and special interest groups (e.g., service delivery groups) can especially fragment support for employment policies. Finally, the interpenetration of labor and management in the political and administrative process solidifies support for ALMP. And although the third point has much less ultimate effect, countries that invest heavily in evaluation research judge policy as efficient or wasteful and slow down policy development, whereas countries that pursue facilitative social research find answers to problems in particular programs, thus aiding policy development.

In presenting the following legislative case studies, I consider West German laws in this chapter and American legislation in the next. I divide the discussion of each country into two parts: the participants in social policy describe the major interest groups and their power base, and the passage of legislation presents the law-making events.

THE PARTICIPANTS IN WEST GERMAN SOCIAL POLICY

The most effective interest groups in West German social policy were the unions and employers' associations. They were connected to political parties who exerted their influence through the chancellor, the Ministry of Labor, and the Bundestag Committee for Labor. All groups funneled influence through the Bundesanstalt für Arbeit, which also had its own bureaucratic interests. In comparison to the United States, unions and employers' associations were strong, and the legislative process was disciplined. Other interests, often powerful in the United States, were extraneous in West Germany.

The DGB dominates the union movement, enrolling about 7.7 million members in sixteen, and more recently seventeen, centralized unions. The two largest are IG Metall, with 33 percent of total DGB membership (steel, automotive, and other metal workers), and the ÖTV, with 15 percent (public office, service, and transport workers).[1] IG Metall, the strongest union within the DGB, has the most radical social policy demands, but ÖTV has grown the most since World War II. The DGB and its two strongest unions have continuously promoted ALMP because ALMP supports high wages and participation rights (Markovits 1986, p. 450).[2]

1. Other unions membership figures are: IG Chemie with 8.2 percent (chemical, paper and ceramic workers); IG Bau with 5.8 percent (construction); DPG with 5.9 percent (postal workers); GdED with 4.9 percent (railways); IG Bergbau und Energie with 4.7 percent (miners and other energy workers); HBV with 4.7 percent (commerce and banking); and the remaining nine unions with less than 4 percent each. These 1983 figures are roughly the same in the mid-1970s (Markovits 1986, p. 460; Weber 1977, p. 108).

2. The White Collar Worker Federation (DAG) has about 470,000 members, but the DGB and ÖTV have three times as many white-collar workers (Weber 1977, p. 116).

Two employer federations are important for ALMP. The Federation of German Employers Associations (BDA) lobbies for business-oriented social policy and provides guidelines for its member associations in collective bargaining. The Federation of German Industry (BDI) stays out of collective bargaining and lobbies for economic policy. Large export-oriented firms dominate these federations through control of more than half the seats in the BDI and a quarter in the BDA (Webber 1983, p. 63). In good times, the BDA and BDI promoted ALMP because of their concerns about the supply of skilled workers, but in bad times they pushed for budget and tax cuts because they believed ALMP threatened investment. Employer support for ALMP helped export-oriented industries who need highly skilled labor to produce high quality exports. Employer opposition to ALMP centered on cutting job creation and reflation measures, which boosted domestic rather than export markets (Markovits 1986; Bunn 1984; Kennedy 1980).[3]

The Christian Democratic Union (CDU) and Christian Social Union (CSU) form a moderately conservative party that combines Catholics and Protestants, usually gains a plurality in the Bundestag, and constitutes a majority in the Bundesrat. Although labeled employer-dominated because it receives major support from the employer associations, the CDU/CSU has a small but important left wing of union officials.[4] The CDU exists in all states save Bavaria, which sponsors the more conservative CSU. With SPD prodding, the CDU/CSU promoted ALMP in prosperity but has favored budget cutting in recessions (Pridham 1977).

The Social Democratic Party (SPD) is the major left party; it has strong ties to blue-collar workers in the DGB. Following the SPD's

3. Two other employer associations had little impact on ALMP. The DIHT, the Association of German Chambers of Industry and Commerce, controls apprenticeship training. A "quasi-employer and employee" organization— the ZDH or Central Organization of German Handwerk—represents craft industries.

4. From 1946 to 1951, Adenauer led a drive to rid the party of its "Christian Socialist" wing, eliminating rivals such as Jakob Kaiser, Karl Arnold, Werner Hilpert, Gunter Gereke, and Joseph Müller. The CDU Ahlen Conference actually proposed a mixed economy; however, by the time Adenauer consolidated his power, the Christian Socialists were gone and only the Christian Trade Union wing remained (Burkett 1975).

decline in popularity throughout the 1950s, at the 1959 Bad Godesberg Conference the SPD redefined itself as a "people's party" (rather than a worker's party), dropped its Marxist connections, and formulated a "positive" democratic socialist program (Smith 1979). Since the 1960s, the party has assimilated large numbers of university graduates and white-collar workers. Although conflicts have occurred between the younger members (JUSO's) and the older union representatives, the party gained strength from 1960 to 1970; however, as the manufacturing sector declined and the oil crisis continued, the SPD suffered losses in the 1980s. The SPD has always promoted ALMP and participation rights (Braunthal 1983).

The Free Democratic Party (FDP), operating as a swing party in coalitions, has trouble reaching the 5 percent minimum vote necessary for Bundestag representation. The FDP peaked at 12.8 percent of the national vote in 1961 but bottomed out at 5.8 percent in 1969 (Smith 1979, pp. 126–46). In the 1950s, it represented voters with little interest in ALMP—farmers, white-collar Protestants, and the self-employed. By 1969, it had shifted considerably to concentrate on professional white-collar workers, civil servants, and the self-employed. Under the liberal leadership of Walter Scheel in the 1970s, the FDP supported social policy expansion. However, since the oil crisis and under Hans-Dieter Genscher's leadership, the FDP in coalition with the CDU/CSU shifted toward business investment and away from ALMP.

The chancellor with his coalition cabinets and ministries develops policy. Although the chancellor's office has increased its staff, it has played only a small role in policy formation (Dyson 1973). The Ministry of Labor drafts ALMP legislation under the chancellor's direction and guides it through the Committee for Labor in the Bundestag. The minister and even subsection chiefs actually participate in the private meetings of the Committee on Labor—an interpenetration of executive and legislative functions. The ministries have the time to formulate legislation because public law corporations and state governments implement most social policy (Nevil Johnson 1973, pp. 60–69, 74–97; Paterson 1982).[5]

5. Ministries played a role in ALMP legislation with the following percentages of appearances in the private Labor Committee sessions in 1968: 58 percent—labor, 13 percent—economics, 6 percent—justice, and 5 percent—finance (BT A für A Protokolls 1968).

The Bundestag Committee for Labor handles bills from the time of their first reading until they are passed or defeated. Like other Bundestag committees, it recommends amendments and tends toward mild autonomy from party and interest groups, but it has no power to pigeonhole or stop legislation (unlike U.S. congressional committees). The Labor Committee, stronger than most Bundestag committees, easily gets the attention of the Labor Ministry partly because unions are strongly represented on the committee. In the late 1970s, union members constituted 44 percent of the Labor Committee but only 14.8 percent of the Agricultural and the Youth/Health Committees and only 25.7 percent of the Economics and the Petitions Committees (Weber 1977, pp. 288–89). The "process of law-making in the Bundestag is essentially a committee process," and unions play a strong role in ALMP legislation with a near majority on the Labor Committee (Johnson 1973, p. 181, 1979).

The final quasi-state actor is the Bundesanstalt für Arbeit (Bundesanstalt). The president of the Bundesanstalt has some influence on legislation and often testifies before Labor Committee hearings. Although all postwar presidents were appointed by CDU chancellors, each president has favored the expansion of ALMP. Because the president's time is limited due to daily administrative tasks, the Administrative Council sends representatives to the Labor Committee meetings. Thus, this organization is deeply involved in legislation, promotes ALMP, and protects its bureaucratic interests.

THE FORMATION OF WEST GERMAN
ACTIVE LABOR MARKET POLICIES

The most important ALMP laws and amendments came in three waves. First, the 1952 Labor Placement and Unemployment Compensation Law demonstrates the staying power of a "work orientation" toward social policy and the SPD's concern for reestablishing participation rights. Second, the 1969 Labor Promotion Law (AFG)—the landmark legislation of the era—shows the left's push for participation rights and the interpenetration of government–bureaucracy–interest group leaders during a period of uncommon cooperation under the Grand Coalition. And third, legislation from 1974 to 1985 demonstrates the resistance of the

SPD, unions, and the Bundesanstalt to budget cuts in ALMP (see Table 4 for a summary of West German political power). In all three cases, social demands more or less prevailed over the hazards of their federal system and bureaucracy.

The 1952 Labor Placement and Unemployment Compensation Act

After 1949, unions and employers agreed that an organization similar to the Reich Office of Labor Placement and Unemployment (Reichanstalt) should be established. Although the social partners disagreed on social insurance, labor placement posed few real difficulties after the employers' federations and the

TABLE 4   *Chancellors, Ruling Coalitions, and Left Party Power in West Germany, 1949 to 1984*

Beginning Date of Coalition	Chancellor and Party	Coalition (% of vote)	Coalition Members	Left Power (% SPD in Bundestag)
9/9/49	Adenauer (CDU)	46.9	CDU/CSU FDP DP	32.6
10/10/53	Adenauer (CDU)	57.9	CDU/CSU FDP Others	32.1
10/24/57	Adenauer (CDU)	53.8	CDU/CSU DP	31.8
11/14/61	Adenauer (CDU)	58.1	CDU/CSU FDP	36.2
10/17/63	Erhard (CDU)	58.1	CDU/CSU FDP	38.1
10/26/65	Erhard (CDU)	57.1	CDU/CSU FDP	38.7
1/12/66	Kiesinger (CDU)	86.9	CDU/CSU SPD[a]	40.7
10/21/69	Brandt (SPD)	48.5	SPD FDP	41.8
12/15/72	Brandt (SPD)	54.2	SPD FDP	46.4
5/18/74	Schmidt (SPD)	48.5	SPD FDP	46.4
12/15/76	Schmidt (SPD)	50.2	SPD FDP	45.7
11/5/80	Schmidt (SPD)	53.5	SPD FDP	43.2
10/1/82	Kohl (CDU)	no vote[b]	CDU/CSU FDP	43.2
3/6/83	Kohl (CDU)	55.7	CDU/CSU FDP	38.4

Sources: These data come from Beyme (1983) and Smith (1979).
[a]This was the "Grand Coalition."
[b]The 1982 constructive vote of no confidence resulted in a change in government without a popular vote.

unions agreed on principles in January 1950. Politicians looked to the safety of a reconstructed Weimar model because West Germany was not fully sovereign until 1955, and leaders wanted to avoid the Nazi labor mobilization organizations. By passing this law, they reestablished participation rights in the labor market according the SPD plans laid during Weimar.

In mid-1950, the Ministry of Labor prepared the Christian government's draft. Initial controversy, concerning which groups would participate in self-administration, surfaced. The DGB and the employers' associations favored bipartite self-administration modeled on social insurance. They reasoned that only those organizations paying for unemployment compensation and the employment service—that is, the unions and employers—should control the administrative council in guiding policy. Contributions legitimated governance. But CDU Minister of Labor Storch proposed an administrative council of unions, employers, *and* governments. He argued that labor exchange, occupational counseling, and unemployment relief were societal programs that exceeded the narrow insurance principles of unemployment compensation. Consequently, the state should be involved at the local and national levels, especially because this same tripartite administration had worked well during Weimar (Höckerts 1980; Hentschel 1983).

In April 1951, the minister of labor presented his draft for the Federal Institute of Labor Exchange and Unemployment Insurance with tripartite administration. At the first reading in the Bundestag, the SPD complained that tripartite administration would create "authoritarian administration." The DGB and employer associations listed three main objections to the plan: the federal government appointed Bundesanstalt presidents, rather than the employers and unions electing them; the federal government approved the Bundesanstalt budget, rather than maintaining budgetary autonomy; and the federal audit office approved Bundesanstalt state and local leadership, rather than organizational independence. In the Bundestag, however, the ruling CDU/CSU-FDP-DP coalition approved the law in July 1951, with one major change: "A hearing rule" allowed the states to object to federal actions and could force the federal authorities to respond to legitimate complaints, except when the federal government had "important reasons to do otherwise." The loophole was rather large; nevertheless, the law passed the Bundestag in July 1951 and was referred to the Bundesrat for approval (Höckerts 1980).

The CDU/CSU–dominated Bundesrat approved the "one-third proportionality principle" because state interests would be promoted by their representation on the Bundesanstalt Administrative Council. But two other state concerns were at issue: The states wanted to eliminate federal power to appoint labor exchange officials and give the federal government large numbers of unqualified professionals (Beamten) who were draining state payrolls. The federal government hardly wanted these employees and proposed that the Bundesanstalt exclude all employees placed after March 31, 1949. The states and the SPD wanted the date advanced two years to March 31, 1951, so the states could transfer more employees. In the states' interests, the Bundesrat filed an objection to the Bundestag law and appealed to the mediation committee between the two legislatures. When the Bundestag defeated the Bundesrat's compromise proposal in the mediation committee, the Bundesrat retaliated by rejecting the Bundestag draft.

In November 1951, the Ministry of Labor began anew and proposed a nearly identical draft. In response, the SPD dropped their demand for bipartite parity representation but still stressed the importance of the social partners' electing the Bundesanstalt president and council members, rather than the federal government's appointing them. When the states dropped the election issue and centered on their own personnel problems, the SPD stood alone on the appointment issue. By March 1952, the Bundesrat and Bundestag agreed, accepting the new government draft with the proviso that the federal government assume most of the underqualified, soon to be pensioned, professionals (Höckerts 1980, pp. 155–61).

The main reason that the Labor Placement and Unemployment Insurance Law passed was unspoken. Although the SPD position on bipartite administration was dropped, tripartite councils and participation rights through self-administration became the bedrock of labor market policy. The new law recreated the Reichsanstalt of 1927. Thus, the work orientation toward social policy of

Weimar Social Democrats dominated policy discussions, despite the Allied occupation. Similar participation rights in bipartite planning and organizational structures were also established in pensions, health insurance, and other areas of the welfare state.[6]

The Premier ALMP Law—the Work Promotion Act of 1969 (AFG)

Just as the 1927 labor market law was the major social policy advance in the Weimar Republic, the 1969 AFG was the most important advance during the Bonn Regime. The Work Promotion Act (AFG), the ALMP law for the past two decades, is often praised, whereas the laws on vocational education, codetermination, and higher education are often criticized.

The initial impetus for ALMP came out of Swedish developments in the early 1950s that eventually reached the attention of OECD and the ILO (Rehn 1948; Meidner 1948). In the early 1960s, both organizations embraced ALMP, and OECD teams actually made visits to member countries to promote such policies (Kühl 1982, p. 252).[7] The OECD stated that the promotion of ALMP in the OECD countries "is one of the most important tasks of the Manpower and Social Affairs Committee" (OECD 1965, p. 170).

The rumblings for basic change in German ALMP and vocational education were heard from the right and the left (Offe 1975, p. 54).[8] Impatient with inadequate reforms of the 1952 law, CDU leaders in January 1966 asked the CDU/CSU–FDP coalition

6. In 1959, the Second Amendment to the AVAVG introduced bad weather and winter work payments for construction workers. Economics Minister Ludwig Erhard (CDU) introduced the bill that passed on December 7, 1959, with little debate (BT. Verhandlungen—Drucksachen: 1240, 1294, and 1392; and BT. Stenographische Bericht: pp. 1523, 2176, 3266, 4563, 4939, and 4408).

7. The ILO proposed *Agreement Number 122 on Employment Policy*, dated July 9, 1964. The OECD adopted their "Recommendation of the Council on Manpower Policy as a Means for the Promotion of Economic Growth" on May 21, 1964. National visits were recorded in the OECD series *Reviews of Manpower Policy*.

8. Examples are: DGB *Programmatic Declaration and Demands of the Trade Unions* (1959), DIHT *Basic Program of 1963*, DIHT *Ground Work and Demands of 1965*, the CDU/CSU *Leading Questions of Vocations and Training* (1962), FDP *Theses of Liberal Cultural Forms* (1962), and SPD *Statements of Training Policy* (1964).

to draft a new law. But the strongest pressure came from SPD desires to totally reform the vocational education system. The initial floor action came three months before the Grand Coalition took office. On August 30, 1966, the SPD introduced the Labor Market Adjustment Law (AMAG) as an opposition proposal to extend participation rights into the vocational education system.

The AMAG draft, the starting point for both the AFG and the Vocational Education Law, contained a number of new ALMP features: labor market research to pinpoint labor market trends, and ALMP to adjust to economic and technological change, rather than through the passive use of unemployment compensation. Active intervention obligated employers to plan for change and to notify the Bundesanstalt in case of important dismissals. Employers would also provide employees with a paid leave of absence to pursue advanced job-training and retraining programs— the work exemption clause (Blankenberg et al. 1976; Offe 1975; Althoff 1971; Hoppe 1966; BT. Verhandlungen—Drucksachen v/ 887, 1966).

Most radically, the AMAG asked for tripartite control of vocational education—the traditional reserve of the employers. The AMAG draft ran a scant twelve pages, of which thirty-nine sections are devoted to the vocational education system, three sections to labor market policy research, and five sections to the prevention of unemployment. Part of the draft addressed social rights to education and employment, but the major sections proposed new participation rights through federal, state, and local vocational education committees. The tripartite committees of fifteen employee, fifteen employer, and fifteen government representatives would replace employer dominance in apprenticeship training. The draft focused on procedural tasks of tripartite regulation and ignored the substance of vocational education. This proposal for far-reaching participation rights eventually became the SPD's bargaining chip to push the CDU/CSU toward a more "active" labor market policy (BT. Verhandlungen—Drucksachen v/887, 1966, p. 7; Kühl 1982, p. 253).

But the political situation was not yet ripe. Six months later on March 10, 1967, the Bundestag passed the Seventh Change in the Labor Placement and Unemployment Insurance Law and raised unemployment benefits and assistance by 7.5 percent (Nahamowitz 1974, p. 158). Amendments were now both tiresome and awkward. But after the SPD proposed the AMAG draft under Erhard's conservative government, the fate of ALMP drastically improved with Kiesinger's Grand Coalition.[9] The new coalition brought the SPD into the government when the SPD wanted to show its ruling capabilities to the electorate. The subsequent events for passage of the AFG took place in the Ministry of Labor and the Bundestag Committee for Labor.

The Grand Coalition's government appointed Hans Katzer (CDU) the new minister of labor. He replaced the passive approach of the Erhard government's economic policy with an activist orientation. Minister of Labor Katzer pushed ALMP and controlled the ministry's bureaucracy to conform to his wishes. The bulk of the labor ministry personnel had been insurance-oriented, especially in Division II, which dealt with labor market policy, unemployment insurance, and foreign workers. These bureaucrats favored incremental adjustments of unemployment insurance policies, while the political economy generalists in planning, Division I, favored ALMP. Although these two sections often fought over policy direction, Labor Minister Katzer sided with the planning division and came down hard on the insurance specialists. The Beamten State Secretary, Kattenstroth, and the head of the basic planning in Division I directed a "personnel politics" strategy that gradually replaced insurance lawyers with labor economists in several sections: basic, planning, and some substantive. The resulting organizational conflict prompted discussions to explain the minister's view and massage hard feelings. These replacements reoriented the ministry toward an active view of labor market policy and set the stage for drafting a fundamental change in policy, not just another amendment (Blankenberg et al. 1976, p. 260).[10]

9. The two largest parties, the CDU/CSU and SPD, formed the Grand Coalition from December 1966 to October 1969. They represented 86.9 percent of the votes cast in the 1965 election.

10. This is a good example of the executive taking active instead of incremental change by controlling the bureaucracy. Such manipulation of the bureaucracy rarely takes place in the United States; instead, bureaucracies spend their time opposing the executive or competing with each other. The German case shows that executive action can overcome incrementalism and pure bureaucratic interest.

The Labor Ministry also created a special section to draft the new labor market and vocational education laws. The new special section leader recognized that a "comprehensive solution was not possible and could fail" because of the complicated division of responsibilities in vocational education between employers, the Ministry of Economics, and the states. He separated the labor market and vocational educational drafts into different bills. Ministry officials publicly backed the section leader with two main arguments. First, although labor market policy was centralized into one organization (the Bundesanstalt), vocational education reform constituted a "brawling situation" that would require cooperation from federal, state, local, and private organizations. Second, labor market funds were regularly derived from joint worker-employer contributions, while vocational education funds accrued in varying amounts from the several states and individual employers. Thus, the ministry wrote a limited vocational education law and a more far-reaching labor market policy law. The separation was crucial because vocational reform proved a messy, emotional, and largely unresolved issue (Blankenberg et al. 1976, pp. 261–62).

Labor Minister Katzer introduced the AFG draft in the Bundestag on December 13, 1967. The draft encouraged spending funds on active job training, job mobility, and some job creation programs, rather than unemployment compensation. Mobility promotion would avoid structural and cyclical changes in the economy. The law made advanced training and retraining a right rather than a government-controlled privilege. But the AFG draft clearly fell short of integrating basic vocational training under participation rights, a measure the SPD had pushed in the AMAG draft (Kühl 1982, pp. 251–52; BT. Verhandlungen—Drucksachen v/2291, 1967).

After the first reading, the AFG draft was passed to the Committee for Labor, which held twenty-six sessions during the next year to rework the draft. Aldolf Müller (CDU, Remscheid), the head of the Labor Committee and a leading member of the CDU labor wing, strongly advocated ALMP:

The goal was to get away from a labor market policy that hindered economic development, and to arrive at a labor market policy that adjusted to structural change. If one wants to make ALMP, one must not only be able to activate the traditional policies of the Bundesanstalt, by then the unemployment has already occurred, but rather before unemployment occurs, institute an improvement of economic structure in affected areas and create new jobs as well as promote qualifications of workers with retraining in their union. (Blankenberg et al. 1976, p. 263)

Müller and Labor Minister Katzer agreed on the value and conception of ALMP, perhaps because they both held leadership positions on CDU social committees and were politically compatible. The other twelve CSU/CDU members of the Labor Committee were also CDU/CSU social committee members. The SPD, holding an equal number of seats on the committee, not only supported ALMP but also wanted to extend participation rights into vocational education.

Katzer and Müller followed a two-part strategy for their AFG draft. First, they actively shared information: the Labor Committee quickly communicated hearing information to the ministry, and then Katzer's ministers contributed their expertise to changes, appendices, and amendments. Although ministries may assume a stewardship role for drafts in the weaker committees, it was a rare action in the Labor Committee. Second, Müller worked hard to create a consensus between the uneasy allies in the Grand Coalition. Positions and demands—called *Nebenkriegsschauplatze* or arenas of the next war—had to be presented in writing well in advance so that they were clear and would not present surprises or emotional reactions. Predictability was necessary because the contentious vocational education reform bill was going through the Labor Committee at that time (Blankenberg et al. 1976, p. 264).

In December 1967, the AMAG and AFG drafts sat before the Labor Committee. The twelve-page AMAG draft, introduced by the SPD before the Grand Coalition as an opposition draft, asked for major changes in the nation's apprenticeship system. The 243-page AFG draft, proposed by the CSU/CDU and technically by the SPD as a coalition draft, was limited to ALMP and unemployment insurance.

The SPD's position in the Labor Committee was awkward. Given West Germany's strong party discipline, the SPD members would have trouble opposing the Grand Coalition and the AFG, especially since the SPD desperately wanted to show competence in governing, rather than political intractability after being out of power since the Weimar Republic. But the SPD also supported the AMAG draft as an opposition bill and an extension of participation rights. The CDU had split the AMAG draft into two laws, which left that draft straddling two forums. The SPD had no hope of passing the AMAG over the wishes of the CDU/CSU, given the political context of the Grand Coalition. Nevertheless, the SPD gingerly supported the AMAG proposal and used it as a wedge to amend the AFG draft toward their own conceptions of ALMP.

The FDP opposition, without a labor wing, opposed most SPD proposals. However, intimidated by the Grand Coalition, the FDP had difficulty defining its role. Schmidt (FDP, Kempten) presented the FDP position in the hearings, which the other FDP representative rarely attended. Following typical FDP strategy, Schmidt searched unsuccessfully for an opportune issue. Later Schmidt and the FDP made controversial claims, based on private discussions in 1966 with the CDU, that they initiated the AFG (BT. Stenographische Bericht 7410, Dec. 13, 1967; FDP 1969, pp. 12–15).

Policy experts discussed the main points of ALMP at the March 6, 1968, public hearings. Dr. Rudolph Meidner from Sweden testified for the AFG bill, which showed the external influence from Sweden. The next day, the interest groups presented their positions on funding and self-administration, issues vital to participation rights.[11]

The unions asked why a general societal benefit—retraining, advanced training, and job creation—should be financed by the social partners. Musa of the DGB stated:

In reply to this [training] question one may refer to the fact that the Bundesanstalt and previously the Reichanstalt . . . have performed vocational training measures from the beginning. But simply from this fact, one should not conclude that it is justifiable to burden contribution payers with a task that is political and therefore ought to be financed by the general public, that is, the totality of state citizens. Thus, the DGB

11. The research program in labor markets was precluded from debate by Bundesanstalt president Anton Sabel (CDU), a former chair of the Labor Committee from 1953 to 1957. In February 1967, he announced that the Institute of Labor and Occupational Research would begin operations on April 1, 1967.

objects to the AFG draft based on constitutional questions. (BT. A für A, Protokoll 56, 1968, p. 6)

The employers' associations questioned the DGB's conception of financing vocational education and objected to their mention of a job-training tax. Assessor Weber (BDA) and Dr. Uthmann (BDI) both claimed that job training was adequately funded from Bundesanstalt coffers and that employers could handle other training needs (BT. A für A, Protokoll 56, 1968, pp. 81–82, 171–74). Expanding the tax base for job training would mean inroads into the employer-dominated vocational education system. Employers and the CDU opposed this, and the SPD did not push for it in the hearings.[12]

Concerned about funding issues, the Administrative Council of the Bundesanstalt was uneasy about vocational education being financed by the social partners rather than the whole society, the use of unemployment reserve funds for ALMP, and vocational education's status as a formal right rather than a discretionary claim. However, despite uneasiness about funding, job retraining became a social right, and the social partners assumed funding for society (Blankenberg et al. 1976, pp. 264–66).

Another issue concerned the integrity of self-administration under the AFG. The Council of Economic Experts provoked this issue in their annual report—*Expansion and Stability* (Sachverständigenrat 1966/67). The council recommended changing the Bundesanstalt into an Office for Employment and Structural Policy that would make central management essential and eliminate self-administration (Kühl 1982, p. 254). The unions and employers strongly defended self-administration. In the hearings, DGB spokesman Musa, also a member of the Bundesanstalt Administrative Council, stood firm on the "original tasks of labor administration" (BT. A für A, Protokoll 56, 1968, p. 4). Walter Henkelmann, the DGB head of social and labor market policy, feared changes in the "proven" form of self-administration, even though the CDU/CSU claimed that "self-administration for the

12. In 1952, countering union arguments for bipartite bargaining, the CDU Minister of Labor argued that the Bundesanstalt involved societywide benefits. In 1968, ironically, the CDU argued against these societywide benefits at the AFG hearings.

most part would be maintained." He said that "self-administration will be seriously damaged through the strengthened supervisory law, shrinkage of Bundesanstalt sovereignty, far-reaching removal of discretionary power over resources, and weakening of discretion over delegated tasks" (Henkelmann 1967, p. 32). The issue of self-administration brought the Bundesanstalt Administrative Council into action to guard the status quo. Unified employer and union representatives opposed any alteration of the balance or amount of power involved. Their fears about changes in Bundesanstalt centralization and federal control were allayed by Labor Minister Katzer's (CDU) assurances, especially because Katzer himself sat on an Administrative Council of the Bundesanstalt. Thus, the SPD and CDU/CSU completely rejected changes suggested by the Council of Economic Experts.

However, the clear union and employer positions at the hearing were matched by an opaque SPD position. The SPD expressed little desire to move on a broader financing of the Bundesanstalt. In fact, DGB spokesman Musa stated that the SPD's AMAG draft contained the same financing assumptions as the CDU's AFG draft (BT. A für A, Protokoll 56, 1968, p. 6). What the SPD wanted on financing was not clear. But the SPD effectively promoted labor market research, training rights, strike neutrality for the Bundesanstalt, and the communication pledge requiring employers to report dismissals. The employers, of course, objected to both the communication pledge and training rights. With the work exemption, under which trainees would be paid regular wages, the SPD was not so successful. Training support would come from the Bundesanstalt, not the employers, and would be roughly equivalent to unemployment pay, not the 120 percent of unemployment benefits the DGB demanded (BT. A für A, Protokoll 56, 1968, p. 6). Thus, the SPD supported and obtained some points, but was vague about its financing demands.

While emotions raged on the vocational education and codetermination bills, the AFG was read for the second and third times on May 13, 1969. Four factors contributed to the "memorable and agreeable unanimity" of the AFG's passage on June 20, 1969 (Kühl 1982, p. 259). First, many leaders interpenetrated the institutions involved in influencing legislation—the Labor Committee, the Bundesanstalt, the Bundestag, political parties, and labor unions. Interpenetration increased cooperation on labor market legislation because leaders had worked together in many other contexts—social legislation, social policy implementation, collective bargaining, and coalition bargaining—and realized that such association furthered their group's interests; as a result, they worked better together.

Committee Chair Müller was an example.

> I was very much impressed by [Ruhr area structural change] because I was the DGB president in North-Rhine-Westphalia, and we were very strongly confronted with the structural crisis in the Ruhr. But also as a participant in the Administrative Council of the State Bundesanstalt— I was at that point in time in a crucial point of negotiations with the representing employer chairman and delegate chairman of the Administrative Council—I can especially understand the problem in the Ruhr and I knew which things would be important. (Blankenberg et al. 1976, p. 263)

Thus, Aldolf Müller was steering the AFG draft through the Committee of Labor, while simultaneously holding positions as president of the North-Rhine-Westphalia DGB, member of a Bundesanstalt Administrative Council, and member of the CDU Social Committee. He held legislative, bureaucratic, party, and interest group positions simultaneously. DGB spokesman Musa and Minister Katzer had similar overlapping memberships. And to a lesser extent, 44.4 percent of the members of the Bundestag Labor Committee had some overlap because they belonged to unions.

Second, bureaucrats cooperated in forming policy because positions in the ministry are career steps for entering politics, especially the Bundestag. In 1976, over 60 percent of all Bundestag members had been civil servants or interest group leaders. Civil servants are represented in Bundestag at a rate of ten times their proportion in the population at large. West German civil servants can be elected to the Bundestag without resigning and can receive a six-week leave of absence with full pay to campaign for office—unlike American public servants.[13] Thus, the interpene-

13. Other benefits include full pension credits and normal promotions during the legislative leave of absence. Thus, civil servants are eligible for civil service and parliamentary pensions—double dipping. Conflict of interest questions are handled by the Domestic Affairs Committee, 80 percent of which are civil servants (Conradt 1978, p. 130).

tration of the bureaucracy and legislature is encouraged (Conradt 1978, pp. 129–30). Lower-level section chiefs in ministries gain experience in private committee hearings with politicians. But more important, bureaucrats who aspire to political office need the help of many politicians with whom they work on the committees. Wise counsel would recommend that bureaucrats court rather than alienate politicians. This interpenetration of West German ministry and the legislative functions produces legislative cooperation through career convergence, while the separation of bureaucracy and legislature in the U.S. system promotes adversarial relationships through career divergence.

Third, the executive controlled the values and orientation of the bureaucracy. Although Katzer's "personnel politics" should not be overrated as a cause of the AFG, he did reorient the Ministry of Labor. A similar bureaucratic intervention occurred during Weimar with the "strengthening professionals." Both interventions were effective. Furthermore, the chancellor can also control the bureaucracy by temporarily retiring top civil servants. Although political purges have been implemented in the United States, changing the basic values of an organization without firing bureaucrats is a much more difficult task. The West German executive can do it.

Fourth, and most important, the AFG garnered left party support. The SPD insistence on participation rights has strongly affected the character of West German social policy, beginning with codetermination in the 1950s and 1970s. The AMAG draft, with provisions for tripartite councils administering vocational education, is a good example of threatening participation rights to build pressure for more advanced programs. In addition, these SPD demands established a firm direction for social policy; the SPD knew where it wanted to go. At the very least, the advocacy of participation rights in the AMAG constituted a bargaining chip that pushed the CDU/CSU toward effective ALMP. Rep. Behrendt (SPD) suggests this tactical view by admitting that "the AMAG draft was only a *skeleton law*" (BT. Stenographische Bericht 7421, Dec. 13, 1967).

The Defense of ALMP, 1974 to 1985

When the oil crisis hit in 1974, federal subsidies to the BAA doubled and accounted for one-third of the federal deficit. During this period of severe budgetary constraints and fair weather coalitions, West German social demands showed their strength in protecting the core of ALMP programs, which were ultimately crippled in the United States. The SPD's rearguard retreat, of course, disappointed and embittered some, but its actions constitute a success, given its occurrence in a politically contentious democracy rather than a more consensual state like Sweden or Japan. Thus, the resistance to cuts in ALMP represents an important and clear difference from the United States.

As the Bundesanstalt deficits increased, the FDP demanded that the SPD transform retraining allowances into loans, restrict retraining to the unemployed, and expand the "reasonableness criteria"—the range of jobs an unemployed person could be compelled to take or face losing his or her unemployment benefits (that is, how much of a pay cut, status loss, or geographical move from home would a worker have to suffer). Labor Minister Arendt (SPD) agreed to restrict retraining to the unemployed but resisted transforming allowances into loans. The DGB and many in the SPD also wanted to abolish the civil servants' exemption from Bundesanstalt contributions, but the FDP opposed this move.

The SPD felt that reducing Bundesanstalt subsidies was necessary to appease the FDP and satisfy lenders financing the federal deficit. The Labor Ministry and FDP drafted the Budgetary Structure Law with cuts in training allowances (but avoiding loans), restrictions on job-training enrollments, and expansions of the reasonableness criteria. The unions reluctantly accepted the cuts (Webber 1982a, 1982b; *Die Zeit*, Sept. 5, 1975; BAA 1979; *Süddeutsche Zeitung*, Jan. 28, 1976).

Observers expected the 1976 Bundesanstalt deficit to exceed 12 billion DM, but it amounted to only 0.29 billion DM; the cuts from the Budgetary Structure Law of 1975 produced more savings than anticipated. With rising unemployment, Bundesanstalt surpluses looked incongruous with a 56 percent reduction in retraining enrollments in 1977–78. Furthermore, workers appealed the violations of the reasonableness criteria to the social courts. Despite opposition by employers, the Bundesanstalt responded with new decrees, protecting workers against occupational downgrading for six months before facing refusal penalties.

Meanwhile, the Labor Ministry heard employers' complaints about job vacancies despite unemployment. An Infratest study supported these claims by identifying many unemployed who were clearly avoiding work.[14] In response, the Labor Ministry with full FDP support presented the Fifth Change in the AFG with new reasonableness criteria; it passed in July 1979. The bill funded higher training allowances for skilled positions with shortages but failed to increase total ALMP expenditures or Bundesanstalt contribution rates. Although the unions and the left-SPD could not convince Chancellor Schmidt to expand ALMP, they were able to give the more union-oriented administrative council the power to implement refusal penalties. In October, the law was supplemented by both a Bundesanstalt decree with new reasonableness criteria and local tripartite committees to hear complaints about penalties. The federal government then increased retraining subsidies (by 25 percent) and job creation (by 65 percent), along with an overall increase in Bundesanstalt spending.

When the rebound to the first oil shock proved sluggish and the second oil shock hit in 1979, ALMP was again put on the cutting block. ALMP was the largest part of the Bundesanstalt budget, and the Bundesanstalt deficits were a large component of the federal deficit. These new conditions offered the ever opportunistic FDP a sure avenue of escape from the coalition's mounting social and financial burdens. Thus, the following discussion of the Labor Market Consolidation Act is inextricably connected to the budgetary process and coalition politics.

The brief spurt of economic growth in 1978 made 1979's disastrous slowdown in economic growth stand out. The balance of payments slumped into deficit in 1979–80, while interest rates were rising instead of falling.[15] Fearing currency decline, the Bundesbank tightened its monetary policy and encouraged budget cutting. At the same time, deficits in the labor market's program ballooned and pushed the total federal deficit to new heights, although declining tax revenues also played a major role. Chancellor Schmidt had just slipped through the 1980 election, mainly on his reputation for "managing the economy," before the

14. The Infratest study was an independent survey. Infratest also studied internal SPD communications from 1977 to 1978 (Braunthal 1983, p. 56).

15. The 1974 oil crisis forced heavy governmental borrowing. When further funds were needed from 1979 to 1981, financial markets were already very crowded, causing interest rates to rise.

full force of the recession dampened the usual postelection SPD-FDP honeymoon. On the heels of the election, a tripartite commission with FDP and SPD members was set up in the Labor Ministry to find spending abuses in the Bundesanstalt, but the savings they imagined evaporated when only 200,000 to 300,000 DM in overspending was uncovered. More painful cuts would have to be found.

As a result of cumulative government borrowing since 1974 for countercyclical employment policy, the state met what the CDU/CSU called "the psychological limits of deficit spending" (Webber 1982a). By May 1981, federal subsidies for the Bundesanstalt reached 8 billion DM, up from 3.65 billion in December, while only 2 billion had been budgeted. The Schmidt government resisted reflation and set up a debate between its ministers. Finance Minister Matthöfer (SPD) said that the state's ability to control the economy must be assessed more modestly; consequently, the state could no longer guarantee full employment (Matthöfer 1981a, 1981b). Labor Minister Ehrenberg (SPD) defended ALMP based on the preservation of the social safety net. However, Chancellor Schmidt had already set up Finance Minister Matthöfer as his budget-cutting pointman. Matthöfer stated his case forcefully: the economy must be restructured, and this required "less energy consumption, more environmental protection, and more jobs for highly skilled employees. This means that the portion of public and private consumption of GNP must return to previous levels, that is, social consumption must decrease" (*Die Zeit*, Sept. 18, 1981, p. 9).

Meanwhile, the DGB, IG Metall, and the left wing of the SPD were demanding increased employment programs. The SPD in summer 1982 wanted an additional tax surcharge on corporations, employees (including civil servants), and private businesses to finance social and labor market policy. The DGB criticized the budget cuts as "unbalanced and negative in terms of labor market policy" and a sure path to "a dead end of decreased growth, less employment, and increased unemployment costs" (*Süddeutsche Zeitung*, Sept. 3, 1981, p. 1).

A serious rift was growing between the SPD and DGB. At a rally in Stuttgart, IG-Metall leader Franz Steinkühler said the government was cutting benefits like a "harvesting machine."

SPD Finance Minister Matthöfer and Steinkühler exchanged biting letters in public. At a DGB demonstration of 700,000 workers in Stuttgart on November 7, 1981, Steinkühler and other leaders soundly criticized the SPD-FDP budget cutting.[16] Two days later the DGB leaders met with Brandt (SPD), the next day with Schmidt, and later even with CDU leader Kohl. DGB head Heinz-Oscar Vetter presented an alternative course of action: decrease interest rates to spur investment; shorten the work week to increase jobs; increase spending on energy, environment, and housing; control prices; and implement a temporary tax surcharge on higher incomes. DGB leaders threatened a series of massive demonstrations "unless there is some government policy for wage earners" (*Die Zeit*, Dec. 18, 1981; *TWIG*, Nov. 13, 1981, Dec. 11, 1981).

Within the SPD, Bundestag representative Coppik (SPD) violently opposed cuts in social policy and distributed a letter to members proposing the reorganization of the party.[17] Even Willy Brandt cautioned that the SPD would suffer an identity crisis if it compromised too much with the FDP. Chancellor Schmidt, especially at the yearly conventions, was having difficulty controlling the party, not only because of the cuts mandated by coalition compromises but also because of Schmidt's managerial rather than democratic leadership style.

The FDP declared that the economists and the general public were on its side. In numerous asides to the press, Economics Minister Lambsdorff (FDP) claimed that a "Trendwende" or "basic change in course" had occurred.[18] The new trend required more reliance on markets, more individual initiative, and less government spending. Hans-Dieter Genscher, the FDP party leader, called for a renewed emphasis on the private sector in all

16. See IG Metall *Metall Nachrichten* Pamphlet Number 1, dated Sept. 30, 1981, for the harvester reference. Matthöfer replied directly to Steinkühler on Oct. 28, 1981, and Steinkühler retorted unrepentantly on Nov. 5, 1981, and in a speech at the Nov. 7, 1981, rally in Stuttgart.

17. As a result of these and other actions, SPD-Whip Peter Glotz proposed Coppik's expulsion from the party. Other expulsions occurred at this time concerning nuclear weapons (*Die Zeit*, Dec. 11, 1981, p. 6). But Coppik later left the party on his own.

18. SPD-Whip Glotz disagreed: "Count Lambsdorff has burdened the discussions over the budget with a general discussion of what he has called a 'trend reversal'. His discussion is rather vague" (*Süddeutsche Zeitung*, Sept. 1, 1981).

aspects of the economy and claimed that "this will be the best employment policy." More specifically, the FDP demanded cuts in ALMP (especially job creation programs), unemployment insurance, and social policy in general. To control unemployment insurance, they wanted tighter "reasonableness requirements" to put more pressure on the unemployed to accept lower-status jobs, longer penalty periods for workers who quit their jobs, and longer working-time requirements to qualify for basic benefits. Of course, this precluded the SPD tax surcharge. The FDP demands had leverage because the FDP threatened to destroy the coalition (*Die Zeit*, Aug. 7, 1981, p. 3; Sept. 13, 1981, p. 10; *Süddeutsche Zeitung*, Sept. 3, 1981).

The CDU/CSU, excluded from the ruling coalition, called for even greater budget cuts. Gerhard Stoltenberg (CDU) criticized the "false estimates of the real burdens of expenditure laws" and presented the party's investment position:

In 1970, investment constituted 28% of GNP, while social insurance expenditures were about 16%. In 1981, investment had decreased to 24%, and social insurance increased to 21%. . . . We can only solve the economic and employment problem of the future if this trend is turned around. (*Die Zeit*, Sept. 4, 1981, pp. 6–8)

Helmut Kohl (CDU) pushed for a free market economy; Franz Joseph Strauß (CSU) had already stated the need for a "radical correction of the country's course" and had rejected the "false cure" of labor market policy (Strauß 1977). In the Bundestag, CDU Rep. George derided the Bundesanstalt budget as a "new Nuremberg funnel" for spending that fed "a barrel without bottom" despite attempts to set limits (BT Stenographische Bericht 1981, p. 2,724).[19]

In the coalition budgetary meetings, sometimes referred to as Operation 82, the SPD and FDP battled over the Bundesanstalt budget. Finance Minister Matthöfer claimed that cuts must come where the federal budget had increased the most—unemployment insurance and ALMP. The FDP presented their savings catalog of 3.5 billion DM, including cuts in ALMP and unemployment in-

19. George refers to the medieval story of the Nuremberg *Trichter* in which instructors poured knowledge into the heads of rather dull students by the use of a funnel. The present-day Bundesanstalt is located in Nuremberg and is funneling public funds for another seemingly useless purpose.

surance, both of which were strongly supported by employers. With the coalition under extreme duress and Lambsdorff proclaiming a "trend reversal," which could be interpreted as either a change in policy or a change in coalition partners, a shaky compromise was reached in September. Although partial and fragile and requiring some later renegotiation, the compromise provided enough so that the Labor Market Consolidation Act could be passed in two months. With a parry toward serious cuts in the social safety net, the SPD gave up its employment program and special tax surcharges and accepted cuts in unemployment insurance, cuts in ALMP, and increases in the unemployment insurance contribution rate. Making the compromise seem sleazy, the FDP also obtained important subsidies and protections for their middle- and upper-class constituencies. Herbert Wehner (SPD) said that the proposals of the "Count of Economics" were "perverse and unreasonable" because they punished the unemployed with "the Count's trend reversal" (*Die Zeit*, Sept. 18, 1981, p. 10). The compromise allowed the Labor Market Consolidation Act to pass on December 22, 1981, and a budget agreement passed in January.

After the severe Bundesanstalt cutbacks in the new law and lowered subsidies for the Bundesanstalt, deficits no longer plagued the federal budget. But in 1982, unemployment rose to new and unprecedented levels, causing the DGB to propose a multiyear 30 to 40 billion DM job creation program. When unemployment finally reached 7.4 percent in December 1982, the FDP and Schmidt began to talk about a new job creation program, despite the FDP's previous opposition to such measures. Wolfgang Mischnick (Bundestag chair, FDP) and Hans-Guenter Hoppe (Bundestag vice-chair, FDP) even publicly discussed possible measures and financing (*TWIG*, Jan. 15, 1982).

In February 1982, Chancellor Schmidt proposed a job creation and economic stimulus program of 12.5 billion DM financed by a 13 percent hike in the value-added tax. Schmidt, staking the coalition on ALMP, connected the plan to a vote of confidence in the Bundestag. Despite winning handily, Schmidt saw his bill blocked by the CDU/CSU in the Bundesrat under their power to control taxes (*TWIG*, Feb. 11, 1982). The CDU/CSU would not accept increases in the value-added tax.

While the job creation program remained under less than enthusiastic consideration in the Bundesrat, the Bundesanstalt proposed and the Schmidt government approved tightened "reasonableness criteria"—an eight-week suspension of unemployment compensation for workers refusing a reasonably downgraded job and an outright suspension of unemployment compensation for workers refusing a second time (*TWIG*, March 12, 1982). These restrictions bought FDP support for a value-added/income tax tradeoff and the chancellor's job creation program. But the employers' associations opposed the job creation bill, especially the value-added tax, because it would raise the prices. The CDU/CSU–dominated Bundesrat rejected the value-added tax increase for the second time on April 30, 1982, and the job creation portion of the bill was sent to die without funding clauses in the mediation committee.

When the CDU/CSU denied the value-added tax increase and the FDP blocked other tax increases, the SPD had a job creation plan financed by thin air. Despite Schmidt's pleas for moderation, the SPD yearly convention made matters worse by proposing a massive job creation proposal with new taxes and increased government borrowing. The FDP was furious, and party leader Genscher denounced the proposal. Given this disagreement and continuous budgetary bickering, the SPD/FDP coalition continued to slide downhill, with further nudges from the indictment of FDP Economics Minister Lambsdorff on corruption charges in the Flick campaign contribution affair; corruption charges pinned on the DGB with the Neue Heimat (New Home Housing Cooperative) scandal; and SPD losses in state elections, especially heavy in Chancellor Schmidt's own state of Hamburg. After the death of the job creation program, the DGB and the left wing of the SPD were disgusted with the FDP and Schmidt's managerial style of politics. Without surprise, except for precise timing, the coalition collapsed in September 1982.

The new chancellor, Helmut Kohl, cut social expenditures but did not dismantle ALMP programs. His cuts involved unemployment benefits, Bundesanstalt pension payments for unemployed workers, health insurance costs, and delays in cost-of-living increases for pensioners. Kohl said that the cuts were needed to reinforce the fiscal foundations of the social safety net and that sacrifices must be made. To create jobs, he proposed tax cuts for industry and individuals, a reprivatization plan for such government-owned industries as Lufthansa, and other investment programs. Kohl's Minister of Labor Blüm stated that "full employment is the most important social-political task," but ALMP was not the policy to alleviate unemployment:

Social politics only has a floor when everyone has work. Unemployment radiates in the social security system. . . . The means for job creation cannot be consumed, therefore, we need policies that make investment possible and get at the roots of unemployment. (Blüm 1983, p. 231)

The DGB protested that government-induced increases in investment were only creating more unemployment despite increased profits. But the employers supported the investment policies of the new government, and some employers even included "election provisions" in collective bargaining contracts—that is, automatic wage cutbacks if the SPD won.

After Kohl and the CDU/CSU won the election, they continued an investment-oriented policy. However, because teenage unemployment was high, Kohl also attempted to increase apprenticeship slots for the young and ease hiring and firing regulations for employers (*TWIG*, Sept. 14, 1984). As unemployment continued to climb to 10.6 percent in January 1985, the Bundesanstalt ironically recorded a modest surplus.[20] The appearance of surpluses began a rather serious intra-CDU battle between Chancellor Kohl and Minister of Labor Blüm. Blüm, who came from the union wing of the CDU, wanted surpluses spent on ALMP, while Kohl was giving in to FDP demands that surpluses be given back to the employers. Blüm even met with Franz-Joseph Strauß, Kohl's archenemy within the CDU/CSU, to advance his case for ALMP. Although the feud was eventually patched, it shows that Blüm does not see investment as a cure-all for unemployment and that technical progress may destroy more jobs than it creates (*Der Spiegel* 1985, p. 20; Blüm 1978).

Despite considerable turmoil, the SPD and unions were moderately successful in their rearguard fight against cuts as ALMP remained at levels higher than ever reached in the United States.

20. Bundesanstalt finances improved because the long-term unemployed disappeared from the rolls and the unemployed young never got on them.

Chapter Eight

The Passage
of ALMP Legislation
in the United States

Why did weaker ALMP laws pass in the United States? This chapter continues the political analysis of ALMP by showing how social demands in the United States gave way to fragmented state structures. I begin with the actors in social policy, proceed to the passage of important ALMP laws, and end with a comparison of ALMP politics in both countries.

THE PARTICIPANTS IN U.S. SOCIAL POLICY

The main actors in U.S. social policy include the major interest groups, special interest groups, political parties in the legislature and committees, the president, and the executive bureaucracy. Unlike West German groups, American groups interact in a highly fragmented political environment.

The AFL-CIO trade union federation and the UAW have supported labor market policy and a moderately left social policy since 1945. The AFL-CIO has been called "the best lobby on the Hill," and in coalitions with civil rights and other groups it has been among the strongest forces for progressive social policy (Wilson 1979, p. 79; Keller 1982a, 1982b).[1] Although trade union

---

1. Progressive trade unionism is somewhat counterbalanced by opportunistic unions such as the Teamsters—the country's largest—and PATCO, who bargains

membership as a percentage of nonagricultural workers has declined over the years, trade unions are a powerful force for ALMP because unions contribute to political campaigns, lobby for ALMP laws, give candidates a grass-roots organization, and represent a large, but unpredictable, voting bloc (Wilson 1979; Rosenbloom 1982).

Three national employer groups are important in national legislation.[2] The National Association of Manufacturers (NAM) has consistently opposed trade unionism in the plant and in legislatures. Its National Industrial Council (founded in 1907), with 250 federations of national, state, and local associations, is a "strike force for business" that shapes and mobilizes business opinion on legislation (Derber 1984, pp. 105–16).[3] Once more moderate and slightly more powerful than NAM, the Chamber of Commerce has occasionally supported ALMP proposals. In 1978, the Chamber of Commerce expanded its political activities by co-sponsoring political action committees and creating the National Chamber Alliance for Politics.[4] Business Roundtable was formed in 1969 out of employer concern about rising construction costs and the deteriorating position of business. It consists of high-level executives who work through special task forces and strategic, personal lobbying. Each employer group has most often fought against ALMP (Derber 1984, pp. 107–8; Loomis 1983, pp. 175–86; Ornstein and Elder 1978, pp. 136–38).[5]

Two status groups are important—racial and veteran organizations. Black groups are represented by the NAACP, the Urban

---

with the Republicans, such as Nixon and Reagan, but rarely took strong stands on social policy.

2. Employer federations are weak in the United States. Often ignored in policy, employer federations only exist in a few industries (Derber 1984, pp. 83–89).

3. The National Association of Manufacturers, the oldest employer group, founded in 1895, has a membership of 13,000 manufacturing firms, a staff of 220 persons, and an annual budget in the range of $5 million.

4. The U.S. Chamber of Commerce, founded in 1912, has 2,700 local chambers, 1,300 trade and professional associations, 8,400 firms, a Washington staff of 500 persons, and an annual budget of $50 million.

5. Other employer organizations are either specialized or research oriented. The National Right to Work Committee concentrates on preventing union organization. The Council for Economic Development and the Conference Board primarily deal with research.

League, the Congress on Racial Equality (CORE), among other groups. Weak in the early 1950s, these organizations gained a foothold in national policy making as the number of black congressional representatives grew from two to eighteen in the House. The Urban League and CORE delved deeply in politics and increased their activities during the 1960s. Black groups have consistently favored ALMP, particularly when it focuses on the disadvantaged. Veterans are mainly organized into the American Legion and the Veterans of Foreign Wars. Both groups are powerful in passing veterans' education and employment legislation, which often competes with ALMP.

As the federal government gained more control over social policy, city, municipal, and governor's groups emerged. Cigler and Loomis believe that this category of groups has "become one of the most important in Washington" (1983, p. 14). Because some large cities have black majorities and have elected black mayors, the city groups interact with black interest groups.

Narrow service deliverer groups, subsumed by unions and employers in West Germany, are common in the United States. The Interstate Conference of Employment Security Agencies represents the interests of the state employment offices. It was formed in 1937 by state employment security administrators who wanted to discuss the implementation of the Wagner-Peyser Act. The Interstate Conference, consisting of agencies controlled by the state employment service administrator, protects the decentralized structure of the U.S. Employment Service and promotes the status quo. Ruttenberg and Gutchess criticize the Interstate Conference as a group that "offers protective cover for those who would use the employment service to prevent change instead of making it a positive instrument for social reform" (1970, p. 52). The Interstate Conference is unique because it receives support from the nation's taxpayers, and its secretary is a federal employee; but the organization holds secret ballots. The Interstate Conference's interests often converge with states rights advocates, and the group sometimes opposes legislation affecting the employment service (Ruttenberg and Gutchess 1970, pp. 52–57; Adams 1969, p. 183; Butler 1951, pp. 52–53, 72, 332).

The American Vocational Association (AVA) represents vocational educators, and since the mid-1960s its main constituency has shifted from high school and private vocational school teachers to instructors in public skills centers and community colleges. Oriented more toward educational than labor interests, the AVA has written and obtained amendments to many job-training laws (Hallman 1977, pp. 19, 38; Davidson 1972, p. 7; Mangum 1968, pp. 12, 15; Sundquist 1968, pp. 88–91).

For the past forty years, the Democratic party has been a consistent supporter of ALMP, while the Republican party has sometimes supported job training but generally opposed job creation because of its expense and its state-driven interference with the normal functioning of the capitalist system. However, Republicans from industrial and urban states will sometimes be solid supporters of ALMP—for example, Senator Jacob Javits (R-N.Y.). With some strategic exceptions and isolated individual cases, the Southern Democrats invariably opposed ALMP.[6] Of course, all three parties have fewer ideological underpinnings and less discipline than West German parties.

The Committee on Labor and Human Resources in the Senate handles most ALMP bills. Headed most often by a Democrat, the bipartisan Senate committee, congenial to ALMP, reports bills in an effective manner.[7] However, the House Committee on Education and Labor has had more trouble handling legislation than the Senate's committee. Although Democrats have always chaired the committee, the range of ideologies on the committee has been enormous. As chair from 1950 to 1960, Southern Democrat Graham Barden (D-N.C.) defeated or delayed liberal bills with his parliamentary skills. The next chair, Adam Clayton Powell (D-N.Y.), quadrupled the number of committee bills reaching the floor in the 1960s, but his "hardball bargaining" prevented reports on the 1967 Anti-Poverty Amendments and the repeal of section 14b of the Taft-Hartley Act. His frequent absences also slowed down action until the committee passed rules to operate

6. I will treat the Southern Democrats as a coalition partner with the other Democrats because their policy preferences are distinctive, and they are the functional equivalent of a party (Shelley 1983).

7. The chairmen have been: Thomas Duncan (D-Utah 1949–51), James Murray (D-Mont. 1951–53), Howard Smith (R-N.J. 1953–55), Lister Hill (D-Ala. 1955–69), Ralph Yarborough (D-Tex. 1969–71), Harrison Williams (D-N.J. 1971–81), and Orrin Hatch (R-Utah 1981–present) (Lindsley 1981, pp. 26–33).

without a chairman. By contrast, Carl Perkins (D-Ky.) has provided long, liberal, and steady leadership for the committee since 1970.

But even when the House Education and Labor Committee reported a bill, the House Rules Committee often killed it (nineteen from 1955 to 1968). The Rules Committee, although ostensibly keeping unpassable bills off the floor, had its own conservative policy agenda. Education and Labor Committee members helped pack the Rules Committee in 1961 and enact the twenty-one-day rule in 1965 that allowed them to bypass the Rules Committee. Nevertheless, the Education and Labor Committee remains partisan and venturous in reporting legislation (Fenno 1973, pp. 128, 229, 236; Unekis and Rieselbach 1984, pp. 4, 7, 90). The differences between the Senate and House committees can be epitomized by the liberal, cooperative Jacob Javits in the Senate and the conservative, contentious Albert Quie (R-Minn.) in the House.[8]

The Democratic presidents have been an effective force for ALMP, but Republican presidents have not. Although ALMP expenditures sometimes increase under Republican presidents, the initiative comes from Congress. Kennedy, Johnson, and Carter all achieved increases in ALMP, while Eisenhower and Reagan opposed, and Ford and Nixon tolerated them.

In the executive branch, policy formation has shifted toward the presidential staff. In the 1950s, the cabinet played a strong role in drafting legislation, especially under Eisenhower, but since then presidential staffs have largely supplanted bureaucratic participation in social policy formation. Because the executive views the departments as having "gone native," presidents have organized staffs to develop their own policy. In comparison to West Germany, U.S. staff development is an admission of inability to control the bureaucracy and cabinet (Hargrove and Nelson 1984, pp. 176–85; Biggart 1984).[9]

8. Orstein and Elder comment that "Republicans on the Senate committee have been much more sympathetic to labor goals than their counterparts on the House panel" (1978, p. 133).

9. Truman used Clark Clifford as a domestic policy adviser; Eisenhower, contrary to the trend, relied on department heads; Kennedy used Theodore Sorenson and policy task forces; Johnson had Bill Moyers and task forces, then

THE FORMATION OF U.S. ALMP LEGISLATION

Left political party power has been important in passing major ALMP laws, but because of ideological confusions, the negative impact of state structures has been more important. During rising Republican party power, the Full Employment Act of 1946 passed without teeth, and the GI Bill of Rights fragmented the working class into veteran/nonveteran categories. Rising Democratic power helped pass the MDTA job-training law but not without amendments due to special interest groups connected to conservatives in the House Rules Committee. The Economic Opportunity Act of 1964 demonstrates both the peak of Democratic party power and the impact of social movements and the Democratic party's confusion on participation rights, which left the act on shaky ground. CETA shows again how the Democratic party produced massive policy advances but was also forced to accept decentralized control, which led to the program's eventual destruction. The formation of JTPA shows the Democratic party losing power and its ideological compass, while Reagan slashed ALMP (Table 5 summarizes U.S. political power). Thus, American social demands tend to fall prey to the strategic influence of state formation.

The Employment Act of 1946 and the GI Bill

After managing job creation during the depression and production during the war, the Democrats were confident that they could eliminate peacetime unemployment. In 1944, President Roosevelt included "the right to a useful and remunerative job" as part of a second Bill of Rights.[10] The 1944 Democratic party

---

moved to more organization with Joseph Califano and the OEO; Nixon used the Ash Council and the Domestic Council under Ehrlichman; Carter used Stuart Eizenstat, interagency councils, and the Domestic Policy Staff; and Reagan used the Office of Policy Development. Kennedy and Johnson also used the Bureau of the Budget to guide and systematize social legislation. But since Nixon, that bureau's policy-molding influence declined (it was renamed the Office of Management and Budget) (Mosher 1984, pp. 119–21).

10. Roosevelt's commitment here was either weak or mitigated by his vision of politics because he appointed Frank Hines as work director of the Retraining and Employment Administration. The agency was criticized and short-lived.

TABLE 5   *Presidents, Mandates, and Left Party Power in the United States, 1949 to 1984*

Beginning Date of Administration	President and Party	Vote Margin of Democratic President (in percentages)	Left[a] Senators in Senate (in percentages)	Left[a] Representatives in House (in percentages)
1950	Truman (D)	+4	29.2	33.3
1952	Eisenhower (R)	−11	25.0	26.7
1954	Eisenhower (R)	—	25.5	23.9
1956	Eisenhower (R)	−13	24.0	28.0
1958	Eisenhower (R)	—	26.8	28.7
1960	Kennedy (D)	+0	41.6	39.1
1962	Kennedy (D)	—	41.0	34.8
1963	Johnson (D)	—	44.0	35.1
1964	Johnson (D)	+23	45.5	44.6
1968	Nixon (R)	−1	38.0	36.1
1970	Nixon (R)	—	37.0	38.4
1972	Nixon (R)	−24	41.0	36.6
1974	Ford (R)	—	43.6	45.7
1976	Carter (D)	+2	43.0	45.9
1978	Carter (D)	—	40.0	43.7
1980	Reagan (R)	−10	32.3	37.9
1982	Reagan (R)	—	31.0	40.8
1984	Reagan (R)	−20	33.0	38.7

[a]Left party power excludes Southern Democrats from Alabama, Arkansas, Florida, Georgia, Kentucky, Louisiana, Mississippi, North Carolina, Oklahoma, South Carolina, Tennessee, Texas, and Virginia.

platform proposed to "guarantee full employment." Although true Republican interest in full employment was small, even Thomas Dewey stated that "government can and must create job opportunities" (Bailey 1950, pp. 41–44).

The pressure for full employment was quickly split. The American Legion demanded that Roosevelt limit the veterans' bonus to mustering-out pay so as not to stunt a larger program, and it then pushed for the GI Bill of Rights and got what they wanted: "Never before has a nation lavished so many material benefits upon its heroes. From subsidized education to privileged ocean travel for their war brides, World War II veterans received a rich bounty" (Ross 1969, p. 3). Although diehard Southern Democrats (Rankin, D-Tenn.) opposed education and other benefits, other Southern Democrats (Barden, D-N.C.) supported the bill. Mainly backed by liberals, the bill was steered toward conservative ends by Southern Democrats and Republicans who headed the House committee that reported the bill. The GI Bill of Rights weakened support for the Full Employment Act by creating a veterans' status group that would pursue its special interests rather than support the welfare state as a whole (Ross 1969, pp. 89–124).

The Democrats introduced the Murray-Wagner Full Employment Act in the Senate on January 22, 1945. Labor was somewhat divided on the bill: because the CIO supported it, the AFL considered opposite action. Although both federations favored full employment, each had an agenda that tended toward social rights and passive labor market policies, such as increasing unemployment compensation, education support, minimum wages, fair employment practices, and price controls. Despite initial lukewarm support, labor leaders testified in support of the bill, supplied amendments, and the CIO even started a grass-roots letter campaign (Bailey 1950, pp. 80–93).

Employers were not so enthusiastic. The National Association of Manufacturers put the full force of its organization against the bill, and its president, Ira Mosher, claimed in the House hearings that the bill "could be no greater discouragement to business" (Bailey 1950, pp. 133–36). The Chamber of Commerce also opposed the bill, but the Chamber did not testify at the hearings because its head, Eric Johnston, was running for president and did not want to go on record as opposing full employment. Nevertheless, the Chamber of Commerce was not friendly: "Labeled in fraud and deception as a bill designed to preserve private enterprise, if enacted, it would be the scaffold on which private enterprise could be dropped to its death" (Bailey 1950, p. 141).

The Murray-Wagner bill passed 71 to 10 in the Senate, but the more conservative House substituted the Whittington-Taft Employment Act of 1946. The enacted compromise replaced "full employment" and economic decision making based upon the unemployment rate with "maximum employment" balanced with minimum inflation. The final Employment Act of 1946 set up the Council of Economic Advisers to the president, but it contained no other operative provisions (Norton 1977).

Bailey (1950) presents the passage of the act as a triumph of pluralism such that the absence of any one supporter would have spelled defeat for the bill. The most powerful force for passage came from the Democratic party and the Union for Democratic Action engaging in political education. Much like the Wagner-Peyser Act, the "social welfare intellectuals" and the Democratic party were more active than unions or other groups.

However, the striking reality was left weakness and retreat rather than pluralistic coordination. The GI Bill had just split the labor movement, and although union membership was on the increase, industrial relations were adversarial. The Employment Act was passed in February 1946 at the peak of an intense strike wave. The National Association of Manufacturers blasted unions in full-page newspaper ads, and the 1946 congressional elections gave the Republicans a "mandate" to stop strikes and labor management discord. A year later, the Republican-dominated Congress struck ALMP from the agenda and passed the Taft-Hartley Act (Millis and Brown 1950, pp. 287, 363). Rather than an advance, the Employment Act of 1946 clearly signaled a retreat on ALMP.

The Manpower Development and Training Act of 1962

After the Republican resurgence, McCarthy purges, and unemployment in two recessions, the Democrats made major gains in the 1958 congressional elections. Labor had completed its consolidation and entered Democratic politics, while black groups were emerging as a political force through civil rights struggles. After the AFL-CIO March on Washington in 1959 and northern liberal pressures, Senate majority leader Lyndon Johnson (D-Tex.) appointed Senator Eugene McCarthy (D-Minn.) to chair a special Senate committee to study unemployment. The committee recommended "a nationwide vocational training program through federal grants-in-aid to the states" (Robertson 1981, p. 190). After Kennedy was elected president, Senator Jennings Randolph (D-

W.V.) submitted a training bill drafted by the AVA and Senator Joseph Clark (D-Pa.) presented a manpower planning bill.

But the administration had a different view. Secretary of Labor Arthur Goldberg, formerly general counsel for the AFL-CIO, sent President Kennedy a draft of the Full Employment Act of 1961 that included job training, taxation, expenditure, housing, and international trade measures. In June, Kennedy ordered the Department of Labor, the Bureau of the Budget, and Senator Clark to produce a new training bill giving training and manpower planning to the Department of Labor. The AVA was not happy.

The main conflicts involved OJT and in-school training. With a proposal oriented to the Department of Labor, the Bureau of the Budget wanted the employment service to identify needs, promote OJT, and contract with public and private schools for training. With an education-oriented proposal, the AVA wanted to add a grant-in-aid category to the Smith-Hughes Vocational Education Act authorizing retraining of adult unemployed workers (Mangum 1968, pp. 13–16). The AVA wanted in-school training run by AVA instructors and opposed OJT because it gave organized labor and the Department of Labor control over vocational education. The AFL-CIO strongly supported OJT and publicly criticized the AVA's conception of vocational education. However, the Department of Labor was curiously divided on job training, and the Department of Health, Education, and Welfare was not particularly interested in it.

President Kennedy and the AFL-CIO saw the vocational education training system in disarray, and Congress and black leaders were unimpressed by the U.S. Employment Service. The fight came down to the AVA versus the administration and the AFL-CIO. AVA lobbyist M. D. Mobley summoned AVA leaders to Washington to demand thirty-four amendments to the bill and to tell Senator Clark that only vocational educators could handle job training. Mobley's connections to a Southern Democrat on the House Rules Committee gave his organization, a minor service delivery interest group, veto power over the administration's training bill—an illustration of the fragmented U.S. legislative process. Although Goldberg was furious, Mobley got most of what he wanted: job training in schools financed with state distribution formulas and matching funds, rather than extensive OJT under the Department of Labor (Sundquist 1968, pp. 85–89). The MDTA bill passed the Senate, 60 to 31, on August 23. In early 1962, Democrats in the House elicited the help of Republican Charles Goodell to support the bill, and after a narrow Rules Committee vote of 8 to 7, it passed the House 354 to 62. Without Mobley's man on the Rules Committee, President Kennedy could not have signed the bill in March 1962.

Although the AFL-CIO preferred OJT, they fully supported the MDTA bill with testimony by Meany, Biemiller, and Ruttenberg. The liberal Americans for Democratic Action supported the bill along with a group of "pragmatic, 'institutional' economists dedicated to 'manpower' issues and the notion of human capital" (Robertson 1981, p. 194).[11]

The passage of MDTA illustrates the negative impact of state structures and the weakness of social demands. First, the fragmented legislative process provided veto power to a small service deliverer group with a connection to one member of the House Rules Committee. In Mobley's words, the AVA prevented vocational education from getting "the last tit on the sow," although educational interests had shown little interest in the bill (Mangum 1968, p. 12).[12] Such access and committee power among special interest groups do not exist in West Germany. Second, the Democratic bill lacked a conception of participation rights. Although the original MDTA bill could be thought of as a back door attempt to give job training to the trade unions and employers through OJT, neither was the plan made clear, nor was the opposition to school control made evident. If a notion of participation rights existed, it was vague or buried under efficiency arguments that OJT does the job better (Menake 1978).

The Equal Opportunity Act of 1964 and Subsequent Amendments

The Equal Opportunity Act of 1964 combined social and participation rights in the Job Corps, Neighborhood Youth Corps,

11. They included Charles Killingsworth, Frederick Harbison, Clark Kerr, Samuel Haber, and Eli Ginzburg.

12. The U.S. Chamber of Commerce expressed fears about federal control of labor markets but never actually fought against passage. Conservatives in Congress viewed MDTA as a step toward socialism, but opposition was moderate.

Operation Mainstream, and other programs. Four intellectual movements prepared the way for the act: the study of juvenile delinquency shifted focus from the individual to the community; theories of urban renewal moved from physical construction to human communities; thoughts on public assistance changed from passive welfare payments to active rehabilitation and employment programs; and economic views of the labor market shifted from cyclical unemployment and unemployment benefits to structural unemployment and ALMP. These four movements converged upon an active approach to poverty.

Just after Kennedy's assassination, his staff consolidated programs into a major poverty effort, introducing community action programs as the unifying device. Community action represented the most radical development of U.S. participation rights after World War II. A new organization, the Office of Economic Opportunity (OEO), would administer the programs. As part of the presidential office, not a department, the OEO gave the president more control over the bureaucracy.

President Lyndon Johnson placed the War on Poverty in the center of his reelection campaign, which proved an effective strategy. His poverty bill, introduced on March 16, 1964, conferred large powers to the OEO director but was vague in many crucial sections (e.g., maximum feasible participation and community action programs). Nevertheless, Johnson started a major lobbying effort with the help of labor, black, religious, and academic groups. In fact, the UAW started a "citizens' drive on poverty," and the Urban League began its own "war on poverty." But business interests opposed the bill.

The hearings were short and carefully engineered. Adam Clayton Powell, chair of the House Education and Labor Committee, pushed the bill through. Democratic liberals had previously blocked Rep. Phil Landrum's (D-Ga.) attempt to sit on the House Ways and Means Committee because Landrum opposed liberal social policy. They offered Landrum, a conservative southern Democrat, a seat on the Ways and Means Committee if he would introduce and support the bill. On August 8, the act passed the House with a 226 to 185 vote, a stronger showing than expected. The bill easily passed the Senate, 61 to 34, in late July. When Johnson signed the Economic Opportunity Act on August 20,

1964, the Job Corps, Operation Mainstream, the Concentrated Employment Program, and the Neighborhood Youth Corps came into being.

Four major currents led to the bill's passage: Democratic party power and two activist presidents committed to eliminating poverty; black pressure for social and participation rights; labor movement pressure for employment and training programs; and intellectual social engineering based on a deep faith in science. First, President Kennedy developed a number of poverty programs during his short term in office. After the assassination and Johnson's landslide victory, the Democratic party had a mandate for these and other poverty programs. Johnson's pragmatic arm twisting and legislative know-how made the bill's passage almost certain, but he lacked a vision of participation rights and a rigorous conception of administration.

Second, blacks fought for political and social rights through social movements and the Democratic party. The civil rights movement picked up steam in the late 1950s, and it was near its peak in 1964 (Blumberg 1984, pp. 99–115; Clark 1966). Turning from the legalistic and tentative strategy of the past, blacks challenged social and economic discrimination. Thus, black movements for social and participation rights demanded equal employment and economic opportunity. Massive demonstrations in St. Louis in 1960 and in New York in 1961 called for state action on economic and employment issues. The civil rights movement, pressing also for legal rights, gained sympathy with national press coverage of blacks being abused by attack dogs and gas, and in 1963 the death of four black girls worshiping in a Birmingham church. As Kotz states, "The civil rights movement at that point had millions of white supporters. It represented ideological commitment to end old abuses and to some extent to make up for them" (1977, p. 50).

Third, the labor movement promoted both employment programs and economic equality. Although unable to control discrimination in the workplace, the AFL-CIO actively supported civil rights and economic opportunity throughout the 1960s and 1970s. In addition to ideological commitment to equality, some union political support was also due to a bargain. President Johnson promised that if labor would support the War on Poverty, he would then push the repeal of section 14(b) of the Taft-Hartley Act or other measures favored by labor. The bargain helped focus union pressure for the War on Poverty (Wilson 1979, pp. 104–5).

Finally, pressure came from increasingly optimistic intellectuals who shifted their policy focus from individual explanations of social problems to new forms of social engineering. Their "deep faith in reason and technology" was probably strengthened by the baby boom reaching college and the growing educational establishment (Liebman 1974; Friedman 1977, p. 31). These intellectual pressures were channeled through the Ford Foundation, presidential commissions, and Kennedy's presidential staff. Although offering little direct pressure for the Economic Opportunity Act, intellectuals provided the theory of reform, and social policy was probably more active than it would have been with just interest groups' input. Nevertheless, confusion on participation rights plagued the act, and this failure must be at least partially attributed to the intellectuals.[13]

The passage of the Equal Opportunity Act strongly supports the view that left party power leads to ALMP. The fragmented legislative process was overcome by a powerful mandate coupled with skillful legislative maneuvering, though a pound of flesh was paid with a Southern Democratic seat on a House committee and the dismissal of Adam Yarmolinsky (a prominent architect of the act). However, the Democratic party revealed a weak conception of participation rights in its inability to define "maximum feasible participation" (Schott and Dugnon 1984, pp. 112–26).[14] This caused a weak foundation that led to confusion and subsequent demise of participation rights in the OEO. I

13. Some scholars on the War on Poverty—Donovan (1980), Moynihan (1969), Lampman (1977), and Levitan (1966)—exaggerate the impact of intellectuals on presidential leadership and downplay group pressures. Why they ignore the social demands of blacks and whites in the late 1950s and early 1960s and the power of media coverage to distill political issues is puzzling (Morris 1984, pp. 280–81).

14. OEO Deputy Director Jack Conway (1964–1965) believed in "organizing the poor against the local political system" (Schott and Dugnon 1984, p. 123). He came the closest to understanding what "maximum feasible participation" meant, although he probably would not have used the term. Conway came from the labor movement and had been an assistant to Walter Reuther at the UAW.

shall analyze this surprising process that occurred after the bill was passed.

Instead of defining the lack of work as the dominant social problem in the early 1960s, the Democratic party focused on "poverty." Though not inherently a social rights' concept, "poverty" tended toward social rights' solutions (i.e., consumption rather than production). Three strategies were presented to attack poverty: a community action strategy offered communities an effective way to implement services and job programs by furnishing the poor with the political power to decide how to escape poverty; a services strategy supplied educational, health, legal, psychiatric, and rehabilitative services to help the poor overcome personal barriers to mainstream life; and a jobs strategy provided a massive employment program for the urban poor. Although the 1964 Economic Opportunity Act contained snippets of a jobs strategy and moderate portions of the services strategy, it totally embraced the community action strategy. While these three strategies were not mutually exclusive, they were also not totally complementary, given limited funds. Community action was seen as "the vehicle" for the War on Poverty because it was cheap, effective, and democratic, while direct provision of jobs and services was considered expensive and ineffective (especially if provided by the moribund USES).

The Community Action Program surprisingly represented a form of "participation rights" oriented toward community consumption rather than organizational production. As such, it buffered firms from workplace democracy and capital control. The participation rights in the War on Poverty did not apply to a particular substantive area, but simply mandated community organizations to eradicate poverty (Toby 1975, pp. 12–13; Moynihan 1970, p. lvii; Lowi 1979, pp. 207–36; Aaron 1978, pp. 16–64).

But community action reflected populist values. Social movements with such grass-roots values often appear in America with an antistate or antimonopoly agenda. The community action programs opposed the "tainted bureaucratic" provision of services and insisted on "pure grass-roots" service delivery and policy making. This democratic populism was not a form of neocorporatism that formed stable institutions; rather, this antistate social movement assumed that grass-roots persons in ghettos knew their needs best, that giving them money allowed them power to move their communities into the mainstream, and that the need for funding withered away as poor people began to compete equally with other Americans. Thus, self-help programs would eradicate poverty and then self-destruct.

The community action programs were flawed attempts to attribute public status to and confer participation rights on interest groups. The state may give public status to an interest group by providing resources, regulating the group's external and internal processes, and giving the interest group a formal role in policy formation (Offe 1980, pp. 136–37). That interest groups for the poor in many areas were nascent or nonexistent does not matter because the state may create them. The federal government provided the resources; however, regulation was largely absent, and the community action programs had little or no formal role in legislation and national planning. The program's vaguely conceived consumptive and community-based role was to receive money and contract for services, which was inherently different from a production-based role (i.e., union self-administration). Community action activities were so diverse and decentralized that they were difficult to organize and coordinate.

The state failed to attribute public status and participation rights to the community action programs because it did not regulate and politically integrate them. But most important, the community action strategy was antistate and contradicted participation rights. It was based on grass-roots democratic theory: bureaucracies are to be avoided because of their inherent vices, and power comes from the bottom and should stay there because protest groups and their leaders are easily coopted by higher-level leadership and elites. The program's radical but confused stance alienated conservative *and* local Democratic leaders. In the end, this grass-roots approach mistrusted the state too much to become an institutional part of it.

With many community action programs ineffective, disorganized, and prone to mismanagement, national policy makers ignored the problem; they simply added Model Cities and Community Development Corporations. Instead of restructuring established organizations, Congress added new ones, hoping the old ones would go away. Radical in conception, the community action programs were conservative in their effects because of the backlash they created, and the Nixon and Ford administrations dismantled them. Although many categorical job-training and job creation programs were nominally given to the Department of Labor, they were decentralized and sent to local and state governments under CETA. The OEO—the symbol of the War on Poverty—disappeared from cabinet-level government. Thus, the one near example of participation rights in post–World War II America eventually led to a conservative decentralization of policy engineered by Nixon (Peterson and Greenstone 1977; Gelfland 1981; Waxman 1968; Lander 1971).

Public Employment in the Emergency Employment Act and CETA

Although public service employment had been proposed in Presidential Commission Reports from 1966 to 1969, it was largely rejected during the War on Poverty.[15] But urban riots and veterans' unemployment gave rise to new demands for jobs beyond training. Senators Joseph Clark and Robert Kennedy (D-N.Y.) proposed the Emergency Employment Act of 1967 to remedy the situation. President Johnson opposed the bill, causing its defeat by five votes in the Senate. Later that year, Rep. James O'Hara (D-Mich.) and Rep. John Conyers (D-Mich.) put forward employment acts; despite enthusiastic support from labor, black, and local government groups, both bills failed in part because of the drain on funds caused by the Vietnam War (Hallman 1977, pp. 7–10).

When Nixon assumed office in 1969, he emphasized revenue sharing with reorganization, management reform, and the consolidation of categorical employment programs. In a message to Congress Nixon requested a comprehensive manpower system that would flexibly and countercyclically fund state and local governments. This system would provide equitable training allow-

15. They included the National Commission on Technology, Automation, and Economic Progress (1966), the President's Commission on Law Enforcement and Administration of Justice (1967), the National Advisory Commission on Rural Poverty (1967), the National Advisory Commission on Civil Disorders (1968), and the President's Commission on Income Maintenance Programs (1969).

ances to individuals with career development plans aided by a
national computerized job bank. But Nixon made no mention of
public service jobs (Hallman 1977, pp. 11–23).

An uneasy compromise bill with both public service jobs and
reorganization was gingerly put together in 1970. Republican
Senators Jacob Javits and Winston Prouty (Vt.) introduced reorganization bills, and then Senator Gaylord Nelson (D-Wis.) upped
the ante with public service employment programs. In committee,
the Republicans wanted decentralized state control, while the
Democrats wanted city and local control with some centralized
categorical programs. The Democratic bill was reported to the
Senate floor with split Republican support, but it easily passed by
68 to 6. However, in the House committee, Republicans were
united against public service employment, and the Democrats
cared little about comprehensive reform. Before the approaching
congressional elections, Secretary James Hodgson and Assistant
Secretary Malcolm Lovell found common ground between the
Republicans, the AFL-CIO, and city groups: the secretary of labor would have the power to move public service workers into
unsubsidized employment or reduce funds to programs that
failed to incorporate public-private transitions. The Democrats obtained public employment programs, while the Republicans retained control and some decentralization. With pressure from Rep.
O'Hara, the bill was passed in the House on September 30, 1970.

During the conference committee meetings, Secretary Hodgson listed three basic concepts that were essential for Nixon's
signature: transition from public service employment to nonsubsidized jobs, moderate public service employment expenditures,
and comprehensive (not categorical) programs at state and local
levels. The Senate and House bills more or less contained all
three requirements; however, the conference committee tinkered
with each one. The Democrats feared that Nixon would impound
job creation funds by having the secretary of labor reduce funds
for programs not meeting specific transition targets. Although
transition remained a goal, the House agreed to strike the clause
but allowed the secretary of labor to transfer 25 percent of funds
from one program to another. On the question of expenditures,
the conference committee settled on $9.5 billion in four years, a
figure midway between the $7.5 billion requested by Nixon and

the $12 billion demanded by the Democrats. Finally, the conference committee decided to give one-third of the funds to comprehensive manpower services, one-third to public service employment, and one-third to categorical programs, research, and a new occupational upgrading program. Interest groups' support seemed to back the bill; both the National League of Cities and the U.S. Conference of Mayors supported public service employment and local control.

On the whole, the bill invited a veto by eliminating most of the secretary of labor's transition powers. Four Republicans charged that the bill went too far on public service employment but not far enough on decategorization. The new bill passed the Senate, 68 to 13, and squeaked by in the House, 177 to 159. Nixon vetoed the bill on December 16, 1970, because it still emphasized categorical programs, contained too much public service employment, and had too few transition measures to nonsubsidized jobs.

In 1971, as unemployment rose to 6 percent, the Democrats began working on new proposals. Twenty-two Democrats and ten Republicans, including Senator Hugh Scott (R-Pa.), sponsored a revised bill with public service employment for two years. The cities testified for the bill, and the AFL-CIO sent strong statements supporting it. Hodgson and Lovell advanced Nixon's recently announced revenue-sharing plan that would eliminate categorical programs. Because Nixon's plan was slow in being introduced by Senator Prouty and Rep. Albert Quie the Senate ignored Nixon's plans and passed their own Emergency Employment Act, 62 to 10. The House heard many of the same groups, and after some debate passed a modified bill, 204 to 182.

In the conference committee, the bill was shortened from five to two years. With AFL-CIO and city groups heavily involved in the negotiations, the House Democrats accepted the transition language from the Senate bill and struck a compromise. After the conference report was easily passed in both the Senate and the House, Nixon signed the Emergency Employment Act on July 12, 1971.

The bill was pushed by city groups, the AFL-CIO, and clearly the Democratic party. The Democrats were most interested in public service employment, while the Republican administration wanted decategorization and a comprehensive revenue-sharing act. Thus, the major innovation of the bill—true job creation— came from the Democrats with support from the cities and unions.

The Emergency Employment Act contained an implicit bargain between Nixon and Congress that "both Houses would move rapidly to consider comprehensive manpower legislation" (Davidson 1972, p. 91; Van Horn 1979, p. 63). In his February 1972 Message on Manpower, Nixon continued to ask for revenue sharing with job-training programs directly supervised by the states and local governments, but he only referred to "temporary" and "transitional" public service employment (CQ, Jan. 12, 1972, p. 293). The Democrats, however, refused to eliminate congressional oversight and emphasized public service employment. In the 1972 election campaign, the Democrats pushed public service employment for such highly skilled jobs as police, fire fighters, teachers, and medical personnel, while the Republicans favored transitional jobs (i.e., unskilled positions) that would temporarily balance the business cycle (CQ, June 17, 1972, pp. 1478–80).

After Nixon swept the 1972 elections, he switched strategies from complex negotiations to unilateral impounding of funds for job creation programs. But the 1973 MDTA and Emergency Employment Act expirations and growing unemployment put pressure on Congress for policy renewal. In an administrative order, Nixon forced the issue by unilaterally curtailing new enrollments in training programs until the Department of Labor implemented his decentralized revenue-sharing plan.

House Democratic leaders responded to Nixon's threats with a public service employment bill that doubled previous efforts, but an immediate veto threat tabled the bill. In the Senate, Nelson and Javits proposed the Job Training and Community Services Act of 1973 that extended MDTA for four years, included prime sponsors consisting of cities and counties with balance-of-the-state programs run by the governors (a form of revenue sharing demanded by Nixon), emphasized veterans, and transferred community action agencies to the Department of Labor (rather than killing them). The training bill passed on July 24, 1973. Another bill, the Emergency Employment Act Extension, which specifically dealt with public service employment, passed on July 31, 1973, despite Nixon's opposition to "dead-end jobs."

The House Labor Committee's deadlock on public job creation was finally broken when Rep. Dominick Daniels (D-N.J.), Rep. Marvin Esch (R-Mich.), and Assistant Secretary of Labor William Kohlberg worked out a compromise that authorized public service employment, included decentralized manpower programs to the state and local governments, and gave strong supervisory powers over decentralized programs to the secretary of labor. On October 18, 1973, the committee reported the Comprehensive Manpower Act of 1973. Of the two versions of the bill reported on the House floor, the Democratic version passed with expenditures on public service employment and safeguards against impoundment.

The House bill and the two Senate bills were sent to the conference committee. The House version was accepted as the Comprehensive Employment and Training Act of 1973 (CETA) with small changes in funding, size of prime sponsors, and triggers attached to levels of unemployment. A few categorical programs were kept, but on the whole the bill was a revenue-sharing program. Threatened by Watergate and rising unemployment, Nixon overlooked his previous opposition to public service employment and signed CETA in December 1973.

Union, black, and urban interest groups strongly supported the House compromise effort, as did many Republicans and most Democrats. The AVA continued to oppose such bills because they gave too much power over job training to the Department of Labor, but AVA power had been surpassed by state and local government groups. The UAW, AFL-CIO, and mayors all stressed the need for more public service employment, while the states and cities wanted decentralization. The Chamber of Commerce even endorsed "properly administered" public service employment (*CQ*, March 4, 1972, p. 502).

As with the Equal Opportunity Act, CETA rested on weak foundations because of a faulty conception of participation rights. The decentralization proposals of the Nixon administration laid the seeds for later difficulties in controlling substitution effects and other program abuses.

The Decline of ALMP:
Amending and Reauthorizing CETA

The recession of 1974 and 1975 pressured CETA to expand public service employment beyond the disadvantaged. As the recession continued, President Gerald Ford was willing to support public service employment "where there is a need for it" (Orfield 1975, p. 246). Labor Secretary Peter Brennan announced a $680 million program, Senator Javits promoted a $4 billion program, and Rep. Richard Van der Veen (D-Mich.) introduced legislation for 900,000 new public service jobs. The AFL-CIO, civil rights groups, and churches all supported the public job creation effort. In late December 1974, Congress enacted the Emergency Jobs and Unemployment Assistance Act, which added countercyclical public service employment for all unemployed persons.

By 1976, the burden of adding tens of thousands of new public service workers to public payrolls within eighteen months had taken its toll in abuses and substitution effects. Congress, facing large budget deficits, was perturbed at reports of large-scale misuse by local sponsors. Furthermore, black groups charged that structural and countercyclical public service employment creamed workers while ignoring the disadvantaged. In October 1976, Congress moved to curtail substitution. The Emergency Jobs Programs Extension Act of 1976 required all new hires to be disadvantaged and limited enrollment to one year. It further reduced community-based organization jobs on the theory that nongovernment jobs did not constitute necessary work. And the countercyclical program was extended another year, but with the expectation that it would be phased out (Bullock 1981, p. 20). Ford signed the bill despite conservative pressures.[16]

When Carter was elected president in 1976, he pledged to fight unemployment. He promptly proposed an economic stimulus package with revenue-sharing, public works, and employment programs. By the midpoint of his term in office, four new laws extended ALMP: The Economic Stimulus Act of 1977 (the Skills Training Improvement Program and supplemental funds for public service employment), the Youth Employment and Demonstra-

16. Under extreme pressure from employers, Ford signed the CETA amendments but vetoed the Common-Situs Picketing Bill in 1976.

tion Projects Act of 1977 (new youth employment programs), the Revenue Act of 1978 (the Targeted Jobs Tax Credit Program), and the CETA Reauthorization Act of 1978 (tightened eligibility requirements). In reality, the CETA Reauthorization Act signaled the decline of CETA and ALMP.[17]

At the 1977 and 1978 CETA Reauthorization hearings, the major battle lines were drawn. The AFL-CIO, UAW, and other unions strongly endorsed an extension of CETA, even though state and local government employee unions expressed serious concerns about the erosion of labor standards, wage rates, and job security; that is, substitution effects directly affected public union jobs. State and local governments wanted more expenditures, local control, and youth programs. In the opposite direction, most Republicans and business groups opposed CETA, especially public service jobs.[18] However, because employers and Republicans thought CETA would be reauthorized, they focused on a stronger employer role in CETA.

On February 22, 1978, President Carter presented his reauthorization message, targeting CETA toward structural and youth unemployment, private sector participation through the Private Sector Initiative Program, and auditing measures that would eliminate substitution effects. Carter believed substitution effects could be eliminated because the economy was on an upswing.

Augustus Hawkins (D-Calif.) reviewed Carter's bill in his Employment Opportunities Subcommittee and presented it on the House floor. The bill added an "Office of Audits, Investigations, and Compliance" in the Department of Labor to curtail substitution effects and proposed a new allocation criteria for prime sponsors, but it lacked the $7,800 average wage and entry level limits on public service jobs. The House mood turned ugly. Reps. David Obey (D-Wis.) and James Jeffords (R-Vt.) led the bipartisan rage against public service employment. Obey called CETA "the second most unpopular program in the country after welfare" (*CQ*, Aug. 12, 1978, p. 2106). When Speaker Tip O'Neill tried to slip

17. The Humphrey-Hawkins Act is not discussed because it is simply another unenforced symbolic gesture (Akard 1988, Keyserling 1981, Currie 1977, and Ginsburg 1979).

18. William Norris of Control Data Corporation was sympathetic to CETA (Bullock 1981, pp. 65–66).

the bill through a late night session, an avalanche of amendments convinced him that opposition to CETA was strong and growing. After losing on a number of important amendment votes, Hawkins postponed further action until more propitious times.

Meanwhile, the Human Resources Employment Subcommittee reported Carter's bill in the Senate. Its amendments established a monitoring procedure, tightened eligibility requirements, and added an Office of Technical Assistance to help prime sponsors deal with the new procedures. The Senate passed moderate limits on CETA that would mollify anger in the House.

The bill was again reported to the House floor after a committee compromise to reduce both structural and cyclical job creation funds, limit individual participation to eighteen months in five years on public service employment, and retain the $7,000 national average for CETA earnings but allow annual adjustments. The House Republicans agreed not to contest the bill, and it passed, 284 to 50.

Democratic party power caused all four Carter bills to pass; however, the restrictions in the Reauthorization Act caused cities and counties to reduce their participation in CETA. When another oil crisis hit in 1979, the newly disciplined CETA offered little help to the unemployed. Targeting on the disadvantaged caused local governments to back out of CETA, leaving its defense to community-based organizations who had little political clout. The basis of CETA's unpopularity—substitution effects exacerbated by decentralization—had its roots in Nixon's and Republicans' antipathy toward the federal bureaucracy. Ironically, the Democrats, who had preferred categorical programs, felt compelled to defend Nixon's decentralization in the hearings. The lack of a firm grasp of program administration and participation rights came back to haunt the Democrats (Franklin and Ripley 1984; Jacobs 1981; Levin and Ferman 1985; Baumer and Van Horn 1985).

The Job-Training Partnership Act
and the Fall of Job Creation

When the Reagan administration slashed social expenditures, ALMP was among the hardest hit. The traditional Republican reticence toward job creation programs plus President Reagan's mandate allowed Republicans to cut CETA job creation programs by 75 percent in 1981–82. When CETA came up for reauthorization in September 1982, Reagan wanted to totally eliminate job creation programs.

Four different proposals were presented in 1982 to replace CETA. Rep. Hawkins proposed the Community Partnership for Employment and Training Act building upon the CETA prime sponsor system; that is, he wanted to give the programs back to the cities and counties. His bill asked for $5 billion but had little chance of surviving the wrath against CETA. Rep. Jeffords presented the innovative Productivity and Human Investment Act, but his bill was least likely to pass. Its "Labor Market Investment Boards" at local, state, and national levels would rationalize and promote comprehensive ALMP (Jeffords 1982a, 1982b).

The Senate and administration bills had more possibilities. The Training for Jobs Act, proposed by Senators Daniel Quayle (R-Ind.) and Edward Kennedy (D-Mass.) as a bipartisan effort to establish business councils to run training programs, gave control to the states and requested $3.9 billion. And Reagan proposed the Job-Training Partnership Act of 1982, with business-dominated private industry councils and power to the states but few guarantees for wages and employment standards; it requested $2.4 billion but was never formally introduced in Congress. All four acts studiously avoided job creation measures, although some conservatives still saw the seeds of job creation in OJT programs.

At the joint hearings, the AFL-CIO cast its support for the Hawkins bill because it built upon CETA, provided labor with a strong voice in implementation and planning, established meaningful labor standards, and spent the most money and consequently would have the greatest effect. City and county groups also supported the Hawkins bill, while the states opposed it. The Chamber of Commerce supported Reagan's bill, while the National Association of Manufacturers supported Quayle and Kennedy's bill. Both the Senate and administration bills gave business a strong position in the planning of job training (CQ, March 17, 1982, pp. 2–28, 536; CQ, March 18, 1982, pp. 526, 727).

These employment and training programs were caught in a complex, three-way negotiation among Reagan, Quayle, and

Kennedy. The administration opposed wage payments to trainees, spending more than 15 percent of funds on support services, the minimum population requirement of four hundred thousand persons, and OJT because it resembled public service employment. Even though OJT has proven the most effective employment program, Reagan questioned House Speaker O'Neill on whether he wanted "make-work or training for lasting jobs?" (*CQ*, Oct. 2, 1982, p. 2427). After agreeing on wage prohibitions for trainees, the Senate passed the Quayle-Kennedy bill, 95 to 0, on July 1, 1982. The House passed the more liberal Hawkins bill, 356 to 52, on August 4, 1982, with an amendment that 70 percent of funds must be spent on training and support services. The two bills were vastly different. After a meeting with Reagan, the conference committee adopted the Senate bill with state controls, 70 percent training requirement (with some exceptions such as child care), no OJT programs, and severely limited trainee wages. Reagan signed the Job Training and Partnership Act on October 13, 1982.

Despite a seemingly bipartisan effort, Tip O'Neill held his own signing ceremony with the media on October 5. House majority leader Jim Wright (D-Tex.) said, "The truth is . . . that the House passed such a bill weeks ago, and the President has only now discovered it and decided he invented it" (*CQ*, Oct. 2, 1982, p. 2427). But although the Reagan administration had not introduced the JTPA, it bore the stamp of business-dominated private industry councils and low expenditures (Robertson 1988, pp. 451–54).

After Democratic attempts to pass a job creation bill proved futile, job creation died. Despite record unemployment levels, the federal government had reduced job training and job placement programs and had destroyed job creation programs. The symbolic mantle of federal responsibility for the unemployed vaguely embodied in the Employment Act of 1946 disintegrated. The irony was that budget deficits soared to record levels, because of tax cuts and military spending, while unemployment rates rose to forty-year highs.

The passage of JTPA and failure of a new job creation law can clearly be put at the feet of the resurgent Republicans and the voters' swing to the right. Nevertheless, JTPA demonstrates the difficulty the Democrats had in protecting ALMP after they had accepted Nixon's radical decentralization. Thus, ALMP was slashed in America, when at the same time, the SPD mounted an effective defense.

COMPARISONS AND CONCLUSIONS: WEST GERMANY AND THE UNITED STATES

Two systematic causes can explain ALMP in these two countries: the social demands of left party power and ideology and the effects of state formation in legislation (see Figures 10 and 11 for a summary of these causal processes). In addition, a less important third cause involves different styles of evaluation research.

First, left party power was a powerful force for ALMP in both countries because both the SPD and Democratic parties clearly promoted and right parties generally opposed ALMP. However, differences between the two countries can be explained by left ideologies. The SPD emphasis on participation rights provided a bargaining chip that forced the conservative parties beyond their social rights programs. The SPD backed their ideology with a disciplined organization and large blue-collar organizational base. During austerity, the SPD shielded labor market laws from onerous budget cutting. The U.S. Democratic party, in contrast, emphasized social rights programs, and as a result their bargaining position was weaker. When U.S. job creation came under heavy criticism, many U.S. Democrats abandoned ship. Their ideological support for full employment was much more uncertain, depending upon the changing winds of media and public opinion. The U.S. Democratic party lacked an ideological framework adequate to handle ALMP; furthermore, left ideology and strategy were not pounded out in yearly party meetings, but they were most often left to elite meetings or private sessions developing presidential campaign strategy. Thus, policy direction is somewhat haphazard or simply incremental.

Segmentation in the American welfare state also weakened social demands for ALMP. The labor market is divided into upper and lower tiers by race and class distinctions, while social policy is partitioned into veteran and nonveteran welfare and educational programs. U.S. labor strongly supported ALMP, with only

10. The Formation of Active Labor Market Policies in West Germany After World War II

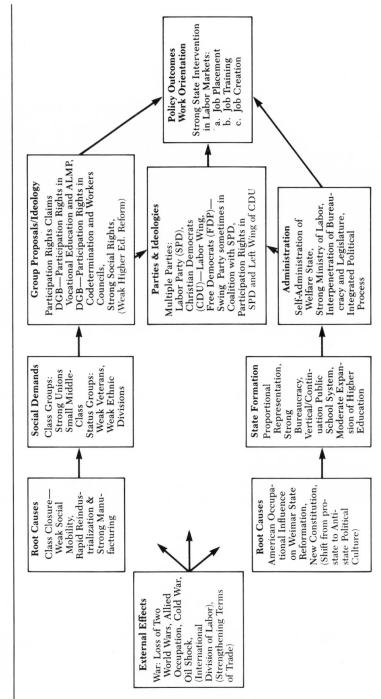

Note: Factors are listed in order of importance, and items in parentheses are less important causes for ALMP not mentioned in the text.

11. The Formation of Active Labor Market Policies in the United States After World War II

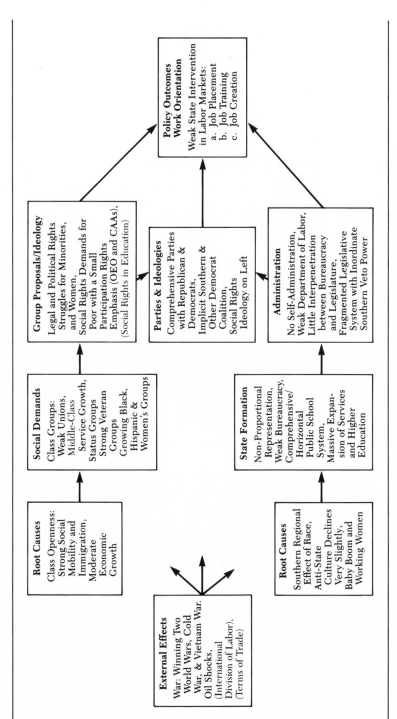

Note: Factors are listed in order of importance, and items in parentheses are less important causes for ALMP not mentioned in the text.

a small base of power in the upper tier of blue-collar labor markets. Remarkably, organized labor still maintained its support for policies that in reality offered them little direct benefit. Despite charges of union racism and self-interest in pursuing collective bargaining, the AFL-CIO has proven itself one of the most altruistic of all large interest groups. Nonetheless, its power was much weaker than the DGB.

Parties of the West German right have had a more positive approach to ALMP than those in the United States. Labor leaders strongly supported ALMP during periods of economic growth, but the CDU/CSU's left wing was largely silent during recessions. No such labor wing exists in the Republican party even though many blue-collar workers would support it. The CDU/CSU tends to mirror employer requests for job training during booms and budget cuts during recessions. Although the American Republican party also reacts to the influence of employers, American employers have been hostile to ALMP. The Chamber of Commerce and especially NAM have consistently opposed ALMP during both economic growth and recessions. Both employer groups tend to lose influence on ALMP issues in good times, but their criticisms are more powerful in recessions. On the whole, parties of the West German right have solidly pursued social rights, but the U.S. right wavers between moderately supporting social rights and definitely pushing citizenship rights back to the legal rights conception of pure insurance and individual employment contracts. Thus, power and ideology of both party and interest group are the most important factors that account for ALMP in West Germany, while these social demand factors are considerably weaker in the United States.

Second, these two countries differ greatly in their state legislative structures, despite similarities in party competition, federal structure, and interest group conflict. The United States has a committee system staffed at crucial points by Southern Democrats who have blocked ALMP legislation. Interest groups, like the AVA, often obtained special leverage on legislation and could veto some bills. This fragmentation encouraged the proliferation rather than aggregation of interest groups. Extraordinary consensus, along with tactical expertise, was needed to pass even diluted ALMP legislation. Major changes in basic structure—such as the employment service—are nearly impossible, despite their need.

The West German legislative process, particularly for ALMP, contained few veto points where special interests could destroy the social demands for legislation. In West Germany, conflict in the legislative process has been intense, but law making was inherently less precarious: committee veto powers are slight; interests are effectively aggregated; and federal ministries develop policy and obtain comments from interest groups rather than compete intensely with each other. Thus, West German law making was much more decisive and less subject to detours than law making in the United States. In fact, the interpenetration of bureaucratic, representative, and interest group personnel throughout the West German government is common (Katzenstein 1987, p. 10). The only West German approximation to American fragmentation was in the coalition government, where the FDP obtained special favors for its own constituency; however, this was not the FDP's practice until the late 1970s and early 1980s.

The bureaucracy in the United States is difficult to control for many reasons: multiple hierarchies, uncertain party discipline, limited bureaucratic career structures, and independent bureaucrats unconstrained by self-administration. Most federal bureaucracies are formally controlled by the president, but congressional committees and interest groups often have more staying power than presidents who come and go. Furthermore, the role of the bureaucracy in formulating policy has dwindled. Interest groups write many bills, and the president has developed a special staff for policy; the executive no longer depends upon bureaucratic policy makers. Bureaucratic contentiousness in the United States stems from low prestige and pay and a career path that does not automatically lead to politics. Consequently, American bureaucrats have an incentive to build and protect their own organizational empires. In West Germany, the chancellor can control the bureaucracy because bureaucrats often use the ministry as a stepping stone to political office, usually through the party lists. Although the chancellor and his ministers may come from opposite sides of the ruling coalition, since World War II the minister of labor has always come from the chancellor's party.[19]

A third cause of ALMP, but one that is difficult to measure, concerns evaluation research. West Germany and most of continental Europe spend money to acquire the knowledge needed to improve programs—facilitation—while the United States focuses on the knowledge needed to judge programs—evaluation (Schwanse 1982; Derlien 1990). These two research styles have entirely different political uses: "knowledge to improve" promotes policy, while "knowledge to judge" criticizes policy. For instance, as late as 1982, no West German studies had effectively calculated substitution effects and the net impact of general job creation measures on employment (Schmid 1982, p. 198). That such a basic control remained undone in the 1980s signals important political differences in how evaluation research proceeds in the two countries. Wilensky (1985) argues that the more evaluation research, the less the effectiveness of the policy; the less evaluation research, the greater the expenditures and the impact of the policy. Moreover, the greater the reporting requirements and evaluation research, the less likely private employers or local governments will participate in ALMP programs. However, "facilitation research" encourages policy improvement and participation. Wilensky (1985) recognizes this "legitimation" function of evaluation research, but its effects are difficult to isolate.

In West Germany, "work" remained the main problem of society, and social demands have had a clear positive effect on ALMP legislation. The state's clear responsibility for the unemployed even has some constitutional claims (Blüm 1983; Vogel 1983). Social demands for employment led to a centralized employment service with monopoly powers in the labor market and further extensions of ALMP programs during the last thirty years. But weaker social demands in the United States are split by many status divisions. The United States enacted a Full Employment Act without operative provisions concerning employment. Since

19. This rosy picture, however, was not always the case with other ministries. Coalition politics often dictate shared party control of the cabinet. For instance, Chancellor Schmidt had trouble controlling FDP Minister of Economics Lambsdorff.

then, state structures have constrained ALMP programs and expenditures even at the height of Democratic party power. During the late 1970s, the temporary consensus brought on by the oil shock gave job creation a major boost, but otherwise the United States has relied upon social rights programs and little ALMP.

Chapter Nine

The Determinants
of ALMP Expenditures

For a historical explanation of ALMP, I followed politicians and interest groups through intense debates and specific bargains in the corridors of power. Often the focal length was short; immediate events sometimes obscure long-term changes. I now refocus on a systematic view of ALMP expenditures over a thirty-year span. Does unemployment have an incremental effect on what governments do about unemployment? Does left party power always cause ALMP? Although the historical evidence may be opaque at times, evidence in time series will show that unemployment and left party power have a strong effect on ALMP in West Germany, while their influence is much weaker or even insignificant in the United States. For West Germany, left party power, unemployment, the manufacturing sector, and the negative impact of the first oil shock explain ALMP expenditures. But in the United States, the explanation is more fragmented and connected to state formation. Labor market pressure and the service sector are the main causes of ALMP, with marginal assistance from left party power and the positive effect of the first oil shock, while the Reagan administration and bureaucratic confusion variables exert a negative impact.

These differences illustrate two different approaches to social policy. In the West German "work model," politicians responded to social demands from the working class: pressure from trade unions caused left party power to fund ALMP to combat unemployment and a declining manufacturing sector. In the U.S. "socialization model," labor market pressures—large numbers of women and young people in the labor market—caused Democratic politicians to fund ALMP in an expanding public sector. The West German model focuses on social demands related to work, while the U.S. model targets state formation focused on social services.

After discussing the theoretical model, data, and methodology, I evaluate and compare the causes of ALMP expenditures. In the final section, I put the most important variables together into path models explaining ALMP expenditures.

THEORY OF ALMP EXPENDITURES

I build on the theory discussed in the previous chapters, but structural constants cannot be included in the time-series analysis because the quantitative analysis is wholly incremental.[1] Consequently, the quantitative model is a subset of the prior theory because it focuses on only incremental variables from the social demand and state formation theories. It consists of six parts (see Figure 12).

The first set of variables concerns the structural causes of social demands. Employment in manufacturing as a percentage of the total labor force declines, pushing workers into unemployment and/or denying younger workers entry into manufacturing jobs. The reality or specter of this decline promotes ALMP expenditures. Although automation and robotics may not directly take jobs away from workers, manufacturing ceases to create new jobs even though production continues to rise. For example, the oil crises accelerated the decline of employment in manufacturing by pushing growth in productivity through labor-saving capital

1. Specific theories on ALMP are rare. Robertson (1988) provides models of egalitarian, guardian, and business-centered strategies toward labor market policy, but he does not provide systematic independent variables. For theories that have a more specific discussion of the quantitative issues involved in explaining expenditures, see Ashford 1978; Burstein 1981; Cameron 1978; Devine 1985; Godwin and Shepard 1976; Griffin, Wallace, Devine 1982, 1983; Griffin, Devine, Wallace 1983; Hage and Hanneman 1980; Korpi 1989; Lewis 1981; Peters and Klingman 1978; Tarschys 1975; and Uusitalo 1984.

12. The Formation of Active Labor Market Policy After World War II—Quantitative Model

Policy Outcome
Size of ALMP
Expenditures:
a. Job Placement
b. Job Training
c. Job Creation

1. Structural Causes
Size of
Manufacturing
Sector,
Trade Union
& DGB Power.

2. Social Demands
Unemployment
Rate,
Economic Misery
Index,
Riots, Protests, &
Strikes

5. Political Power
Left Party Power
in Legislature &
Executive,
Administration
Dummy Variables

4. Labor Market Pressures
Baby Boom Generation Enters
Labor Market & Service
Sector,
Women enter Labor Market
and Service Sector,
Guestworkers & Immigrants
Intensify Service Sector

3. State Administration
Size of Bureaucracy—
State/Local and ALMP
Bureaucracy,
Bureaucratic Confusion,
Service Sector Growth:
Higher Education and
Other Services

6. External Effects
Oil Shock Effects:
1st Oil Shock,
2nd Oil Shock
(War Dummy Variable)

investment and the relocation of plants in third world countries. As unemployment reaches new heights, unions must either respond through political action or lose members. ALMP is one political course. In a purely industrial society, unions with political clout should respond to the decline in the manufacturing sector and unemployment with successful pressure for ALMP (Gourevitch et al. 1984).

Second, hypotheses concerning social demand involve the effect of more short-term pressures. The business cycle—the fluctuations in unemployment, inflation, and economic growth—have an impact on politics and social welfare programs including ALMP. Unemployment clearly increases expenditures on unemployment compensation, but the relationship of unemployment to ALMP is most often assumed to be positive. Because ALMP aims to reduce unemployment, high unemployment should lead politicians to increase expenditures on ALMP—a countercyclical hypothesis. However, if unemployment reduces resources and the cooperation of capital, the state's response should be procyclical with less expenditure. Thus, the business cycle may produce opposite responses. In the countercyclical theory, the state responds to social demands by increasing spending during economic crisis to reduce unemployment. Inflation is included because ALMP may remove production bottlenecks by increasing the supply of scarce skills, which then increase production and economic growth. Thus, the state creates ALMP in response to unemployment and low growth.

In the procyclical hypothesis, social demands fail as conservative pressures to constrain governmental expenditures prevail during periods of low economic growth, profits, and tax revenues. Economic growth ensures more spending on ALMP during good times and allows the left to press for expansion of the welfare state. Low economic growth constrains government expenditures and ALMP during inevitable economic downturns, and this gives capital an upper hand, as the government and most of society look to business for more jobs. In effect, the state has coopted the unions during good times and straitjacketed them during bad times (Nolan and Sabel 1982, pp. 12–16). Social protest in the form of riots, demonstrations, and strikes can emerge out of this bottling up of discontent and create pressures for increased ALMP expenditures (Piven and Cloward 1971).

Third, state formation and bureaucratic growth may cause higher ALMP. As citizens obtain higher disposable income, they demand more state and private services. As more women enter competitive employment, the service sector expands through the growth of female-dominated semi-professions—teaching, nursing, social work—and the demand for services for working mothers— child care, cleaning, and food services. The education system that produces larger numbers of white-collar workers creates a surplus of workers that must be absorbed by the state. As the state and local governments reach the fiscal limits of absorbing labor market slack, they turn to the federal government for subsidies. The federal government, while controlled by the left and concerned about the disadvantaged, subsidizes local government expansion for white-collar workers through public service employment. Consequently, most ALMP job creation comes in the form of government services, and the service sector "pulls" ALMP into its financially needy arms.

The state may also be involved because bureaucracies protect their own survival, growth, and stability; but bureaucratic interests differ in elite or common civil service systems. Elite systems, like those of West Germany, keep the size of the bureaucracy lean to exert upward pressure on bureaucratic wages and benefits; their power and prestige depend on scarcity. Common systems, like those of the United States, operate in the opposite way because mere bureaucratic employment does not entail special privilege. Only expanding the common system—more duties, employees, and programs—will yield higher wages and further promotions (Peters 1978). Thus, the labor market's bureaucracies should push for greater ALMP, with such pressure being higher in the United States.

Fourth, a number of factors strain labor markets: working women, young adults, and immigrants. The rise of married women in the labor force increases job competition;[2] the baby

2. The tremendous rise in rates of female participation in the labor force has come from married women from the middle and upper classes. Single

boom places a tremendous burden on the labor market to absorb large cohorts of new workers; and immigration also crowds the civilian labor force. Labor market pressure has two effects: indirectly, it influences policy by increasing the unemployment rate, which can be a cause of ALMP; and directly, it influences policy through worker's insecurity on the job (this factor can be shown when equations control for unemployment). Workers experiencing the labor market pressure through organizational crowding react with political attitudes and demand increasing employment.

Rates of female participation in the labor force should be strongly connected to ALMP in two ways. As women work, they become more conscious of labor market issues and demand equal employment opportunity; their demands should include ALMP. Politicians respond slowly because some may see women in the labor force according to old stereotypes—exceptional childless and career-oriented women or married women needlessly competing for male jobs—rather than more recent realities—dual career families with wives often pursuing fragmented careers and single mothers forced into the labor market and desperate for decent paying work. Increases in rates of female participation and affirmative action may also threaten males through tighter conditions in the labor market. Concern for unemployed males initiates political demands for ALMP, while concern for females prompts protection of civil rights. ALMP expenditures should increase because employed men want insurance against competition in the labor market and women want fairness at work and access to jobs (Gelb and Palley 1982; Kessler 1982).

A bulge of young persons crowds the labor market. In the mid-1970s, the American baby boom entered the labor market, caused higher unemployment, and then demanded ALMP. By the 1980s, the peak of the baby boom had passed; most of the youthful cohort reached stable employment, while succeeding cohorts were smaller and less politically demanding. Immigration should exert similar pressures. In West Germany, the steady

---

women, black women, and lower-class married women have always had high rates of participation in the labor force.

growth of guestworkers caused the government to recognize the possibility of guestworkers taking jobs from natives. They used ALMP to promote the native labor force over the guestworkers. Similar governmental tendencies concerning immigrants in the United States may have operated, although no such explicit policy existed.[3]

Fifth, political power hypotheses regard governmental processes as an independent causal force, rather than as a superstructural reaction to societal cleavages or economic fluctuations.[4] In many analyses of social spending, political variables have often been operationalized crudely.[5] As a result, dummy variables for party majorities and party control of the presidency appear to have had little effect on "education, manpower, and social services" or "social consumption" expenditures (Browning 1981, pp. 99, 155; Devine 1985). However, by dividing American parties into their ideological components—Southern Democrats and Republicans on the right, and other Democrats on the left—and by separating executive from legislative power, left political power should have a positive effect on ALMP. The political party's power directly determines public expenditures in two ways: an increase of expenditures by step function through new legislation, and the incremental, year-to-year increase in expenditures through budgetary decisions.

Sixth, the external effects of major crises may have a tremendous influence on the welfare state. After World War II, the major external event was the oil shock, which drastically reduced the terms of trade, caused mass unemployment, and made a sig-

---

3. This hypothesis applies even though most illegal immigrants and guestworkers do not take jobs from native workers. Employers reorient future investment and reallocate tasks in the face of immigration and possibilities of cheap labor. This often pressures native men and women in the secondary sector and even lower tiers of the primary sector to seek better work or else be subject to downward wage pressures. The fact is that native Germans were on the automobile assembly lines in the 1950s, and now guestworkers are in many of those jobs. But no guestworker took a job away from a unionized German worker.

4. Some claim that socioeconomic conditions are more powerful than party power in cross-sectional and time-series analysis (Lewis-Beck 1977, Dye 1981).

5. An exception is Wilensky (1981) who demonstrates in a crosssectional analysis of nineteen countries that cumulative left-party and Catholic-party power from 1919 to 1976 produces democratic corporatist bargaining structures that, in turn, promote higher public expenditures.

nificant impact on ALMP in both countries. War, however, did not occur after 1950 in West Germany, and although participation in wars was more frequent for the United States, the wars had only a moderate (negative) impact on ALMP.

This model follows earlier models in emphasizing social demands, state formation, and external events. However, it does not directly measure citizenship rights as an independent variable and cannot operationalize structural constants such as proportional-versus-nonproportional election procedures. For instance, the strong differential effects of the war and veterans as a status group were discussed in the previous chapter, but their effects cannot be seen here. Nevertheless, the quantitative model in a reduced theoretical form answers important questions that the documentary analysis does not. In a sense, it not only tests elements in common with the documentary models (political power of parties, organizational confusion, and unemployment), but it also tests variables not in the documentary models (pressure on the labor market and bureaucratic growth).

VARIABLES, METHODS, AND LAG STRUCTURES

Efforts to measure ALMP— the dependent variable—are described in both the introduction and the Appendix. But unlike previous chapters I will increase the comparability of the two cases by excluding programs that exist in only one country and are somewhat marginal to ALMP, that is, the youth services programs for high school students in the United States and the job maintenance programs in West Germany. Rather straightforward data for the other variables for both countries come from the federal government's statistical sources (see Appendix).

Indices were created to reduce the complexity of the data and avoid multicollinearity problems: the "economic misery index"— unemployment plus inflation minus economic growth rates; the "labor market pressure index"—the percentage of women in the labor force, plus the percentage of young adults in the labor force, plus immigrants as a percentage of the population; the "left party power" index—Bundestag plus chancellor's party power in West Germany, and the House and Senate party power in the United States; and the "service sector index"—the combination of private and public service sectors in the United States. The indices, composed of rates and percentages, are not standardized (each component has a different weight), except for the left party power index which is standardized (each component has equal weight).

I divided ALMP expenditures by GNP to provide comparability and refer to it as ALMP throughout the rest of this chapter. I did not use rate-of-change variables because social pressures do not mechanistically affect spending; that is, the policy process is not such an immediate stimulus-response relationship. Economic variables may react quickly and consistently, but political and social variables often develop time cushions and percolator effects. Only inflation, the money supply, and economic growth are rates of change because that is their common meaning.[6]

Because time-series data on public expenditures are not independent, traditional regression procedures could not be used. Autocorrelation violates the assumptions of ordinary least squares regression: error terms are not normally distributed with a mean of zero, may not have constant variance, and are in fact correlated. When autocorrelated error exists, the coefficients are inefficient, and levels of significance are inflated. Consequently, I used a version of the Cochrane-Orcutt method to control for autocorrelation.[7]

6. Jennings justifies not using rates of change: "Many analysts (e.g., Cook and Campbell 1979) recommend that time-series data always be detrended (rates of change) before analysis. That seems appropriate when one is conducting quasi-experimental research based on stimulus-response models; however, much of the work on the relationship between socio-economic development and public policy is inappropriately represented by stimulus-response models, so there is little reason to detrend the data. In fact, doing so could undermine any attempt to detect relationships between levels of system components" (1983, p. 1232).

7. I used the AUTOREG program in SAS, which generalizes the Cochrane-Orcutt method into a "two step full transform" method to control for autocorrelation (SAS 1982; Pindyck and Rubinfeld 1981). I chose this method over simple regression with a lagged dependent variable as a means of controlling for autocorrelation because this correction consumes variance in the unlagged dependent variable that independent variables would have explained (Jennings 1983). I did not use ARIMA models because they require at least fifty cases (McCleary and Hay 1980, p. 20).

Lags provide theoretical and causal structure to models and represent a more realistic build-up of social demands to which politicians and bureaucrats can respond (Isaac and Kelly 1981, p. 1365).[8] Prior time-series research has used one-year lags, but I use longer and more distributed lags. Politics clearly lengthens and diversifies lags in three ways: the bureaucracy takes time to spend money, activate plans, and hire employees; new legislation may take one to three years depending upon support; and executive administrations may take four years or more to replace. The autocorrelation function already covers the incremental effects of budgetary decisions that depend on the previous year in a one-year lag. A two-year lag would take into account the effects of congressional elections. The legislative process itself accounts for two- and three-year lags, while bureaucratic implementation and regime changes could take as much as a four-year lag. Thus, the arbitrary assignment of one-year lags clearly distorts political reality.

Lags in complex policy processes are distributed, spreading the influence of each variable in a particular pattern over a number of years. Weights for distributed lags, generally supported by statistical tests with polynomial and geometrical lags, specify the years that have the most effect.[9] Political variables have distributed lags that follow a four-year inverted U-curve. They build up and decline with their peak influence coming in the second and third years, although a few political variables in the United States operate one year faster. Thus, the distributed lag was initially 15 percent (year 1), 30 percent (year 2), 40 percent (year 3), and 15 percent (year 4); I then simplified it to 30 percent (year 2) and 40 percent (year 3) because the 15 percent figures did not significantly affect correlation coefficients. Economic variables, however, have a peak influence in the first year because economic

8. Some differences in the length of lags are due to the nature of the dependent variable. For instance, wage/capital ratios are rather immediate phenomena; that is, wages are paid, and profits are generated during the same year in which they occur—they do not have two-to-four-year gestation periods. Even public assistance expenditures are much more responsive to needs than ALMP because they must be paid immediately, but ALMP can be delayed.

9. I constructed formal polynomial (Almon) lags for the political variables and geometric (Koyck) lags for economic variables. Although the formal lags support my theory, they were not statistically significant (Pindyck and Rubinfeld 1981).

information is quickly disseminated throughout society, but then variables decline in the second year when new economic reports are issued. Unemployment and other economic variables that are widely publicized in the media may quickly increase discretionary bureaucratic expenditures on existing programs. This lag was 70 percent (year 1) and 30 percent (year 2). Demographic variables are clearly indirect because they do not signal an immediate problem requiring political action; they enter the political spotlight only when they cause something else like overcrowded schools or unemployment. Demographic variables follow an inverted U-curve like political variables, but their peak influence comes later in the third and fourth years.

DETERMINANTS OF ALMP EXPENDITURES

In this section, I test the social demand, state formation, and effects of external variables against the data (see Table 6 for correlation coefficients).[10]

Structural Social Demands.   The two structural variables are the percentages of manufacturing-sector employment and trade union power. In the United States, the decline in the manufacturing sector clearly has had a large impact on ALMP (r=−0.76),[11] but American union membership as a percentage of the nonagricultural labor force is strongly negative with ALMP (r=−0.69), contradicting the theory. AFL-CIO and UAW lobbying and electoral expenditures as a percentage of GNP were also unrelated to ALMP (r=+0.07). I tried eight different lags on union membership ratios and lobbying expenditures over GNP without significant effect. West Germany fits this model much better. The manufacturing sector and union density ratios are highly

10. Industrial development theory focuses on socioeconomic development as the cause of public expenditures, but I have not used this theory because GNP per capita (the usual measure) is a widely based societal resource that could be used for many purposes, and it does not differentiate between results in these two countries (Wilensky 1975, p. 26; Grønbjerg 1977; Stinchcombe 1985). But, real GNP per capita is correlated with ALMP in both countries (r=+0.83; r=+0.77).

11. In the 1980s, manufacturing still accounted for 41 percent of the nonagricultural labor force in West Germany but only 22.5 percent in the United States.

TABLE 6   *The Determinants of Expenditures on Active Labor Market Policy, 1950 to 1985: Hypotheses with Zero-order Correlation Coefficients*

Hypotheses	United States	West Germany
Structural Causes:		
Percentage of manufacturing employees in the civilian labor force	−0.76[a]	−0.52[a]
Union membership ratio	−0.84[a]	+0.78[a]
Union—other measures[b]	+0.09	+0.86[a]
Social Demands:		
Unemployment rate	+0.44[a]	+0.51[a]
Inflation rate	+0.56[a]	+0.72[a]
Real growth rate	+0.36	−0.25
Economic misery index	+0.57[a]	+0.81[a]
Riot frequency	+0.08	+0.23
Demonstration frequency	+0.34	+0.16
Strike frequency	−0.23	+0.17
State Administration:		
Percentage of service sector employees in the civilian labor force	+0.75[a]	+0.73[a]
USES or BAA employees as a percentage of labor force	+0.34	+0.76[a]
State and local employees as a percentage of labor force	+0.79[a]	—
Labor Market Pressure Hypotheses:		
Female labor force participation rate	+0.68[a]	+0.31
Young worker percentage of labor force	+0.79[a]	+0.02[c]
Immigrant or guestworker percentage of population	+0.50[a]	+0.82[a]
Labor market pressure index	+0.84[a]	+0.74[a]
Political Power:		
Left party power index	+0.69[a]	+0.81[a]
Right party power index	−0.77[a]	−0.75[a]
Left executive power	+0.06	+0.70[a]
External Effects:		
Oilshock dummy variable	+0.74	+0.56
War dummy variable	−0.18	—

[a]The statistic is significant at the $p<0.05$ level.

[b]Other union measures are for union political expenditures in the U.S. and DGB membership rations in West Germany.

[c]This correlation is for young workers aged fifteen to twenty-five; other correlations for workers aged fifteen to twenty ($r=+0.58$) and twenty to twenty-five ($r=−0.25$) are reported in the text.

correlated with ALMP expenditures ($r=-0.52$, $r=+0.76$), and the service sector is not correlated with manufacturing employees ($r=-0.24$) or unemployment ($r=-0.08$).[12] Furthermore, of all the West German political variables DGB power alone has the strongest correlation with ALMP ($r=+0.86$). Thus, union power cannot account for U.S. ALMP, but it is powerfully connected to the West German manufacturing sector and ALMP.

Social Demands. West German economic variables are much more countercyclically related to ALMP than those of the United States. In the United States, ALMP is only moderately correlated with unemployment ($r=+0.44$)—not as high as expected for a direct cause of ALMP. The same West German correlation is slightly stronger ($r=+0.51$). Although ALMP is countercyclically related to unemployment in both countries, we see in the discussion of the oil shock that this relationship is more complicated in the United States. The impact of the rates of economic growth is totally different in the two countries: U.S. economic growth is positive and moderately correlated with ALMP ($r=+0.36$), while West German economic growth is negative and not strongly correlated with ALMP ($r=-0.25$). Economic growth in the United States supports the procyclical hypothesis: more is spent on ALMP during periods of high growth. But West German growth rates are countercyclical with ALMP because slow growth and recession mildly promoted West Germany ALMP expenditures.

An economic misery index tests whether overall economic effects produce a demand for ALMP. The results are moderate in the United States ($r=+0.57$) but much stronger in West Germany ($r=+0.81$). Unemployment, inflation, and misery are economic problems.[13] When the state responds to problems by increasing

12. The definition of the service sector for West Germany includes the state and service industries.

13. Inflation can play a role with ALMP, but I do not believe it is very large. If Swedish labor economists who developed ALMP in part to combat inflation are correct, inflation should have a positive impact on ALMP expenditures (Rehn 1948, Meidner 1948, Piore 1979). From the "fiscal crisis" perspective, the state uses or creates inflation to generate a higher tax rate for greater social spending, or it can use inflation to disguise cuts in real expenditures (O'Connor 1973, pp. 43, 232). The correlation could go either way in this neo-Marxist approach. A negative correlation between inflation and ALMP would be predicted

ALMP spending, it reacts to social demands and confirms the countercyclical hypothesis. The results tend to verify the social demand hypothesis; it is strong in West Germany but less so in the United States. Growth rates are economic resources that should have negative correlations with ALMP to support the countercyclical hypothesis. This is confirmed in West Germany but not in the United States. However, evidence of intense social demands through strikes, riots, or demonstrations is not supported in either country because none of these correlations are significant with ALMP. Thus, the overall evidence for the countercyclical operation of social demands is strong in West Germany but mild or even contradictory in America.

State Administration and Growth.   In the United States, the service sector and state/local employees are strongly correlated with ALMP ($r=+0.75$, $r=+0.79$), and so are women and young workers in the labor force ($r=+0.68$, $r=+0.79$). The West German service sector is strongly correlated with ALMP ($r=+0.73$), but neither women ($r=+0.31$) nor young workers ($r=+0.02$) show strong correlations. West Germany clearly did not open the sluice gates of higher education to encourage a rush of college graduates to enter government employment. Instead, guestworkers are highly correlated with ALMP in West Germany ($r=+0.82$), but guestworkers, like illegal aliens in the United States, demand less from state services. Thus, in the United States, the service sector pulled in workers and necessitated ALMP, unlike the West German service sector.

The effect of the bureaucracy on ALMP expenditures can be estimated by the ratio of employment service workers to the civilian labor force. The bureaucracy hypothesis, however, is weak with the U.S. Employment Service ($r=+0.34$) because it grew little with ALMP—a result befitting an elite rather than a com-

---

by those who place weight on the negative correlation of inflation with unemployment in the Phillips curve (Laidler and Parkin 1975, pp. 753–66). The correlations of ALMP with inflation are positive and strong in both the United States ($r=+0.56$) and West Germany ($r=+0.72$). But in the end, I believe inflation has too weak a theoretical connection to ALMP to be considered an important cause of ALMP.

mon system. State and local bureaucracies, rather than USES, implemented CETA and are more directly connected to ALMP (r=+0.79). In West Germany, the employment service ratio is strongly correlated with ALMP (r=+0.76) because Bundesanstalt employees actually implemented ALMP programs, rather than subcontracting them to local governments.[14]

However, the causal connection between ALMP and bureaucratic growth has the potential for going in both directions. A causal order test in West Germany disproves the bureaucratic hypotheses (Granger 1969). The two bureaucratic variables (total Bundesanstalt and permanent Bundesanstalt employees as a percentage of the labor force), each lagged two years, explain 31 percent and 19 percent of the variance in the unlagged ALMP variable, but ALMP lagged two years, explains 37 percent and 48 percent of the variance in each of the unlagged bureaucracy variables. Because ALMP causes the West German employment service bureaucracy to grow, rather than the other way around, it cannot be used as a cause of ALMP. In the United States, the causal ordering of the state administration variables is different. ALMP's two-year lag explains only 15 percent of the variance in local and city government employees as a percentage of the labor force (unlagged), while local and city government employees with the same lag explain 45 percent of the variance in the unlagged ALMP variable—three times as much. The city and local bureaucracy is a much more powerful predictor of American ALMP than vice versa.

The results of the bureaucratic variables generally support the elite/common hypotheses. On the one hand, the West German bureaucracy grows because of increased ALMP, not its own inertia. On the other hand, American state and local governments form a strong and positive cause of increased ALMP expenditures. Although this variable had its strongest effect during the CETA period (1973 to 1982), the strength of U.S. state and local government employment leads to a much wider set of statements

14. Incrementalist theory is related to state-based theories, but I do not use it (Lindblom 1980, Wildavsky 1979). It can be tested by correlating the lagged dependent variable with the unlagged dependent variable. Although this relation is strong in the United States and West Germany (r=+0.82 and 0.83), it cannot explain reversals in expenditures.

about the service sector. As a result, I will use state and local
governmental employment in the United States as an indirect
effect in the path analysis of the service sector on subsequent
supply of labor. USES, however, is clearly being bypassed for
duties; and this supports the discussion of institutional weakness
in Chapter 4.

Labor Market Pressure Models.   Participation rates of females
in the labor force are strongly correlated with ALMP in the
United States ($r= +0.68$) but not in West Germany ($r= +0.31$). In
multivariate equations with unemployment, the direct effects of
women in the American labor force on ALMP are stronger than
unemployment, but participation rates of females in West Germany turn weak and negative. This is mainly because West German female participation rates have only increased by 2 percent
from 1962 to 1982, while U.S. rates have increased by 21 percent
in the same period. Consequently, the hypothesis of female participation in the labor force has support independent of unemployment only in the United States.

In the United States the size of the cohorts aged sixteen to
nineteen and/or twenty to twenty-four as a percentage of the total
population are both highly correlated with ALMP ($r= +0.88$ and
$+0.77$), and I combined them into a youth variable aged sixteen
to twenty-four ($r= +0.80$). In West Germany, although the correlation of twenty- to twenty-five-year-olds with ALMP is negative
($r= -0.25$), the correlation for the fifteen to twenty age group is
high and positive ($r= +0.58$). This shows that young adults are
quickly assimilated into the work force through the education system's strong connections with the labor market. Again political
pressure is separated from economic need by controlling for unemployment. In the United States regressions on ALMP, the percentage of young persons in the labor force (aged sixteen to
twenty-four) is stronger than the unemployment rate, while in
West Germany the reverse of the equations holds with young
persons (aged fifteen to twenty) being weak and negative. Like
female participation rates, the baby boom hypothesis is stronger
than unemployment in the United States but not in West
Germany.

The correlation between ALMP and guestworkers as a percentage of the labor force in West Germany is strong ($r = +0.82$), but only moderate between ALMP and immigrants in the United States ($r = +0.50$). Even controlling for unemployment in West Germany, guestworkers are a stronger factor than unemployment in explaining ALMP. Similar regression results in the United States are reversed. Thus, the direct, independent effects of guestworkers in West Germany are large, while the similar effects of immigrants in the United States are small.

These three pressures, combined into a weighted labor market pressure index, have a strong positive impact on ALMP in the United States ($r = +0.84$) but weaker influence in West Germany ($r = +0.74$); the West German differential mainly results from the low participation rate of women in the labor force and a small baby boom. When regressing labor market pressure and unemployment on ALMP, labor market pressure is much stronger than unemployment in the United States but weaker in West Germany. Thus, labor market pressure has strong, direct effects on American ALMP independent of unemployment, while labor market pressure in West Germany does not.

The Political Power.   The American left party power index, excluding Southern Democrats and combining both houses, is significantly correlated with ALMP ($r = +0.69$). In West Germany, left party power, including the Bundestag and chancellor, is more strongly correlated with ALMP ($r = +0.81$). Both right parties are negative and strong with ALMP ($r = -0.77$ in the United States, and $r = -0.75$ in West Germany). However, the left executives in each country have not been equally responsive to ALMP.[15] The left presidency dummy variable ($r = +0.16$) and

15. The executive may manipulate the economy (via the money supply or fiscal spending) a year before the election to insure reelection through short-term economic growth (Tufte 1978; Monroe 1979, 1984). The president, according to Macesich, is the "principal political influence behind Federal Reserve policy" (1984, p. 120). This hypothesis of a political business cycle worked moderately well in the United States with high correlations between the money supply and ALMP ($r = +0.65$ for M1, $r = +0.70$ for M2), but not in West Germany, where the Bundesbank is more independent ($r = -0.22$ for M1, $r = -0.12$ for M2) (Koenig 1988).

left presidency ideological index (r=+0.06) are both weak with American ALMP, while the left chancellor is strong with West German ALMP (r=+0.70 for a dummy variable). The strong correlation in West Germany reflects the unity of West German politics, where the chancellor is chosen by the legislature; the weak American correlations demonstrate the fragmentation of U.S. politics, where the legislature and presidency are chosen independently. But more important, it shows that left chancellors have had a strong impact on ALMP; however, American Democratic presidents have had little effect, largely because the Truman administration had almost no ALMP, the Johnson/Kennedy administrations had small but growing ALMP, and the Nixon/ Ford administrations presided over major increases in ALMP. If I had excluded the Southern Democratic presidents, this would have left only six years for the left presidency and an even lower correlation coefficient.[16]

External Events.   The 1974 to 1981 oil shock played economic havoc throughout the Western industrialized world. But the correlation of the oil shock dummy variable and ALMP is more strongly countercyclical in the United States (r=+0.74) than in West Germany (r=+0.56). The oil shock is stronger in the United States because unemployment was perceived two ways: externally induced unemployment brought about by the oil shock (1974 to 1981), and internally induced unemployment due to the business cycle (1950 to 1973 and 1982 to 1984). Americans viewed internally induced unemployment individualistically: if the unemployed really wanted jobs, they could get them. Consequently,

16. The political variables in this section involve a number of issues. The index of the American left's political power, based on ideological voting, produced results similar to the party membership variable so I did not use it. Also, the left's power on the House Rules Committee (with a one-fifth weight) in combination with the left's legislative power results in a stronger relationship (r=+0.77), and this accurately reflects the fragmented nature of U.S. politics. But I did not use this due to multicollinearity problems. West German left and right legislative power relationships with ALMP formed a parabola, so they were transformed by squaring the independent variable. The nontransformed relationships with ALMP were r=0.52 and −0.48. This transformation means that legislative power is curvilinear with ALMP—an inverted U-curve— because the multitude of parties in the early 1950s caused left party power to be seriously underestimated when it was really somewhat high.

job creation by the state was not necessary, although job training was permissible as part of the individual's attempt to advance into more highly skilled jobs. However, Americans saw externally induced unemployment in the 1970s as a foreign threat from hostile countries dramatized by the Iranian hostage crisis. The oil shock produced a temporary consensus to invest heavily in job creation programs. This influence subsided by 1982 when the hostages were released, oil prices dropped, and the CETA program disappeared. The correlations of externally induced unemployment and internally induced unemployment with ALMP are opposite and strong (r= +0.80 external, and r= −0.87 internal).[17] Thus, the oil shock produced a temporary countercyclical response with ALMP in the United States.

In West Germany, the relationship of unemployment to the oil shock is strong and consistent. West German policy analysts argued that the heavy costs of passive policies—transfer payments for unemployment compensation, public assistance, increased health and other payments—could be saved through ALMP.[18] Consequently, unemployment consistently produces higher ALMP expenditures.

From these correlations of independent variables with ALMP, West Germany and the United States fit into completely different models. West German ALMP has a strongly countercyclical reaction to social demand variables. The United States is more weakly correlated with unemployment and procyclical with growth. West Germany demonstrates the industrial push of structural variables; both the manufacturing sector and unions are strong. The United States, however, illustrates a service society model where service sector employment and labor market pressure play a strong role. The initial tests support the West German work model, with more emphasis on social demands where left parties and unions

17. These two variables represent the unemployment rate in the years indicated and zero in the other years, but they were only used to emphasize this single point.

18. This argument was forcefully made in West Germany; however, in the United States the possible trade-off between transfer payments and ALMP was more transparent because much less money was paid in transfer payments to the unemployed. In fact, some states do not have public assistance programs for the able-bodied unemployed who have exhausted their unemployment compensation payments.

fund ALMP in response to working-class decline in manufacturing and unemployment, and the U.S. socialization model, where the state's service sector creates demographic pressures that fuel ALMP. The multivariate analysis rigorously tests these results.[19]

MULTIVARIATE TIME-SERIES ANALYSIS OF ALMP

The Determinants of West German ALMP Expenditures

Variables representing left political power, both legislative and executive, are the most powerful determinants of West German ALMP expenditures, closely followed by unemployment and the declining manufacturing sector. Both the left's control of the chancellorship and the unemployment rate are strong and explain 84 percent of the variance in ALMP expenditures (equation 1, Table 7). The left party power index combining legislative and executive power does less well with unemployment, but it still explains 69 percent of the variance; and right party power is in between and negative. Clearly, left party power has led to higher ALMP expenditures, while right party power has reduced them. Unemployment is a strong positive predictor of ALMP, which is consistently countercyclical with the government responding to unemployment with greater ALMP.

The left chancellor and the declining manufacturing sector are also strong. They explain 81 percent of the variance—also a high percentage for only two variables. During the 1950s, when the manufacturing sector was struggling to get on its feet after the war, ALMP was high. When the economic miracle boosted

19. Time-series data are especially prone to multicollinearity, especially for trend-dominated variables. Although neither dependent variable is trend-dominated—ALMP in West Germany forms a U-curve and in the United States an inverted U-curve—many independent variables are trend-dominated. The presence of multicollinearity considerably restricts the analysis and the number of variables that can be put into one equation. Thus, the analysis must proceed within the restraints imposed by multicollinearity. In order to detect disqualifying multicollinearity, I used the following rule: the correlation between independent variables should not be more than the correlation of each independent variable with the dependent variable. I made exceptions for correlations higher than the direct correlation if the intercorrelations were below 0.70, and the results were stable in multiple equations. Instability was detected by sign reversals, large fluctuations in significance level, and drastic changes in the size of coefficients (Achen 1982; Pindyck and Rubinfeld 1981).

TABLE 7 *The Multivariate Determinants of Expenditures on Active Labor Market Policy*

Variables	Unstandardized β's Predicting ALMP over GNP[a]				

	West Germany[b]				
	(1)	(2)	(3)	(4)	(5)
Left chancellor	0.280 (0.0001)	0.286 (0.0001)	0.321 (0.0001)	0.320 (0.0001)	0.320 (0.0001)
Unemployment rate	4.05 (0.0001)	—	4.34 (0.0001)	4.33 (0.0001)	4.33 (0.0001)
Manufacturing sector employment	—	−8.78 (0.0001)	—	—	—
First oil shock variable	—	—	−0.137 (0.0001)	—	−0.136 (0.0001)
Second oil shock variable	—	—	—	0.060 (0.104)	0.005 (0.854)
R^2	0.84	0.81	0.96	0.86	0.96

	United States[c]				
	(1)	(2)	(3)	(4)	(5)
Labor market pressure	3.10 (0.0002)	4.02 (0.0001)	2.71 (0.0001)	3.39 (0.0001)	3.33 (0.0001)
Left party power	0.041 (0.069)	0.025 (0.132)	0.031 (0.030)	0.023 (0.052)	0.028 (0.017)
Reagan presidency	—	−0.131 (0.004)	—	—	−0.082 (0.014)
First oil shock variable	—	—	0.145 (0.0005)	0.147 (0.0002)	0.121 (0.0006)
Bureaucratic confusion	—	—	—	−0.06 (0.039)	−0.049 (0.064)
R^2	0.67	0.82	0.87	0.90	0.93

[a]Significance levels are in parentheses. Read down for each equation.
[b]Figures derived from 1952 to 1984; n=33.
[c]Figures derived from 1950 to 1984; n=35.

the manufacturing sector to unparalleled levels, ALMP hit a low. But in the 1970s, when the oil crisis reduced the manufacturing sector, ALMP rose again. The manufacturing sector, which is not correlated with the service sector ($r = -0.24$), plays an important role in the West German economy, especially because it is larger than any other sector and strongly correlated with unemployment ($r = -0.87$).

One could argue that the left chancellor variable is simply a proxy for the oil shock. The total oil shock and the left chancellorship variables are too highly correlated to include in the same regression equation to settle the question. However, left party power (a standardized index of left Bundestag and executive power) and the oil shock variables can be put together. In an equation that explains 88 percent of the variance in ALMP, the direct effects of the oil shock are woefully insignificant, while left party power and the unemployment variables are both significant. Thus, in West Germany the oil shock simply does not match the strong effect of left party power.

The oil shock has a complex relationship to ALMP in West Germany, which is disguised by its poor performance with unemployment in regression equations. The oil shock actually consists of three completely different reactions. Based on prior political and unemployment patterns, the government optimistically spent well over its predicted income in 1975, which drained budgets and produced overwhelming deficits. As a result, the government spent much less than predicted from 1976 to 1978 and even produced some embarrassing Bundesanstalt budget surpluses. When the second oil shock appeared from 1979 to 1981, the West German government spent much more on ALMP than expected. If the oil shock period is divided into two variables of three years each and if the overly optimistic first year is eliminated, the oil shock variables produce opposite and significant results with the left chancellorship and unemployment. The first oil shock reduces ALMP (in helping to explain 95 percent of the variance in ALMP—see Table 7, equation 3), but in a similar equation, the second oil shock increases ALMP but is much less significant (it drops out of the four-variable equation—see Table 7, equations 4 and 5). Thus, the first oil shock constricted ALMP, the opposite of its effect in the United States.

DGB power, unlike that of the AFL-CIO, has faced only a mild decline in membership figures, and its strength helps motivate the SPD to respond to the twin threats of unemployment and manufacturing decline. However, despite a strong correlation with ALMP, DGB power does not work well with unemployment and other variables to explain ALMP. Although the coefficients are significant, the explained variance is low. The SPD must be in power for the DGB to exert its direct influence; therefore, the effects of unions are more indirect and will appear later in the path analysis.

Thus, West Germany has a parsimonious political economy model in which three variables—left power, unemployment, and the first oil shock—explain more than 95 percent of the variance in ALMP. The declining manufacturing sector can also replace unemployment in a three-variable equation with good results. Other variables fail to explain much variance in West German ALMP. The index of labor market pressure is weak, even altering the index to accent guestworkers. A dummy variable representing bureaucratic confusion—disruption in ALMP implementation caused by new laws—worked for neither major changes nor amendments. Political economy variables represent an internal set of connected forces that determined ALMP under the diverse effects of war recovery and oil shocks. Thus, West Germany exhibits a social demand model in which the left's political power responds in a regular fashion to workers' needs.

Explaining U.S. ALMP Expenditures

If the strongest two variables from the West German model—left party executive power and the unemployment rate—are used in U.S. equations, a striking difference appears. While the left chancellor and the unemployment rate explained 84 percent of the variance in West German ALMP, the Democratic president and the unemployment rate explain only 15 percent of the variance in U.S. ALMP. Substituting a measure of presidential ideology does no better, and replacing the Democratic president with Democratic party power increases the variance explained to 21 percent, still well short of the mark. American unemployment simply does not predict ALMP. On the contrary, when unemployment is perceived to be cyclical, it generates a procyclical response with ALMP (i.e., higher unemployment means less ALMP); when unemployment is perceived to be caused by OPEC, it generates a countercyclical response (i.e., higher unemployment means more ALMP). Consequently, the West German model fails in the United States.

Variables more connected to state growth—demographic and service sector variables—explain American ALMP. The index of U.S. labor market pressure alone explains the most variance in ALMP, and with the left's legislative power it explains 61 percent of the variance in ALMP. If we decrease the political lags from two and three years to one and two years on left party power, and the demographic lags from three and four years to two and three years on the labor market pressure index, the amount of variance explained increases six points to 67 percent (equation 1, Table 7). Furthermore, the regression coefficient for labor market pressure is strong, while left party power is close to significance. Thus, the left legislative index, not the left presidency, and labor market pressure explain ALMP in the United States.

Three additional variables were needed to approach the power of the West German explanation because the U.S. model lacks parsimony. First, a total oil shock variable, although only marginally significant, explains an additional 10 percent variance; this brings the total variance explained with the political and labor market variables to 77 percent. However, the increases in ALMP due to the crisis ended prematurely in 1980–81. Using a dummy variable for the first oil shock, the positive effect of the oil crisis can be more precisely singled out (Table 7, equation 3). Controlling for labor market pressure and left party power, the first oil shock adds 20 percent to the variance explained; the total explanation reaches 87 percent. But the second oil shock, instead of boosting ALMP, brought its demise. Only the first oil shock created the massive consensus to pass job creation programs and foster a countercyclical reaction to unemployment. Thus, the first oil shock created opposite effects in each country.

Labor market pressure and left party power created a demand for ALMP in the 1970s, but when demographic pressures stabilized and Democratic power decreased in the early 1980s, ALMP dropped at a much greater rate than expected. Only a Reagan administration dummy variable can explain the precipitous decline in ALMP that takes place from 1980 to 1984. Reagan prematurely cut ALMP when labor market pressure trends were only tipping in this direction. The Reagan presidency is strongly negative and brings the total explained variance to 82 percent, 15 percent more than the original equation with labor market pressure and left legislative power (Table 7, equation 2).

A third variable focuses directly on state formation. Bureaucratic confusion, detailed in Chapter 8, is represented by the passage of the most important American ALMP laws—MDTA, Economic Opportunity Act, Emergency Employment Act, CETA, CETA Reauthorization, and JTPA. Each year—1962, 1964, 1971, 1973, 1978, and 1982—represents the bureaucratic confusion caused by new organizational structures introduced with each law: the skills centers, the community action agencies, the community-based organizations, the private industry councils, the prime sponsors, and the myriad of other agencies. Bureaucratic confusion reduces ALMP and explains surprising shortfalls in the total explanation (Table 7, equation 4). It adds 3 percent more variance explained to the index of labor market pressure, left party power, and the first oil shock, but bureaucratic confusion is the weakest of the three additional variables.

The most powerful American equation explains 93 percent of the variance in ALMP (Table 7, equation 5). Labor market pressure is the strongest explanatory variable with the highest significance. The first oil shock, left party power, and the Reagan presidency are all strong and significant, and the bureaucratic confusion variable comes close to significance.[20] However, 1977 with the highest expenditure of the period still remains a difficult year to explain. In 1977 CETA, bloated on job creation policies, overstepped its political and economic support, was constrained in 1978, and then destroyed in 1982.

Two other variables were also strong predictors of ALMP, but they are both too highly related to the index of labor market pressure. State and local government employment as a percentage of civilian employment and private service sector employees as a percentage of civilian employment were impossible to include in the same equation with labor market pressure. I used each vari-

---

20. Bureaucratic confusion declines in significance in this last equation because it shares 1982 with the Reagan administration variable.

able in place of the labor market pressure index, but the results were always weaker with less variance explained. Instead I use them with appropriate lags as indirect effects in the path analysis to follow.

Instead of a tightly grouped system of political economy variables, the United States fits a fragmented socialization model that emphasizes variables connected to state formation (labor market pressure, the service sector, the Reagan administration, and bureaucratic confusion) and external effects (the oil shock), while social demands (left party power) play a smaller role.

Path Models for West Germany and the United States

These regression equations can be arranged into a causally ordered sequence of variables in an overall model (see Figure 13).[21] The purpose here is not to increase variance explained but to place variables into a causally consistent and structural model. In West Germany, the path model explains 97 percent of the variance in ALMP and shows the strong connections of unemployment, the left chancellor, and the first oil shock. The indirect paths show that union power—the DGB's membership ratio—leads to left chancellor power and that the decline in manufacturing sector employees contributes to unemployment.[22] West Germany demonstrates social demands for ALMP, where changes in unions and manufacturing lead to left political action concerning unemployment, but little in the way of state administration is present (i.e., there are no state expansion variables below the oil shock path in Figure 13).

21. This path analysis does not add to the total variance explained; rather it aims to show the connections between variables. I do not include error terms for indirect regressions because variables explained by only one connection actually represent correlation coefficients. Their error terms would naturally be high.

22. Union power in West Germany is also connected to unemployment, but unions do not cause unemployment. Why? West German unions have a small presence on the shop floor and must voluntarily obtain union dues because closed shops are illegal (Hanson et al. 1982). When important questions come up—future layoffs or collective bargaining issues—membership increases. Fears of unemployment cause membership to go up, leaving a correlation between union membership and unemployment. Thus, the threat of unemployment causes union membership to go up, not vice versa.

A. West Germany: Work-Based Social Demand Model: Total R² = 0.97

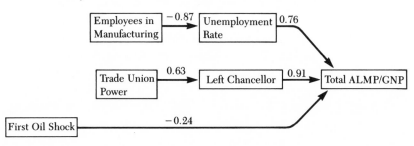

B. United States: Socialization-Based State Model: Total R² = 0.89

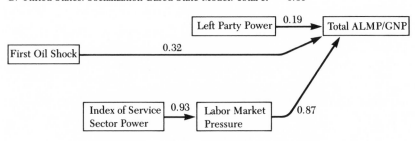

In the United States, the emphasis is reversed with strong state administration but less in the way of social demands. Both public and private bureaucracies in the service sector control large amounts of funds and vast numbers of jobs. Because the two sectors are strongly related, I combine them in an index of service sector power. The service sector also represents the professional interests of teachers, nurses, professors, social workers, and others who have organized into associations. Similarly, state and local employment represents the state, county, and city interest groups that have become an important force in postwar politics. The labor market pressure index and the first oil shock are strong, and the left's legislative power is still significant. Service sector power increases labor market pressure. This path model explains 89 percent of the variance in ALMP. Thus, the United States demonstrates a "socialization model" because service sector and labor market pressure lead to ALMP, rather than the manufacturing sector and unemployment (i.e., there are few social demand variables above the oil shock path in Figure 13).[23]

The causal order between labor market pressure and service sector power could be questioned in this model; however, with appropriate lags the causal order can go either way. I argue that the strong service sector in the United States produced labor market pressures and absorbed them through ALMP. As I showed in Chapter 1, the formation of the service sector with strong influence from social work in the first half of the century clearly preceded labor market pressure in the last thirty years. These service institutions began at the turn of the century, long before the baby boom, and pulled women and young persons into the labor market for services. Eventually the service sector over-

23. This does not mean that social demands are totally absent from the U.S. model but rather that they are weak and do not help explain ALMP. However, female participation in the labor force is connected to ALMP, and a social demand variable could be collected on the strength of womens' movement organizations. Furthermore, blacks have been adversely affected by unemployment, and black representatives have consistently supported employment policies. Blacks in the House are strongly correlated with ALMP ($r = +0.78$ lagged two years) and to left party power ($r = +0.53$). Thus, a structural variable could be constructed out of female, black, and union power that could then be connected to left party power. However, because it remains weak in explaining ALMP, this exercise would not improve the model.

produced students for its own employment capacity. Indeed, as the West German case shows, the service sector can avoid labor market pressure. Thus, middle-class reformers were able to expand the government and other services to women and the baby boomers in the United States, and as a result, service sector power led to large labor market pressures. But with opposite lags, a case can also be made for labor market pressure fueling the growth of the service sector. Thus, my model emphasizes the service sector creating labor supply, rather than labor market pressure creating labor demand in the service sector.[24]

CONCLUSION AND SUMMARY

The determinants of ALMP in these two countries are strikingly different. West German ALMP, with its work approach to social policy, has a work model strongly driven by left politics (left chancellor), social demands (unemployment), and structural causes (manufacturing and union power). The government clearly generates ALMP funds in a countercyclical manner. The state and its service sector, along with demographic pressures from women and the baby boom, play little or no part in generating West German ALMP. West Germany lends itself to a tight social demand model focused on work issues and labor institutions.

The U.S. socialization model is based on the state and expanding service sector increasing the number of women, baby boomers, and immigrants needing services and employment. Bureaucratic limits on financing service sector jobs and demographic pressures powerfully increased ALMP intervention. American ALMP operated procyclically, until the first oil shock caused the relationship to operate countercyclically. Unemployment should represent a strong cue to governments to intervene in labor markets with ALMP, but changes in unemployment rates have little systematic effect on U.S. ALMP. At some points after

24. The causal impact of the service sector in creating excess labor supply among those with a rather high level of education has been a popular theme (Berg 1970). However, this factor does not operate in many countries like Sweden and West Germany because they regulate the number of people who can go into different postsecondary fields. This reduces but does not eliminate the labor market's pressures on the service sector.

World War II, job loss and higher prices were accompanied by aggressive moves to manipulate U.S. labor markets; at other points, these economic downturns signaled stable or declining ALMP expenditures. In short, U.S. responses to unemployment and inflation are sufficiently inconsistent that cyclical economic fluctuations fail to predict policy expenditures.

Political economy variables play a small role in the United States. The left party power demonstrates the fragmentation of the U.S. system because the presidency has no effect, and the left's legislative power often barely achieves significance. American union power is even further removed from the West German work model. Instead of a structural cause, unions could even be grouped with the Republican party as a factor operating against ALMP. While this is preposterous, given trade union efforts on behalf of ALMP, these results suggest that union power simply cannot be a systematic determinant of ALMP.

The fragmentation of American politics is also demonstrated by the additional variables needed to approach the explanatory power of the West German model. The bureaucratic confusion variables show the weakness of U.S. labor market institutions in explaining the dips in expenditures in the year of ALMP law passage. And, of course, bureaucratic confusion is compounded by the declining USES, which is only weakly associated with ALMP. Finally, only the Reagan administration variable—not Republican or right-wing party power—could adequately account for the decrease of ALMP in the 1980s.

The opposite reactions of the first oil shock to ALMP in these two countries, however, require some explanation. An external shock can be divided into two parts. The oil shock can be divided into separate time periods because of a worldwide increase in prices on definite dates, and the 1928–39 depression can also be divided into parts with exact dates depending on the country. The first and second shocks produce different effects. In the United States, the stinginess of the Hoover administration offered fewer social expenditures than expected, and then the Roosevelt administration in the second depression proposed more than expected. Sweden reacted similarly with deflation followed by dramatic expenditures (Gourevitch 1986, pp. 131–35). But Germany already had high social welfare expenditures from 1926 to 1930, and some blamed the depression on social spending. The emergency governments from 1930 to 1933 subsequently spent less than expected and were unable to get job creation measures off the ground. Thus, the early policies during a crisis are labeled failure, policy abuse, or even as a cause of the crisis.

During the oil crisis, similar principles operated, but the countries are reversed. After 1975, West Germany was tightfisted and spent less than expected on ALMP, which legitimated more spending when the second oil shock arrived. In the opposite direction, the United States spent much money during the first oil shock, and CETA was labeled a gluttonous abuse. This caused ALMP expenditures to drop even before Reagan took office in the midst of the second oil shock. Thus, low expenditures in the first crisis are labeled as stingy, but they then legitimate higher expenditures later. Conversely, high expenditures in the first crisis are labeled abusive, and they cause expenditures to drop during the second crisis. The generality of this hypothesis is tentative, but it helps explain the opposite reactions to crisis in these two countries.[25]

This quantitative analysis provides a strong explanation for ALMP expenditures that emphasize social demands for West Germany and state formation for the United States. These results complement previous analyses that relied on structural constants that cannot be entered into regression equations. I also expect them to be somewhat rigorous in holding into the near future. The strongest American relationship should stay strong because labor market pressures and ALMP will decline together as the baby boom and women are largely absorbed into the labor force. However, the connection of ALMP with Democratic legislative power will weaken with additional years in the time series because Democrats have gained seats but ALMP remains low. In West Germany, the correlation of ALMP expenditures and unemployment should remain moderately high, but left power depends on a new coalition, which is difficult to predict. The biggest changes could come from the push of guestworkers and their offspring into the welfare state, bringing a stronger and larger service sector and the possibilities of greatly expanded ALMP aimed at newly dislocated workers in a unified Germany.

25. This explanation is at variance with Gourevitch (1986, p. 227) who seems to see more uniform responses to the crises (especially for Weimar Germany).

Chapter Ten

Conclusion: Promises, Possibilities, and Proposals

Active labor market policy promises to deliver a better trained and more productive work force than passive policies would deliver. It also promises the combination of low unemployment and low inflation through eliminating skill bottlenecks in production; indeed, that was the very intention of the Swedish economists who formulated it (Rehn 1948; Meidner 1948). These macroeconomic and production-oriented aims are also coupled with efforts to avoid the deterioration of workers' skills and motivation, which are inherent in passive policies, and to establish a more equitable and fully employed society. In practice, Sweden has come much closer to this promise than either the United States or West Germany. However, given the lack of consensus on unemployment and the competition of political parties in the federal systems of both countries, West Germany has done a remarkable job implementing ALMP, both equitably and efficiently. In this conclusion, I review the reasons why West Germany effectively pursued ALMP, while the United States fell short; then I address possibilities and proposals for change in America.

EXPLAINING ALMP IN THE UNITED STATES AND WEST GERMANY

In a comprehensive review of ALMP, Garth Mangum and others claim that the United States "spent too much" and "went too far" on labor market policy from 1960 to 1980 (1981, p. 509; Burtless 1984). My study of active labor market policy puts such assertions in cross-national context. Compared to West Germany, the United States clearly spent little and took only small steps toward an effective ALMP; but compared to Sweden, both countries spent a pittance. West German programs in job placement, job training, and job creation were not only better funded than similar programs in the United States but also much stronger. I briefly review these policy conclusions and then turn to the causes of these major differences.

First, concerning job placement, the stable West German organizational structure of a powerful employment bureaucracy, largely but not totally independent of political fluctuations, provided stable administration for a large array of active labor market policies and established monopoly control over job placement. Implementation processes worked smoothly because of a clear view of participation rights in labor, management, and government direction of the employment service.

In contrast, U.S. employment bureaucracies and programs often stagnated with inadequate funding or were confused by repeated organizational changes. The U.S. Employment Service only touched the fringes of the labor market; after the mid-1960s, USES was bypassed by most new policies, causing an ever-changing parade of organizations through the labor market. Politicians constantly complicated the implementation process with their frequent policy changes, ambiguous demands, administrative changes, and lack of guiding ideas about ALMP. This political interference in ALMP administration left a scattered trail of programs, laws, and implementing organizations. In the end, it led to a political backlash against ALMP. Thus, the stability of the West German system and the fragmentation of temporary American organizations is a major difference in ALMP.

Second, beginning in the early 1950s, the West Germans established highly skilled ALMP job-training programs, building on the apprenticeships in the compulsory school; since 1969, their mix of job-training programs expanded. In contrast, U.S. ALMP job-training programs started later in the mid-1960s as short-term socialization measures aimed at the unskilled and scattered among different administrative agencies. Many of these categorical programs declined during the oil shock and reemerged after pruning in the 1980s. Although job training programs have been an evaluated success—much more successful in West Germany than in the United States—West German politicians recognize that success, but U.S. politicians focus more on the shortcomings of evaluative research.[1]

Third, West Germany also started job creation programs in the early 1950s, while the United States again began ten years later. Pure job creation programs in West Germany were modest in scale and carefully monitored, but job maintenance programs like short-time work and bad weather payments were heavily funded. In the United States, job creation policies were largely ignored until an external shock from OPEC inspired hasty legislation and large funding in the 1970s. However, the decentralized administration of job creation programs in the 1970s allowed abuses and confusion that created a backlash against public employment programs in the 1980s. West Germany carefully monitored job creation policies, watched expenditures in the 1970s, and controlled a similar backlash.

Job creation policies have definite limits in a contentious, capitalist economy.[2] Citizens often demand job creation policies, and governments may promise them. But continuous political support for job creation programs is fragile. The working population, vastly outnumbering the unemployed even in the worst depression, easily becomes ambivalent about its taxes supporting the unemployed in suspect work, that is, publicly created jobs. Government job creation policy faces a dilemma. If the government performs useful work, private employers and conservatives claim government competition with private industry.[3] If the govern-

1. Some participants in the massive controversy over experimentation as an evaluation tool dispute the positive results of job-training programs. However, even studies with experimentation show positive results (Ashenfelter 1988, p. 284), and Heckman and Hotz even dispute whether costly experimentation is needed (1988, pp. 291–302). We should not be confused by the methodological disputes in academia or the negative results in a few studies. Job training programs have had moderate but positive results. .

2. A capitalist country that can reach a consensus about unemployment, like Sweden, can transcend these limits.

3. In West Germany, conservative politicians claimed that sprucing up government grounds took away "possible" contracts with gardening firms. Ironically, "leaf-raking"—the critique of the WPA—was even claimed for the private sector.

ment avoids such real or imagined competition, private firms and conservatives claim that public jobs constitute useless work. With the choppy and often irrational implementation of job creation policies in the United States, the political survival of public service employment was in doubt from the start. West Germany limited spending on pure job creation but spent heavily on job maintenance policies that affected a broader and more powerful spectrum of citizens. Consequently, their job creation programs are still in effect long after American programs are gone.

What accounts for these differences? Why did West Germany spend considerable money on ALMP and make its programs effective, while the United States spent little on ALMP and accepted only moderately effective measures? The answers come from the social demands of interest groups and political parties expressed within both particular ideological frameworks and state and institutional structures that formulate and implement ALMP. The interaction of these two factors provides a powerful explanation of ALMP.

These themes are captured in my three-stage explanation of ALMP. In the analysis of the roots of labor market policy, the German work approach to citizenship rights and education—emphasizing high skill training and direct union participation in the welfare state—led to strong labor market institutions, while the U.S. socialization approach—focusing on acculturating ethnics and blacks with little union participation in the welfare state—did not. In the analysis of legislation after World War II, left party power caused the passage of ALMP legislation in both countries, but West Germany's farther-reaching legislation came from the SPD's participation rights ideology of self-administration in the welfare state and the interpenetration of elites in policy-making institutions. And finally, the systematic analysis of ALMP expenditures from 1950 to 1985 showed that a parsimonious work model based on social demands (left party power, unions, and unemployment) produced ALMP expenditures in West Germany, while a more complex socialization model based on state formation (state services and labor market pressures) and weaker social demands explains ALMP expenditures in the United States. I summarize these conclusions to show that, although both social demands and state formation are prominent factors in explaining

ALMP in each country, the German case more clearly emphasizes the positive force of social demands while the American case
emphasizes the negative impact of state formation.

The Roots of ALMP, 1800 to 1945

In Weimar Germany, a work orientation toward social policy emphasized participation rights—workers' control and state intervention in firms and labor markets. The labor movement and the
SPD sought and achieved workers' control over national pension,
health insurance, and accident insurance programs, and they provided workers' councils in the plant and workers' representatives
on corporate boards. Germany established strong labor market
institutions reflecting the work orientation: a centralized and autonomous employment service with monopoly powers over job
placement; a job-training system oriented toward high skill training that incorporates both the continuation school and apprenticeships in private firms; and a wide range of job creation
policies housed in the employment service. These institutions,
pushed by the SPD and unions, were administered through tripartite labor-management-government councils. ALMP legislation was also achieved through collaboration between the SPD
and the Catholic Center party, which was connected to Catholic
unions with their own conception of participation rights. The
German work orientation was largely based on class divisions
manifested in politics and education, but management, labor, and
the government worked together to produce an efficient orientation to social policy, despite their conflicting interests.

In the United States, a socialization orientation to social policy
supported social rights rather than participation rights. This approach emphasized policy administration by third-party bureaucrats, rather than workers' participation—a result pushed by
Secretary of Labor Perkins. The orientation toward social rights
focused on several areas: a weak employment service, late in ar-
riving and split between the individual states and the federal government; a secondary education system, imparting few technical
skills and offering tenuous connections between school and work
for most manual workers; and job creation programs, distinct
from the employment service and permanently dismantled before

World War II. The Democratic party emphasized a social rights ideology without labor-management participation, and even at the peak of their power, the Democrats had trouble passing ALMP laws.

After World War II, social demands and state institutional structures profoundly affected ALMP. Despite some post–World War II changes in each country's social policy orientation, the work and socialization approaches remained dominant in each country. The West German Ministry of Labor was powerful; the U.S. Department of Labor was weak. The education system constrained policy in both countries: the West German apprentice system with the Berufschule accentuated highly skilled apprenticeship training, while the U.S. high school continued to avoid technical training for manual workers. Finally, winning wars reinforced conflicts in status; a veterans' status group and bureaucracy in the United States created a veterans' labor market policy to compete with ALMP. Losing wars submerged veterans within class groups and general social policy in West Germany. Only within the limitations of these institutional and structural constraints can post–World War II variations in politics and economics explain fluctuations in ALMP.

The Passage of ALMP Legislation, 1945 to 1984

U.S. and West German political cultures became much more similar after the war: Roosevelt made big government somewhat palatable to Americans, while Hitler created a distaste for state interference (Roberts 1984). Nevertheless, labor and management participation in the direct guidance of social policy played an important role in passing West German ALMP legislation. Not only were participation rights directly involved in the actual ALMP legislation, but the SPD's threat to advance participation rights into the secondary education system also contributed to the passage of the most important ALMP law of the post–World War II period—the AFG. Furthermore, an integrated political process, with the interpenetration of class and interest group representatives in the Bundestag and the employment service, led to extensive and well-funded ALMP, along with efforts to keep the bureaucracy from taking an independent course of action.

However, American difficulties during the 1960s over participation rights in community action agencies and "maximum feasible participation" led to unmanageable decentralization and the ultimate destruction of ALMP. In the late 1960s and early 1970s, the effects of administrative confusion in the decentralized CETA system produced a rush of severe criticism. The problem was most apparent in the Democratic party, which had participation rights on its political agenda in the 1960s. In addition to ideological problems, the diffuse American polity, comprised of many status groups, and a weak but independent federal bureaucracy could do little to promote or defend ALMP measures. Political fragmentation often gave Southern Democrats veto power over ALMP legislation. Lobbyists representing service-provider groups— the American Vocational Association and the Interstate Conference of Employment Security Agencies—obtained enough disproportionate leverage on Southern Democrats in powerful congressional committees to block or alter ALMP. The fragmentation of the political process allowed status cleavages of race, gender, region, and war service to have inordinate influence, causing policy to be handled piecemeal or not at all. Finally, evaluation researchers supplied ammunition to contending parties in the United States by further polarizing the politics of ALMP (Wilensky 1985).

The Systematic Analysis of ALMP Expenditures, 1950 to 1984

The quantitative analysis of ALMP in these two countries provides two completely different explanations of ALMP. West German ALMP is fueled by political reactions to economic conditions important to the working class. Trade unions and left party power respond to increasing unemployment and a declining manufacturing sector with effective ALMP. The first oil shock, as an external effect, had a negative impact on ALMP. This work model of ALMP emphasizes the social demands of my social policy model.

The American model is neither tightly knit nor based on social demands. Instead, the American socialization model of ALMP is mainly composed of demographic pressure in the labor market, Democratic legislative power, the oil shock, and two other variables. First, labor market pressure, focusing on the insecurity of workers who face a crowded labor market, elevates concern about unemployment. Second, though not nearly as strong as the SPD, American left party power in the legislature played a role in enacting and funding ALMP. Third, higher unemployment usually signaled a relative drop in U.S. ALMP expenditures, except when the first oil shock produced enough consensus to raise ALMP through job creation policies. Fourth, rather than Republican resurgence or economic trends, only the special influence of the Reagan administration could explain the shortfalls that occurred in ALMP during the 1980s. And fifth, bureaucratic confusion, measured by the passage of six major ALMP laws, explained otherwise surprising declines in ALMP expenditures. The American model is weaker on social demands because it contains few union or unemployment measures, and its demographic emphases can be explained through state formation by a growing service sector.

In short, West German trade unions and left parties responded to social demands to produce a strong ALMP. In the United States, liberal politicians reacted to pressures of the labor market and needs of the service sector to create weak ALMP, but extensive ALMP only came under the pressure of an externally caused oil crisis. The West German work model shows how political parties embracing participation rights responded to unemployment by investing heavily in ALMP. The U.S. socialization model often ignored unemployment and responded to demographic pressures that were mainly connected to the service sector. The results of strong ALMP are highly skilled workers, high productivity, and efficient use of human resources and capital; the consequences of weak ALMP resemble the labor force of third world or declining countries.

Thus, this study has shown how social demands and state formation have led to ALMP. Although no quantitative criteria are available to differentiate between structural constants and incremental variables in two countries, I argue for the following causal priorities (see Figure 14 for a summary).[4] West German ALMP is

4. Although reliable cross-sectional data on ALMP in OECD countries is not available (see Table 1 for what is available), cross-sectional data would be appropriate for discovering these structural constants.

14. A Summary of Causes of Active Labor Market Policy in the
    United States and West Germany

Analysis Period	1. Documentary Analysis Before World War II		2. Documentary Analysis After World War II		3. Quantitative Analysis After World War II		Summary Comparison
	(West) Germany	USA	(West) Germany	USA	(West) Germany	USA	
Social Demands	+ + + (Class group power)	+	+ + + (Class group power)	+ +	+ + + (Class group power)	+	(West) Germany > USA
	0 (Status group power)	−	0 (Status group power)	−	0 (Status group power)	−	
State Formation	+ + (Self-administered & strong bureaucracy)	− − −	+ + + (Self-administered & strong bureaucracy)	− − −	nt (Self-administered & strong bureaucracy)	nt	USA > (West) Germany
	+ + (Party structure)	− −	+ + (Party structure)	− − −	nt (Party structure)	nt	
	0 (Bureaucratic control of policy)	−	0 (Bureaucratic control of policy)	− −	0/0 (Size of bureaucracy/ bureaucratic confusion)	+ + +/−	
Ideology	+ + + (Participation/ rights emphasis)	− −	+ + + (Participation/ rights emphasis)	−	nt (Participation rights emphasis)	nt	(West) Germany > USA
	+ + (Social rights emphasis)	+	+ + (Social rights emphasis)	+ +	nt (Social rights emphasis)	nt	
External Events	+ + (War)	−	+ + (War)	− −	0 (War)	−	USA > (West) Germany
	+/− (1st & 2nd depression)	−/+	−/+ (1st & 2nd oil shock)	+ +/−	+/− (1st & 2nd oil shock)	+/−	

Notes: + + +, + +, and +: Very strong, strong, and mild positive factor causing more ALMP
− − −, − −, and −: Very strong, strong, and mild positive factor causing less ALMP
0: Not a factor
nt: Not tested

better explained by social demands—mainly because class groups (trade unions and the SPD) consistently showed strong support for ALMP—while American social demands were complicated by blacks' and womens' movements, and clearly competed with veterans' demands. Furthermore, U.S. social demand variables failed to produce much ALMP at the peak of Democratic party power. Roosevelt presided over the passage of a weak employment service act, and he had to hide the WPA in a general spending bill. Johnson had to sell a seat on the Ways and Means Committee to a Southern Democrat in order to help pass the Economic Opportunity Act, legislation that soon became mired in administrative confusion. Moreover, Johnson allowed the amendment to the employment service act to be easily defeated, and he thwarted efforts by the secretary of labor to strengthen the federal role in the employment service.

Rather than social demands, state formation is more useful in explaining American ALMP. Throughout the analysis, aspects of state formation kept intervening with U.S. legislation. The cross-cutting action of class and status groups often left a social policy vacuum that third-party bureaucrats and "social welfare intellectuals" could fill (Robertson 1981). Secretary of Labor Perkins overrode self-administrative councils embodied in the Wagner-Peyser Act and went to court on civil service requirements that were not in the act. Southern Democrats lodged on Ways and Means and other committees allowed special interests unusual access to powerful policy levers. These are some instances of state structures that deterred American ALMP.

In contrast, Germany did not allow such bureaucratic discretion, despite having a strong bureaucracy. Bismarck could not override social demands on social insurance to provide for complete third-party bureaucratic control on social insurance, and this formed the basis for self-administration in the employment service. Later during Weimar, the government discredited the federal labor market's bureaucracy with the "strengthening professional's" damning report. In 1969, the newly formed Grand Coalition government and its minister of labor were able to turn the organizational culture of the employment service around by replacing lawyers with labor economists. Unlike U.S. congressional committees, the Bundestag Committee for Labor did not allow veto power to small groups of service providers. Finally, throughout the postwar period, bureaucrats were brought into the political process through a convergence of career lines causing their cooperation with, not opposition to, social demands. Thus, social demands were often opposed or contorted by legislative committees or the bureaucracy at the state and federal levels in the United States, while social demands at least partially molded the bureaucracy and legislative committees to class interests in West Germany.

In addition to social demands and state formation, citizenship ideology has an independent effect on a lower level of causation in focusing or diffusing class or status group interests. In effect, class and status group interests and state formation variables are the "tracklaying vehicles" in the development of social policy with ideology operating at times as the "switchmen" of history, but group interests always have the power to override ideology and lay new track (Mann 1986, pp. 22–28; Sewell 1985; Skocpol 1985). In both periods, we saw how American difficulties with participation rights caused major problems with the administration of labor market policies. Secretary Perkins swept the Wagner-Peyser Act councils under the rug of the civil service, and community action's years of confused meandering in the urban wilderness show where the lack of clear participation ideology can lead. Ideology has been somewhat neglected in previous analyses of social policy, but we should not be blinded to negative causes or nonissues. We also should not attribute ideology to simply a reflection of group power, although the two are closely intertwined.

And finally, both countries were affected, but in different ways, by external events because these are interpreted within the context of each country's social policy. The oil shocks in both countries had almost opposite effects, when unemployment and politics are controlled. And wars had opposite effects in determining whether powerful status groups are created by winning or losing.

In conclusion, all four factors cause differences in direct intervention by the state to prevent unemployment. Although social demands emanating from class divisions with strong unions in Germany led to strong pressures for ALMP, American unions also showed considerable support for ALMP, especially after World

War II. Later, black and other status groups also pressed for ALMP. After pinpointing structural constraints, I have shown that the power of political parties has a significant yearly effect in both countries, unlike previous analyses that have discounted the effects of politics (Lewis-Beck 1977). Differences in state formation led to strong and participative bureaucratic structures in West Germany and weak and professionalized bureaucracies in the United States. Furthermore, multiple political parties in Germany with specific ideologies led to a party that emphasized participation rights and trade unions, while the dual party system in the United States led to vague and general ideologies that largely ignored participation rights. Citizenship rights theory helps differentiate ideologies of social policy into work and socialization agendas emphasizing different aspects of my social policy model.

Thus, the debate between the social demand theorists and the state formation theorists is neither won nor lost here (Korpi 1989; Quadagno 1987; and Skocpol and Orloff 1986). In part, the two sides often use different methods while I have used them both; in part, the debates do not distinguish between the pressures for policy formation and the forms of policy implementation. In many cases, the two can be compatible. For instance, black and labor interest groups along with civil rights demonstrations and sit-ins may cause a law to pass, but the legislative committees, bureaucracy, and advisers may determine much of that particular law's form and implementation. Form and pressure must be differentiated. Although either theory may outweigh the other in particular countries and historical periods, social demands and state formation can be compatible.

WHAT IS POSSIBLE IN THE UNITED STATES?
BARRIERS AND LEVERS

Rather than compare the United States to the consensual political structures of the more centralized governments in Sweden and Japan, I chose to compare the United States and West Germany because of their similarity. Although I have pointed out important differences between these two countries, their politics have operated under the tough conditions of federalism, high military expenditures, and alternating power between political parties.

This section directs attention to the main stumbling blocks to enacting stronger ALMP in the United States and asks whether they can be surmounted. Can cultural and institutional barriers be removed by accessible levers, or are their roots so deep that we can expect little change? I shall consider three questions concerning effective ALMP: Do U.S. values prevent employment protections? Does business dominate policy and thwart effective ALMP? And does the fragmentation of the political system inevitably frustrate reasonable change?

On the first question, American political and economic values have not prevented major government offensives against unemployment. During this century, the United States started two "wars" against unemployment: Roosevelt produced job creation policies of unprecedented scope and funding during the New Deal, and Carter accelerated the CETA program so that ALMP expenditures in 1977 actually exceeded West German expenditures as a percentage of GNP. Therefore, U.S. values were not an impenetrable bar to extensive government policies toward full employment in two periods.

However, U.S. political and economic demands are unstable and at times contradictory. For every poll that shows that Americans want the government to solve social problems, another poll reflects citizen demands that government get off their backs (Hamilton and Wright 1986, pp. 327–73; Smith 1987, pp. 409–21; Peretz 1983, pp. 71–212). The public wants it both ways (Coughlin 1980, pp. 14–15; Free and Cantril 1967). This antinomy, seen in demands for many U.S. social policies, is also reflected in the passage of two laws that were never enforced: the Full Employment Act of 1946 and the Humphrey-Hawkins bill of 1978 (Currie 1977; Keyserling 1981). Wilensky sums up the evidence on U.S. values and the welfare state spending:

It is tempting to attribute this reluctance to cultural values—our economic individualism, our unusual emphasis on private property, the free market, and minimum government—because they permeate so many areas of American life. Although they certainly shape our public debates, these values do not explain much of our resistance to public spending and taxing. (in Coughlin 1980, p. xi)

He goes on to say that because modern populations embrace contradictory values and are ambivalent about taxes and spending, politicians can play it either way: harangue government to reduce expenditures and taxes, or mobilize humanitarian and community sentiments to solve social problems.

Coughlin (1980) showed that eight OECD countries were not much different in their public opinion on specific issues and even their broader ideologies throughout the post–World War II period. Many conservative "American" values can also be seen in West Germany: beliefs in minimum government after World War II, trust in economic individualism, and faith in the free market after the "economic miracle." Indeed the University of Chicago's free market school can find its analog at the University of Kiel. With 1985 data, Tom Smith (1987, p. 413) found that 40 percent of the American and West German public strongly favored cuts in government spending, and only 2 percent separated U.S. and West German public support for governmental financing to create new jobs (69 percent in the United States, 71 percent in West Germany). Thus, U.S. and West German beliefs about the economy and society are not so different as to preclude extensive ALMP.

However, institutional differences in each country are distinct forces for the status quo. National differences in the definition of and approach to social problems have congealed into concrete institutions: the structure of the educational system and the employment service. These structures have a major impact on the levels of funding and on the success or failure of ALMP. Although many cultural beliefs and values may differ little between the United States and West Germany, labor market institutions differ so greatly that little convergence may be expected. Differences in the structure of the school systems, the power of the employment services, and the fragmentation of the political systems will be hard to dislodge. Left unchanged, the U.S. school system will produce a homogeneous manual work force ill-suited to flexible, specialized, and highly skilled work, while West German schools, despite stratification problems, will more adequately match workplace needs. And a weak and unreformed USES will be trailed by other agencies trying to take up the slack, while the West German Bundesanstalt will continue its steady implementation of ALMP.

Thus, U.S. values and culture do not rule out the achievement of full employment policies, but the institutional and structural environment for ALMP is hostile to a national policy for full employment. Values concerning government guarantees of employment in both countries are ambiguous, but structures and institutions are vastly different.[5]

The second question asks whether business dominates politics in either country. Capitalist domination in the United States does not explain surges of spending during the 1930s depression and the 1960s to 1970s—two periods of high ALMP growth. Business manipulation does not explain the Grand Coalition in West Germany in which working-class and middle-class parties cooperated to produce truly progressive policies in the mid-1960s. Rather than focusing on union weakness and employer interests (Quadagno 1984; Currie 1977), I emphasize the unique American socialization approach to education of immigrants and the structure of the legislative process. Moreover, I emphasize the ideological problems of the Democratic party with participation rights. Thus, business, which has strong but not dominant influence, was unable to prevent extensive employment policies in the 1930s or 1970s. Instead, many of these efforts self-destructed through bureaucratic confusion and political inability to induce labor and management cooperation in ALMP.[6]

Nevertheless, important differences in class structure exist between these two countries. The U.S. school system emphasizes socialization and homogeneity, while the West German school system promotes class closure, unions, and working-class consciousness. As a result, West German unions, stronger than U.S. unions, play a direct role in implementing policy in the employment service. There are also big differences in employers' power. West German employers are heavily involved in competitive international trade and cannot afford crippling strikes. U.S. employers who depend more on the domestic market, which they can

5. The generation of these structures lay in diverse values prior to World War II; however, today's values could not produce such structural differences.

6. Business in the United States clearly had inordinate power in the 1800s, but this power has eroded as state power increased after World War I (Jacoby 1989).

control, are less affected by strikes. As a result, German employers are often more cooperative concerning ALMP (Jacoby 1989). But with huge American trade deficits, the ability of American employers to control domestic markets is shrinking, and American business may become more tractable.

Although business is a strong influence in both countries, West Germany set up institutional structures to effectively mediate divisiveness, while the United States has not. The tripartite control of an independent public law corporation brings labor and employers together in West Germany. The third-party executive control of the U.S. Employment Service leaves labor and employers competing for influence and ignored in implementation. Furthermore, the dual state/federal control of the employment service is an irrationality that national labor markets can ill afford. Consequently, business does not dominate politics in each country, but it can play either a constructive or an obstructive role toward ALMP.

The third question deals with federalism blocking ALMP. Both West Germany and the United States have federal systems of government, and neither country is likely to become more centralized in the near future. However, Germany overcame federalism with clever legislative maneuvering and a compromise on independent control to establish a national employment service in 1927. West Germany also overcame federalism to establish a national employment service again in 1952. Although states in a federal system may not accept direct control by the federal government, they may accept a national but independent agency with provisions for appropriate participation by labor, management, and local government. Although both countries have a federal system in which the states jealously guard their rights, one has enacted a centralized employment service, while the other has a weak impostor. Federalism is not the reason for the difference.

In a similar vein, U.S. politicians have had a difficult time controlling the bureaucracy. While ignoring existing bureaucracies like the Department of Labor, U.S. leaders have added ad hoc agencies—the Works Progress Administration, the Community Action Agencies, and the Office of Economic Opportunity to name only a few—that subsequently disappear. The Germans used "strengthening professionals" during Weimar and "personnel politics" during the late 1960s to control their bureaucracy. Although the United States cannot exactly follow these examples, at least they demonstrate that political control of the bureaucracy is possible in a federal system.

Both the SPD and the Democratic party have had to broker coalitions. Northern Democrats built coalitions with the South, blacks, and whatever progressive elements they could find. However, my arguments do not emphasize differences in coalition building. The Northern Democratic–Southern Democratic coalition is roughly similar to the SPD-FDP coalition, and the percentage of the votes garnered by the Northern Democrats is roughly equivalent to SPD percentages. The SPD has also had problems similar to those of the Democratic party in brokering the North and South.

The biggest differences between the countries are neither the cultural values of the masses nor the structures of federal systems but rather the substance of its political party ideologies. The left party plays a stronger role in West Germany than in the United States. Why?

The Democratic party in America has hindered effective ALMP; its inability to understand participation rights upset the War on Poverty and harmed the passage of subsequent ALMP. The SPD has a theory of participation rights; Northern Democrats do not. I chronicled both the effectiveness of the SPD's AMAG draft in pushing participation rights as a bargaining chip to produce stronger ALMP and the Northern Democrats' great difficulty and ultimate failure at the height of their power to define participation rights in "maximum feasible participation." This ideological confusion, embedded in the Democratic party but also fostered by reformers, limits the support for ALMP.[7]

Recent changes in the post–World War II period have reduced political fragmentation in the United States. Because the House Rules Committee has lost power, the Education and Labor Committee in the House can more easily report bills. The Con-

7. Part of this failure may come from a lack of participation in the party itself. Where West Germany has annual party conventions to debate ideology, the United States relies on presidential primary campaign and media definitions of domestic concerns, which often dwell on personalities rather than issues.

gress reformed its seniority system, removing the lock on important committees held by Southern Democrat chairs. Other sources of fragmentation include bureaucratic incentives due to isolated career development, the divergence of presidential and congressional interests, and the special role of interest groups. Overall fragmentation in the U.S. system has been slightly reduced.

Thus, in explaining the weakness of American ALMP policies, I emphasize that U.S. and West German political parties are ideologically divergent. Unlike the West German SPD, the U.S. Democrats are unable to articulate participation rights as a foundation of government intervention into labor markets. Because the value systems of whole societies are not particularly amenable to change, it is fortunate that these values are not now vastly different. Although the fragmentation of the political process in the United States has altered, remaining checks and balances are not easily modified because of constitutional protections. But the institutional problems of the comprehensive school and the employment service and the particular political ideology of the "reconstructed" Democratic party are more open to debate. It remains to be seen whether the Democratic party can fashion a response to unemployment with a sophisticated emphasis on interest mediation and economic guidance, or whether it gets mired in other problems. Rebuilding institutions could only follow such a redrawing of the labor market's issues.

What is possible? Although federalism will not change in the United States, some legislative streamlining has taken place, and more is possible; the high school will not disappear, but more meaningful vocational tracks could be introduced within it. The U.S. Employment Service is unlikely to become a centralized agency with monopolistic powers over the labor market, yet it could become an independent public law corporation under the right political conditions. And although the Democratic party will not become a labor party, participation rights could be placed on the public agenda, especially with the Democratic party's concern to redefine itself and balance its rapport with business. Thus, with this optimistic view of possibilities, I turn to more specific policy options.

OPENING UP THE DEBATE ON POLICY

Policy recommendations in comparative research are always subject to the criticism that proposals generated from another country could not possibly work here. Comparative researchers know only too vividly that no two countries are the same and that the direct importation of policies is certainly hazardous. But comparative work can bring a wider range of options to view. In this regard, I discuss policy alternatives in three areas: administration of the labor market and job placement; job training and high school education; and job creation policies.

First, in the area of job placement and administration, the United States needs a national institution able to make an impact on the broad range of human resources and employment problems. USES is capable of neither fulfilling its role in job placement nor implementing the full range of ALMP. Because federalization will not work given states' interests, an independent employment service system should be established. Critics agree that USES is an abomination, and some regard reform as impossible (Osterman 1988, pp. 153–55; Burton et al. 1986; Ruttenberg and Gutchess 1970; Beimiller 1966). Nevertheless, a full employment policy in the United States, no matter what the phase of the business cycle, demands a centralized employment service that implements the vast majority of labor market policies. (Imagine the inevitable financial chaos of a decentralized federal reserve system, with each state having its own rules for controlling the money supply!) Why should the United States promote rationality in financial markets but accept chaos in labor markets? A national and centralized employment service is needed, and for political reasons it should be an independent agency much like the federal reserve system.[8]

Tripartite participation—labor, management, and government—should be established for ALMP. Each group should be involved in the actual planning and implementation of labor mar-

8. Suggestions for a strong and comprehensive employment service were embodied in President Kennedy's Community Manpower Centers (1962), President Johnson's Comprehensive Manpower Service Centers (1965), and Representative Jefford's Labor Market Investment Boards (1982).

ket policy. This would create a basis for trust between these three parties and promote efficient policy implementation. Because many workers are not organized in the United States, the direction of the national employment service would be more complicated than it is in West Germany, and issues of representation would have to be worked out. Nevertheless, labor, employers, and government should guide policy at the national, state, and community levels. High schools should be effectively represented on the councils as part of the government section to assure transition to work programs.

The British created a tripartite employment service organization that has been effective under difficult labor market conditions.

The Manpower Services Commission (MSC) . . . has proved a remarkable institutional innovation. Established in 1973 by the Heath administration, it is one of those tripartite, interventionist, consensus-seeking QUANGOs that Thatcherite Conservatism seems so much to despise; and yet it has gained enormously in influence under the present Government. And unlike many tripartite bodies, it has by no means been a passive talking shop, but a highly active and innovative force. (*Political Quarterly* 1986, p. 227)

Although this commission was abolished in 1988 after the Thatcher government tried to double the number of employer seats, this tripartite organization worked well in an Anglo-Saxon country.[9] Admittedly, the United States is much more ethnically and racially diverse than either the United Kingdom or West Germany, but the creation of fair and flexible job placement is still possible. For example, Senator Paul Simon recommends appointing thirteen-member councils for job creation programs with four representatives from business, four from labor, and the remaining five from government units within the district (1987, pp. 132–35). The appointment of powerless advisory councils is not difficult; but the United States needs councils that are highly in-

9. The Manpower Services Commission was transformed into the Training Commission and then abolished in September 1988 (Grant 1989, p. 16). The precipitating factor in the commission's demise was the Conservative Party's plans to double the number of employers' representatives, which prompted the trade unions to withdraw (Longstreth 1988, p. 417).

novative and empowered to make decisions. And councils for the labor market need a coordinated organization, similar to the West German Bundesanstalt, to run effective and stable programs.

Once tripartite councils are established to lead a comprehensive ALMP organization, then specific policy issues can be addressed in all areas of ALMP. Most critical for the unemployed is job placement. To be effective, the employment service needs employers' notification of plant closings. Most European countries have such policies, and, with adequate confidentiality within the employment service and tripartite councils, they should not pose problems for employers and would prepare the way for adequate planning for workers. A displaced workers' program with adequate warning could ease workers' hardships and aid in transitions to new and more productive jobs.[10]

The foremost responsibility of the new employment service is to hire representatives who actively canvass employers and work with them to develop their needs in training and human resources. In the short run a national computerized system could also address regional imbalances in job skills through job placement and mobility benefits, and it could foresee employer training needs for specific skills. All this, of course, requires the active participation of employers and labor representatives to build a spirit of consensus and make planning possible, even under difficult economic conditions.

Second, in the area of job training, specific technical training should be provided in the high school, done on the job, and followed with specific skills tests. The general and vocational tracks in the high school should be totally revised and upgraded. Vocational education is in disastrous shape in the United States, and as Semple states "the comprehensive schools often have blended the worst of the general and vocational tracks" (1986, pp. 70, 87). Programs for students interested in craft or technical labor markets should emphasize skills—reading, calculating, and craft—in concrete vocational procedures. Just as some high school students take college placement exams at the end of high school, each stu-

10. The Senate considered a modest notification provision in the Trade Adjustment Act, but President Reagan vetoed the measure. The act was later passed and signed without the plant closings and notification provision (Tarullo 1989).

dent in vocational and technical courses should be tested on academic and technical skills at the end of training. A vocational certificate in a specific skill should be given to each successful graduate.

High school vocational training should also be provided on the job because it works best there. Schools cannot purchase a wide variety of equipment and be expected to duplicate fast-paced technological change in firms. Vocational training programs should be based in the high school, but physical training should occur as much as possible on the job. This will require an effective and broad-ranged integration of high school vocational education with employers and trade unions. This also integrates interested students into the world of work as opposed to an organizational culture of sports and dating (Rumberger and Daymont 1984).

Rather than keeping post–high school vocational schools separate from the realities of employment and the labor market, retraining, built on certifiable skills and on-the-job training, should provide high levels of skills along with initial training. Employers should encourage workers to attend programs with full wages, not only to prepare workers for new jobs but also to promote flexibility within their own company. Unions, employers, employee associations, and government agencies should work together to design such programs so that they provide the advanced skills that employers can use rather than the minimal skills programs that exist now. Individual workers should be actively assisted to improve their skills and flexibility while they are on the job. Workers in dead-end jobs should be offered basic and advanced skills training so that they may respond when new opportunities arise. The government should identify dead-end jobs and give workers in them presumptive eligibility for new training programs.

These changes will of course require labor-management-government integration into high school training and retraining. The world of work—unions, employers, employee associations, and government agencies—needs to be represented in the high school (Bronfenbrenner 1973). Formal classes in the job market, as in Sweden, could also be established in the secondary schools.

The United States is now engaged in a national debate on the quality of education, but the debate focuses on improving teachers and motivating students, rather than on making skills applicable to the labor market.[11] Americans like to ignore vocational education, but they do so at their own peril. Researchers studying employers have discovered that American business is not even interested in vocational education (Wilms 1983). This attitude reflects the present state of American vocational education; it is an attitude not expressed in West Germany or Sweden, where most employers strongly support vocational education.[12] The outlook of American business and even its product mix would change with a different job training system.

The issue of competitiveness in world markets demands that we look at the manual labor force. James Fallows makes this point while comparing the Japanese and U.S. secondary schools:

We don't need to pour more money into the Harvards and Berkeleys, where we're already strong. The battle should instead be fought where we're now the weakest: in the big-city public high schools and the mediocre elementary schools. In the past twenty years the best bottom half of the world has been up against the best upper half, and the bottom half is winning. (1987, p. 20)

The training and productivity of the manual work force is of great importance and must be supported. The promotion of effective job training for the bottom half of the labor force should be not a residual outcome; it should be a national priority.

Some basic points about the interaction of labor market structure and basic cultural values must be understood to underscore the need for reform in the American educational system. Japan and West Germany produce the best manual and lower-technical workers in the world. Japan copied the American system of com-

11. Debates about secondary education have focused on four areas (in decreasing order of attention): rigorous skills—reading, writing, and mathematics; political and religious values; social skills including sex education; and labor market skills—job training and cooperative education.

12. Amitai Etzioni even finds a bias against vocational education among industry leaders: " 'Vocational education is not a priority,' lamented Richard Arnold, . . . division manager . . . of AT&T. 'Business Round Table decided not to take it on,' confided one of my colleagues. . . . When Carl D. Perkins launched hearings on possible renewal of the massive five-year program of federal aid to vocational education . . . the opposing views did not make the network news, indeed were barely reported at all. Vocational education may not be a prestigious or 'in' subject, but it requires attention in this era of national turnabout" (1983, p. 209).

prehensive schools and made it work. However, the Japanese system will not work in the United States because Japanese employers have near monopolistic controls over primary labor markets for manual workers. If a worker quits a primary sector firm—the employers that pay so well, have lifetime employment, and provide copious benefits—he or she will rarely get back into the primary sector to see those high wages again. Primary sector firms only recruit workers who have not worked in other competitive firms. Consequently, Japanese firms can safely provide extensive training in specific and general topics without fear that workers will quit and benefit another company. Thus, employers' controls over the labor market in Japan strongly encourage job training. American companies lack protected investments because they have neither sought nor been able to obtain such a monopoly over primary sector labor markets. American employers often steal well-trained employees from other firms, which produces a strong disincentive toward employers' investment in training. American schools attempt to compensate for the disincentives on firm training, but my discussion of the high school has shown that vocational education has been stagnant and ineffective. Hence, exhorting U.S. employers to invest in more training will not work unless employers' interests are protected.

In the opposite direction, the West German continuation school system also produces excellence in the bottom half of the labor force. But the West German labor markets and school system operate entirely differently than those in the United States. West German employers have little need to establish monopolistic controls over the labor market because they do not have to fear losing workers. Employers participate in basic vocational education and spend large amounts of money on job training. The apprenticeship system allows employers to train workers for society as a whole and to test a continuous stream of apprentices for potential employment. If workers do well, employers hire them after the apprenticeship. Because West German workers are accurately certified for their skills, employers can hire new workers with known levels of skill at various points in their careers. West German firms do not need elaborate testing procedures and probation periods because the apprenticeship and continuation school already provide this information. Furthermore, employers are involved in and can control the training process, and hence the school system is not going to produce people irrelevant to their needs. But the West German system will not work in the United States either. The branding of working-class children at the age of fourteen or earlier is anathema to American beliefs in social mobility and equality. Indeed, the West German school system has been under fire on this point during much of the 1960s and 1970s. What can be done?

Sweden is perhaps the only country since World War II that has turned its education system totally around to meet both high skills requirements of the manual work force and demands for equality (Stenholm 1984; SÖ 1986). It has combined the socialization of a comprehensive school, the demands for higher education, and the need for specific and certified vocational programs. This is not simply a tracking system of college prep, business, and general programs; instead, it prepares many students for the detailed skills needed to work at specific jobs, and at the same time it prepares other students for higher education. Swedish secondary schools avoid being a holding tank for noncollege-bound students, and yet they keep diverse students in the same school. Secondary education not only provides general education for these noncollege students, but it also gives them the near equivalent of an apprenticeship education. When students have been comprehensively tested, have finished actual work experience, and are certified by the schools to possess critical skills, employers want them, especially if the workers have been previewed on the job.[13] The real world is further introduced into these comprehensive/continuation schools through work counseling by the employment service and follow-up activities by other agencies (SÖ 1988).

Thus, American vocational education in the high school could go in the direction of the Swedish rather than the Japanese or West German model. College preparatory and vocational education would take place in the same schools; they would not, as in West Germany, be totally divorced from each other. Students

13. Employers will flock to job-retraining schools if they are properly run. During my visit to Sweden in 1989, employers were recruiting directly at the ALMP training schools (AMU training centers) and at the Gymnasium in Stockholm.

who initially enter a vocational curriculum could change to a college preparatory program without problems, only making up courses they missed; students who transfer from the academic curriculum to the vocational courses would do the same.[14] Thus, highly intensive skills can be given to vocational students so they can enter labor markets prepared for work. The doors remain open for students to transfer between systems if they so desire, but the system would not drop unprepared manual workers into an unsympathetic labor market.[15]

These are not isolated recommendations. In a study appropriately labeled "a bridge too long" the National Commission on Youth (1980, pp. 1–6, 187–89) recommends a dual addition to the high school: transition schools for the last two years of high school, operated by the public school system to provide career options, introduce new skills, and test competency in internships and apprenticeships; and optional learning centers operated by the community to provide a safety net of jobs, service opportunities, and vocational apprenticeships for students who drop out of or cannot handle mainstream schooling. Osterman (1988, p. 158) and Becker (1988) propose similar changes based on the West German model.[16] Their recommendations on schooling point in

14. The Swedish system cannot be entirely taken as an example for the United States. Transferring between academic and vocational courses tends to be from the top down in Sweden, and in general, upward transferring is not easy because of educational planning. West Germany and Sweden limit the number of students that can go into various areas so that they match labor demand (i.e., available jobs) in the future. This increases the efficiency of labor markets, but it would probably be politically impossible in the United States. American schools would have to drop tight planning and accentuate transferring between vocational and college preparatory courses.

15. Vocational training is often criticized in the United States for its narrowness; however, West German employers believe that an employee who has completed an apprenticeship has acquired the self-discipline and analytic abilities to learn other trades or jobs. Oddly enough, American employers express the same thoughts about college graduates in fields unrelated to the company's area of business. Rigorous training, whether manual or college, can lead to both flexible and disciplined workers.

16. Osterman implies that West Germany targets mainstream employees and ignores others. This is somewhat misleading. First, West Germany serves the disadvantaged with ALMP programs. Second, the United States creates a massive sector of disadvantaged workers through its training system, while West Germany minimizes the creation of disadvantaged workers. And third, separate

the right direction, but I suggest a more systematic approach, beginning with the high school freshman rather than the high school dropout.

Lifelong training and flexibility are necessary for fluid retraining and transitions in the labor market. In this regard, both the West German and Japanese labor markets have advantages over the U.S. system. With entirely different industrial relations systems, they provide flexibility within the working environment to do many different jobs—a sort of informal job rotation program where workers not only learn many different kinds of skills but where managers can use workers more productively. American internal labor markets have jobs with very specific tasks, but workers with very general skills or low levels of literacy. Matching tasks with skills is difficult, and the system of job classification fights against the flexible use of labor. Although new union-management contracts incorporate flexibility, bargaining at the plant level is not sufficient. Workers' participation and an employment service with tripartite boards would lead to flexibility through a different approach to job training.

These recommendations will revive turn-of-the-century debates about "corporate hegemony" versus "pedagogic liberation" in the United States (Wirth 1972, 1985; Jamieson 1985). Educational interest groups have traditionally favored humanistic or liberal education over work or vocational education, especially if employers play a strong role. Etzioni goes so far as to recommend that we "reduce the role of general education, which tends to foster an antivocational educational orientation" (1983, p. 217).[17]

---

services for the disadvantaged stigmatize programs and mitigate against universalistic principles that are much more helpful in giving legitimacy to social programs.

17. Black groups may oppose vocational education in the schools because of their past experience with the industrial training movement (discussed in Chapter 2). And even with my recommendations, they will have to be vigilant in pressing for increased college enrollments and in keeping black students from being too easily pushed into lower programs than they deserve. However, too many disadvantaged students profit too little from the present structure of the high school. Pushing everyone toward college does not do much to help dropouts. Properly applied, "high skill vocational programs" would benefit more technically inclined students in the labor market whose interests are currently ignored.

Just as third-party bureaucrats in the government would oppose participation of labor and employers, third-party educators may do the same. However, Americans can no longer afford to ignore the manual labor force's needs for training and employment. Foreign competition is showing us that financial wizards and engineering geniuses, though necessary, are not sufficient in highly competitive world markets, and well-trained and flexible technical workers are also indispensable.[18]

Third, in the area of job creation, the federal/state governments should establish work creation programs for those who need them in place of unemployment compensation, but they must be careful to monitor programs very closely so that they are politically defensible. Unemployment compensation promotes passivity. Why not replace it almost totally with job training and job creation measures? The people who most need these programs are teenagers, especially the disadvantaged, unemployed workers in depressed areas, and workers laid off during economic downturns.

A national youth service for full-time employment to benefit the nation and its communities is one proposal for teenagers. A one-year mandatory service requirement to the nation is not too much to ask of affluent teenagers, while we simply cannot continue to accept 50 percent unemployment rates among disadvantaged teenagers. Such projects form a base for community caring and promote the benefits of mixing subcultures and classes; they also provide a way to fulfill citizenship obligations, which are often ignored in comparison to rights. Part-time and full-time options would be available, and a moderate pay schedule would be maintained. Youth service programs have been recommended by

18. The United Kingdom tends to ignore manual workers in an analogous way to the United States. It may be instructive to ask how much of the following statement about the "resurgence" of the British economy might apply to job training in the United States: "it is more interesting to ask why these [Japanese] firms are building their factories in Britain rather than Bavaria or Barcelona. . . . The real reason is not entirely complimentary. Britain offers the best combination of low labor costs . . . and relevant skills. . . . By and large British skills are relevant because the country's workforce is less well educated and less well trained than that in France or West Germany, for instance. In other words, at present wage levels, Britons are better suited for fairly hum drum tasks—like assembling Japanese cars" (*Economist* 1989, pp. 18–19).

the National Commission on Youth (1980, pp. 35–62), and they are on the legislative agenda in a number of states. Antecedents to a youth service are the Peace Corps, VISTA, the National Youth Service, and the Youth Conservation Corps.

A less ambitious program for youth would be a "job guarantee for teenagers." Sweden guarantees teenagers a job for four hours a day in place of unemployment compensation. Coupled with "job clubs"—self-help job-finding groups with professional job assistance—the youth guarantee keeps teenagers in the work force and socializes them toward work (Johannesson 1989, pp. 12–13). It does not provide them with skills other than what is learned on the job, but often teenagers have a renewed interest in training after their first job. And perhaps more important, it keeps teenagers from becoming discouraged and susceptible to crime, drugs, or welfare dependence.

Second, job creation programs could be targeted for depressed areas severely affected by plant closings or economic neglect. With adequate warning, these efforts could be coupled with a form of industrial policy for the area. The least vulnerable workers, usually with more skills and fewer responsibilities, will obtain jobs elsewhere and perhaps move; but the most vulnerable workers most often simply sink in an area of stagnation. Job creation rather than passive transfer payments can help keep these people motivated and active. Furthermore, they can be a bridge to new industries. For instance, the government could create temporary firms to clean up waste, train unemployed workers for these jobs, and then demonstrate the feasibility of such projects.[19] Private firms would then be invited to take over the projects for profit. Some projects would become full-fledged businesses, while others would simply end. Nevertheless, a transition process would be provided to bridge the public-private chasm in job creation. Similar projects could be provided in services. However, these kinds of programs require a cooperation that would have to be nurtured over time. With the state's

19. DGB President Ernst Breit has pointed out that intensified environmental protection could mean many more jobs for the unemployed. The Bundesanstalt Research Institute has calculated multiplier effects of three DM for every one invested in environment-related jobs (*TWIG*, May 27, 1988). Job creation has a large potential in this area.

current competitive industrial policies, a nationally coordinated policy would be unlikely.

Third, cyclical job creation measures could be targeted for rebuilding infrastructure during economic downturns. Senator Paul Simon recommends WPA-like boards that would supply short-term temporary jobs rather than assigning workers to state and local governments. Some of these jobs could be subcontracted to private industry, while others would be directly funded by the state. Consensual planning would be essential. As Simon suggests, tripartite councils could provide jobs on a project-by-project basis; supervisors would be hired for each project, and workers would be paid the minimum wage or 10 percent above welfare, whichever is higher. A project could be vetoed by two of the four representatives for either employers or labor. The jobs would provide a thirty-two-hour week and thus allow workers to look regularly for other employment (Simon 1987, pp. 132–35). Therefore, the projects would be temporary and avoid the paralyzing substitution effects of the CETA program, where some state and local governments subsidized a portion of their wage bill with federal funds.

Nevertheless, critics of job creation programs always abound. Job creation programs must be kept small to moderate in size and carefully audited. Publicity on actual costs must stress that job creation saves money by reducing unemployment compensation and welfare costs, by increasing or maintaining workers' skills and self-discipline, and by keeping workers out of the underground economy. Crime ultimately costs society much more money than the job creation programs themselves. A new employment service with an efficient organization, rather than different and temporary job creation organizations, would be vital to the success and monitoring of such programs. And the actual participation of business and labor in the direction of these programs would increase their effectiveness and reduce political opposition.

Despite the barriers I have specified, the United States can take steps toward reform in three areas: a strong, centralized, and independent employment service; effective vocational education in the high school and retraining in high skills; and carefully crafted and limited job creation policies. U.S. productivity and foreign trade problems demand new approaches to labor markets and the workplace. Perhaps the key to these recommendations and to change is an understanding of participation rights in this country. People work better if they participate in both the planning and the work. Employers and labor get along better if they participate in policy direction. On both levels, participation builds on the strong points of democracy.

Appendix
Variable Construction
and Data Sources

The ALMP data were constructed from national sources in both countries, and other data came from diverse sources. The following abbreviations are used:

FEDERAL REPUBLIC OF GERMANY

BAA-AN and BAVAV-AN: Bundesanstalt für Arbeit *Amtliche Nachrichtung der Bundesanstalt für Arbeit* from 1952 to 1984

BAA-GB and BAVAV-GB: Bundesanstalt für Arbeit *Geschaftsbericht* from 1952 to 1984

BAA-AA: Bundesanstalt für Arbeit *Auslandische Arbeitsnehmer* for 1981

BMA-HAS: Bundesministerium für Arbeit *Hauptergebnisse der Arbeits- und Sozialstatistik* from 1954 to 1984

SJ-BRD: Bundesrepublik Deutschland *Statistisches Jahrbuch für die Bundesrepublik Deutschland* from 1948 to 1984

JG: Sachverständigenrat *Jahresgutachten* for 1970–71 and 1984–85

SB: Bundesrepublik Deutschland, Statistisches Bundesamt *Bevölkerung und Kultur - Reihe 2.* for 1975

UNITED STATES

AFL-CIO/BCR: AFL-CIO *Biannual Convention Reports* from 1948 to 1984

BUSG: U.S. Government, *Budget of the United States Government* from 1946 to 1986

ECRP: U.S. President, *The Economic Report of the President* from 1984 to 85

ETRP: U.S. President, *The Employment and Training Report of the President* from 1962 to 1982

DOL-EHE: U.S. Department of Labor, *Employment, Hours and Earnings: U.S. 1909–1984, Volume II* for 1985

DOL-HLS: Department of Labor, *Handbook of Labor Statistics* for 1980

DOL-MLR: Department of Labor, *Monthly Labor Review*

INS: U.S. Immigration and Naturalization Service, *1981 Annual Report*

UAW/AAR: UAW, *Annual Audit Reports* from 1948 to 1984

BOTH COUNTRIES

OECD-NAS: OECD, *National Accounts Statistics, Main Aggregates* from 1960 to 1985

Active Labor Market Policy Expenditures

FRG: ALMP expenditures are the sum of job placement, job retraining, and job creation programs: BAVAV-AN and BAA-AN for most years, BMA-HAS for 1965–67, and Wittich (1966) to clarify the early periods.

U.S.: U.S. ALMP expenditures are scattered in the DOL, USES, HEW, OEO, and elsewhere: ETRP for most data since 1962, an "internal DOL budget office report" for the CETA years, and BUSG for USES and OEO expenditures. All U.S. expenditures were reported in fiscal years and had to be converted into calendar years.

Government Employment

FRG: Total BAA permanent employees, BAA-GB and BAVAV-GB. The figures were divided by the total civilian labor force. Other government employees were taken from Flora (1983) and supplemented by the SJ-BRD.

U.S.: USES federal and state national staff years (i.e., full-time employee equivalents) were obtained from an "internal DOL Budget Department Memorandum." Total federal, state, and local government employment were taken from the DOL-EHE.

Political Variables

FRG: Party power in the chancellorship was measured by a dummy variable that was 1 when the SPD was in power and zero otherwise. Party power in the Bundestag was taken from the SJ-BRD. The yearly figures are adjusted to reflect midyear election dates and representatives who crossed over to other parties (Burkett 1975, Conradt 1978).

U.S.: Presidential party power is measured by a dummy variable where the Democratic president is 1. Party power in the legislature is measured separately for each branch. Three parties are involved: Mainstream Democrats, Republicans, and Southern Democrats (Shelley [1983] identifies Ala., Fla., Ga., Ky., La., Miss., N.C., Okla., S.C., Tenn., Tex., and Va.). Each legislative variable was divided by total members. A standardized index of the left's party power in the U.S. was constructed from House and Senate party power.

Trade Unions

FRG: Trade union power is DGB membership as a percentage of the civilian labor force: the SJ-BRD.

U.S.: The two measures of trade union political power are: (1) total union membership, taken from the AFL-CIO/BCR and UAW/AAR, is divided by the civilian labor force, and (2) combined AFL-CIO and UAW lobbying and political expenditures, taken from the same sources, is divided by GNP at factor cost.

Social Movement Variables

FRG: Protest demonstrations and riots are from Taylor and Hudson (1975) and Taylor and Jodice (1983). Each variable measures frequency. Days lost in strikes and lockouts are from the SJ-BRD.

U.S.: Social movement variables come from the same sources as West Germany. Strikes as days idle and days idle as a percentage of estimated working time come from the DOL-MLR.

Occupational Structure of the Labor Force

FRG: The number of employees in each occupational sector of the labor force come from the BAA-GB and BAVAV-GB, and this figure is divided by the total civilian labor force.

U.S.: Occupational sectors of the labor force were taken from the ECRP: the percentage of the labor force in mining, construction, manufacturing, finance, service industries, federal government employment, and state and local employment. More precise variables in the service sector were taken from the DOL-EHE: the percentage of the labor force in the private and state and local service sectors.

Economic Variables

FRG: Unemployment and inflation rates with 1970 as the base year figures are from the JG. GNP at factor cost, computed from the OECD-NAS, was deflated and divided by the population for GNP per capita. Economic growth is the yearly rate of change in GNP at factor cost.

U.S.: The unemployment and inflation rates are from the ECRP. The inflation rate is the consumer price index with 1967 as the base year. GNP at factor cost was calculated from OECD-NAS. Economic growth is the yearly rate of change in GNP at factor cost.

Demographic Variables

FRG: The total West German population and civilian labor force is from the BMA-HAS. The labor force participation rates came from the JG. The female labor force participation rate was calculated from the BMA-HAS, and for 1950 to 1951 and 1983 from the SJ-BRD. The percentage of the population by age groups came from the SJ-BRD and the SB. Guestworkers in the labor force came from the BAA-AA and the SJ-BRD; guestworkers for 1950 to 1953 were estimated from immigration figures.

U.S.: The total U.S. population and labor force participation rates—total, female and male—came from the ECRP. The civilian labor force figures by age and totals come from the DOL-HLS. Total immigration divided by population was taken from the INS.

Bibliography

Aaron, Henry
 1978 *Politics and the Professors.* Washington, D.C.: Brookings.
Abbott, Grace
 1908 "The Chicago Employment Agency and the Immigrant Worker." *American Journal of Sociology* 14:289–305.
Abraham, David
 1981 *The Collapse of the Weimar Republic.* Princeton, N.J.: Princeton University Press.
Achen, Christopher
 1982 *Interpreting and Using Regression.* Beverly Hills, Calif.: Sage.
Adams, Leonard
 1969 *The Employment Service in Transition, 1933–1968.* Ithaca, N.Y.: Cornell University Press.
AFL-CIO
 1955–68 *Biannual Convention Report.* Washington, D.C.: AFL-CIO.
Akard, Patrick
 1988 "Economic Policy in a Capitalist State: the Humphrey-Hawkins Bill and the Revenue Act of 1978." Presented on August 26, 1988 at the Annual Meeting of the American Sociological Association in Atlanta, Georgia.
Alber, Jens
 1981 "Government Responses to the Challenge of Unemployment." In *The Development of Welfare States in Europe and America,* ed. Peter Flora and Arnold Heidenheimer, 151–53. New Brunswick, N.J.: Transaction Books.
Albritton, Robert
 1979 "Social Amelioration through Mass Insurgency." *American Political Science Review* 73:1003–12.

Allen, William
    1966   *The Nazi Seizure of Power*. London: Eyre and Spottis-
                woode.
Almond, Gabriel, and G. B. Powell
    1978   *Comparative Politics*. Boston: Little Brown.
Althoff, Heiner
    1971   "Die Entstehung des Berufsbildungsgesetzes im Bundes-
                tag und seinen Ausschussen, 1966–1968." Diplomarbeit,
                Free University of Berlin.
Amons, Peter
    1975   "Work Incentive Program." In *The Impact of Government
                Manpower Programs*, ed. Charles Perry et al., 360–96.
                Philadelphia: Industrial Research Unit—University of
                Pennsylvania.
Anderson, C. Arnold
    1963   *Industrialization and Society*. Mouton: UNESCO.
Anderson, James
    1982   "The Historical Development of Black Vocational Educa-
                tion." In *Work, Youth and Schooling*, ed. H. Kantor and
                D. Tyack, 180–222. Stanford, Calif.: Stanford University
                Press.
Ashenfelter, Orley
    1988   "The Case for Evaluating Training Programs with Ran-
                domized Trials." In *Industrial Relations Research Asso-
                ciation Series Proceedings*, 283–90. Madison, Wis.:
                Industrial Relations Research Association.
Ashford, Douglas
    1978   *Comparing Public Policies*. Beverly Hills, Calif.: Sage.
Backer, Gerhard, Reinhard Bispinck, Klaus Hofemann, and Gerhard
Nägele
    1980   *Sozialpolitik: Eine Prolementierte Einführung* (Social Poli-
                cy: A Problem-Oriented Introduction). Köln: Bund Verlag.
Bailey, Stephen
    1950   *Congress Makes a Law*. New York: Columbia University
                Press.
Bailey, Thomas
    1988   "Market Forces and Private Sector Processes in Govern-
                ment Policy: The Job Training Partnership Act." *Journal
                of Policy Analysis and Management* 7:300–315.
Barclay, David
    1974   "Social Politics and Social Reform in Germany, 1890–
                1933." Ph.D. diss., Stanford University.

Barlow, Melvin
   1971   "Changing Goals." In *Vocational Education*, ed. G. Somers and J. K. Little, 9–32. Madison, Wis.: Center for Studies in Vocational Education.

Barnow, Burt
   1987   "The Impact of CETA Programs on Earnings." *Journal of Human Resources* 22:157–93.

Barocci, Thomas
   1980   "Employment and Training Programs in the 1970s." In *Industrial Relations Research in the 1970s*, ed. Thomas Kochan, Daniel Mitchell, and Lee Dyer, 95–147. Madison, Wis.: Industrial Relations Research Association.

Bäthge, Martin, et al.
   1976   *Sozialpolitik und Arbeiterinteresse.* Frankfurt: Campus Verlag.

Baum, John, and Joseph Ullman
   1976   *The Impact of Mandatory Listing on the Labor Market Role of the Public Employment Service.* Washington, D.C.: U.S. Department of Labor.

Baumer, Donald, and Carl Van Horn
   1985   *The Politics of Unemployment.* Washington, D.C.: Congressional Quarterly Press.

Beck, Nathaniel
   1982   "Parties, Administration, and American Macroeconomic Outcomes." *American Political Science Review* 76:83–93.

Becker, Gary
   1989   "Tuning into the Needs of High School Dropouts." *Business Week*, July 3.

Behr, Marhild von
   1982   *Die Entstehung der industriellen Lehrwerkstatten.* Frankfurt: Campus Verlag.
   1985   "Compilation and Analysis of Documents and Materials on the History of Apprentices Training in German Industry." Presented at the Conference on the Social Structure of the European Working Class in the Nineteenth Century: Berlin.

Beideman, Geraldine
   1976   "How Should the Public Employment Service be Financed?" In *The Role of the Employment Service, 1975–1985*, Joint Conference of the DOL Employment and Training Administration and the ICESA, 3–77 to 3–92. Washington, D.C.: Department of Labor.

Beimiller, Andrew
1966 "Statement on the Manpower Services Act of 1966 and Employment Service Act of 1966." In *Joint Meeting of the Employment and Manpower Subcommittees of the Senate Committee on Labor and Public Welfare* and the *Select Subcommittee on Labor of the Committee on Education and Labor*, 301–26. March 17, 1966. Washington, D.C.: GPO.

Bendix, Reinhard
1964 *Nation Building and Citizenship*. New York: Wiley.
1968 *State and Society*. Boston: Little Brown.

Benenson, Harold
1982 "Skilled Labor and Working-Class Consciousness." Paper for 10th World Congress of Sociology. Mexico City.

Berg, Ivar
1970 *The Great Training Robbery*. Boston: Basic Books.

Berg, Axel van den, and Joseph Smucker
1989 "Labor Market Policies and Industrial Change." Unpublished manuscript.

Berkowitz, Edward, and Kim McQuaid
1980 *Creating the Welfare State*. New York: Praeger.

Besters, Hans
1981 *Ist Arbeitslosigkeit unser Shicksal?* Baden-Baden: Nomos.

Beveridge, W. H.
1908 "Public Labor Exchanges in Germany." *Economic Journal* 18:1–18.

Beyme, Klaus von
1983 "Coalition Government in Western Germany." In *Coalition Government in Western Europe*, ed. Vernon Bogdanor, 16–37. London: Heinemann.
1985 "Policy-making in the Federal Republic of Germany." In *Policy and Politics in the Federal Republic of Germany*, ed. Klaus von Beyme and Manfred Schmidt, 1–26. New York: St. Martin's.

Biggart, Nicole
1984 "A Sociological Analysis of the Presidential Staff." *Sociological Quarterly* 25:27–44.

Bishop, John
1989 "Toward more Valid Evaluations of Training Programs Servicing the Disadvantaged." *Journal of Policy Analysis and Management* 8:205–28.

Björklund, Anders
1988 "What Experiments are Needed for Manpower Policy." *Journal of Human Resources* 23:267–77.

Blair, P. M.
1981   *Federalism and Judicial Review in West Germany.* Ox-
          ford: Oxford University Press.
Blanke, Bernhard, Hubert Heinelt, and Carl-Wilhelm Macke
1984   "Arbeitslosigkeit und Kommunale Sozialpolitik." In *Ar-
          beitslosigkeit in der Arbeitsgesellschaft,* ed. Wolfgang
          Bonß and Rolf Heinze, 299–330. Frankfurt: Suhrkamp
          Verlag.
Blankenburg, Erhard, Günther Schmid, and Hubert Treiber
1976   "Legitimäts- und Implementierungsprobleme 'aktive Ar-
          beitsmarktpolitik.' " In *Burgerlicher Staat und politische
          Legitimätion,* ed. Rolf Ebbinghausen, 247–80. Frankfurt:
          Suhrkamp Verlag.
Blumberg, Rhoda
1984   *Civil Rights: The 1960s Freedom Struggle.* Boston:
          Twayne.
Blüm, Norbert
1978   "Der DGB muß endlich umdenken." *Manager Magazin*
          5:19–24.
1983   "Gibt es Alternativen zum Sozialstaat?" In *Chancen und
          Grenzen des Sozialstaats,* ed. P. Koslowski, P. Kreuzer,
          and R. Löw, 229–37. Tübingen: J. C. B. Mohr.
Bogart, E. L.
1908   "Public Employment Offices in the U.S. and Germany."
          Quarterly Journal of Economics 19:341–77.
Borus, Michael
1980   "Assessing the Impact of Training Programs." In *Employ-
          ing the Unemployed,* ed. Eli Ginzburg, 25–40. New York:
          Basic Books.
Braunthal, Gerard
1983   *The West German Social Democrats, 1969–1982.* Boulder,
          Colo.: Westview Press.
Breitman, Richard
1981   *German Socialism and Weimar Democracy.* Chapel Hill,
          N.C.: University of North Carolina Press.
Briggs, Asa
1961   "The Welfare State in Historical Perspective." *Archives
          Européennes de Sociologie* 2:221–58.
Briggs, Vernon
1982   "The Revival of Job Creation Programs in the 1970s: Les-
          sons for the 1980s." In *Proceedings of the Industrial Rela-
          tions Research Association—1981.* Pp. 258–73. Madison:
          Industrial Relations Research Association.

Brilliant, Eleanor
1986   "Social Work Leadership: A Missing Ingredient?" *Social Work* 31:325–31.
Brinkman, Gerhard
1981   *Ökonomik der Arbeit, Band 1 und 2.* Stuttgart: Klett Cotta Verlag.
Briscoe, Alden
1972   "Public Service Employment in the 1930s: The WPA." In *The Political Economy of Public Service Employment,* ed. H. Sheppard, B. Harrison, and W. Spring, 95–115. Lexington, Mass.: D. C. Heath.
Brody, David
1983   "On the Failure of U.S. Radical Politics: A Farmer-Labor Analysis." *Industrial Relations* 22:141–63.
Bronfenbrenner, Urie
1973   *Two Worlds of Childhood.* New York: Pocket Books.
Browning, Robert
1981   "Political and Economic Predictors of Policy Outcomes." Ph.D. diss., University of Wisconsin at Madison.
Bruche, Gerd, and Sabine Kroker
1982   *European Labor Placement.* West Berlin: IIM-Wissenshaftsentrum.
Bruche, Gert, and Bernd Reissert
1985   *Die Finanzierung der Arbeitspolitik—System, Effectivität, Reformansatze.* Frankfurt: Campus Verlag.
Bry, Gerhard
1960   *Wages in Germany, 1871–1945.* Princeton, N.J.: Princeton University Press.
Buck, Gerhard
1983   "Die Entwicklung der Freien Wohlfahrspflege von den ersten Zusammenschlüssen der freien Verbände im 19. Jahrhundert bis zur Durchsetzung des Subsidaritätsprinzips in der Weimarer Fürsorgegesetzgebung." In *Geschichte der Sozialarbeit,* ed. R. Landwehr and R. Baron, 139–72. Weinheim and Basel: Beltz Verlag.
Bullock, Paul
1981   *CETA at the Crossroads.* Los Angeles: IIR-UCLA.
Bundesanstalt für Arbeit (BAA)
1969–84   (or Bundesanstalt für Arbeitsvermitt-lung und Arbeitslosenversicherung [BAVAV] 1954–1968). *Amtliche Nachrichten der Bundesanstalt für Arbeit-Jahreszahlen.* Nuremberg: BAA.

1952–84   *Geschaftsbericht.* Nuremberg: BAA.
1971, 1973–75, 1979, 1981   *Förderung der Berufliche Bildung.* Nuremberg: BAA.
1979   *Federal Employment Institute.* Nuremberg: BAA.
1981   *Auslandische Arbeitnehmer.* Nuremberg: BAA.
Bundesinstitut für Berufsbildung (BIBB)
1983   *For Your Information: The Federal Institute of Vocational Education and Training.* West Berlin: BIBB.
1984   *Further Vocational Training as a Means of Coping with Structural Change in the Economy.* West Berlin: BIBB.
Bundesministerium für Arbeit (BMA)
1952–84   *Hauptergebnisse der Arbeits und Sozialstatistik.* Bonn: Bundesminister für Arbeit und Sozialordnung.
1972 and   *Arbeits- und Sozialstatistik.* Bonn: Bundesminister für Ar-
1984   beit und Sozialordnung.
1972   *Survey of Social Security in the Federal Republic of Germany.* Bonn: BMA.
1983   *Statistisches Taschenbuch 1983.* Bonn, Bundesminister für Arbeit und Sozialordnung.
Bundesministerium für Bildung und Wissenschaft (BMBW)
1984   *Berichtsystem Weiterbildungs Verhalten 1982.* Bonn: Bundesministerium für Bildung und Wissenschaft.
Bundesrepublik Deutschland (BRD)
1950–85   *Statistisches Jahrbuch der Bundesrepublik Deutschland.* Stuttgart: Kohlhammer.
1952–84   *Bundeshaushaltsplan für das Haushaltsjahr 1952–1982.* Bonn: Bundesdruckerei.
1975   *Bevölkerung und Kultur.* Mannheim: Statistisches Bundesamt.
1982   *Minicensus.* Wiesbaden. Typescript.
Bundestag (BT)
1952–84   *Stenographische Bericht.* (BT. SB.) Bonn: Bundestag der Bundesrepublik Deutschland.
1952–84   *Verhandlungen—Drucksachen* (BT. Dr.). Bonn: Bundestag der Bundesrepublik Deutschland.
1967–68   *Stenographisches Protokoll offentliche Informationssitzung.* Bonn: Ausschuße für Arbeit [confidential committee reports, unpublished].
Bunn, Ronald
1984   "Employers Associations in the Federal Republic of Germany." In *Employers Associations and Industrial Rela-*

tions, ed. John Windmuller and Alan Gladstone, 169–201. Oxford: Clarendon Press.

Burghardt, Anton
    1979   *Kompendium der Sozialpolitik* (The Compendium of Social Policy). Berlin: Duncker and Humblot.

Burkett, Tony
    1975   *Parties and Elections in West Germany.* London: C. Hurst.

Burstein, Paul
    1981   "The Sociology of Democratic Politics and Government." *Annual Review of Sociology* 7:291–319.

Burtless, Gary
    1984   "Manpower Policies for the Disadvantaged: What Works." *The Brookings Review* 3:18–22.

Burtless, Gary, and Larry Orr
    1986   "Are Classical Experiments Needed for Manpower Policy?" *Journal of Human Resources* 21:606–39.

Burton, Daniel, John Filer, Douglas Fraser, and Ray Marshall
    1986   *The Jobs Challenge.* Cambridge, Mass.: Ballinger.

Butler, Arthur
    1951   "The Public Employment Service in the U.S." Ph.D. diss., University of Wisconsin at Madison.

Buttler, Friedrich
    1984   "West Germany: On the Road toward Deactivation by the State." In *Public Policies to Combat Unemployment in a Period of Economic Stagnation*, ed. K. Gerlach, W. Peters, and W. Sengenberg, 141–70. Frankfurt: Campus Verlag.

Button, James
    1978   *Black Violence.* Princeton, N.J.: Princeton University Press.

Cameron, David
    1978   "The Expansion of Public Economy." *American Political Science Review* 72:1243–61.

CAMIL
    1975   *Job Search and the Employment Service.* Washington, D.C.: CAMIL.

Christian, David
    1964   "The National Apprenticeship Program: Unfinished Business." *Monthly Labor Review* 87:625–32.

Church, Robert, and Michael Sedlak
    1976   *Education in the United States.* New York: Free Press.

Cigler, Allan, and Burdett Loomis
1983   "The Changing Nature of Interest Group Politics." In *Interest Group Politics*, ed. A. Cigler and B. Loomis, 1–30. Washington, D.C.: Congressional Quarterly Press.
Clark, Kenneth
1966   "The Civil Rights Movement: Momentum and Organization." *Daedalus* 95:239–67.
Cohen, Robert
1976   *New Careers Grow Older*. Baltimore, Md.: Johns Hopkins University Press.
Commons, John R.
1928   "Statement of Dr. John R. Commons." U.S. Senate Hearings, Committee on Education and Labor, 70th Congress, S. 219. *Unemployment in the United States*.
Congressional Budget Office (CBO)
1982   *CETA Training Programs: Do They Work for Adults?* Washington, D.C.: CBO-NCEP Joint Study for the U.S. Congress.
Congressional Quarterly (CQ)
1966–85   *Congressional Quarterly Weekly Report*. Washington, D.C.: Congressional Quarterly Press.
Conradt, David
1978   *The German Polity*. New York: Longmans.
Cook, Thomas, and Donald Campbell
1979   *Quasi-Experimentation*. Chicago: Rand-McNally.
Cook, Robert, Charles Adams, V. Lane Rawlins
1985   *Public Service Employment*. Kalamazoo, Mich.: Upjohn.
Coughlin, Richard
1980   *Ideology, Public Opinion and Welfare Policy*. Berkeley, Calif.: Institute of International Studies, Monograph No. 42.
Cremin, Lawrence
1961   *The Transformation of the School*. New York: Random House.
Crouch, Colin
1979   "The State, Capital and Liberal Democracy." In *State and Economy in Contemporary Capitalism*, ed. Colin Crouch, 13–54. New York: St. Martin's Press.
Cuban, Larry
1982   "Enduring Resiliency." In *Work, Youth and Schooling*, ed. H. Kantor and D. Tyack, 45–78. Stanford, Calif.: Stanford University Press.

Currie, Elliot
>   1977   "The Politics of Jobs: Humphrey-Hawkins and the Di-
>   lemmas of Full Employment." *Socialist Revolution* 32:
>   93–114.

Dahrendorf, Ralf
>   1974   "Citizenship and Beyond: the Social Dynamics of an
>   Idea." *Social Research* 41:673–701.

Davidson, Roger
>   1972   *The Politics of Comprehensive Manpower Legislation.* Bal-
>   timore, Md.: Johns Hopkins University Press.

Davis, Mike
>   1980   "Why the U.S. Working Class is Different." *New Left Re-
>   view* 123:3–46.

Davis, Philip
>   1920   *Immigration and Americanization.* Boston: Ginn.

Dawson, William
>   1912   *Social Insurance in Germany, 1883–1911.* London:
>   Fischer-Unwin.

Dembo, Jonathan
>   1983   *Unions and Politics in Washington State, 1885–1935.* New
>   York: Garland.

Denison, Edward
>   1967   *Why Growth Rates Differ.* Washington, D.C.: Brookings
>   Institution.

>   1979   *Accounting for Slower Economic Growth.* Washington,
>   D.C.: Brookings Institution.

Derber, Milton
>   1984   "Employers Associations in the U.S." In *Employers Asso-
>   ciations and Industrial Relations*, ed. John Windmuller
>   and Alan Gladstone, 79–114. Oxford: Clarendon Press.

Der Spiegel
>   1982   "Küzere Arbeitszeit—Jobs für alle." *Der Spiegel* 49:40–50.
>   1985   "Ins Wespennest." *Der Spiegel* 38:20–22.

Derlien, Hans-Ulrich
>   1990   "Program Evaluation in the Federal Republic of Ger-
>   many." In *Program Evaluation and the Management of
>   Government*, ed. Ray Rist, 37–51. New Brunswick, N.J.:
>   Transaction.

Dertouzos, Michael, Richard Lesler, Robert Solow, and the MIT Commission on Productivity
>   1989   *Made in America: Regaining the Productive Edge.* Cam-
>   bridge, Mass: MIT Press.

Devine, Joel
  1983   "Fiscal Policy and Class Income Inequality." *American Sociological Review* 48:606–22.
  1985   "State and State Expenditures." *American Sociological Review* 50:150–65.

Deutsche Reich
  1922–33 *Statistisches Jahrbuch für das Deutsche Reich.* Berlin: Statistischen Reichsamt.

Dewey, John
  1914   "A Policy of Industrial Education." *The New Republic* 1:11–12.

Dickinson, Katherine, Terry Johnson, and Richard West
  1986   "An Analysis of the Impact of CETA Programs on Participant's Earnings." *Journal of Human Resources* 21:64–91.

Dineen, Donal
  1984   "Anti-Unemployment Policies in Ireland since 1970." In *Unemployment: Policy Responses of Western Democracies*, ed. Jeremy Richardson and Roger Henning, 238–76. Beverly Hills, Calif.: Sage.

Director, Steven
  1979   "Underadjustment Bias in the Evaluation of Manpower Training." *Evaluation Quarterly* 3:190–218.

Domurad, Frank
  1981   "The Politics of Corporatism." In *Social Change and Political Development in Weimar Germany*, ed. R. Bessel and E. Feuchtwanger, 174–206. London: Croom-Helm.

Donnison, David
  1979   "Social Policy Since Titmus." *Journal of Social Policy* 8:145–56.

Donovan, John
  1980   *The Politics of Poverty.* Washington, D.C.: University Press of America.

Droz, Jacques
  1983   "In Search of Prussia." *Journal of Modern History* 55: 71–77.

Dryzek, John, and Robert Goodin
  1985   "Risk-Sharing and Social Justice: The Motivational Foundations of the Post-War Welfare State." *British Journal of Political Science* 16:1–34.

Durman, Eugene
  1973   "Have the Poor been Regulated?" *Social Service Review* 47:339–59.

Dückert, Thea
  1982   "Arbeitsbeschaffungsmaßnahmen — Ein Beschäftigungs-
            politisches Instrument?" Ph.D. diss., Universität Regens-
            burg.
Dye, Thomas
  1981   *Understanding Public Policy*. New York: Prentice-Hall.
Dyson, Kenneth
  1973   "Planning and the Federal Chancellor's Office in West
            German Federal Government." *Political Science* 21:
            348–62.
  1980   *The State Tradition in Western Europe*. Oxford: Martin
            Robertson.
  1982   "West Germany: The Search for a Rationalist Consensus."
            In *Policy Styles in Western Europe*, ed. J. Richardson et
            al., 17–46. London: Allen Unwin.
  1982   "The Politics of Economic Recession in West Germany."
            In *Politics, Policy and the European Recession*, ed. An-
            drew Cox, 32–64. London: MacMillan.
Economist
  1989   "The End of the Beginning: A Survey of Business in Brit-
            ain." *The Economist*, May 20–26.
Erhard, Ludwig
  1963   *The Economics of Success*. Princeton, N.J.: Van No-
            strand.
Esping-Andersen, Gøsta
  1985   *Politics against Markets*. Princeton, N.J.: Princeton Uni-
            versity Press.
Etzioni, Amitai
  1983   "The Reindustrialization of Vocational Education." In *The
            World of Work*, ed. Howard Didsbury, 209–18. Bethesda,
            Md.: The World Future Society.
Eucken, Walter
  1951   *This Unsuccessful Age*. Edinburgh: Hodge and Company.
Eyck, Erich
  1967   *A History of the Weimar Republic*. Cambridge, Mass.:
            Harvard University Press.
Fallows, James
  1987   "East Asia: Gradgrind's Heirs." *Atlantic* 259:16–24.
Faust, Anselm
  1981   "State and Unemployment in Germany, 1890–1918." In
            *The Emergence of the Welfare State in Britain and Ger-
            many*, ed. W. J. Mommsen, 150–63. London: Croom-
            Helm.

1984   "Arbeitsmarktpolitik in Deutschland: Die Entstehung der öffentlichen Arbeitsvermittlung, 1890–1927." In *Historische Arbeitsmarketforschung*, ed. T. Pierenkemper and R. Tilly, 253–75. Göttingen: Vandenhoeck and Ruprecht.

Fechter, Alan
1975   *Public Employment Programs.* Washington, D.C.: Urban Institute Report 198-963-41.

Feder, Leah
1936   *Unemployment Relief in Periods of Depression.* New York: Russell Sage.

Feldman, Elliot
1978   "Comparative Public Policy: Field or Method." *Comparative Politics* 10:287–305.

Feldman, Gerald
1966   *Army, Industry and Labor in Germany.* Princeton, N.J.: Princeton University Press.
1970   "German Business between War and Revolution." In *Entstehung und Wandel der Modernen Gesellschaft*, ed. Gerhard Ritter, 312–41. Berlin: Walter de Gruyter Verlag.

Fenno, Richard
1973   *Congressmen in Committees.* Boston: Little Brown.

Fine, Sidney
1963   *The Automobile Under the Blue Eagle.* Ann Arbor: University of Michigan Press.

Fink, Arthur
1942   *The Field of Social Work.* New York: Henry Holt.

Finland
1966–82   *Finnish Statistical Yearbook.* Helsinki: Central Statistical Office.

Fischer, Cornelia
1981   *Staatliche Arbeitsfördergung.* Frankfurt: Campus Verlag.

Flamm, Franz
1974   *Social Welfare Services and Social Work in the FRG.* Troisdorf: Deutsche Vereins für öffentliche und private Fursorge.

Flora, Peter
1983   *State, Economy and Society.* Chicago: St. James Press.
1986   *Growth to Limits.* Berlin: Walter de Gruyter Verlag.

Flora, Peter, and Jens Alber
1981   "Modernization, Democratization, and the Development of Welfare States in Western Europe." In *The Development of Welfare States in Europe and America*, ed. P. Flora and A. Heiderheimer, 37–80. New Brunswick, N.J.: Transaction Books.

Flora, Peter, and Arnold Heidenheimer
1981   *The Development of Welfare States in Europe and America.* New Brunswick, N.J.: Transaction Books.
Form, William, and Delbert Miller
1960   *Industry, Labor and Community.* New York: Harper.
Fraker, Thomas, and Rebecca Maynard
1987   "The Adequacy of Comparison Group Designs for Evaluations of Employment-Related Programs." *Journal of Human Resources* 22:194–227.
Franklin, Grace, and Randall Ripley
1984   *CETA: Politics and Policy, 1973–1982.* Knoxville: University of Tennessee Press.
Free, Lloyd, and Hadley Cantril
1967   *The Political Beliefs of Americans.* New York: Simon and Schuster.
Friedlander, Walter, and Earl Myers
1940   *Child Welfare in Germany before and after Naziism.* Chicago: University of Chicago Press.
Freie Demokratische Partei (FDP) Bundestag Fraktion
1969   *FDP im 5. Deutschen Bundestag: Stichwort zur Bundespolitik 1965–1969.* Beuel-Bonn: Röge-Druck.
Friedman, Lawrence
1977   "The Social and Political Context of the War on Poverty." In *A Decade of Federal Antipoverty Programs*, ed. Robert Haveman, 21–47. New York: Academic Press.
Fryer, David, and Roy Payne
1986   "Being Unemployed: A Review of the Literature on the Psychological Experience of Unemployment." *International Review of Industrial and Organizational Psychology* 1986.
Führ, Christian
1983   "Bound to the Now Established Autonomy of the Lander." *Western European Education* 15:27–35.
Gagel, Alexander
1984   "Einführung." In *AFG—Arbeitsförderungsgesetz*, 10. *Auflage*, 11–35. München: Beck-Texte.
GAO
1986   *Employment Service: More Job Seekers Should Be Referred to Private Employment Agencies.* Gaithersburg, Md.: GAO.
Garraty, J. A.
1973   "The New Deal, National Socialism, and the Great Depression." *American Historical Review* 78:907–44.

1978   *Unemployment in History*. New York: Harper & Row.
Gates, Robert A.
1974   "Von der Sozialpolitik zur Wirtschaftspolitik? Das Di-
         lemma der deutschen Sozialdemokratie in der Krise 1929–
         1933." In *Industrielles System und politische Entwicklung
         in der Weimarer Republik*, ed. H. Mommsen, D. Petzina,
         and B. Weisbrod, 206–25. Düsseldorf: Droste Verlag.
Gelb, Joyce, and Marian Palley
1982   *Women and Public Policies*. Princeton, N.J.: Princeton
         University Press.
Gelfland, Mark
1981   "The War on Poverty." In *Exploring the Johnson Years*,
         ed. Robert Divine, 126–54. Austin: University of Texas
         Press.
Gennard, John
1979   *Job Security and Industrial Relations*. Paris: OECD.
Gerlach, Knut, Wilhelm Peters, and Werner Sengenberger
1984   *Public Policies to Combat Unemployment in a Period of
         Economic Stagnation*. Frankfurt: Campus Verlag.
Giddens, Anthony
1982   "Class Division, Class Conflict and Citizenship Rights." In
         Profiles and Critiques in Social Theory, 164–80. Berkeley:
         University of California Press.
Ginsburg, Helen
1979   "Full Employment as a Policy Issue." *Policy Studies Jour-
         nal* 8:359–68.
Glover, Robert
1974   *Apprenticeship in America: An Assessment*. Madison,
         Wis.: Industrial Relations Research Association.
Godwin, R. K., and W. B. Shepard
1976   "Political Process and Public Expenditures." *American Po-
         litical Science Review* 70:1127–35.
Goldberg, Harriet
1975a   "Job Corps." In *The Impact of Government Manpower
         Programs*, ed. Charles Perry et al., 397–422. Phila-
         delphia: Industrial Research Unit—University of Pennsyl-
         vania.
1975b   "Neighborhood Youth Corps." In *The Impact of Govern-
         ment Manpower Programs*, ed. Charles Perry et al., 423–
         50. Philadelphia: Industrial Research Unit—University of
         Pennsylvania.

Gordon, David, Richard Edwards, and Michael Reich
1982   *Segmented Work, Divided Workers.* Cambridge: Cambridge University Press.
Gottschalk, Peter
1983   "U.S. Labor Market Policies since the 1960s." Madison, Wis.: Institute for Research on Poverty Discussion Paper 730-83.
Gourevitch, Peter
1986   *Politics in Hard Times.* Ithaca, N.Y.: Cornell University Press.
Gourevitch, Peter, Andrew Martin, George Ross, Christopher Allen, Stephen Bornstein, and Andrei Markovits
1984   *Unions and Economic Crisis.* London: Allen Unwin.
Granger, C. W.
1969   "Investigating Causal Relations by Econometric Models and Cross-Spectral Methods." *Econometrica* 37:424–38.
Grant, Wyn
1989   "The Erosion of Intermediary Institutions." *Political Quarterly* 60:10–21.
Graveson, R. H.
1953   *Status in the Common Law.* London: Althone.
Green, Alfred
1966   *Manpower and the Public Employment Service in Europe.* Washington, D.C.: Department of Labor.
Griffin, Larry, Michael Wallace, and Joel Devine
1982   "The Political Economy of Military Spending." *Cambridge Journal of Economics* 6:1–14.
1983   "On the Economic and Political Determinants of Welfare Spending in the Post-WWII Era." *Politics and Society* 12:331–72.
Griffin, Larry, Joel Devine, and Michael Wallace
1983   "Monopoly Capital, Organized Labor, and Military Expenditures in the U.S., 1949–1976." *American Journal of Sociology Supplement* 88:s113–s153.
Grossman, Jonathan
1967   *The Department of Labor.* New York: Praeger.
Grottian, Peter, and Rolf Paasch
1984   "Arbeitslose: Von der gesellschaftlichen Randsgruppe zum politischen Faktor?" In *Arbeitslosigkeit in der Arbeitsgesellschaft*, ed. Wolfgang Bonß and Rolf Heinze, 331–48. Frankfurt: Suhrkamp.

Grønbjerg, Kirsten
    1977   *Mass Society and the Extension of Welfare*. Chicago: University of Chicago Press.

Grubb, W. N., and M. Lazerson
    1982   "Education and the Labor Market." In *Work, Youth and Schooling*, ed. H. Kantor and D. Tyack, 110–41. Stanford, Calif.: Stanford University Press.

Guillebaude, Claude
    1971   *The Social Policy of Nazi Germany*. Cambridge: Cambridge University Press.

Gutek, Gerald
    1983   *Standard Education Almanac*. Chicago: Professional Publications.

Guttman, Robert
    1983   "Job Training Partnership Act: New Help for the Unemployed." *Monthly Labor Review* 106:3–10.

Guzda, Henry
    1983   "The U.S. Employment Service at 50." *Monthly Labor Review* 106:12–19.

Haber, William, and Daniel Kruger
    1964   *The Role of the United States Employment Service in a Changing Economy*. Kalamazoo, Mich.: Upjohn.

Hage, Jerald, and Robert Hanneman
    1980   "The Growth of the Welfare State in Britain, France, Germany and Italy." *Comparative Social Research* 3:45–70.

Hallman, Howard
    1977   *Emergency Employment: A Study in Federalism*. University: University of Alabama Press.

Hamilton, Steven
    1985   "Apprenticeship as a Transition to Adulthood in West Germany." Paper presented at the American Educational Research Meetings. Chicago.

Hamilton, Richard, and James Wright
    1986   *The State of the Masses*. Chicago: Aldine.

Hanson, Charles, Sheila Jackson, and Douglas Miller
    1982   *The Closed Shop*. New York: St. Martin's Press.

Hargrove, Erwin, and Michael Nelson
    1984   *Presidents, Politics and Policy*. Baltimore, Md.: Johns Hopkins University Press.

Haveman, Robert
    1979   "Direct Job Creation: Potentials and Realities." Madison,

Wis.: University of Wisconsin Institute for Research on Poverty, Discussion Paper 570-79.

Hayes, John, and Peter Nutman

1981   *Understanding the Unemployed.* London: Tavistock.

Hearndon, Arthur

1974   *Education, Culture and Politics in West Germany.* Oxford: Pergamon.

Heclo, Hugh

1974   *Modern Social Politics in Britain and Sweden.* New Haven, Conn.: Yale University Press.

Heckman, James, and Joseph Hotz

1988   "Are Classical Experiments Necessary for Evaluating the Impact of Manpower Training Programs." In *Industrial Relations Research Association Proceedings,* 291–302. Madison, Wis.: Industrial Relations Research Association.

Heidenheimer, Arnold

1981   "Unions and Welfare State Development in Britain and Germany." West Berlin: International Institute for Comparative Social Research, Wissenschaftszentrum.

1983   "Education Policy." In *Comparative Public Policy,* ed. A. Heidenheimer, H. Heclo, and C. Teich Adams, 21–53. New York: St. Martin's Press.

Heinemann, Eduard

1929   *Soziale Theorie des Kapitalismus.* Frankfurt: Suhrkamp Verlag.

Henderson, W. O.

1975   *The State and the Industrial Revolution in Prussia.* Liverpool: Liverpool University Press.

Henkelmann, Walter

1967   "AFG—Reform des AVAVG? Eine Kritik aus gewerkschaftlicher Sicht." *Arbeit und Sozialpolitik* 10:318–22.

Hentschel, Richard

1983   *Sozialpolitik.* Frankfurt: Suhrkamp Verlag.

Hibbs, Douglas

1977   "Political Parties and Macroeconomic Policy." *American Political Science Review* 71:1467–87.

Hibbs, Douglas, R. Douglas Rivers, and Nicholas Vasilatos

1982   "On the Demand for Economic Outcomes." *Journal of Politics* 44:426–62.

Hicks, Alexander

1984   "Elections, Keynes, Bureaucracy and Class." *American Sociological Review* 49:145–82.

Hofbauer, Hans
1984a   "Untersuchungen des IAB über die Wirksamkeit der Beruflichen Weiterbildung." In *Konzepte der Arbeitsmarkt- und Berufsforschung*, ed. Dieter Mertens, 514–40. Nuremberg: Beiträge zur Arbeitsmarkt- und Berufsforschung des IAB.
1984b   "Ausbildungs- und Berufsverläufe." In *Konzepte der Arbeitsmarkt- und Berufsforschung*, ed. Dieter Mertens, 474–513. Nuremberg: Beiträge zur Arbeitsmarkt- und Berufsforschung des IAB.

Hofstadter, Richard
1955   *The Age of Reform*. New York: Knopf.

Hogan, David John
1985   *Class and Reform*. Philadelphia: University of Pennsylvania Press.

Holloway, William, and Michael Leach
1985   *Employment Termination*. Washington, D.C.: Bureau of National Affairs.

Hoppe, Albert
1966   "Der SPD-Entwurf zum 'Arbeitsmarkt- Anpassungsgesetz.' " *Zeitschrift für Sozialreform* 12:641–52.

Holzer, Harry
1987a   "Informal Job Search and Black Youth Unemployment." *Industrial Relations Research Association Proceedings*. Madison, Wis.: Industrial Relations Research Association.
1987b   "Hiring Procedures in the Firm." NBER Working Paper No. 2185. Cambridge, Mass.: National Bureau of Economic Research.

Höckerts, Hans-Gunter
1980   *Sozialpolitische Entscheidungen im Nachkriegsdeutschland*. Stuttgart: Klett-Cotta.

Huber, Ernst
1981   *Deutsche Verfassungsgeschichte seit 1789, Band IV-VI*. Stuttgart: Kohlhammer Verlag.

IG Metall
1981   *Metall Nachrichten*, Pamphlet No. 1. September 30.

ILO
1931   *Unemployment and Public Works*. Geneva: ILO Series C.
1935   *Public Works Policy*. Geneva: ILO Series C.

International Monetary Fund
1983   *International Financial Statistics*. Washington, D.C.: International Monetary Fund.

Isaac, Larry, and William Kelly
  1981   "Racial Insurgency, the State and Welfare Expansion."
            American Journal of Sociology 86:1348–96.
Jacobs, Bruce
  1981   *The Political Economy of Organizational Change*. New
            York: Academic Press.
Jacoby, Sanford
  1989   "American Exceptionalism Revisited: the Importance of
            Management." In *American Employers*, S. M. Jacoby.
            New York: Columbia University Press.
Jahoda, Marie
  1982   *Employment and Unemployment*. Cambridge: Cambridge
            University Press.
Jamieson, Ian
  1985   "Corporate Hegemony or Pedagogic Liberation." In *Edu-
            cation, Training and Employment*, ed. R. Dale, 23–40.
            Oxford: Pergamon Press.
Jeffords, James M.
  1982a   "Introduction of the Productivity and Human Investment
            Act." *Congressional Record*, February 4, 1982: E239–E240.
  1982b   "Summary of the Productivity and Human Investment Act."
            Congressional Record, February 8, 1982: E263–E265.
Jennings, Edward
  1983   "Racial Insurgency, the State and Welfare Expansion."
            American Journal of Sociology 88:1220–36.
Jerrett, Robert, and Thomas Barocci
  1979   *Public Works, Government Spending and Job Creation*.
            New York: Praeger.
Jochimsen, Reimut
  1978   "Aims and Objectives of German Vocational and Profes-
            sional Education." *Comparative Education* 14:199–209.
Johannesson, Jan
  1989   "On the Composition and Outcome of Swedish Labour
            Market Policy, 1970–88." Stockholm: The Delegation for
            Labor Market Policy Research—Ministry of Labor.
Johannesson, Jan, and Günther Schmid
  1980   "The Development of Labour Market Policy in Sweden
            and in Germany." *European Journal of Political Research*
            8:387–406.
Johnson, Miriam
  1973   *Counterpoint: The Changing Employment Service*. Salt
            Lake City, Utah: Olympus.

Johnson, Nevil
  1973   *Government in the FRG: The Executive at Work.* Oxford: Pergamon.
  1979   "Committees in the West German Bundestag." In *Committees in Legislatures: A Comparative Analysis,* ed. J. Lees and M. Shaw, 102–47. Durham, N.C.: Duke University Press.
Kaim-Caudle, P. R.
  1973   *Comparative Social Policy and Social Security.* London: Martin Robertson.
Kantor, Harvey
  1988   *Learning to Earn.* Madison: University of Wisconsin Press.
Karr, Werner, and Rudolf Leupoldt
  1976   *Strukturwandel des Arbeitsmarktes 1950 bis 1970 nach Berufen und Sektoren.* Nuremberg: IAB-BAA Beiträge zur Arbeitsmarkt- und Berufsforschung.
Katzenstein, Peter J.
  1984   *Corporatism and Change.* Ithaca, N.Y.: Cornell University Press.
  1987   *Policy and Politics in West Germany.* Philadelphia: Temple University Press.
Katzman, David
  1973   *Before the Ghetto.* Champaign-Urbana: University of Illinois Press.
Katznelson, Ira, and Margaret Weir
  1985   *Schooling for All.* New York: Basic Books.
Keller, Bill
  1982a   "Once a Washington Power, Labor Now Plays Catch-up in Lobbying and Politics." *CQ Weekly Report,* September 4.
  1982b   "Organized Labor's Vital Signs Show Waning Political Clout." *CQ Weekly Report,* August 28.
Kellman, Mitchell, and Oded Izraeli
  1985   "Rhythms in Politics and Economics." In *The Political Business Cycle: An International Perspective,* ed. P. Johnson and W. Thompson, 71–83. New York: Praeger.
Kendrick, John
  1977   *Understanding Productivity.* Baltimore, Md.: Johns Hopkins University Press.
Kennedy, Thomas
  1980   *European Labor Relations.* Lexington, Mass.: D. C. Heath.

Kesselman, Jonathan
  1978   "Work Relief Programs in the Great Depression." In
            Creating Jobs, ed. J. Palmer, 153–229. Washington, D.C.:
            Brookings Institution.
Kessler-Harris, Alice
  1982   *Out to Work: A History of Wage-Earning Women in the
            United States.* New York: Oxford University Press.
Kett, Joseph
  1982   "The Adolescence of Vocational Education." In *Work,
            Youth and Schooling*, ed. H. Kantor and D. Tyack, 79–
            109. Stanford, Calif.: Stanford University Press.
Keyserling, Leon
  1981   "The Humphrey-Hawkins Act Since Its 1978 Enactment."
            In *Solutions to Unemployment*, ed. David Colander, 225–
            29. New York: Harcourt Brace Jovanovich.
Kieser, Alfred
  1989   "Organizational, Institutional, and Societal Evolution: Me-
            dieval Craft Guilds and the Genesis of Formal Organiza-
            tions." *Administrative Science Quarterly* 34:540–64.
Kirchlechner, Berndt
  1978   "New Demands or the Demands of New Groups?" In *The
            Resurgence of Class Conflict*, ed. C. Crouch and A. Piz-
            zorno, 161–76. London: MacMillan.
Kirkland, Edward
  1951   *A History of American Economic Life.* New York:
            Appleton-Century Crofts.
Kitchen, Martin
  1978   *The Political Economy of Germany, 1815–1914.* London:
            Croom-Helm.
Kittner, Michael
  1982   *Arbeitsmarkt—ökonomische soziale und rechtliche Grund-
            lagen.* Heidelberg: Muller Juristischer Verlag.
Klatzky, S. R.
  1970   "Organizational Inequality: The Case of the Public Employ-
            ment Agencies." *American Journal of Sociology* 76:
            472–91.
Klönne, Arno
  1984   "Arbeitslosigkeit und politische Systemkrise. Ein Rück-
            blick auf die Weimarer Republick." In *Arbeitslosigkeit in
            der Arbeitsgesellschaft*, ed. Wolfgang Bonß and Rolf
            Heinz, 191–213. Frankfurt: Suhrkamp.
Kocka, Jürgen
  1980   "Class Formation, Interest Group Articulation and Public

Policy." In *Organizing Interests in Western Europe*, ed. Suzanne Berger, 48–51. Cambridge: Cambridge University Press.

Kommers, Donald
1976   *Judicial Politics in West Germany*. Beverly Hills, Calif.: Sage.

Kommunalverband Ruhrgebiet
1983   *Dokumentation regionaler Initiativen gegen Arbeitlosigkeit*. Essen: Brink and Company.

Koenig, Peter
1988   "Seven Men on the Twelfth Floor." *Euromoney*, March, 62–74.

Kornblum, William
1978   *Blue-Collar Community*. Chicago: University of Chicago Press.

Korpi, Walter
1989   "Power, Politics, and State Autonomy in the Development of Social Citizenship." *American Sociological Review* 54:309–28.

Kotz, Nick
1977   "Discussions." In *A Decade of Federal Antipoverty Programs*, ed. Robert Haveman, 48–51. New York: Academic Press.

Krasner, Stephen
1984   "Approaches to the State." *Comparative Politics* 16:223–46.

Krause, Paul
1982   *Division of Labor: A Political Perspective*. Westport, Conn.: Greenwood Press.

Krautkramer, Uta
1978   *Labor Market Administration in the Federal Republic of Germany*. West Berlin: IIM-Wissenschaftszentrum.

Kusmer, Kenneth
1976   *A Ghetto Takes Shape*. Champaign-Urbana: University of Illinois Press.

Kühl, Jürgen
1982   "Das Arbeitsförderungsgesetz (AFG) von 1969." *Mitteilungen aus der Arbeitsmarkt- und Berufsforschung*, March, 251–60.
1984   Interview with Thomas Janoski, Nuremberg, June 14.

Kühl, Jürgen, A. G. Paul, and D. Blunk
1980   *Employment Policy in Germany*. Nuremberg: Bundesanstalt für Arbeit.

Laidler, David, and Michael Parkin
  1975   "Inflation: A Survey." *The Economic Journal* 85:741–806.
Lambert, Norbert
  1979   *Arbeitsmarktpolitik in der Wirtschaftskrise.* Frankfurt:
            Institut für Marxistischen Studien und Forschungen.
Lampert, Heinz
  1979   *Arbeitsmarktpolitik.* Stuttgart: Fischer.
  1980   *Sozialpolitik.* West Berlin: Springer Verlag.
  1982   "Arbeitsmarktpolitische Aspekte der Strukturberichter-
            stattung." *Mitteilungen aus der Arbeitsmarkt- und Beruf-
            sforschung* March, 338–44.
  1983   *Die Wirtschafts- und Sozialordnung der BRD, 9. Auflage.*
            München: Olzog Verlag.
Lampman, Robert
  1977   "Discussions." In *A Decade of Federal Antipoverty Pro-
            grams,* ed. Robert Haveman, 51–54. New York: Academic
            Press.
Lander, Byron
  1971   "Group Theory and Individuals: The Origin of Poverty as
            a Political Issue." *Western Political Quarterly* 24:514–26.
Landwehr, Rolf, and Rüdiger Baron
  1983   *Geschichte der Sozialarbeit.* Basel: Beltz Verlag.
Lempert, Wolfgang
  1981   "Perspectives of Vocational Education in West Germany
            and Other Capitalist Countries." *Economic and Industrial
            Democracy* 2:321–48.
Lenoir, J. J.
  1940   "Judicial Review under the Weimar Republic." *Tulane
            Law Review* 14:361–83.
Lescohier, Donald
  1919   *The Labor Market.* New York: MacMillan.
Lessman, Sabine
  1987   *Budgetary Politics and Elections.* Berlin: Walter de
            Gruyter.
Levin, Henry
  1977   "A Decade of Policy Developments in Improving Educa-
            tional Training for Low Income Populations." In *A Decade
            of Federal Anti-Poverty Programs,* ed. Robert Haveman,
            123–88. New York: Academic Press.
Levin, Martin, and Barbara Ferman
  1985   *The Political Hand.* London: Pergamon.

Levitan, Sar
1966   "Is this War on Poverty Different?" In *Dimensions of Manpower Policy*, ed. S. Levitan and I. Siegel, 43–60. Baltimore, Md.: Johns Hopkins University Press.
1976   *The Promise of Greatness*. Cambridge, Mass.: Harvard University Press.
1980   *Programs in Aid of the Poor*. Baltimore, Md.: Johns Hopkins University Press.
Levitan, Sar, and Frank Gallo
1988   *A Second Chance: Training for Jobs*. Kalamazoo, Mich.: Upjohn.
Levitan, Sar, and Benjamin Johnston
1975   *The Job Corps*. Baltimore, Md.: Johns Hopkins University Press.
Levitan, Sar, and Garth Mangum
1981   "Summary of Findings and Recommendations." In *The T in CETA*, ed. S. Levitan and G. Mangum, 1–91. Kalamazoo, Mich.: Upjohn.
Lewis, Michael
1981   "The Welfare Response to Black Americans." *Research in Social Problems and Public Policy* 2:243–82.
Lewis-Beck, Michael
1977   "The Relative Importance of Socioeconomic and Political Variables for Public Policy." *American Political Science Review* 71:559–66.
Lidtke, Vernon
1985   *The Alternative Culture*. New York: Oxford University Press.
Lieberson, Stanley
1980   *A Piece of the Pie*. Berkeley, Calif.: University of California Press.
Liebfried, Stephen
1978   "Public Assistance in the U.S. and F.R.G." *Comparative Politics* 11:59–76.
Liebman, Lance
1974   "Social Intervention in a Democracy." *The Public Interest* 34:14–29.
Lijphart, Arend
1968   *The Politics of Accommodation*. Berkeley, Calif.: University of California Press.
1975   "The Comparative Cases Strategy in Comparative Research." *Comparative Political Studies* 8:158–77.

Lindblom, Charles
1977   *Politics and Markets.* New York: Basic Books.
1980   *The Policy Making Process.* 2d ed. Englewood Cliffs, N.J.:
          Prentice-Hall.
Lindsley, Thomas
1981   *History of the Committee on Labor and Human Re-*
          sources. Washington, D.C.: U.S. Government Printing
          Office.
Lipset, Seymour Martin
1977   "Why No Socialism in the United States?" In *Radicalism*
          in the Contemporary Age, ed. S. Bialer and S. Sluzar, 31–
          149. Boulder, Colo.: Westview Press.
Lombardi, John
1942   *Labor's Voice in the Cabinet.* New York: Columbia Uni-
          versity Press.
Long, David, Charles Mallar, and Craig Thornton
1981   "Evaluating the Benefits and Costs of the Job Corps."
          Journal of Policy Analysis and Management 1:55–76.
Longstreth, Frank
1988   "From Corporatism to Dualism?" *Political Studies* 36:
          413–32.
Loomis, Burdett
1983   "A New Era: Groups and the Grassroots." In *Interest*
          Group Politics, ed. Allan Cigler and Burdett Loomis, 169–
          90. Washington, D.C.: Congressional Quarterly Press.
Lowi, Theodore
1979   *The End of Liberalism.* New York: Norton.
1984   "Why is there No Socialism in the United States? A Fed-
          eral Analysis." In *The Costs of Federalism,* ed. R. Golem-
          biewski and A. Wildausky, 37–53. New Brunswick, N.J.:
          Transaction Books.
Lutz, Burkart
1981   "Education and Employment: Contrasting Evidence from
          France and the FRG." *European Journal of Education*
          16:73–86.
Macesich, George
1984   *The Politics of Monetarism.* Totowa, N.J.: Rowman and
          Allanheld.
MacMahon, Arthur, John Millet, and Gladys Ogden
1941   *The Administration of Federal Work Relief.* Chicago: Pub-
          lic Administration Service.

Maier, Charles
1975   *Recasting Bourgeois Europe.* Princeton, N.J.: Princeton
            University Press.
1987   "The Economics of Facism and Nazism." In *In Search of
            Stability,* ed. Charles Maier, 70–120. Cambridge: Cam-
            bridge University Press.
Maier, Hans
1982   "Experimentelle Arbeitsbeschaffungsmassnahmen." Ber-
            lin: Wissenschaftzentrum IIM Discussion Paper 82-20.
Mangum, Garth
1968   *MDTA: Foundation of Federal Manpower Policy.* Balti-
            more, Md.: Johns Hopkins University Press.
1981   "Twenty Years of Manpower Training and Economic De-
            velopment." In *Proceedings of the Industrial Relations
            Research Association,* 508–14. Madison, Wis.: Industrial
            Relations Research Association.
Mangum, Garth, and John Walsh
1973   *A Decade of Manpower Development and Training.* Salt
            Lake City, Utah: Olympus.
Mangum, Stephen, and David Ball
1987   "Military Skill Training: Some Evidence of Transferabil-
            ity." *Armed Forces and Society* 13:425–41.
Markovits, Andrei
1986   *The Politics of the West German Trade Unions.* Cam-
            bridge: Cambridge University Press.
Markovits, Andrei, and Christopher Allen
1980   *Trade Unions and Politics in Western Europe.* London:
            Frank Cass.
Marris, Peter, and Martin Rein
1969   *Dilemmas of Social Reform.* Chicago: University of Chi-
            cago Press.
Marsden, Peter
1980   *Analysen der Verändergungen der Lohnstruktur in der
            Industrie beschäftigten Arbeiter in sechs Gemein-
            schaftsländern seit 1966.* Sussex: Eurostat Research.
Marshall, T. H.
1963   *Society at the Crossroads and Other Essays.* London:
            Heinemann.
1964   *Class, Citizenship and Social Development.* Chicago: Uni-
            versity of Chicago Press.
1981   *The Right to Welfare and Other Essays.* London: Heine-
            mann.

Martin, George
  1976   *Madame Secretary*. Boston: Houghton Mifflin.
Martinez, Tomas
  1976   *The Human Market Place*. New Brunswick, N.J.: Transaction Books.
Matlack, Larry
  1975a   "Public Service Careers and New Careers." In *The Impact of Government Manpower Programs*, ed. Charles Perry et al., 202–21. Philadelphia: Industrial Research Unit—University of Pennsylvania.
  1975b   "Operation Mainstream." In *The Impact of Government Manpower Programs*, ed. Charles Perry et al., 451–73. Philadelphia: Industrial Research Unit—University of Pennsylvania.
Matthöfer, Hans
  1981a   "Speech to the Bundestag on June 2, 1981." *Protokoll der Verhandlungen des Deutschen Bundestages* 118:2139.
  1981b   "Rede zur Einbringung des Bundeshaushaltes 1981." Bonn: Bundesministerium der Finanzen.
Max Planck Institute
  1984   *Between Elite and Mass Education*. Albany, N.Y.: State University of New York Press.
Mayntz, Renate, and Fritz Scharpf
  1985   *Policy-making in the German Federal Bureaucracy*. Amsterdam: Elsevier.
McCleary, Richard, and Richard Hay
  1980   *Applied Time-Series Analysis for the Social Sciences*. Beverly Hills, Calif.: Sage.
Meckstroth, Theodore
  1975   "Most Different Systems and Most Similar Systems." *Comparative Political Studies* 8:132–57.
Meidner, Rudolf
  1948   "Lönepolitikens dilemma vid full sysselsättning." *Tiden* 9:464–70.
  1984   "Sweden: Approaching the Limits of Active Labor Market Policy." In *Public Policies to Combat Unemployment in a Period of Economic Stagnation*, ed. K. Gerlach, W. Peters, and W. Sengenberger, 249–65. Frankfurt: Campus Verlag.
Melone, Albert, and George Mace
  1988   *Judicial Review and American Democracy*. Ames: Iowa State University Press.

Menake, George
1978   *Policy-Making in the American System*. Washington, D.C.: University Press of America.
Meyer, Stephen
1981   *The Five Dollar Day*. Albany, N.Y.: State University of New York Press.
Michaels, Heinz
1985   "Ausbildung tut Not." *Die Zeit*, August 16.
Mill, John Stuart
1936   *A System of Logic*. London: Longmans, Green.
Miller, Gale
1986   "Unemployment as a Dramaturgical Problem: Teaching Impression Management in a Work Incentive Program." *Sociological Quarterly* 27:479–93.
Miller, Mark
1981   *Foreign Workers in Western Europe: An Emerging Political Force*. New York: Praeger.
Millis, Harry, and Emily Brown
1950   *From the Wagner Act to Taft-Hartley*. Chicago: University of Chicago Press.
Mintz, Alex, and Alexander Hicks
1984   "Military Expenditures in the U.S., 1949 to 1976." *American Journal of Sociology* 90:411–17.
Mirengoff, William, and Lester Rindler
1978   *CETA: Manpower Programs Under Local Control*. Washington, D.C.: National Academy of Sciences.
Mirengoff, William, Lester Rindler, Harry Greenspan, and Scott Seablom
1980   *CETA: Assessment of Public Service Employment Programs*. Washington, D.C.: National Academy of Sciences.
Mirengoff, William, Lester Rindler, Harry Greenspan, and Charles Harris
1982   *CETA: Accomplishments, Problems and Solutions*. Kalamazoo, Mich.: Upjohn.
Mishra, Ramesh
1981   *Society and Social Welfare*. Atlantic Highlands, N.J.: Humanities Press.
Monroe, Kirsten
1979   "Economic Analysis of Electoral Behavior." *Political Behavior* 1:137–73.

1984   *Presidential Popularity and the Economy.* New York: Praeger.

Morris, Aldon
1984   *The Origins of the Civil Rights Movement.* New York: Free Press.

Moses, John
1982   *Trade Unionism in Germany from Bismarck to Hitler, 1869–1933, Volumes 1 and 2.* London: G. Prior.

Mosher, Frederick
1984   *A Tale of Two Agencies.* Baton Rouge: Louisiana State University Press.

Moynihan, Daniel
1969   *Maximum Feasible Misunderstanding.* New York: Free Press.

Münch, Joachim
1984   *Vocational Training in the Federal Republic of Germany.* West Berlin: European Center for the Development of Vocational Education.

Murphy, Richard
1983   *Guestworkers in the German Reich.* Boulder, Colo.: East European Monographs.

Mushaben, Joyce
1985   "Cycles of Peace Protests in West Germany." *West European Politics* 8:24–40.

Myrdal, Gunnar
1960   *Beyond the Welfare State.* New Haven, Conn.: Yale University Press.

Nahamowitz, Peter
1978   *Gesetzgebung in den kritischen Systemjahren 1967–1969.* Frankfurt: Campus Verlag.

Napthali, Fritz
1928   *Wirtschafts-Demokratie: Ihr Wesen, Weg und Ziel.* Berlin: Verlag des ADGB.

Nathan, Richard
1983   "State and Local Governments under Federal Grants." *Political Science Quarterly* 98:47–57.

Nathan, Richard, Robert Cook, and Viviane Rawlins
1981   *PSE: A Field Examination.* Washington, D.C.: Brookings Institution.

National Commission for Employment Policy
1987   *The Job Training Partnership Act.* Washington, D.C.: National Commission for Employment Policy.

National Commission on Youth
   1980   *The Transition of Youth to Adulthood.* Boulder, Colo.:
              Westview Press.
Neumann, Franz
   1966   *Behemoth.* New York: Harper & Row.
Nolan, Mary, and Charles Sabel
   1982   "Class Conflict and the Social Democratic Reform Cycle
              in Germany." *Political Power and Social Theory* 3:145–73.
Nordlinger, Eric
   1981   *On the Autonomy of the Democratic State.* Cambridge,
              Mass.: Harvard University Press.
Norton, Hugh
   1977   *The Council of Economic Advisors.* Columbia: University
              of South Carolina Press.
O'Connor, James
   1973   *The Fiscal Crisis of the State.* New York: St. Martin's
              Press.
Organization for Economic Co-operation and Development (OECD)
   1949–85   *National Accounts, Main Aggregates.* Paris: OECD.
   1965   *Active Manpower Policy: International Management Sem-*
              inar. Paris: OECD.
   1966   *Manpower Policy and Programs in the United States.*
              Paris: OECD.
   1972   *Review of National Policy on Education—Germany.* Paris:
              OECD.
   1974   *Manpower Policy in Denmark.* Paris: OECD.
   1978   *A Medium Term Strategy for Unemployment and Man-*
              power Policies. Paris: OECD.
   1979   *Policies for Apprenticeship.* Paris: OECD.
   1980   *Youth Unemployment.* Paris: OECD.
   1981   *Educational Statistics in OECD Countries.* Paris:
              OECD.
   1982   *The Challenge of Unemployment.* Paris: OECD.
   1985a   *Historical Statistics, 1960 to 1983.* Paris: OECD.
   1985b   *Main Economic Indicators.* Paris: OECD.
   1988   *Employment Outlook, September 88.* Paris: OECD.
Offe, Claus
   1975   *Berufsbildungsreform: Eine Fallstudie über Reformpoli-*
              tik. Frankfurt: Suhrkamp Verlag.
   1980   "The Attribution of Public Status to Interest Groups." In
              Organizing Interests in Western Europe, ed. S. Berger,
              123–58. Cambridge: Cambridge University Press.

Orfield, Gary
1975   *Congressional Power.* New York: Harcourt, Brace, Jo-
          vanovich.
Orloff, Ann Shola, and Theda Skocpol
1984   "Explaining the Politics of Public Social Spending." *Amer-
          ican Sociological Review* 49:726–50.
Ornstein, Norman, and Shirley Elder
1978   *Interest Groups, Lobbying and Policymaking.* Washing-
          ton, D.C.: Congressional Quarterly Press.
Osterman, Paul
1988   *Employment Futures.* New York: Oxford University
          Press.
Pankoke, Eckart
1981   "Gesellschaftlicher Wandel sozialer Dienste." In *Hand-
          buch Praxis der Sozialarbeit und Sozialpädagogik,* 3–30.
          Düsseldorf: Pädagogischer Verlag.
Pantich, Leo
1980   "Recent Theorizations of Capitalism." *British Journal of
          Sociology* 31:159–87.
Paterson, William
1982   "The Chancellor and His Party." In *The Political Economy
          of West Germany,* ed. Andrei Markovits, 3–17. New York:
          Praeger.
Peretz, Paul
1983   *The Political Economy of Inflation.* Chicago: University of
          Chicago Press.
Perlman, Selig
1928   *A Theory of the Labor Movement.* New York: Augustus
          Kelley.
Perry, Charles
1975a   "Job Opportunities in the Business Sector." In *The Impact
          of Government Manpower Programs,* ed. Charles Perry
          et al., 186–201. Philadelphia: Industrial Research Unit—
          University of Pennsylvania.
1975b   "Manpower Policies and Programs." In *The Impact of
          Government Manpower Programs,* ed. Charles Perry et
          al., 3–24. Philadelphia: Industrial Research Unit—Univer-
          sity of Pennsylvania.
1975c   "Manpower Development and Training Act." In *The Im-
          pact of Government Manpower Programs,* ed. Charles
          Perry et al., 149–85. Philadelphia: Industrial Research
          Unit—University of Pennsylvania.

Peters, B. Guy
1978   *The Politics of Bureaucracy.* New York: Longmans.
Peters, Guy, and David Klingman
1978   "Patterns of Expenditure Development in Sweden, Norway and Denmark." *British Journal of Political Science* 7:387–412.
Peters, Tom
1989   "German Companies Prove Bigger Isn't Better." *Business Week*, August 7.
Peterson, Paul
1985   *The Politics of School Reform, 1870–1940.* Chicago: University of Chicago Press.
Peterson, Paul, and J. D. Greenstone
1977   "Racial Change and Citizen Participation." In *A Decade of Federal Anti-Poverty Programs*, ed. Robert Haveman, 241–78. New York: Academic Press.
Pfaffenberger, Hans
1981   "Zur Situation der Ausbildung für das Praxisfeld." In *Handbuch Praxis der Sozialarbeit und Sozialpädagogik*, ed. E. Kerkhof, 61–103. Düsseldorf: Schwann Pädagogischer Verlag.
Pindyck, Robert, and Daniel Rubinfeld
1981   *Econometric Models and Economic Forecasts.* 2d ed. New York: McGraw Hill.
Piore, Michael
1979   *Unemployment and Inflation.* White Plains, N.Y.: M. E. Sharpe.
Piven, Frances Fox, and Richard Cloward
1971   *Regulating the Poor.* New York: Pantheon.
Political Quarterly, editor
1986   "Commentary: The Manpower Services Commission." *Political Quarterly* 57:227–30.
Pollard, Sidney
1974   "The Trade Unions and the Depression of 1929–1933." In *Industrielles System und politische Entwicklung in der Weimarer Republik*, ed. H. Mommsen, D. Petzina, and B. Weisbrod, 237–48. Düsseldorf: Droste Verlag.
Preller, Ludwig
1949   *Sozialpolitik in der Weimarer Republik.* Frankfurt: Franz Mittelbach Verlag.
1970   *Praxis und Probleme der Sozialpolitik* (Practice and Problems of Social Policy). Tübingen: J. C. B. Mohr.

Preston, Michael
  1984   *The Politics of Bureaucratic Reform.* Urbana-Champaign:
              University of Illinois Press.
Pridham, Geoffrey
  1977   *Christian Democrats in West Germany.* London: Croom-
              Helm.
Quadagno, Jill
  1984   "Welfare Capitalism and the Social Security Act of 1935."
              American Sociological Review 49:632–47.
  1987   "Theories of the Welfare State." *Annual Review of Sociol-
              ogy* 13:109–28.
Ragin, Charles
  1981   "Comparative Sociology and the Comparative Methods." *In-
              ternational Journal of Comparative Sociology* 22: 102–20.
  1987   *The Comparative Method.* Berkeley: University of Califor-
              nia Press.
Rayback, Joseph
  1966   *A History of American Labor.* New York: Free Press.
Rehn, Gösta
  1948   "Ekonomisk politik vid full sysselsättning." *Tiden* 3:
              135–42.
  1952   "The Problem of Stability: An Analysis and Some Policy
              Proposals." In *Wages Policy Under Full Employment*, ed.
              Ralph Tuvey, 30–54. London: William Hodge.
  1982   "Anti-Inflationary Expansion Policies with Special Refer-
              ence to Marginal Employment Premiums." Institutet för
              Social Forskning. Meddelande, August. University of
              Stockholm.
Reissert, Bernd
  1983   "Langfristarbeitslosigkeit und temporärer Ersatzarbeits-
              markt." *Wirtschaftsdienst* 4:178–84.
Renetzky, Alvin
  1980   *Standard Educational Almanac.* Los Angeles: Media
              Press.
Reubens, Beatrice
  1973   "German Apprenticeship: Controversy and Reform." *Man-
              power* 11:12–20.
  1974   "Vocational Education for All in High School?" In *Work
              and the Quality of Life*, ed. J. O'Toole, 299–337. Cam-
              bridge, Mass.: MIT Press.
Revelle, Roger
  1981   *Select Commission on Immigration and Refugee Policy.*
              Washington, D.C.: GPO.

Reyher, Lutz, and Eugen Spitznagel
1979   "Job Creation in the Federal Republic of Germany." In *Work Creation*, ed. M. Jackson and V. Hanby, 69–99. Westmead, England: Saxon House.

Reyher, Lutz, Martin Koller, and Eugen Spitznagel
1979   *Employment Policy Alternatives to Unemployment in the FRG*. London: Anglo-German Foundation for the Study for Industrial Society.

Richardson, J., Gunnel Gustafsson, and Grant Gordon
1982   "The Concept of Policy Style." In *Policy Styles in Western Europe*, ed. J. Richardson, 1–16. London: Allen Unwin.

Riche, Martha
1964   "Public Policies and Programs: An Assessment of Apprenticeship." *Monthly Labor Review* 87 (January):143–48.

Rimlinger, Gaston
1971   *Welfare Policy and Industrialization in Europe, America and Russia*. New York: Wiley.

Ringenbach, Paul
1973   *Tramps and Reformers*. Westport, Conn.: Greenwood Press.

Ringer, Fritz
1979   *Education and Society in Modern Europe*. Bloomington: Indiana University Press.

Ritter, Gerhard, and Klaus Tenfelde
1975   "Der Durchbruch der Freien Gewerkschaften Deutschlands zur Massenbewegung im letzten Viertel des 19. Jahrhunderts." In *Vom Sozialistengesetz zur Mitbestimmung*, ed. Heinz Oskar Vetter, 61–121. Köln: Bund Verlag.

Roberts, Geoffrey
1984   " 'Normal' or 'Critical'? Progress Reports on the Condition of West Germany's Political Culture." *European Journal of Political Research* 12:423–31.

Robertson, David
1981   "Politics and Labor Markets." Ph.D. diss., Indiana University.

1987   "Labor Market Surgery, Labor Market Abandonment: the Thatcher and Reagan Unemployment Remedies." In *Political Economy*, ed. J. Waltman and D. Studlar, 69–97. Jackson: University of Mississippi Press.

1988   "Governing and Jobs: America's Business-Centered Labor Market Policy." *Polity* 20:426–56.

Rogosa, D.
1978   "Causal Models in Longitudinal Research." In *Longitudinal*

Research in Human Development, ed. John Nesselroade and Paul Baltes, 263–302. New York: Academic Press.

Roman, Frederick
1915   *The Industrial and Commercial Schools of the U.S. and Germany.* New York: Putnam.
1930   *The New Education in Europe.* London: Routledge and Kegan Paul.

Roomkin, Myron
1974   "Chicago." In *Emergency Employment Act: The PEP Generation*, ed. S. Levitan and R. Taggart, 59–89. Salt Lake City, Utah: Olympus.

Rose, Hilary
1981   "Rereading Titmus: The Sexual Division of Labor." *Journal of Social Policy* 10:477–502.

Rosenbloom, Steven
1982   "The AFL and the Politics of Employment." Ph.D. diss., Columbia University.

Rosenhaft, Eve
1981   "Working Class Life and Working Class Politics." In *Social Change and Political Development in Weimar Germany*, ed. R. Bessel and E. Feuchtwanger, 207–40. London: Croom-Helm.
1983   *Beating the Facists?* Cambridge: Cambridge University Press.

Ross, Davis
1969   *Preparing for Ulysses: Politics and Veterans During World War II.* New York: Columbia University Press.

Rumberger, Russell, and Thomas Daymont
1984   "The Economic Value of Academic and Vocational Training Acquired in High School." In *Youth and the Labor Market*, ed. Michael Borus, 157–91. Kalamazoo, Mich.: Upjohn.

Ruttenberg, Stanley, and Jocelyn Gutchess
1970   *The Federal-State Employment Service: A Critique.* Baltimore, Md.: Johns Hopkins University Press.

Sabel, Charles
1982   *Work and Politics.* Cambridge: Cambridge University Press.

Sachverständigenrat
1966–67 *Jahresgutachten: Expansion und Stabilität.* Stuttgart: Kohlhammer.
1970–71 *Jahresgutachten: Konjunktur im Umbruch—Risken und Chancen.* Stuttgart: Kohlhammer.

1984–85   *Jahresgutachten: Chancen für einen langen Aufschwung.* Stuttgart: Kohlhammer.

Sagarra, Eda

1977   *A Social History of Germany, 1648–1914.* New York: Homes-Meier.

Sanders, Elizabeth

1982   "Business, Bureaucracy and the Bourgeoise." In *The Political Economy of Public Policy*, ed. A. Stone and E. Harpham, 115–40. Beverly Hills, Calif.: Sage.

Sanders, Heywood

1980   "Paying for the 'Bloody Shirt': The Politics of Civil War Pensions." In *Political Benefits*, ed. Barry Rundquist, 137–60. Lexington, Mass.: D. C. Heath.

SAS

1982   *SAS/ETS Users Guide: Econometric and Time-Series Library.* Cary, N.C.: SAS Institute.

Sauter, Edgar

1982   "Berufliche Weiterbildung und Arbeitslosigkeit." *BIBB BWP*, January, 1–6.

1984   "Fortbildung und Umschulung." In *Kein Arbeit—Keine Zukunft*, ed. H. Apel et al., 166–87. Frankfurt: Diesterweg.

Sautter, Udo

1986   "Government and Unemployment: The Use of Public Works before the New Deal." *Journal of American History* 73:59–86.

Scharpf, Fritz

1981   "Die Implementation des Sonderprogrammes vergleich." In *Implementationsprobleme Offensiver Arbeitsmarktpolitik*, ed. Fritz Scharpf, Freidrike Maier, and Hans Maier, 273–310. Frankfurt: Campus Verlag.

Schefter, Martin

1977   "Party and Patronage: Germany, England, and Italy." *Politics and Society* 7:403–51.

Schindler, Peter

1983   *Datenhandbuch zur Geschichte des deutschen Bundestages 1949–1982.* Bonn: Abteilung Wissenschaftliche Dokumentation des Deutschen Parliament.

Schlesinger, Arthur

1986   "Affirmative Government and the American Economy." In *The Cycles of American History*, 219–55. Boston: Houghton Mifflin.

Schmid, Günther

1980   *Strukturierte Arbeitslosigkeit und Arbeitsmarktpolitik.*
        Königstein: Athenaum.

1981   "Employment Policy in the FRG: Lessons to be
        Learned." In *Conference on European and American La-
        bor Market Policies*, 1–26. Washington, D.C.: Depart-
        ment of Labor.

1982   "Public Finance Measures to Generate Employment for
        Hard to Place People." In *Public Finance and Public Em-
        ployment*, ed. the International Institute of Public Fi-
        nance, 189–209. Detroit, Mich.: Wayne State University
        Press.

Schmidt, Manfred

1983   "Two Logics of Coalition Policy: The West German Case."
        In *Coalition Government in Western Europe*, ed. Vernon
        Bogdanor, 38–58. London: Heinemann.

Schmitter, Philippe

1977   "Modes of Interest Intermediation and Models of Change
        in Western Europe." *Comparative Political Studies* 10:
        7–38.

1982   "Reflections on Where the Theory of Neo-Corporatism
        Has Gone and Where the Praxis of Neo-Corporatism May
        be Going." In *Patterns of Corporatist Policy-Making*, ed.
        G. Lehmbruch and P. Schmitter, 259–79. Beverly Hills,
        Calif.: Sage.

Schneider, Michael

1975a   *Das Arbeitsbeschaffungsprogramm des ADGB.* Bonn-Bad
        Godesberg: Verlag Neue Gesellschaft.

1975b   *Unternehmer und Demokratie.* Bonn-Bad Godesberg:
        Verlag Neue Gesellschaft.

1986   "The Development of State Work-Creation Policy in Ger-
        many, 1930–33." In *Unemployment and the Great Depres-
        sion in Weimar Germany*, ed. Peter Stachura, 163–86.
        New York: St. Martin's Press.

Schneider, Saundra, and Patricia Ingraham

1984   "The Impact of Political Participation on Social Poli-
        cy Adoption and Expansion." *Comparative Politics* 17:
        107–22.

Schöfer, Rolf

1981   *Berufsausbildung und Gewerbepolitik.* Frankfurt: Cam-
        pus Verlag.

Schott, Richard, and Hamilton Dugnon
1984   *People, Positions and Power*. Chicago: University of Chicago Press.

Schorske, Carl
1955   *German Social Democracy, 1905–1917*. Cambridge, Mass.: Harvard University Press.

Schwanse, Peter
1982   "European Experience." In *Jobs for Disadvantaged Workers*, ed. Robert Haveman and John Palmer, 297–324. Washington, D.C.: Brookings Institution.

Semple, Nathaniel
1986   "Vocational Education: the Missing Link." *Peabody Journal of Education* 63:70–102.

Sengenberger, Werner
1982   "Federal Republic of Germany." In *Workforce Reductions in Undertakings*, ed. Edward Yemin, 79–105. Geneva: ILO.

1983   "Vocational Worker Training, Labor Market Structure and Industrial Relations." Paper presented at Second German-Japanese Conference on Industrial Relations, Darmstadt.

Sewell, William
1985   "Ideologies and Social Revolutions: Reflections on the French Case." *Journal of Modern History* 57:57–85.

Shalev, Michael
1985   "Labor Relations and Class Conflict: A Critical Survey of the Contributions of John R. Commons." *Advances in Industrial and Labor Relations* 2:319–63.

Shelley, Mack
1983   *The Permanent Majority*. University: University of Alabama Press.

Sheppard, Howard, and A. Harvey Belitsky
1966   *The Job Hunt: Job-Seeking Behavior of Unemployed Workers in a Local Economy*. Baltimore, Md.: Johns Hopkins University Press.

Shibutani, Tamotsu
1978   *The Derelicts of Company K*. Berkeley, Calif.: University of California Press.

Shorter, Edward, and Charles Tilly
1974   *Strikes in France 1830–1968*. Cambridge: Cambridge University Press.

Simon, Paul
  1987   *Let's Put America Back to Work.* Chicago: Bonus Books.
Simons, Diane
  1967   *George Kerschensteiner.* London: Methuen.
Sinfield, Adrian
  1978   "Analyses of the Social Division of Welfare. *Journal of Social Policy* 7:129–56.
Sipe, Daniel
  1981   "A Moment of the State." Ph.D. diss., University of Pennsylvania
Skocpol, Theda
  1985   "Bringing the State Back In: Strategies of Analysis in Current Research." In *Bringing the State Back In,* ed. Peter Evans, Dietrich Rueschemeyer, and Theda Skocpol, 3–37. Cambridge: Cambridge University Press.
Skocpol, Theda, and Ann Orloff
  1986   "Explaining the Origins of Welfare States." In *Approaches to Social Theory,* ed. S. Lindenberg, J. Coleman, and S. Nowak, 229–54. New York: Russell Sage Foundation.
Smelser, Neil
  1976   *Comparative Methods in the Social Sciences.* Englewood Cliffs, N.J.: Prentice-Hall.
Smith, A. T.
  1975   *The Comparative Policy Process.* Santa Barbara, Calif.: ABC-Clio.
Smith, Gordon
  1979   *Democracy in Western Germany.* New York: Holmes Meier.
Smith, Tom W.
  1987   "The Welfare State in Cross-National Perspective." *Public Opinion Quarterly* 51:404–21.
Snedeker, Bonnie, and David Snedeker
  1978   *CETA: Decentralization on Trial.* Salt Lake City, Utah: Olympus.
Soltwedel, Rüdiger
  1984   *Mehr Markt am Arbeitsmarkt.* München: Philosophia Verlag.
SÖ (ÖGY)
  1986   *En treårig yrkesutbildning. Del I. Riktlinjer för fortsatt arbete.* Stockholm: Liber Tryck AB
SÖ
  1988   "Measures Employed in Sweden to make Working Life

Visible to Students." Stockholm: National Board of Education Information: 88:20.

Sparrough, Michael
1975   "Public Employment Program." In *The Impact of Government Manpower Programs*, ed. Charles Perry et al., 252–300. Philadelphia: Industrial Relations Unit—University of Pennsylvania.

Spitznagel, Eugen
1980   *Globale und strukturelle Auswirkungen von Allgemeinen Maßnahmen zur Arbeitsbeschaffung*. Nuremberg: BAA Beiträge zur Arbeitsmarkt- und Berufsforschung.

Spring, Joel
1972   *Education and the Rise of the Corporate State*. Boston: Beacon.

Stachura, Peter
1986   "The Development of Unemployment in Modern German History." In *Unemployment and the Great Depression in Weimar Germany*, ed. Peter Stachura, 1–28. New York: St. Martin's Press.

Stearns, Peter
1967   *European Society in Upheaval*. New York: MacMillan.
1975   *Lives of Labor*. New York: Holmes-Meier.

Stenholm, Britta
1984   *The Swedish School System*. Uppsala: The Swedish Institute.

Stinchcombe, Arthur
1985   "The Functional Theory of Social Insurance." *Politics and Society* 14:411–30.

Streek, Wolfgang
1982   "Guaranteed Employment, Flexible Manpower Use and Cooperative Manpower Management." International Conference on Industrial Relations in Transition, Sendai, Japan.

Strauß, Franz Josef
1977   "Es gibt keine Wunderdroge—Der Patient is durch eine falsche Therapie verpfuscht." In *Wegweiser in die Vollbeschäftigung*, 3–6. München: Süddeutscher Zeitung Dokumentation.

Stürmer, Michael
1967   *Koalition und Opposition in der Weimarer Republik*. Düsseldorf: Droste Verlag.

Sundquist, James
1968   *Politics and Policy*. Washington, D.C.: Brookings Institution.

334   *Bibliography*

Süddeutsch Zeitung
  1977   *Wegweiser in die Vollbeschäftigung.* München: Süd-
            deutsch Zeitung Dokumentation.
Swedish Government
  1976   *Riksgäldskontoret—Budgetaret 1976/76 Arsbok.* Stock-
            holm: Libertryck.
Syrup, Friedrich
  1939   *Hundert Jahre Staatliche Sozialpolitik.* Frankfurt: Kohl-
            hammer Verlag.
Taggart, Robert
  1981a   "A Review of CETA Training." In *The T in CETA,* ed. Sar
            Levitan and Garth Mangum, 93–144. Kalamazoo, Mich.:
            Upjohn.
  1981b   *A Fisherman's Guide: An Assessment of Training and Re-
            mediation Strategies.* Kalamazoo, Mich.: Upjohn.
Tampke, Jürgen
  1981   "Bismarck's Social Legislation: A Genuine Breakthrough?"
            In *The Emergence of the Welfare State in Britain and
            Germany,* ed. W. Mommsen, 71–83. London: Croom-
            Helm.
Tarschys, Daniel
  1975   "The Growth of Public Expenditures." *Scandinavian Polit-
            ical Studies* 2:9–31.
Tarullo, Daniel
  1989   "Public Policy and Employment Security." In *Industrial
            Relations Research Association Proceedings,* 430–38. Mad-
            ison, Wis.: Industrial Relations Research Association.
Taylor, Charles, and Michael Hudson
  1975   *Political and Social Indicators.* New Haven, Conn.: Yale
            University Press.
Taylor, Charles, and David Jodice
  1983   *Political and Social Indicators.* New Haven, Conn.: Yale
            University Press.
Tenfelde, Klaus
  1977   *Sozialgeschichte der Bergarbeiterschaft an der Ruhr im
            19. Jahrhundert.* Bonn-Bad Godesberg: Verlag Neue Ge-
            sellschaft.
Tennstedt, Florian
  1977   *Geschichte der Selbstverwaltung in der Krankenver-
            sicherung.* Bonn: Verlag der Ortskrankenkassen.
This Week in Germany (TWIG)
  1980–88   Bonn: West German Information Service.

Thurow, Lester
 1975 *Generating Inequality.* New York: Basic Books.
Titmuss, Richard
 1963 *Essays on the Welfare State.* London: Allen Unwin.
Toby, Jackson
 1975 "The War on Poverty: Politics of Unrealistic Expectations." *Contemporary Sociology* 4:11–18.
Toews, Emil
 1955 "The Life and Professional Works of George Michael Kerschensteiner." Ph.D. diss., University of California at Los Angeles.
Tollkühn, Gertrude
 1926 *Die Planmäßige Ausbildung des gewerblichen Fabriklehrlings in den Metal- und holzverarbeitenden Industrien.* Jena: Gustav-Fischer.
Tufte, Edward
 1978 *The Political Control of the Economy.* Princeton, N.J.: Princeton University Press.
Turner, Bryan
 1986 *Citizenship and Capitalism.* London: Allen Unwin.
U.A.W.
 1952–84 *Annual Audit Report.* Detroit, Mich.: U.A.W.
United Nations
 1983 *U.N. Yearbook of International Trade Statistics.* New York: United Nations.
U.S. Department of Commerce (DOC)
 1923–33, *Statistical Abstract of the United States.* Washington,
 1950–85 D.C.: GPO.
 1976 *Historical Statistics of the U.S.* Washington, D.C.: GPO
 1981 *Business Conditions Digest.* Washington, D.C.: GPO.
U.S. Department of Health, Education and Welfare (HEW)
 1977 *The Condition of Education.* Washington, D.C.: GPO.
U.S. Department of Justice (DOJ)
 1981 *Immigration and Naturalization Service, Annual Report.* Washington, D.C.: GPO.
U.S. Department of Labor (DOL)
 1950–64 *Annual Report of the Bureau of Employment Security.* Washington, D.C.: GPO.
 1950–64 *Labor Market and Employment Security.* Washington, D.C.: GPO.
 1979 *Apprenticeship Past and Present.* Washington, D.C.: GPO.

1980   *U.S. Handbook of Labor Statistics.* Washington, D.C.:
          GPO.
1985   *Employment, Hours and Earnings: U.S. 1909–1984.* Vol-
          ume II, Bulletin 1312–12. Washington, D.C.: GPO.
U.S. Government
1950–82   *Budget of the United States Government.* Washington,
          D.C.: GPO.
1950–83   *United States Government Manual.* Washington, D.C.:
          GPO.
U.S. President
1964–82   *Employment and Training Report of the President* (U.S.
          ETRP). Washington, D.C.: GPO.
1984–85   *Economic Report of the President (ECRP).* Washington,
          D.C.: GPO.
U.S. Senate
1969   *Senate Justice Subcommittee on Antitrust and Monopoly.*
          Washington, D.C.: GPO.
U.S. Supreme Court
1916   *Adams vs. Tanner.* 244, 605.
Unekis, Joseph, and Leroy Riselback
1984   *Congressional Committee Politics.* New York: Praeger.
Uusitalo, Hannu
1984   "Comparative Research on the Determinants of the Wel-
          fare State." *European Journal of Political Research* 12:403–
          22.
Van Horn, Carl
1979   *Policy Implementation in the Federal System.* Lexington,
          Mass.: D. C. Heath.
Vogel, Hans-Jochen
1983   "Die Haltung der SPD." In *Chancen und Grenzen des So-
          zialstaats,* ed. Peter Koslowski, Philip Kreuzer, and Rein-
          hard Löw, 238–47. Tübingen: J. C. B. Mohr.
Waxman, Chaim
1968   *Poverty, Power and Politics.* New York: Grosset and Dunlap.
Webber, Douglas
1982a   "Zwischen programmatischem Anspruch und politischer
          Praxis." *Mitteilungen aus der Arbeitsmarkt- und Berufs-
          forchung,* March, 261–75.
1982b   "Combatting and Acquiescing in Unemployment." *West
          European Politics* 5:23–43.
1983   "A Relationship of 'Critical Partnership?' " *West European
          Politics* 6:61–86.

Webber, Douglas, and Gabriele Nass
1984   "Employment Policy in West Germany." In *Unemploy-ment: Policy Responses of Western Democracies*, ed. Jer-emy Richardson and Roger Henning, 167–92. Beverly Hills, Calif.: Sage.

Weber, Jürgen
1977   *Die Interessengruppen im politischen System der Bundes-republik Deutschland.* Stuttgart: Kohlhammer Verlag.

Weigert, Oscar
1934   *Administration of Placement and Unemployment In-surance in Germany.* New York: Industrial Relations Counselors.

Weinstein, James
1968   *The Corporate Ideal in the Liberal State, 1900–1919.* Bos-ton: Beacon Press.

Weir, Margaret, Ann Shola Orloff, and Theda Skocpol
1988   *The Politics of Social Policy in the United States.* Prince-ton, N.J.: Princeton University Press.

Weisbrod, Bernd
1981   "The Crisis of German Unemployment Insurance in 1928/ 29 and its Political Repercussions." In *The Emergence of the Welfare State in Britain and Germany*, ed. Wolfgang Mommsen, 188–204. London: Croom-Helm.

Wietzel, Renate
1983   "Berufliche Bildung nach dem Arbeitsförderungsge-setz." West Berlin: Wissenschaftszentrum-IIM/LMP 83-12.

Wildavsky, Aaron
1979   *The Politics of the Budgetary Process.* 3d ed. Boston: Lit-tle Brown.

Wilensky, Harold L.
1975   *The Welfare State and Equality.* Berkeley, Calif.: Univer-sity of California Press.

1976   *The New Corporatism: Centralization and the Welfare State.* Beverly Hills, Calif.: Sage.

1981   "Leftism, Catholicism and Democratic Corporatism." In *The Development of Welfare States in Europe and Amer-ica*, ed. Peter Flora and Arnold Heidenhiemer, 341–78. New Brunswick, N.J.: Transaction Books.

1983   "Political Legitimacy and Consensus." In *Evaluating the Welfare State*, ed. S. E. Spiro and E. Yuchtman-Yaar, 51–74. New York: Academic Press.

1985a   "Nothing Fails Like Success: The Evaluation-Research In-
             dustry and Labor Market Policy." *Industrial Relations*
             24:1–19.
1985b   *Welfare State and Equality Data Set.* Berkeley: University
             of California, Berkeley. Manuscript.
Wilensky, Harold L., and Charles Lebeaux
1965   *Industrial Society and Social Welfare.* New York: Free
             Press.
Wilensky, Harold L., and Lowell Turner
1987   *Democratic Corporatism and Policy Linkages.* Berkeley,
             Calif.: University of California Institute of International
             Studies.
Wilms, Wellford
1981   "The Non-System of Education and Training." In *Jobs and
             Training in the 1980s*, ed. P. Doeringer and B. Ver-
             meulen, 19–49. Boston: Martinus Nijhoff.
1983   "The Limited Utility of Vocational Education." *Public Af-
             fairs Report* 24:1–7.
Wilson, Graham
1979   *Unions in American National Politics.* New York: St. Mar-
             tin's Press.
Wilson, William Julius
1980   *The Declining Significance of Race.* 2d ed. Chicago: Uni-
             versity of Chicago Press.
1987   *The Truly Disadvantaged.* Chicago: University of Chicago
             Press.
Windolf, Paul
1981   "Strategies of Enterprises in the German Labour Mar-
             ket." *Cambridge Journal of Economics* 5:351–67.
Wirth, Arthur
1972   *Education in the Technological Society.* Scranton, Pa.: In-
             text.
Wittich, Günther
1966   "The German Road to Full Employment." Ph.D. diss.,
             University of California at Berkeley.
Wolffsohn, Michael
1981   "Creation of Employment as a Welfare Policy." In *The
             Emergence of the Welfare State in Britain and Germany*,
             ed. W. J. Mommsen, 205–44. London: Croom-Helm.
Wrigley, Julia
1982   *Class Politics and the Public Schools.* New Brunswick,
             N.J.: Rutgers University Press.

Woytinsky, W. S.
 1961   *Stormy Passage*. New York: Vanguard Press.
Zastrow, Charles
 1982   *Introduction to Social Welfare Institutions*. Homewood,
         Ill.: Dorsey.
Zelditch, Morris
 1971   "Intelligible Comparisons." In *Comparative Methods in
         Sociology*, ed. Ivan Vallier, 267–308. Berkeley: University
         of California Press.
Zöllner, Detlev
 1982   "Germany." In *The Evolution of Social Insurance, 1881–
         1981*, ed. P. Koehler and H. Zacker, 1–92. New York: St.
         Martin's Press.

Subject Index

Name Index

Compositor:	BookMasters, Inc.
Text:	Caledonia
Display:	Caledonia
Printer:	Braun-Brumfield, Inc.
Binder:	Braun-Brumfield, Inc.